THEORISING MEDIA AND PRACTICE

Anthropology of Media
Series Editors: John Postill and Mark Peterson

The ubiquity of media across the globe has led to an explosion of interest in the ways people around the world use media as part of their everyday lives. This series addresses the need for works that describe and theorize multiple, emerging, and sometimes interconnected, media practices in the contemporary world. Interdisciplinary and inclusive, this series offers a forum for ethnographic methodologies, descriptions of non-Western media practices, explorations of transnational connectivity, and studies that link culture and practices across fields of media production and consumption.

Volume 1
Alarming Reports: Communicating Conflict in the Daily News
Andrew Arno

Volume 2
The New Media Nation: Indigenous Peoples and Global Communication
Valerie Alia

Volume 3
News as Culture: Journalistic Practices and the Remaking of Indian Leadership Traditions
Ursula Rao

Volume 4
Theorising Media and Practice
Edited by Birgit Bräuchler and John Postill

Theorising Media and Practice

Edited by
Birgit Bräuchler and John Postill

Berghahn Books
New York • Oxford

Published in 2010 by

Berghahn Books

www.berghahnbooks.com

Library of Congress Cataloging-in-Publication Data
Theorising media and practice / edited by Birgit Bräuchler and John Postill.
 p. cm. – (Anthropology of media ; v. 4)
 Collection of papers, some of which were presented at a media anthropology
network workshop, organised by the editors as part of the European
Association of Social Anthropologists' (EASA) conference held in Bristol,
U.K., September, 2006.
 ISBN 978-1-84545-741-9 (hardback : alk. paper) – ISBN 978-1-84545-745-7
(pbk. : alk. paper)
 1. Mass media and anthropology–Congresses. 2. Mass media and
culture–Congresses. 3. Mass media–Research–Congresses. I. Bräuchler,
Birgit. II. Postill, John, 1965- III. European Association of Social
Anthropologists. Conference (2006 : Bristol, England)
 P96.A56T44 2010
 302.23–dc22

2010019545

British Library Cataloguing in Publication Data
A catalogue record for this book is available from the British Library.

Printed in the United States on acid-free paper.

ISBN: 978-1-84545-741-9 (Hardback)
ISBN: 978-1-84545-745-7 (Paperback)

To Jörg and Sarah

Contents

List of Figures

Preface

Theorising Media and Practice originates in a Media Anthropology Network workshop organised by the editors as part of the European Association of Social Anthropologists' (EASA) conference in Bristol, U.K., in September 2006. As always with such events, the challenge when preparing the call for papers was to find a theme for the workshop that would be broad enough to interest most of our colleagues and yet not so broad that the session would lack focus. With the deadline looming and few ideas forthcoming, we decided to browse through the online profiles posted by Network members and soon made two interesting discoveries. First, we found that many colleagues declared a keen interest in 'media practices' related to blogging, film-making, journalism, gaming, telework, web forums and so on. At the same time, we also realised that the key notion of 'practices' was being neither defined nor problematised – something which we later understood as signalling a wider neglect of practice theory in the media studies and media anthropology literature, not least in our own work!

So we put out a call for proposals in which we asked the following questions: What do we actually mean by 'media practices'? What are the key theoretical and methodological problems attending their study? How do different theories of practice aid or hinder anthropological analyses of media practices? In what ways do different media practices overlap with one another and with non-media practices? How can we begin to map and theorise the bewildering diversification of media practices in recent years?

We are very pleased to report that we received a large number of proposals from across Europe and beyond and that the session was a great success. This encouraged us to embark on the arduous but hugely rewarding process leading to the publication of *Theorising Media and Practice*. While some of the book's chapters started as EASA workshop papers, others are the result of the subsequent call for chapters or were commissioned especially for this volume. All chapters are published here for the first time save for two, namely Nick Couldry's essay 'Theorising Media as Practice', originally published in the journal *Social Semiotics* in 2004, and Christopher Kelty's 'The Movement', a chapter in his 2008 book *Two Bits: The Cultural Significance of Free Software*. These texts are reprinted below with the kind permission of Taylor and Francis and Duke University Press respectively.

We are immensely grateful to all contributors for their commitment to this book and to other colleagues who have participated in different ways since the Bristol session, including two anonymous readers for their helpful comments. We are very fortunate to have embarked on this work at a time when the anthropology of media is flourishing, as can be seen by the recent publication of no less than four media anthropological overviews (see references in the Introduction) and by the phenomenal growth of the EASA Media Anthropology Network, which started as a small group of enthusiasts in Vienna in September 2004 but today has close to 700 mailing list subscribers and shows no signs of slowing down. We thank all those colleagues and students who have participated in the lively mailing-list seminars and other discussions over the years. These exchanges have been integral to the making of this book, for they have provided most of us with a conducive environment and sounding board to develop our ideas on mediated practice. Although we have been unable to include all the excellent chapter proposals we received, we hope that this will not discourage people from joining us in what is still very much early days in the collective theorising of media and practice.

Birgit Bräuchler would like to thank the Asia Research Institute (ARI), National University of Singapore, for supporting her trip to Bristol and for providing her with a pleasant and challenging intellectual environment in which she could, among other things, pursue this project.

Birgit Bräuchler and John Postill
Frankfurt and Sheffield, July 2009

Introduction: Theorising Media and Practice*

John Postill

This book rethinks the study of media from the perspective of practice theory, a branch of social theory centred on 'practices' rather than structures, systems, individuals or interactions. Practices are the embodied sets of activities that humans perform with varying degrees of regularity, competence and flair. Although practice theory has been a mainstay of social theory for nearly three decades, so far it has had very limited impact on media studies. By linking practice theory and media studies, *Theorising Media and Practice* offers media scholars and students – and indeed anyone with a professional or personal interest in what people actually do with media – a link with the often abstract practice theory literature. It also provides a link for practice theorists wishing to travel in the other direction, towards media research and theory, an area of scholarship largely overlooked by practice theorists. Drawing on case studies of media-related practices from places such as Zambia, India, Hong Kong, the United States, Britain, Norway and Denmark (see Figure 0.1), the contributors to this volume show some of the myriad ways in which humans make use of media technologies. The practices covered in the book include making news, reading newspapers, playing and modifying computer games, watching television, listening to the radio, teaching film-making, sharing videos on YouTube, working from home, using mobile phones to 'hold things together', and developing free software (see Figure 0.2). Collectively, these chapters make a strong case for the importance of theorising the relationship between media and practice.

Theorising Media and Practice contributes, therefore, to two bodies of literature: practice theory and media studies. One main source of inspiration for this project has been Nick Couldry's call for a new paradigm in media research that takes as its starting point the 'practice turn' in

Norway (9)
UK (14)   Denmark (10, 11)
France (12)
Spain (12)

USA
(Intro, 4, 13)

Hong Kong (12)

India (6,7)

Malaysia (Intro)

Bali (2)

Zambia (5)

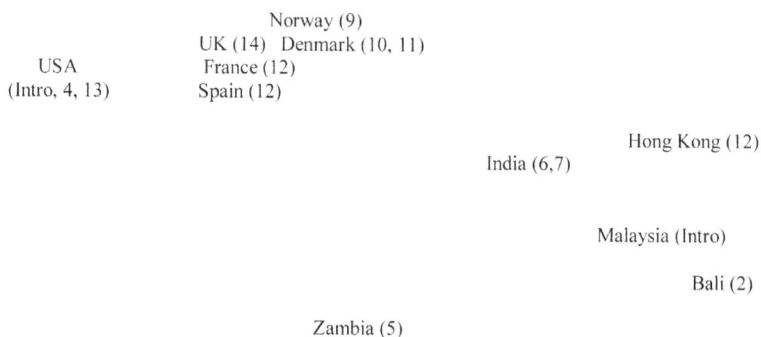

Figure 0.1. Geographical distribution of main examples of media practices given in the present study by chapter (in brackets). See also Index.

sociology (Couldry 2004), reprinted here as Chapter 1. This book is also firmly aligned with Shaun Moores's recent publication *Media/Theory* (Moores 2005) – discussed later in this Introduction – which builds on Giddens's theory of practice. It further shares the concerns of David Hesmondalgh and Jason Toynbee (2008) who, in a recent collection on media theory, stress the need to strengthen the theoretical backbone of media studies, a field of research with an empiricist and positivist track record in which social theory is often used superficially. Like these authors, the contributors to the present book see theories as 'useful abstractions' (ibid.: 3) that should not be divorced from empirical research.

The present study approaches media and practice primarily from the anthropology of media, a subfield that has expanded dramatically since the late 1980s.[1] Most contributors to *Theorising Media and Practice*, including its coeditors, are indeed media anthropologists; in addition, there are chapters by a media sociologist, a semiotician, a film-maker, and two technologists. What marks this volume off from existing media anthropological collections is that rather than being a broad introduction to the subfield, the present collection addresses a single problem, namely how we may go about theorising media as practice.[2]

In this Introduction I review the relevant media studies and practice theory literature to argue not for a new 'practice paradigm' in media studies (*pace* Couldry and Hobart this volume) but rather to argue for practice theory as a new strand to add to existing strands of media theory. Drawing from the practice theories of Giddens, Bourdieu and

Warde, as well as from my own research in Malaysia, I sketch out a field-of-practice approach to media around three main questions: media in everyday life, media and the body, and media production. I then note some of the limitations of any practice perspective on the study of media, ending with an outline of the book.

backyard/indie wrestling	Bird (4)
BASE jump videoing	Postill (Intro)
computer gaming	Ardèvol et al. (12)
digital practices	Bird (4), Helle-Valle (9), Kjaerulff (10), Christensen & Røpke (11), Ardèvol et al. (12), Kelty (13), Greenhalgh (14)
domestic media practices	Postill (Intro), Hobart (2), Helle-Valle (9), Kjaerulff (10), Christensen & Røpke (11)
film and video-making	Postill (Intro), Bird (4), Rao (7), Greenhalgh (14)
ICT practices	Helle-Valle (9), Christensen & Røpke (11)
internet practices	Postill (Intro), Bird (4), Kjaerulff (10), Ardèvol et al. (12), Kelty (13)
machinima	Ardèvol et al. (12)
media rituals	Postill (Intro), Couldry (2), Bird (4)
mobile phone practices	Christensen & Røpke (11), Ardèvol et al. (12)
news-making	Bird (4), Rao (7)
newspaper reading	Peterson (6)
radio listening	Spitulnik (5)
semiosis (sign-making)	Ipsen (8)
software production	Kelty (13)
telework	Kjaerulff (10)
TV reporting	Bird (4)
TV viewing	Hobart (2), Bird (4)
YouTube sharing	Ardèvol et al. (12)

Figure 0.2. Main examples of media practices by author(s) and chapter (in brackets). See also Index.

Doing Ethnography through 'Media Practices'

The anthropology of media is an ideal place to start a review of the media studies literature on practice because its specialists have already studied and participated in a plethora of media-related practices around the world. This practical knowledge, though, is strewn across a dispersed ethnographic record where it has been deployed in relation to a broad range of theoretical aims only implicitly related to theories of practice. Hence my use of the preposition 'through' in this section's heading: media anthropologists have regarded media practices not as objects of study in their own right but rather as conduits through which to reach other research objects.

Over the past twenty years or so, media anthropologists have used the notion of 'practices' and its countless variants ('media practices', 'cultural practices', 'discursive practices' and so on) both profusely and to great effect, vastly expanding media studies beyond its traditional Euro-American heartland. The main topics studied by anthropologists via the notion of '(media) practices' include indigenous media activism in white-settler countries; media and cultural politics in postcolonial states; mainstream media production in both rich and poor countries; ethnic minority media; ritual, performance and media; and the 'social life' of media artefacts (Hughes-Freeland 1998; Ginsburg, Abu-Lughod and Larkin 2002; Rothenbuhler and Coman 2005).

But what do anthropologists actually mean by 'media practices'? (see also Hobart this volume). A survey of all instances in which the word 'practices' appears in four influential media anthropological collections is revealing.[3] The term 'practices' is used in these reference books 190 times in 93 different ways, with a great variety of single qualifiers ('media practices', 'cultural practices', 'social practices', 'symbolic practices') and double qualifiers ('minority media practices' or 'media consumption practices') being employed. The most commonly used of these combinations is 'media practices' (occurring 34 times),[4] followed at a considerable distance by 'cultural practices' (8 times) and 'social practices' (6 times). Not only is 'media practices' the most frequently used variant, it is also given pride of place in the edited collections surveyed. Some examples include (italics added):

> [W]e have attempted to use anthropology to push media studies into new environments and examine diverse *media practices* that are only beginning to be mapped. (Ginsburg, Abu-Lughod and Larkin 2002: 1)

[T]he different kinds of *media practices* represented in this volume can be placed on a sociopolitical continuum reflected in the different sections of the book. (ibid.: 7)

Anthropologists categorically reject the common tendency to treat media as separate from social life and in ethnographic case after case highlight the interconnections between *media practices* and cultural frames of reference. (Askew and Wilk 2002: 10)

[M]edia practices have tended to be analysed with reference to consumption ... In this book, *media practices* are analysed in terms of agency, in some cases with reference to performance. (Hughes-Freeland 1998: 4–5)

One fundamental problem with the term 'media practices' as it is used in the media anthropological literature is that it is nowhere defined or problematised. Rather this term and its cognates are used as lexical means towards ethnographic ends. To reiterate: it is through the study of (media) practices that anthropologists are taking media studies beyond the affluent North and into the 'media worlds' of subaltern people in the South. For instance, in my own ethnographic work among the Iban of Borneo I use the phrase 'media practices' to track the spread of nationalist ideals across rural Sarawak (Postill 2006: 91), but in typical ethnographic fashion I do not define what I mean by 'practices', let alone problematise this notion.

Although numerous kinds of practices are mentioned in the media anthropological literature, these practices are seldom unpacked. One of the few exceptions to this rule is Hobart's differentiation of (discursive) practices into 'practices of knowing, explaining, justifying and so on' and, at a different point in his exposition, into 'practices of asserting, denying, questioning, deceiving and so forth' (Hobart 2005: 26, 31). A further problem is semantic slippage.[5] For instance, Ginsburg, Abu-Lughod and Larkin use the terms 'practices', 'formations' and 'processes' interchangeably:

[T]he different kinds of media practices represented in this volume can be placed on a sociopolitical continuum ... On one end are the more classic *formations* of mass media produced through large governmental and commercial institutions ... In the middle range are more reflexive *processes* [related to] a variety of subaltern social and cosmological worlds ... On the other end are more self-conscious *practices*, often linked to social movements, in which cultural material is ... strategically deployed as part of a broader project of political empowerment by indigenous and other disenfranchised groups. (Ginsburg, Abu-Lughod and Larkin 2002: 7, italics added)

Meanwhile, in the same volume, Hamilton conflates 'activities', 'practices' and 'behavior' in a passage about television viewers in Thailand: 'The demeanor of viewers changed during the Royal News; they stopped their other *activities* and fell silent. This *behavior* was consistent with other *practices* expected when ordinary people are brought in conjunction with Royalty' (Hamilton 2002: 162, italics added).

More importantly, there is a general lack of explicit engagement with practice theory. In a comprehensive survey of eighty-five media anthropological chapters I found only four references to practice theory (Schieffelin 1998; Coman 2005; Couldry 2005; Peterson 2005) – all four, interestingly, to Bourdieu's *Outline of a Theory of Practice* (1977).

To summarise, although the term 'practices' and its vast progeny have performed a sterling service for the anthropology of media[6] as research tools, the theoretical promise of this concept remains unrealised. If we are to begin to understand what people actually do with media we need to engage with practice theory.

What is Practice Theory?

Social theorists agree that there is no such thing as a coherent, unified 'practice theory', only a body of highly diverse writings by thinkers who adopt a loosely defined 'practice approach'. Theodor Schatzki (2001) distinguishes four main types of practice theorists: philosophers (such as Wittgenstein, Dreyfus, or Taylor), social theorists (Bourdieu, Giddens), cultural theorists (Foucault, Lyotard) and theorists of science and technology (Latour, Rouse, Pickering). It is also possible to distinguish two 'waves' or generations of practice theorists. Whilst the first generation, led by some of the foremost theorists of the twentieth century (e.g., Bourdieu 1977; Foucault 1979; Giddens 1979, 1984; de Certeau 1984), laid the foundations of what we now regard as practice theory, the second generation is currently testing those foundations and building new extensions to the theoretical edifice (Ortner 1984, 2006; Schatzki 1996; Schatzki, Knorr Cetina and von Savigny 2001; Reckwitz 2002; Warde 2005). In this section I review the main questions addressed by the more influential members of each generation, concluding with some contemporary trends in practice theory.

The first generation of practice theorists sought a virtuous middle path between the excesses of methodological individualism – explaining social phenomena as a result of individual actions[7] – and those of its logical opposite, methodological holism – the explanation of phenomena by means of structures or social wholes (Ryan 1970). Put differently, they wished to liberate agency – the human ability to act upon and change the world – from the constrictions of structuralist and systemic models while avoiding the trap of methodological individualism. These theorists regarded the human body as the nexus of people's practical engagements with the world.[8] Thus the French sociologist Pierre Bourdieu (1977) developed the notion of 'habitus' to capture 'the permanent internalisation of the social order in the human body' (Eriksen and Nielsen 2001: 130) whilst recognising 'the agent's practice, his or her capacity for invention and improvisation' (Bourdieu 1990: 13). In Bourdieu's theory of practice, the world's structural constraints form 'permanent dispositions'. These are

> schemes of perception and thought, extremely general in their application, such as those which divide up the world in accordance with the oppositions between the male and the female, east and west, future and past, top and bottom, right and left, etc., and also, at a deeper level, in the form of bodily postures and stances, ways of standing, sitting, looking, speaking, or walking. (Bourdieu 1977: 15, quoted in Eriksen and Nielsen 2001: 130)

Bourdieu borrows the Greek word 'hexis' to refer to the way in which social agents 'carry themselves' in the world – their gait, gesture, postures and so on (Jenkins 2002: 75). He exemplifies this idea with his early research in Kabylia (Algeria) where he observed that men and women carried themselves in markedly different ways. Where women's bodies were oriented down in keeping with '[t]he female ideal of modesty and restraint', men's bodies were oriented towards other men (ibid.: 75). Bourdieu concluded that Kabyle bodies are 'mnenomic devices' that help to reproduce fundamental cultural oppositions and are integral to a cultural habitus learned more through observation than formal teaching (ibid.: 75–76). In Mark Peterson's summary of Bourdieu's account of practice (this volume): 'Social life is a constant struggle to construct a life out of the cultural resources one's social experience offers, in the face of formidable social constraints. By living in a society structured by such constraints, and organised by the successful practices of [others], one develops predispositions to act in certain ways'.

Later in his career Bourdieu added the notion of 'field' to his theoretical vocabulary (see Bourdieu 1992, 1993, 2005; Bourdieu and Wacquant 1992; Swartz 1997; Reed-Danahay 2005). Fields are specialist domains of practice (such as art, photography, sociology) with their own 'logic' that are constituted by a unique combination of species of capital; for example, financial capital, symbolic capital (prestige, renown) or social capital ('connections'). An apt metaphor for a field is that of a game. Only players with sufficient 'know-how' and belief in the game ('illusio') will be willing to invest time and effort playing it.[9] Skilled players acquire over time a 'feel for the game' or 'practical sense' that allows them to improvise in a structured but seemingly effortless manner. Field agents' successful strategies may appear to the casual observer rational and conscious but in reality, says Bourdieu, they are only possible when there is a good fit between the habitus and the field. The habitus

> produces strategies which, even if they are not produced by consciously aiming at explicitly formulated goals ... turn out to be objectively adjusted to the situation. Action guided by a 'feel for the game' has all the appearances of the rational action that an impartial observer ... would deduce. And yet it is not based on reason. You need only think of the impulsive decision made by the tennis player who runs up to the net, to understand that it has nothing to do with the learned construction that the coach, after analysis, draws up ... The conditions of rational calculation are practically never given in practice: time is limited, information is restricted, etc. (Bourdieu 1990: 11)

Another fundamental notion in Bourdieu's practical apparatus is 'doxa',[10] those deeply internalised societal or field-specific presuppositions that 'go without saying' and are not up for negotiation (Bourdieu 1998: 66–67, 2005: 37). For Bourdieu, in sum, practice is 'based on the dispositions inherent in habitus' and unfolds as 'strategic improvisations – goals and interests pursued as strategies – against a background of doxa that ultimately limits them' (Parkin 1997: 376).

A closely related notion to Bourdieu's habitus is Michel Foucault's concept of 'discipline' (Foucault 1979). Like habitus, discipline 'is structure and power that have been impressed on the body forming permanent dispositions' (Eriksen and Nielsen 2001: 130). In contrast to Bourdieu, though, Foucault laid particular emphasis on the violence through which modern regimes impress their power (or 'biopower') on bodies (ibid.: 130). In Europe, the introduction of mental asylums and prisons allowed the replacing of earlier hierarchical and centralised forms of control with more diffuse and insidious forms of 'governmentality' and 'disciplinary power'. Disciplinary power works through the body; subjects learn to self-regulate their bodily practices, making it less necessary for states to intervene directly in their lives (Gledhill 2000: 149).

Like Bourdieu, the British sociologist Anthony Giddens (1979, 1984) first developed an original version of practice theory in the 1970s, but he arrived there via a very different route. Where Bourdieu prided himself in grounding his theories in empirical research, Giddens is more concerned with the history of philosophy and social theory than with sociological data (Eriksen and Nielsen 2001: 129). In *The Constitution of Society*, Giddens sets out to unify structure and agency through the notion of the 'duality of structure', the idea that structure is both 'the medium and outcome it recursively organizes' (Giddens 1984: 374). Social relations are structured across space and time thanks to the duality of structure – this is what Giddens calls 'structuration' (ibid.: 376). His structuration theory demonstrated 'how principles of order could both produce and be reproduced at the level of practice itself' and not through some 'ordering' society which impinges upon individual actors from above (Couldry this volume). Critically building on Hägerstrand's (1967) geographical work, Giddens argues that we cannot separate 'individuals' from the day-to-day contexts they help to constitute. Rejecting what he regards as Hägerstrand's weak notion of power as 'authority constraints' to human action, he stresses instead the transformational power of human action, which operates both with the limitations and possibilities afforded by societal constraints (Giddens 1984: 116–7). For Giddens, the routinisation of day-to-day life is fundamental to humans who derive a sense of 'ontological security' from the familiar contours of the social worlds they have helped to (re)create (ibid.: 23, 50).

Turning now to the second generation of practice theorists, these thinkers have continued to stress the centrality of the human body to practice while paying closer attention to questions of culture and history as well as developing new concepts – such as 'dispersed' versus 'integrative' practices (see below) – and applying practice theory to new areas such as consumption studies, organisational theory, the material culture of the home, or neuroscience.

In the mid 1980s, the American cultural anthropologist Sherry Ortner published a germinal essay titled 'Theory in Anthropology Since the Sixties' (Ortner 1984) that is often regarded by anthropologists as marking the discipline's 'turn to practice' (Eriksen and Nielsen 2001; Ortner 2006; Bird this volume). Ortner questioned the three 'theories of constraint' that dominated U.S. cultural anthropology in the early 1980s, namely interpretive anthropology (Geertz), Marxist political economy and structuralism. She found that these approaches remained silent about human agency and 'the processes that produce and reproduce constraints – social practices' (Ortner 2006: 2). Dissatisfied with this situation, Ortner sought inspiration in Bourdieu (1977), Giddens (1979) and Sahlins (1981), whom she saw as putting actors back into social processes yet without neglecting the larger structures that enable and constrain their actions.[11] On the other hand, Ortner was critical of practice theory for lacking 'a recognisable concept of culture' (Ortner 2006: 11) and for its limited purchase on questions of power and history. In this regard, she found Gramsci's notion of 'hegemony' more useful than Foucault's totalising account of disciplinary power, as hegemony, for Gramsci, is 'strongly controlling but never complete or total' (2006: 7).[12] Leaning on Sahlins's work, Ortner concluded that 'a theory of practice is a theory of history' and that therefore social practices can only be understood in their articulations with historical events.

If Ortner's 1984 essay is still essential reading for anthropologists interested in practice theory, Theodor Schatzki (1996, 2001) is a more central figure among second-wave practice theorists. Schatzki is a Wittgensteinian social philosopher for whom the idea of a 'total field of practices' is fundamental (Schatzki 2001). By this term Schatzki appears to mean – though this is not entirely clear – the dense tangle of human practices that spans the globe. In order to be able to work with this massive web, says Schatzki, practice theorists have had to either narrow down the inquiry to more manageable subfields of the 'total field' – for example, science or photography – or transform existing subject matter into a practice theory question – such as Swidler's (1986) notion of 'culture as practice' or Couldry's 'media as practice' (this volume). For Schatzki, 'the social is a field of embodied, materially interwoven practices centrally organized around shared practical understandings' (Schatzki 2001: 3). The maintenance of practices over time depends on 'the successful inculcation of shared embodied know-how' (ibid.: 3) as well as on their continued performance (Schatzki 1996). Because activities (or actions) and bodies are 'constituted' within practices, 'the skilled body' is where activity and mind as well as individual and society meet (Schatzki 2001: 3). It follows that we can only understand actions within their specific practical contexts.[13]

Most practice theorists, according to Schatzki (ibid.: 2), minimally define practices as 'arrays of activity' in which the human body is the nexus. Although he subscribes to this curt definition, Schatzki (1996) also introduces an important distinction between what he calls 'integrative' and 'dispersed' practices. Integrative practices are 'the more complex practices found in and constitutive of particular domains of social life' (ibid.: 98), such as cooking, farming or business. By contrast, dispersed practices include 'describing … explaining, questioning, reporting, examining and imagining' (ibid.: 91), and they can take place within and across domains or subfields (Peterson this volume).

Another contemporary author, Andreas Reckwitz (2002), synthesises elements from Schatzki, Bourdieu, Giddens and other thinkers to

build an 'ideal type' of practice theory. With Giddens, Reckwitz empha-
sizes the importance of routines – 'social practices are bodily and mental routines' (ibid.: 256) – whilst noting that we should not lose sight of
'crises of practice' that can bring about significant changes – that is,
new routines. Reckwitz also notes that practice theorists have, by and
large, neglected the individual (cf. Helle-Valle's 'in/dividual', this volume), even though there is 'a very precise place for the 'individual' – as
distinguished from the agent – in practice theory ... As there are
diverse social practices, and as every agent carries out a multitude of different social practices, the individual is the unique crossing point of
practices, of bodily-mental routines' (ibid.: 256).

Where Reckwitz is often abstract and philosophical, Alan Warde (2005)
– who inspired Nick Couldry's turn to practice[14] – approaches practice theory with a far more concrete, empirical aim in mind: the sociology of consumption. He finds Schatzki's notion of 'integrative practices' of more relevance to this research area than that of 'dispersed practices' and illustrates
his argument with examples from the practice of motoring in Britain. For
Warde, the rewards of practice can be of different kinds: they can be social,
as in Bourdieu's social recognition; psychological, as in Csíkszentmihályi's
(1990) notion of 'flow'; or of other kinds. Complex practices offer practitioners more levels of self-development and a stronger sense of well-being
than simple practices, which to Warde may explain why many people appear
to be satisfied cultivating low-status practices. Practices are internally differentiated and distinctions among practitioners can matter a great deal, not
least in the differing qualities and degrees of commitment to the practice
(Warde 2005: 138). No practice is 'hermetically sealed' from other practices:
innovations are diffused, copying and borrowing are common (ibid.: 141).
Nor are practices understandable without regard to the broader political,
infrastructural and technological environments in which they are sustained
(Randles and Warde 2006: 229).

In the wake of this second wave of thinkers, practice theory is currently being put to numerous new uses across a range of disciplines, such as the
study of domestic and leisure practices (Shove 2003; Shove and Pantzar
2005; Shove et al. 2007), social and political anthropology (Nuitjen 2003;
Evens and Handelman 2006), ecological economics (Røpke 2009), strategy research (Whittington 2006; Jarzabkowski, Balogun and Seidl 2007),
management accounting (Baxter and Chua 2008), occupational therapy
(Lee, Taylor and Kielhofner 2009) and neuroscience (Lizardo 2007).

To summarise, *practice theory is a body of work about the work of the body.*
With one or two exceptions, this loose network of approaches to social
theory takes the human body to be the nexus of arrays of activities, or
practices, that agents perform with greater or lesser commitment, dex-

terity and grace. Whilst some of these practices are widely diffused across social space and time, others are found clustered in configurations that change over time through the socially (re)productive agency of practitioners. Practice theory itself has diffused across epistemic space since its emergence in the 1970s and today we find practice-based approaches in subfields as diverse as strategy theory, political anthropology, material culture studies, the sociology of consumption, ecological economics and neuroscience.

Theorising Media and Practice: Prospects and Limitations

In this section I argue that practice theory can be greatly beneficial to media studies, albeit not as the field's next paradigm (*pace* Couldry and Hobart this volume). Rather, I am suggesting that practice theory offers media studies new ways of addressing questions that are central to the field, such as media in everyday life, media and the body, and media production. At the same time, we cannot expect practice theory (or any other theory, for that matter) to be a panacea, and in the latter part of this section I discuss one set of media questions that practice theory is not better suited to answering than existing theoretical models, namely questions about mediated processes such as global media events, media dramas or digital epidemics.

Let us first examine the question of media in everyday life. A helpful starting point is Shaun Moores's *Media/Theory* (2005). Moores devotes the first part of this book to extending Giddens's (1984) structuration theory to the study of media. Giddens contrasts the irreversibility of human biographical time with the reversibility (or cyclicity) of modern clock-and-calendar time. For Giddens, the predictability of modern time cycles contributes to people's sense of 'ontological security' – that is, a 'confidence or trust that the natural and social worlds are as they appear to be' (ibid.: 375). Any major disruption to these familiar cycles can lead to an acute sense of insecurity and disorientation. As they go about their rounds of activities, human agents 'stop' and interact with others in what Giddens, following Hägerstrand, calls 'stations' – for example, workplaces, schools, homes, shops. Stations can be studied along three main dimensions: how encounters are distributed across space and time, how the station is internally 'regionalised', and how these regions are contextualised by agents (ibid.: 135). Thus time-space is 'zoned' in relation to the routinised practices of social agents:

[A] private house is a locale which is a 'station' for a large cluster of interactions in the course of a typical day. Houses in contemporary societies
are regionalized into floors, halls and rooms. But the various rooms of
the house are zoned differently in time as well as space. The rooms down-
stairs are characteristically used most in daylight hours, while bedrooms
are where individuals 'retire to' at night. (ibid.: 119)

Building on Giddens's ideas about modern time and space, Moores follows
Ellis (1982), Scannell (1988, 1991), Silverstone (1993) and other media
scholars to explain how broadcasting in Britain was built on clock-and-calendar cycles through devices such as seriality and scheduling. Thus, fixed
schedules made audiences expect an 'ordered and predictable' output
(Moores 2005: 20). After a historical process of routinisation all but forgot-
ten today, radio and television – in contrast to film – came to be regarded
as 'profoundly "ordinary" media' (ibid.: 22). Although most programme
production is studio-based, from the outset broadcasters 'attempted to produce programmes that fitted into the domestic sphere and the daily round'
(Scannell 1991: 3, quoted in Moores 2005: 19).

These ideas, firmly embedded as they are in British sociology and
media studies, may seem irrelevant to 'media-poor' countries in the South.
Yet in my own research in the late 1990s among the Iban of Sarawak, in
Malaysian Borneo (Postill 2002, 2006), I found the same close intertwin-
ing of broadcasting schedules with people's 'round-and-round movements
in time-space' (Moores 2005: 34). For instance, in the more urbanised
longhouses – the 'villages under one roof' where most Iban live – watching television had its own regular evening slot (roughly between 7 and 10
P.M.) and preferred 'region' within the geography of the longhouse: the
semi-private family living room. Moreover, as in the British case, Malaysian
broadcasting is built on modern clock-and-calendar time, and I found no
evidence of an indigenous 'Iban time' running out of synch with national
broadcasting cycles. As Alfred Gell concludes in his comprehensive review
of the cross-cultural literature on time:

There is no fairyland where people experience time in a way that is markedly unlike the way in which we do ourselves, where there is no past, present
and future, where time stands still, or chases its own tail, or swings back and
forth like a pendulum. All these possibilities have been seriously touted in
the literature on the anthropology of time ... but they are all travesties,
engendered in the process of scholarly reflection. (Gell 1992: 315)

The Giddensian stress on day-to-day recursivity and modern forms of
scheduling does not mean, however, that we can take for granted the

creation and maintenance of routine media practices. Moores regards the 'ordinariness' of broadcasting as the regular outcome of the 'seemingly effortless practical accomplishments' of both broadcasters and their audiences (Moores 2005: 23). But what of media practices outside the 'typical' routines of twentieth-century television viewing? Do these ideas apply to today's far more diverse, mobile and ubiquitous media technologies (see Hawk, Riedler and Oviedo 2008)? Two recent case studies from Denmark suggest that they do.[15] Toke Christensen and Inge Røpke (this volume) describe how families in urban Denmark use mobile phones to try to coordinate their activities – not always successfully – and 'hold things together' whilst individual family members make their rounds through what Giddens would call their day-to-day 'stations' (schools, workplaces, shops, car parks, and so forth). By contrast, the rural teleworkers studied by Kjaerulff (this volume) face the opposite challenge: how to 'keep things apart', as it were, when 'work' and 'family life' share the same locale – the home. Both cases demonstrate that under conditions of swift technological and economic change, domestic media-related practices are not always 'seemingly effortless'. Yet regardless of the technologies employed, these practices are invariably tied to the relentless cycles of clock-and-calendar time. Like the Iban families I knew in Borneo, these Danish families have no timeless 'fairyland' to repair to, no magical world 'where time stands still, or chases its own tail, or swings back and forth like a pendulum' (Gell 1992: 315).

A second key media question that practice theory is well equipped to address is the relationship between media and the body. As discussed earlier, practice theorists have stressed the powerful imprint of the state (Foucault's 'discipline') and the family or kin group (Bourdieu's 'habitus') on the body. Whilst homes, schools, prisons and hospitals are no doubt important stations in which to study the disciplined habitus and its technological mediations, we should not neglect other stations in which people seek to discipline their bodies on a regular basis, such as dance schools, weightwatchers' groups, yoga sects, fitness centres or boxing clubs (on the latter, see Wacquant 2006).

Let us compare, for instance, the subcultural worlds of BDSM (bondage and discipline, domination/submission, and sadomasochism) and BASE jumping (the illegal practice of jumping with a parachute from fixed structures such as bridges or skyscrapers). At first sight, these two 'integrative practices' may seem to have little in common. A closer inspection through a media practice lens, however, reveals striking commonalities as well as contrasts. In two separate ethnographies of such worlds (both in the United States) we find people who are tirelessly 'working at play' (Weiss 2006), investing time, money and effort in highly technical, often mediated, embodied practices. Thus growing numbers of BASE jumpers now fit small video cameras onto their helmets and/or bodies to become 'stars of their own in-flight movies' which they later replay and share with others. This being a fiercely competitive milieu, becoming a skilled film-maker as well as a skilled jumper can enhance a practitioner's reputation. However, these relatively new 'media practices' (Ferrell, Milovanovic and Lyng 2001) have had some unintended effects as well: what in the BASE scene is customarily regarded as an ephemeral, private and ineffable practice – the jump – is transformed by means of new media technologies into an enduring, public and visible practice. In contrast, although we are told that BDSM practitioners in San Francisco are regular users of e-mail, websites and print media, Weiss (2006) is silent about media uses during their sexual practices. It is fair to assume, nonetheless, that audiovisual technologies will have found their way into these practices as well, with consequences for the wider social field of BDSM that only empirical research can establish (on BDSM practices in the virtual world of Second Life, see Boellstorff 2008: 114, 162).

At any rate, both BASE jumping and BDSM furnish their more advanced practitioners with a sense of self-development and well-being, as Warde (2005) suggests for complex integrative practices in general. The grounded micro-study of embodied practices should not make us lose sight, however, of the wider infrastructural, legislative and political factors that both enable and constrain practice (Randles and Warde 2006). Just as the very British practice of trainspotting is unthinkable in Sarawak (where there are no trains), BASE jumping without America's colossal man-made structures would lose much of its appeal. The evidence also suggests that both BASE and BDSM leading practitioners deploy the rhetoric of 'community'[16] strategically across different public media as they strive to legitimise these 'alternative' practices vis-à-vis the authorities and the general public. By analogy with Ginsburg's (1993) indigenous film-makers' 'cultural activism', we could call this a form of 'subcultural activism' that objectifies a set of practices partly for reasons of public relations (see Bob 2005).

Moving on now to the possible uses of practice theory in the study of media production, in recent years a number of researchers working on the media industries have turned to Bourdieu's field theory for inspiration (e.g., Moeran 2002; de Nooy 2003; Benson and Neveu 2005; see also Peterson 2003). A field, as we said earlier, is a domain of practice in which differently positioned practitioners compete and cooperate over the same prizes and rewards: money, pleasure, recognition and so on (cf. Martin 2003). In his own research on French journalists,

Bourdieu (1998) argued that these media professionals constitute a highly influential field with tangible effects on other fields of cultural production such as science and literature. As Rao (this volume) aptly puts it, Bourdieu insisted that 'only an internal analysis of the embodied practices of media professionals and their relationships to each other can open up an understanding of the way the social is constituted in the contemporary world'.

A major stumbling block in the development of a practice approach to media production is Bourdieu's aversion to interactionism – the sociological approach centred on people's social interactions that informs Giddens's structuration theory. Whilst Giddens (1979, 1984) was influenced by early interactionist theorists such as Goffman and Frederik Barth[17] (Eriksen and Nielsen 2001: 129), Bourdieu was adamantly opposed to all forms of interactionism. He argued that interactionists fail to grasp the importance of the invisible objective relations binding social agents' relative positions within fields of practice and the broader 'social space' in which these fields are embedded, such as the social space of France. Thus two professors of sociology living in different parts of France may have never 'interacted' but can still occupy neighbouring positions in the field of sociology and wider French social space (Knox, Savage and Harvey 2006; Postill 2008).[18]

In my own ongoing study of internet activists in a suburb of Kuala Lumpur (Malaysia) I have ignored Bourdieu's objections and used the notion of interaction as part of a practice theory framework, for I can see no logical incompatibility between this notion and Bourdieu's invisible 'network' of objective relations binding all field practitioners (see also de Nooy 2003). Moreover, it is hard to envisage an internet without interactivity – think, for instance, of the ease with which users of blogs or Twitter can reply to previous posts. Although the focus of my research is media and 'the production of locality' (Appadurai 1996) rather than media production, I believe my analysis also has implications for this latter area of research. In the study I concentrate on what I call the suburb's 'field of residential affairs'. This is an invisible 'field of practices' in which activists, politicians, councillors, journalists and other interested parties compete and collaborate over issues of concern to local residents, such as traffic congestion, street lighting or crime (Postill 2008). Here I use the plural form 'practices' not out of ethnographic habit (as I did in Postill 2006) but to signal that the field is internally differentiated into a plethora of practices: patrolling the streets, posting on Web forums, attending meetings or organising local events. This plurality extends to field practitioners: different agents carry out different arrays of activities at different field stations with varying degrees of commitment, embodied skill and publicness (cf. Warde 2005). As a result, each practice has evolved its unique blend of sociality, 'mediated interaction' (Thompson 1995) and articulations with the rest of the field. Additionally, cutting across these diverse practices there are field-wide forces at work, such as the 'fundamental law' (Bourdieu 1993) of selfless volunteerism – that is, the doxic expectation that leading residents will freely volunteer their time and labour for the good of 'the community' (Postill 2008).

What is the relevance of this practice theory model to the study of media production? First, it allows for more nuanced accounts of field practices and their specific mediations than existing theoretical models. Contrast, for instance, my stress on the plurality of field practices with Wittel's (2001) dichotomous sociality model in which Wittel posits 'network sociality' (as opposed to 'community sociality') as the predominant mode of sociality in London's new media industries. The model I am proposing also enables us to theorise the kinds of skilled embodied practices of media professionals that ethnographers have documented in recent years but which lack a firm grounding in practice theory (see Ginsburg, Abu-Lughod and Larkin 2002; Peterson 2003; Paterson and Domingo 2008). If we further add a spatio-temporal strand to the model, the result is a frame of analysis in which the agency of media practitioners can be tracked across Giddensian 'stations' and 'regions' within the workplace and beyond. Finally, as with all other field theory models, the synthesis I am advocating here permits the historical analysis of fields of media production and their changing power relations vis-à-vis other fields (Bourdieu 1992; cf. Couldry 2003).

One neglected area in the study of fields of media production is the dispersal of practices (and elements of practice) to and from such fields (cf. Schatzki 1996; Warde 2005). A few ethnographic examples will clarify this point. In May 1997 I participated in the invention of a media-derived practice during my fieldwork among the Iban of Sarawak. As part of the annual Dayak Festival celebrations, a kind of longhouse quiz show was introduced that year. The woman who dreamed up this innovation had seen many quiz shows on Malaysian television. Her aim was to test the 'school knowledge' of local children and publicly reward the more diligent among them (Postill 2006: 179–83). This new practice was scripted and staged 'as seen on television', with all the necessary props and impeccable timekeeping. Although this may be a rare case of direct appropriation of a media practice, there is ample ethnographic evidence to suggest that ritual and other performative practices around the world are being influenced by practices seen on television and other media (see Eisenlohr 2006; van de Port 2006; Pype 2008; Bird this volume). Thus, early 1990s Balinese theatrical audiences 'increasingly expected plays to be as-seen-on-TV and actors to replicate favourite routines from television performances' (Hobart 2002: 377). In some cases a single element of a media practice will be appropriated. For instance, in Zambia the English meta-pragmatic device 'Over to you!' diffused from a popular 1980s radio show by that name to a wide range of practices, including weddings, singing rehearsals and letter writing. Debra Spitulnik (1996) makes the intriguing point that discursive items such as 'Over to you!' may have an inherent 'detachability' and 'reproducibility' that allows them to spread widely across practices well beyond their original contexts. In other cases, the practical elements will migrate in the opposite direction, from domains of amateur practice to the professional mass media. It is important, however, not to draw too sharp a divide between 'the media' and 'the public', especially given the recent proliferation of 'user-generated content' across multiple Web and mobile platforms, these often being shared by media professionals and amateurs (Kücklich 2005; Ardèvol et al. this volume).

To recap: a practice theory approach to media suggests that people use a range of media partly to try to maintain – not always with success – a sense of ontological security in a modern world in which biological death and the predictable cycles of clock-and-calendar time are among the only certainties. In going about their embodied engagements with the world, people traverse and (re)produce a variety of internally regionalised, variously mediated 'stations' (homes, schools, gyms, bars, newsrooms, studios and so forth). This day-to-day and biographical work and play of cultural (re)production and change occurs within and across specialist fields (law, BDSM, journalism, film-making) whose practitioners differ greatly in the degree and quality of their embodied know-how, self-discipline and commitment to the 'games' played in the field. Media practitioners, practices and technologies migrate and circulate across field boundaries unevenly, with some practical elements exhibiting a greater in-built 'detachability' and 'reproducibility' than others.

This sketch of a theory of media practice brings us to the limitations of practice theory for media studies. To reiterate my earlier point, I am arguing that practice theory cannot be a theoretical cure-all. For example, it is unlikely that practice theory will help us to explain the events surrounding the publication in September 2005 of a set of cartoons of the prophet Mohammed in a Danish newspaper (Hervik and Peterson forthcoming). Practice theory is certainly equipped to handle some of the multiple articulations of this global media event with (inter)local practices (posting on a blog, talking on TV, sharing a YouTube video, debating the issue in coffee-shops, and so on). Where practice theory cannot help, though, is with the study of this world-historical moment in its own right, as what members of the Manchester School of anthropology (Evens and Handelman 2006) would call not a social practice but rather a 'political process' – that is, an unpredictable political conflict whose main arenas can shift at great speed across social fields and geographical space (Swartz, Turner and Tuden 1966). These irregular episodes, some of which are known as 'social dramas' (Turner 1974, 1996; Eyerman 2008) or 'media dramas' (Wagner-Pacifici 1986) possess their own dynamics and 'processual forms', not those of regular embodied practices (Bourdieu's bodily hexis). Provided that the empirical data are sufficiently rich, such episodes are amenable to detailed stage-by-stage analysis, but practice theory can be of little assistance here.

Other types of media process that practice theory cannot help us with include global media events around catastrophes such as the Indian Ocean tsunami of 2004 or the Chinese earthquakes of 2008; the instant formation of 'smart mobs' enabled by new mobile technologies, such as the 2001 People Power II demonstrations in the Philippines that led to a change of government (see Rafael 2003); or the 'pandemic' spread of urban legends, rumours or hoaxes across internet and mobile networks (Cortázar Rodríguez 2004). Again, I am not suggesting that practice theory has nothing to tell us about these mediated processes, only that it does not equip us to study them as processes any better than existing theoretical models. What practice theory can do in all these instances is lend us tools with which to study (especially ethnographically) some of the practical ramifications of these processes – for example, how they can disrupt the daily practical rounds of people affected by them (see Moores 2005: 31) or how certain media professionals and amateurs may use these events to modify existing media practices or invent new ones.

Outline of the Book

Theorising Media and Practice opens with a debate in Part 1 between two media theorists who advocate different 'turns to practice' and regard their own proposals as being 'instrumental' (Couldry) and 'radical' (Hobart) respectively. Then, in Part 2, a group of contributors argue for the need to retain holistic notions such as 'culture' and/or 'structure' in approaches to media that draw from practice theory. By contrast, the chapters in Part 3 reject any notion of an overarching social structure, placing media squarely in the situated contexts of their practical uses. The last section of the volume, Part 4, considers the implications of new digital technologies for a practice theory approach to media production.

Part 1, 'Media as Practice', is an exchange about practice theory and its implications for media studies between two British media theorists: the media sociologist Nick Couldry and the media anthropologist Mark Hobart. These disciplinary identities frame some of their disagreements, particularly around the politics, possibilities and limits of a practice approach to media research in non-Western locales where anthropologists have long had a presence, such as in Bali, the focus of Hobart's own research. In Chapter 1, Nick Couldry proposes a new media studies paradigm based on practice theory that will bring media scholars closer to the practical actualities of social life in a 'media-saturated world'. Couldry suggests that this turn to practice theory will help media scholars overcome old impasses around media effects, political economy and audience research, enabling them to take up instead the study of 'the open-ended range of practices focused directly or indirectly on media'. The chapter starts by situating the proposed paradigm in relation to the history of media research, after which it discusses the advantages of this approach with particular reference to the limitations of existing audience studies. Of special interest to Couldry is the study of 'media-oriented practices' and the question of whether certain media practices 'anchor' other practices across social space.

Mark Hobart (Chapter 2) responds to Couldry's proposal with a call for a more 'radical' practice turn in media studies that does away with notions such as structure and system that are deeply rooted in Western thought. Hobart is critical of what he regards as the way Couldry privileges media as an 'anchor' for other social practices (cf. Swidler 2001) and doubts that scholars enjoy a special insight into media power regardless of ordinary people's own discursive practices. In place of Couldry's 'media-oriented practices' Hobart proposes 'media-related practices' as an open-ended notion that does not confine us to the seemingly bounded worlds of media organisations (but see Ardèvol et al., Chapter 12). The term media-related practice can refer, for Hobart, to anything from film- or news-making to cooking in time for the family's favourite soap opera to discussing the purchase of a domestic media artefact. Arguing that Schatzki's (1996) notion of practices as 'organized nexuses of activities' downplays human beings' ability to articulate and order their own practices, Hobart defines practices as 'those recognised, complex forms of social activity and articulation, through which agents set out to maintain or change themselves, others and the world around them under varying conditions'. The mass media are crucially important in this regard, says Hobart, because they are centrally implicated in such articulations.

Chapter 3 is a brief exchange between Couldry and Hobart on some of the issues raised in their respective chapters and on the futures of media scholarship, with special reference to the 'media as practice' paradigm proposed by Couldry.[19] Both theorists agree that media scholars need to gain a greater understanding of the philosophical underpinnings and presuppositions that shape much media research, a field with a long history of empiricism and positivism. They also concur about the urgent need to internationalise media studies. They disagree, however, on a number of issues, including the question of whether certain (media) practices organise or hierarchise other practices.

When reviewing the history of practice theory earlier, I discussed the American anthropologist Sherry Ortner's (1984, 2006) call for a practice theory that extends its remit to questions of power, culture and history. These questions are central to Part 2, 'Media, Culture and Practice', whose contributors (three of them American cultural anthropologists) concur about the need to retain the notion of 'culture' in spite of its troubled history. To argue their cases they draw on media examples from the United States, Zambia and India. Elizabeth Bird (Chapter 4) explores the potential uses of practice theory for an anthropology of media audiences not limited to the immediate contexts of media reception (see also Bird 2003). In contrast to Hobart, Bird does not favour a 'radical' turn to practice theory that would jettison the key notions of culture and structure. Instead she follows Ortner in arguing that a practice approach must hold together both 'the constraints of structure and the power of audience agency'. Bird develops her argument with examples of three cultural practices in the United States: weddings, backyard wrestling and television reporting, suggesting that old media-effects models cannot capture the manifold ways in which the media subtly alter existing practices. Distinguishing her approach from that of mainstream media scholars, Bird stresses the importance of practices that are not ostensibly centred on media.

In Chapter 5, Debra Spitulnik conducts a thought experiment based on her media anthropological research in Zambia. She invites us to imagine a group of young men listening to the radio in a provincial Zambian marketplace. To analyse this practice one could either follow standard ethnographic procedure by taking this to be a 'core' media practice and contextualising it through an ever-widening lens (youth culture, provincial marketplace, modern Zambia and so on), or adopt a more reflexive, unbounded and 'rhizomatic' approach (Deleuze and Guattari 1987). Although Spitulnik favours the second, more experimental, option she also aligns herself with Brightman (1995), Hannerz (1992) and other social theorists – not least with Ortner – who argue for the retention of a non-essentialist notion of culture. This combination of practical rhizomes and cultural milieux, suggests Spitulnik, affords 'more complex analyses of what is going on within so-called "sets of meanings and practices"', such as radio listening in a Zambian marketplace.

Practice theorists have overlooked what practitioners themselves make of their own cultural practices, argues Mark Peterson in Chapter 6. In other words, we lack metacultural accounts of practice (see also Chapter 13). Grounding the discussion in his anthropological fieldwork in New Delhi, Peterson sketches a vernacular theory of the practice of reading newspapers. One significant folk distinction is that between 'taking' and 'reading' a newspaper. Whilst taking a prestigious English-language paper is part of one's 'personalia' (Gell 1986) as a modern educated Indian, privately reading a low-status paper is justified as merely a 'habit' or 'addiction' – one of the 'little heterodoxies' through which social agents deviate from local regimes of value. The chapter concludes with a reflection on Peterson's own effect on the practices he was studying – for example, by introducing 'dispersed practices' (Schatzki 1996) such as asking informants to comment on their reading practices.

Ursula Rao's discussion (Chapter 7) is, like Peterson's, based on ethnographic research on the news media in North India, but here the focus is on media production rather than consumption. Rao brings an interest in the performative nature of public life to her analysis of the controversy surrounding the making of a Hindi film in the holy city of Banaras. The analysis reveals how ambitious local men used the populist 'open-door policy' of the vernacular press to launch their political careers by capitalising on the Banaras drama. Finding the practice models of Bourdieu (1998) and Couldry (2004, this volume) too orderly, Rao argues that in the 'culture in flux' of India's ever more commercialised press, we must pay close attention not to regulated domains but to the contingent border-crossing 'tactics' (de Certeau 1984) of grassroots practitioners. She also contends that although folk versions of a Habermasian public sphere certainly inform widely shared democratic ideals about the Indian press, the actual news-making practices of local journalists differ quite markedly from the cherished ideals. In India, the 'performative politics' of making visible a political leader's heroism, benevolence and effective networking is inextricable from the practices related to news-making.

The chapters in Part 3, 'Media Practices in Context', appear to follow 'radical contextualism' (Ang 1996: 69) as their tacit guiding principle. Their authors focus on the context-specific ways in which people make use of media. To these contributors meanings do not travel well across social situations – but see Spitulnik's (1996) earlier mentioned meta-pragmatic discourse – so that the meaning of a medium is always emergent and contingent on the microhistorical circumstances of its use, regardless of whether a given medium allows users to communicate with others across vast stretches of time and/or space (cf. Thompson 1995; Moores 2005). Some of these authors also warn against the cryptic structuralism of much media scholarship, and indeed of social theory generally. In this respect they come closer to Hobart's than to Couldry's position in the media-as-practice debate. Thus the media semiotician Guido Ipsen builds on the ideas of the founder of American pragmatism, Charles S. Peirce (1839–1914) to propose a semiotic pragmatist approach to theorising media as practice (Chapter 8). Distancing himself both from structuralist semiotics and from what he sees as media studies' sociotechnocentrism (which he partly blames on McLuhan), Ipsen places instead sign-making (or semiosis) at the forefront of a practice theory approach to media. For Ipsen, meaning cannot reside in media artefacts or technologies. Because media, like signs, bear 'the fundamental quality of something in between' we can only know what a medium actually means 'within the process and practice of its usage'.

Like Ipsen, Jo Helle-Valle (Chapter 9) has little time for structuralism. Helle-Valle argues that structuralist assumptions still shape (media) anthropological research, in particular the tacit idea that an invisible *langue* (system of meaning) orders our visible practices. To release himself from the grip of structuralism, Helle-Valle conjoins the Wittgensteinian notion of 'language-games' ('the practically formed communicative contexts that provide statements with meaning') with the anthropological concept of 'in/dividual' (the idea that our self is at times unitary and at other times divided; see LiPuma 1998), to develop an original practice theory model for media research. Combined, he argues, the notions of language game and in/dividual let us track people's media uses and meaning-making as they move across social contexts. He illustrates this abstract model with examples from his research into the uses of information and communication technologies (ICTs) in Norwegian households.

Following Fredrik Barth, a Norwegian social anthropologist whose name is not readily associated with practice theory, Jens Kjaerulff (Chapter 10) argues for a radically empirical take on the question of media as practice. The ethnographic examples are taken from Kjaerulff's research among teleworkers in rural Denmark. His analytical starting point is a naturalistic definition of social practice as 'what people actually do'. With this deliberately broad definition, Kjaerulff intends to capture the open-endedness of his research participants' (internet-related) practices. Like Barth, he is more interested in how people attempt – but often fail – to order their lives than in classic social theoretical concerns with how social order is possible in the first place. He argues that ordering is always an unending, partial and untidy process. For instance, rural teleworkers' best efforts at separating work from family life were often undermined by events beyond their control. Regarding work as a 'cultural stream' (Barth) that shapes local practices, Kjaerulff illustrates this influence with the case of a weekly lunch that brought together all local teleworkers. Because this lunch was framed as 'work' this determined the timing of the event, the types of food and beverages consumed, the topics of conversation deemed appropriate, and so on.[20]

Still in Denmark, Toke H. Christensen and Inge Røpke (Chapter 11) examine the daily uses of ICTs by Danish families through examples of practices such as shopping, 'holding things together', maintaining social networks, or 'killing time'. Questioning Reckwitz's (2002) depiction of individuals as the 'carriers' of practices, they stress the importance of social interaction and situated context. In most cases, they suggest, 'the successful performance of a practice depends on the active participation of several persons, for instance, when micro-coordinating a family meal over several mobile phones. Whilst concurring with Shove and her associates (e.g., Shove and Pantzar 2005) on the need to address the neglect of materiality by leading practice theorists, they also point out that Shove et al., like Reckwitz, downplay social interaction (see the earlier discussion of this term). The chapter closes with some remarks on the challenges of applying practice theory to the study of ICTs in day-to-day life, including the analytical difficulties of separating out one practice from another (such as shopping versus 'holding things together') or of ascertaining whether a given mediated activity belongs with more than one practice simultaneously.

The chapters in Part 4, 'New Media Production Practices', consider the implications of the rapid proliferation of digital technologies for practice theory analyses of social change within specific domains of cultural production: online games, other ludic media forms, free software and film-making.

The aim of Elisenda Ardèvol and colleagues' piece (Chapter 12) is to understand the relationship between popular and professional media practices as a way of understanding media as practice. Ardèvol et al. entreat media theorists to regard 'play' (cf. Weiss 2006 and above) as a key aspect of the current global shift in media production towards 'user-generated content'. Through the ludic appropriation of internet and mobile technologies, today's media consumers are often simultaneously producers, distributors and consumers of new media contents.

Exemplifying their analysis with computer gaming and other audiovisual practices in France, Hong Kong and Spain, they caution that Mark Hobart's notion of 'media-related practices' assumes a sharp separation between professional and amateur (or popular) media practices at odds with today's media environments. For instance, in April 2006 a mundane Hong Kong bus scene captured with a mobile phone camera 'went viral', morphing at great speed across the porous boundaries separating the 'traditional' mass media from myriad new media platforms. Ardèvol and colleagues conclude that any practice-based approach to media should recognise that today virtually all of us are 'the media'.

In Chapter 13, Christopher Kelty teases out the historical threads of a highly specific domain of new media production – free software – and reviews the particularities of what he regards as its five key practices (sharing source code, conceptualising open systems, writing licenses, coordinating collaborations and fomenting movements). Kelty argues that over time these practices have given rise to a 'recursive public' – a type of public characterised by 'the maintenance and modifiability of the medium or infrastructure by which it communicates' (Kelty 2008: 256). Kelty's focus in this chapter is on 'the movement', which he defines as 'the practice, among geeks, of arguing about and discussing the structure and meaning of free software'. The fact that this includes discussions about the other four practices suggests that the movement may be what Peterson (this volume) calls a 'metapractice': a practice about practice.

Finally, in Chapter 14 Cathy Greenhalgh approaches practice theory as a film-maker, ethnographer and teacher. She argues that film and media theorists have rarely acknowledged the collaborative character of film-making, as they have focused on forms, texts and authorship and not on how the crew shape the making of the final product. Her chapter describes in detail two cinematographic practices – 'cheating' ('the constant coordination of bodies and sets with different lens views') and 'visualisation' ('the visual concept of a sequence or whole film') – with particular reference to how digital technologies have transformed the ways in which films are visualised today. Following the practice theorist de Certeau (1984), Greenhalgh distinguishes between the long-term 'strategies' of the film industry and the semi-autonomous 'tactics' of the crew. She ends by suggesting that theories of practice tend to be too general to capture the bottom-up, contingent emergence of actual (mediated) practices.

To conclude, collectively the chapters in this book further our understanding of media as practice by critically engaging with the work of a range of practice theorists (Peirce, Wittgenstein, Bourdieu, Foucault, de Certeau, Barth, Ortner, Schatzki, Reckwitz, Warde and others) in order to address a set of closely interrelated questions, namely the epistemological implications for media studies of a prospective turn to practice theory; the power/knowledge asymmetries that define the mutually constitutive practices of media researchers and researched; the uses and abuses of key concepts such as 'practices', 'media practices', 'structure' and 'culture'; the radically situated nature of people's embodied, mediated practices; the study of media practices under conditions of swift technological change; the relationship between mainstream and marginal media practices; and the gulf between media theorists' and media practitioners' understandings of mediated practice.

Notes

*   I wish to thank Birgit Bräuchler, Sarah Pink, Dorle Dracklé and an anonymous reader for their thoughtful comments on previous drafts of this Introduction.
1.   For a series of overviews of the anthropology of media, see Dickey (1997), Askew and Wilk (2002), Ginsburg, Abu-Lughod and Larkin (2002), Peterson (2003) and Rothenbuhler and Coman (2005).
2.   There is also an overlapping literature known as 'the ethnography of media' to which this volume is linked, albeit rather more tenuously. For instance, like Paterson and Domingo's (2008) recent ethnographic collection on online news-making, a number of contributors to the present book discuss media production (see especially Part 4). The key difference is that they do so in both empirical and theoretical terms and not solely empirically, as is the case with most chapters in Paterson and Domingo.
3.   This analysis is based on a Google Book search of the word 'practices' through online versions of four textbooks (Hughes-Freeland 1998; Askew and Wilk 2002; Ginsburg, Abu-Lughod and Larkin 2002; and Rothenbuhler and Coman 2005) followed by a direct inspection of the printed versions of these books. This method yielded a complete set of instances in which the word 'practices' appears along with the contexts of its numerous usages. A copy of this set is available at: http://johnpostill.wordpress.com/2008/08/06/media-anthropological-uses-of-keyword-practices/.
4.   This figure includes double qualifiers.
5.   See Amit (2002) on common anthropological slippages around key notions such as 'community', 'group', 'network' and so on.
6.   The same applies to the ethnography of media: see, e.g., Paterson and Domingo (2008).
7.   *Stanford Encyclopedia of Philosophy*, http://plato.stanford.edu/entries/methodological-individualism/. Retrieved 11 August 2008.

8. But see the 'post-humanist challenge' (Schatzki 2001) posed by Bruno Latour and his former Actor Network Theory associates (Hinkelbein 2008; Couldry n.d.).
9. This passage is based on a text from the now inaccessible carnalsociology.org website. The text is now available at: http://johnpostill.wordpress.com/2008/05/14/fields-capital/.
10. From the Greek for 'belief or judgment' (see Guthrie 1962: 155).
11. For media-anthropological versions of Ortner's position, see Part 2 (this volume).
12. This preference for Gramsci is shared by political anthropologists (e.g., Gledhill 2000; Nuitjen 2003) and media anthropologists (e.g., Mankekar 1999; Ginsburg, Abu-Lughod and Larkin 2002).
13. However, see Christensen and Røpke (this volume) on the analytical difficulties of attempting to do so 'in practice'.
14. Couldry acknowledges Warde's inspiration in Couldry (2004: 130).
15. See also Christensen and Røpke (this volume) on the routinisation of computer and internet technologies (in affluent countries) and how today 'most people feel comfortable using a computer' (cf. Hinkelbein 2008 on foreign immigrants in Germany and their ICT uses).
16. A rhetoric uncritically reproduced in both ethnographic accounts cited here.
17. On Fredrik Barth as a practice theorist of sorts, see Kjaerulff (this volume).
18. One interesting digital media instance of these two sociological principles at work is the music sharing site Last.fm (http://www.last.fm/) in which users are related to one another as 'friends' (i.e., anyone with whom they recognise a social tie) and/or 'neighbours' (users with whom, on the basis of their digital trail, they share a similar taste in music).
19. For reasons of space the original exchange had to be abridged. See the full version at: http://www.criticalia.org/Debate_on_Media_Practices.htm. Retrieved 27 August 2008.
20. See my discussion of a suburban Malaysian 'field of practices', above.

References

Amit, V. 2002. 'Anthropology and Community: Some Opening Notes', in V. Amit and N. Rapport (eds), *The Trouble with Community*. London: Pluto Press, pp.13–25.

Ang, I. (ed.). 1996. *Living Room Wars: Rethinking Media Audiences for a Postmodern World*. London: Routledge.

Appadurai, A. 1996. *Modernity at Large: Cultural Dimensions of Globalization*. Minneapolis: University of Minnesota Press.

Askew, K. and R.R. Wilk (eds). 2002. *The Anthropology of Media: A Reader*. New York: Blackwell.

Baxter, J. and W.F. Chua. 2008. 'Be(com)ing the Chief Financial Officer of an Organisation: Experimenting with Bourdieu's Practice Theory', *Management Accounting Research* 19(3): 212–30.

Benson, R. and E. Neveu (eds). 2005. *Bourdieu and the Journalistic Field*. Cambridge: Polity Press.

Bird, S.E. 2003. *The Audience in Everyday Life: Living in a Media World*. London: Routledge.

Bob, C. 2005. *The Marketing of Rebellion: Insurgents, Media and International Activism*. Cambridge: Cambridge University Press.

Boellstorff, T. 2008. *Coming of Age in Second Life*. Princeton: Princeton University Press.

Bourdieu, P. 1977. *Outline of a Theory of Practice*. Cambridge: Cambridge University Press.

―――― 1990. *In Other Words*. Cambridge: Polity.

―――― 1992. *The Rules of Art: Genesis and Structure of the Literary Field*. Cambridge: Polity Press.

―――― 1993. *The Field of Cultural Production*. Cambridge : Polity Press.

―――― 1998 *On Television and Journalism*. London: Pluto.

―――― 2005. 'The Political Field, the Social Science Field, and the Journalistic Field', in R. Benson and E. Neveu (eds), *Bourdieu and the Journalistic Field*. Cambridge: Polity Press, pp.29–47.

Bourdieu, P. and L. Wacquant 1992. *An Invitation to Reflexive Sociology*. Cambridge: Polity.

Brightman, R. 1995. 'Forget Culture: Replacement, Transcendence, Relexification'. *Cultural Anthropology* 10(4): 509–46.

Coman, M. 2005. 'Cultural Anthropology and Mass Media', in Rothenbuhler, E. and M. Coman (eds), *Media Anthropology*. London: Sage, pp.46–55.

Cortázar Rodríguez, F.J. 2004. 'Rumores y Leyendas Urbanas en Internet', *Archivo del Observatorio para la CiberSociedad*. Retrieved 14 July 2009 from: http://www.cibersociedad.net/archivo/articulo.php?art=194.

Couldry, N. 2003. 'Media Meta-capital: Extending the Range of Bourdieu's Field Theory', *Theory and Society* 32: 653–77.

―――― 2004. 'Theorising Media as Practice', *Social Semiotics* 14(2): 115–32.

―――― 2005. 'Media Rituals: Beyond Functionalism', in E.W. Rothenbuhler and M. Coman (eds), *Media Anthropology*. London: Sage, pp.59–69.

―――― n.d. 'Actor Network Theory and Media: Do they Connect and on What Terms?' Retrieved 6 July 2009 from: http://www.lse.ac.uk/collections/media@lse/pdf/Couldry_ActorNetworkTheoryMedia.pdf .

Csíkszentmihályi, M. 1990. *Flow: The Psychology of Optimal Experience*. New York: Harper and Row.

De Certeau, M. 1984. *The Practice of Everyday Life*. Berkeley: University of California Press.

Deleuze, G. and F. Guattari. 1987. *A Thousand Plateaux: Capitalism and Schizophrenia*. Minneapolis: University of Minnesota Press.

De Nooy, W. 2003 'Fields and Networks: Correspondence Analysis and Social Network Analysis in the Framework of Field Theory', *Poetics* 31: 305–27.

Dickey, S. 1997. 'Anthropology and its Contributions to Studies of Mass Media'. *International Social Science Journal* 49(3): 413–27.

Eisenlohr, P. 2006 'As Makkah is Sweet and Beloved, so is Madina: Islam, Devotional Genres, and Electronic Mediation in Mauritius', *American Ethnologist* 33(2): 230–45.

Ellis, J. 1982. *Visible Fictions.* London: Routledge and Kegan Paul.

Eriksen, T.H. and F.S. Nielsen. 2001. *A History of Anthropology,* London: Pluto Press.

Evens, T.M.S. and D. Handelman (eds). 2006. *The Manchester School: Practice and Ethnographic Praxis in Anthropology.* Oxford: Berghahn.

Eyerman, R. 2008. *The Assassination of Theo Van Gogh: From Social Drama to Cultural Trauma.* Durham, NC: Duke University Press.

Ferrell, J., D. Milovanovic and S. Lyng. 2001. 'Edgework, Media Practices, and the Elongation of Meaning: A Theoretical Ethnography of the Bridge Day Event', *Theoretical Criminology* 5(2): 177–202.

Foucault, M. 1979. *Discipline and Punish: The Birth of the Prison.* Harmondsworth: Peregrine Books.

Gell, A. 1986. 'Newcomers to the World of Goods: Consumption among the Muria Gonds', in A. Appadurai (ed.), *The Social Life of Things: Commodities in Cultural Perspective,* Cambridge: Cambridge University Press, pp.110–38.

——— 1992. *The Anthropology of Time: Cultural Constructions of Temporal Maps and Images.* Oxford: Berg.

Giddens, A. 1979. *Central Problems in Social Theory: Action, Structure and Contradiction in Social Analysis.* Berkeley: University of California Press.

——— 1984. *The Constitution of Society.* Cambridge: Polity.

Ginsburg, F. 1993. 'Aboriginal Media and the Australian Imaginary', *Public Culture* 5(3): 557–78.

Ginsburg, F., L. Abu-Lughod and B. Larkin (eds). 2002. *Media Worlds.* Berkeley: University of California Press.

Gledhill, J. 2000. *Power and its Disguises: Anthropological Perspectives on Politics.* London: Pluto.

Guthrie, W.K.C. 1962. *A History of Greek Philosophy, Vol. I.* Cambridge: Cambridge University Press.

Hägerstrand, T. 1967. *Innovation Diffusion as a Spatial Process.* Chicago: University of Chicago Press.

Hamilton, A. 2002. 'The National Picture: Thai Media and Cultural Identity', in F. Ginsburg, L. Abu-Lughod and B. Larkin (eds), *Media Worlds: Anthropology on New Terrain.* Berkeley: University of California Press, pp.152–70.

Hannerz, U. 1992. *Cultural Complexity: Studies in the Social Organization of Meaning.* New York: Columbia University Press.

Hawk, B., D. Riedler and O. Oviedo (eds). 2008. *Small Tech: The Culture of Digital Tools.* Minneapolis: University of Minnesota Press.

Hervik, P. and M.A. Peterson. Forthcoming. *Cartoon Violence? Media, Muslims and the Making of a Global Controversy.* Oxford: Berghahn.

Hesmondhalgh, D. and J. Toynbee (eds). 2008. *The Media and Social Theory*. New York: Routledge.

Hinkelbein, O. 2008. 'Strategien zur Digitalen Integration von Migranten: Ethnographische Fallstudien in Esslingen und Hannover', Ph.D. dissertation. Bremen: University of Bremen.

Hobart, M. 2002. 'Live or Dead? Televising Theater in Bali', in F. Ginsburg, L. Abu-Lughod and B. Larkin (eds), *Media Worlds*. Berkeley: University of California Press, pp.370–82.

——— 2005. The Profanity of the Media', in E. Rothenbuhler and M. Coman (eds), *Media Anthropology*. London: Sage, pp.26–35.

Hughes-Freeland, F. (ed.) 1998. *Ritual, Performance, Media*. London: Routledge.

Jarzabkowski, P., J. Balogun and D. Seidl. 2007. 'Strategizing: The Challenges of a Practice Perspective', *Human Relations* 60(1): 5–27.

Jenkins, R. 2002. *Pierre Bourdieu*. London: Routledge.

Kelty, C.M. 2008. *Two Bits: The Cultural Significance of Free Software*. Durham, NC: Duke University Press.

Knox, H., M. Savage and P. Harvey. 2006. 'Social Networks and Spatial Relations: Networks as Method, Metaphor and Form', *Economy and Society* 35(1): 113–40.

Kücklich, J. 2005. 'Precarious Playbour: Modders and the Digital Games Industry', *Fibreculture* 3(5). Retrieved 26 June 2009 from: http://journal.fibreculture.org/issue5/kucklich.html.

Lee, S.W., R. Taylor and G. Kielhofner. 2009. 'Choice, Knowledge, and Utilization of a Practice Theory: A National Study of Occupational Therapists Who Use the Model of Human Occupation', *Occupational Therapy In Health Care* 23(1): 60–71.

LiPuma, E. 1998. 'Modernity and Forms of Personhood in Melanesia', in M. Lambek and A. Strathern (eds), *Bodies and Persons: Comparative Perspectives from Africa and Melanesia*. Cambridge: Cambridge University Press, pp.53–79.

Lizardo, O. 2007. '"Mirror Neurons", Collective Objects and the Problem of Transmission: Reconsidering Stephen Turner's Critique of Practice Theory', *Journal for the Theory of Social Behaviour* 37(3): 319–50.

Mankekar, P. 1999. *Screening Culture, Viewing Politics. An Ethnography of Television, Womanhood, and Nation in Postcolonial India*. Durham: Duke University Press.

Martin, J.L. 2003. 'What Is Field Theory?' *American Journal of Sociology* 109: 1–49.

Moeran, B. 2002. 'Fields, Networks and Frames: Advertising Social Organization in Japan', *Global Networks* 16: 371–86.

Moores, S. 2005. *Media/Theory*. London: Routledge.

Nuitjen, M. 2003. 'Family Property and the Limits of Intervention: The Article 27 Reforms and the PROCEDE Programme in Mexico', *Development and Change* 34: 475–97.

Ortner, S.B. 1984, 'Theory in Anthropology Since the Sixties', *Comparative Studies in Society and History* 26(1): 126–66.

———— 2006. *Anthropology and Social Theory: Culture, Power and the Acting Subject.* Durham, NC: Duke University Press.

Parkin, R. 1997. 'Practice Theory', in T. Barfield (ed.), *The Dictionary of Anthropology.* Oxford: Blackwell, pp.375–77.

Paterson, C. and D. Domingo. 2008.*Making Online News: The Ethnography of New Media Production.* New York: Peter Lang.

Peterson, M.A. 2003. *Anthropology and Mass Communication: Media and Myth in the New Millennium.* Oxford: Berghahn.

———— 2005 'Performing Media: Toward an Ethnography of Intertextuality', in E. Rothenbuhler and M. Coman (eds), *Media Anthropology.* London: Sage, pp.129–38.

Postill, J. 2002. 'Clock and Calendar Time: A Missing Anthropological Problem, *Time and Society* 11: 251–70.

———— 2006. *Media and Nation Building: How the Iban Became Malaysian.* Oxford: Berghahn.

———— 2008. 'Localizing the Internet Beyond Communities and Networks', *New Media and Society* 10(3): 413–31.

Pype, K. 2008. 'The Making of the Pentecostal Melodrama: Mimesis, Power, and Agency in Kinshasa's Media World', Ph.D. dissertation. Leuven: Catholic University of Leuven.

Rafael, V. 2003. 'The Cell Phone and the Crowd: Messianic Politics in the Contemporary Philippines', *Public Culture* 15(3): 399–425.

Randles, S. and A. Warde. 2006. 'Consumption: The View from Theories of Practice', in K. Green and S. Randles (eds), *Industrial Ecology and Spaces of Innovation.* Cheltenham: Edward Elgar, pp.220–37.

Reckwitz, A. 2002. 'Toward a Theory of Social Practices: A Development in Culturalist Theorizing', *European Journal of Social Theory* 5: 243–63.

Reed-Danahay, D. 2005. *Locating Bourdieu.* Bloomington: Indiana University Press.

Røpke, I. 2009. 'Theories of Practice: New Inspiration for Ecological Economic Studies', *Ecological Economics* 68: 2490–7.

Rothenbuhler, E. and M. Coman (eds). 2005. *Media Anthropology.* London: Sage.

Ryan, A. 1970. *The Philosophy of the Social Sciences.* London: Macmillan.

Sahlins, M., 1981. *Historical Metaphors and Mythical Realities.* Ann Arbor: University of Michigan Press.

Scannell, P. 1988. 'Radio Times: The Temporal Arrangements of Broadcasting in the Modern World', in P. Drummond and R. Paterson (eds), *Television and its Audience.* London: British Film Institute, pp.15–29.

———— 1991. 'Introduction: The Relevance of Talk', in P. Scannell (ed.), *Broadcast Talk.* London: Sage, pp.1–13.

Schatzki, T. 1996. *Social Practices: A Wittgensteinian Approach to Human Activity and the Social.* Cambridge: Cambridge University Press.

———— 2001. 'Introduction: Practice Theory', in T. Schatzki, K. Knorr Cetina and E. von Savigny (eds), *The Practice Turn in Contemporary Theory.* London: Routledge, pp.1–14.

Schatzki, T., K. Knorr Cetina and E. von Savigny (eds). 2001. *The Practice Turn in Contemporary Theory*. London: Routledge.

Schieffelin, E. 1998. 'Problematizing Performance', in F. Hughes-Freeland (ed.), *Ritual, Performance, Media*. London: Routledge, pp.194–207.

Shove, E. 2003. *Comfort, Cleanliness and Convenience: The Social Organization of Normality*. Oxford: Berg.

Shove, E. and M. Pantzar. 2005. 'Consumers, Producers and Practices: Understanding the Invention and Reinvention of Nordic Walking', *Journal of Consumer Culture* 5: 43–64.

Shove, E. et al. 2007. *The Design of Everyday Life*. Oxford: Berg.

Silverstone, R. 1993. 'Television, Ontological Security and the Transitional Object', *Media, Culture and Society* 15(4): 573–98.

Spitulnik, D. 1996. 'The Social Circulation of Media Discourse and the Mediation of Communities', *Journal of Linguistic Anthropology* 62: 161–87.

Swartz, D. 1997. *Culture and Power: The Sociology of Pierre Bourdieu*. Chicago: University of Chicago Press.

Swartz, M., V. Turner and A. Tuden (eds). 1966. *Political Anthropology*. Chicago: Aldine.

Swidler, A. 1986. 'Culture in Action: Symbols and Strategies', *American Sociological Review* 51: 273–86.

——— 2001. 'What Anchors Cultural Practices', in T. Schatzki, K. Knorr Cetina and E. von Savigny (eds), *The Practice Turn in Contemporary Theory*. London: Routledge, pp.74–92.

Thompson, J.B. 1995. *The Media and Modernity: A Social Theory of the Media*. Cambridge: Polity Press.

Turner, V.W. 1974. *Dramas, Fields and Metaphors: Symbolic Action in Human Society*, Ithaca, NY: Cornell University Press.

——— 1996[1957]. *Schism and Continuity in an African Society*. Oxford: Berg.

Van de Port, M. 2006 'Visualizing the Sacred: Video Technology, "Televisual" Style, and the Religious Imagination in Bahian Candomblé', *American Ethnologist* 33(3): 444–61.

Wacquant, L. 2006. *Body and Soul: Notebooks of an Apprentice Boxer*. Oxford: Oxford University Press.

Wagner-Pacifici, R. E. 1986. *The Moro Morality Play: Terrorism as Social Drama*. Chicago: University of Chicago Press.

Warde, A. 2005. 'Consumption and Theories of Practice', *Journal of Consumer Culture* 5: 131–53.

Weiss, M.D. 2006. 'Working at Play: BDSM Sexuality in the San Francisco Bay Area' *Anthropologica* 48: 229–45.

Whittington, R. 2006. 'Completing the Practice Turn in Strategy Research', *Organization Studies* 27(5): 613–34.

Wittel, A. 2001. 'Toward a Network Sociality', *Theory, Culture and Society* 18(6): 51–76.

PART I

Media as Practice

CHAPTER I

Theorising Media as Practice

Nick Couldry

Media research has been a thing of fits and starts.[1] As we look back over more than a century of reflection on media, can we say the subject has now broken into a steady rhythm running in a clear direction? Not yet, because media research remains marked by its episodic history. The time is nonetheless ripe to attempt to formulate a new paradigm of media research that can draw together some of the more interesting recent work, but at the same time achieve a decisive break with the unprofitable disputes of the past. This new paradigm sees media not as text or production economy, but first and foremost as practice. Some of the stimulus for this comes from the recent growth of practice theory in sociology; indeed this new paradigm insists on a much closer relationship with central debates in the social sciences than previously in media studies, with the advantage that the major contribution of media research to those wider social science debates becomes clearer.

This is no place for a history of media research. To set the scene, however, it is worth recalling that theoretical discussion about the social consequences of media goes back well into the nineteenth century (de Tocqueville 1994; Kierkegaard 1962), although it remained completely marginal in mainstream sociology until after the Second World War with only rare exceptions (Tarde 1969). The contemporary landscape of 'media studies' is the residue of at least five distinct currents of work: first, U.S. mass communications research (Merton, Lazarsfeld, Katz) which was set firmly in the tradition of the experimental social sciences but took its cue from wider intellectual debates on mass media and their consequences for democracy and social order; second, critical Marxist commentary (Benjamin, Adorno) which also took its cue from mass culture debates but within an agenda based on the critique of capitalism (this in turn developed into the political economy tradition);

third, semiotic analysis which in its dominant form developed in the context of European structuralism and poststructuralism and applied the most radical theoretical innovations of postwar literary theory to media texts; fourth, the critical research, particularly on media audiences (Hall, Morley, Ang), that emerged in Britain in close association with semiotics and Marxism but quickly developed into a broader empirical tradition which has continued through the 1990s; and fifth, and most recently, the line of anthropological research into media that has emerged out of postmodern versions of symbolic anthropology (Ginsburg 1994; Ginsburg, Abu-Lughod and Larkin 2002). Needless to say, there is not always common ground between these traditions: for example, the third has developed largely independently of the others with its own extensive theoretical framework drawing particularly on psychoanalysis, while the fourth is sharply critical of the first and second and has only a limited interest in the third; the fifth meanwhile has some difficulty acknowledging how much it has in common with the fourth (Abu-Lughod 1999).

These traditions disagree of course as to their primary theoretical focus: for the first, it is problems of large-scale social effects; for the second, processes of commodification; for the third, the polysemy of the text; for the fourth, the process of interpretation; and for the fifth, open-ended practices of media production, circulation and consumption. At the same time, there are of course cross-currents: so the problems of the U.S. mass communications field with effects have serious implications for critical theory and audience research, even if they are blissfully ignored by semiotic analysis; while the processual complexities uncovered by audience research are irrelevant for anthropological narratives of media practice. With such profusion, why call for a further paradigm? One aim is to put behind us some of the internecine disputes of the past: between audience research and screen theory over the determining status of the text (Morley 1980); between audience research and political economy over the importance of audience practices of meaning-making (Garnham 1995; Grossberg 1995). Another aim is to help clarify where might lie the epicentre of new research questions, if (as I would argue) this no longer lies directly above the media text or the media's production economy.

The proposed new paradigm is disarmingly simple: it treats media as the open set of practices relating to, or oriented around, media.[2] The potential of this reformulation only becomes clear when we look more closely at recent debates over 'practice' in the social sciences. The aim, however, can be stated directly: to decentre media research from the study of media texts or production structures (important though these are) and to redirect it onto the study of the open-ended range of practices focused directly or indirectly on media. This places media studies firmly within a broader sociology of action and knowledge (or if you prefer, cultural anthropology or cognitive anthropology), and sets it apart from versions of media studies formulated within the paradigm of literary criticism.

Why Practice?

This proposal needs some unpacking: first, in terms of questions of media analysis; and second, in terms of questions of social theory.

Practice as an Emerging Theme in Media Research

The new paradigm decentres the media text for a reason: to sidestep the insoluble problems over how to prove 'media effects' – that is, a convincing causal chain from the circulation of a media text, or a pattern of media consumption, to changes in the behaviour of audiences. The classic version of this debate concerned cultivation analysis, which has been unfairly vilified for at least being explicit and methodical in its attempt to prove a causal chain between heavy television viewing and cognitive and moral shifts in those viewers, which was extremely difficult to establish at a statistically significant level (Signorielli and Morgan 1990). But hidden assumptions about 'media effects' abound in media analysis and everyday talk about media. Indeed they are hard to avoid if you start from the text itself: outside literary approaches, why else study the detailed structure of a media text as your primary research focus unless you can plausibly claim that those details make a difference to wider social processes? But it is exactly this that is difficult to show. As Justin Lewis put it: 'The question that should be put to textual analysis that purports to tell us how a cultural product "works" in contemporary culture is almost embarrassingly simple: where's the evidence? Without evidence, everything else is pure speculation' (Lewis 1991: 49). It is better, surely, to focus our research paradigm somewhere else.

A popular alternative has been to start from the institutional structures that produce media, as in the political economy and (more recently) the cultural economy traditions (Garnham 1990; du Gay et al. 1997; Hesmondhalgh 2002). Clearly, the analysis of industrial and market structures in the media and cultural sectors is valid in its own right as a contribution to policy debates and to the analysis of the wider economy, as well as being vital to our understanding of the pressures which limit participation in those sectors on various scales and also limit the range of outputs they produce. Here, there is no question of speculation (quite the contrary) and in my view such work is important. But in considering what should be the general paradigm for media research and media theory, there is a difficulty in situating it in media production, obvious though that might be in one respect (this is where media products start their life). The difficulty is that the structures of media production, and particularly the dynamics of concentration and conglomeration, do not, of themselves, tell us anything about the uses to which media products are put in social life generally. Even from a Marxist perspective, which insists on the causal primacy of economic relations, it is difficult to make the leap from arguing that economic factors determine the nature of media production to arguing that the (economically determined) nature of media production determines the social consequences of media texts. Unlike the primary case of labour conditions, there is a crucial uncertainty about how media texts (or any texts produced in an economy) causally mediate between the world they represent and the world where they are consumed. This was precisely the force of the challenge to the dominant ideology thesis (Abercrombie, Hill and Turner 1981): Where is the evidence that the holding of beliefs associated with a dominant ideology adds anything to the structuring of social relations by what Marx called the dull compulsion of economic life? The point applies a fortiori if we consider the consequences of media texts, since the relationship between consumption of a media text (however it may be read as reproducing an ideology) and transmission of belief in that ideology is also uncertain (Lewis 1991, quoted above). Unless, therefore, you reduce media texts to being a conduit for economic signals (absurd in all but the crudest case), we are forced once again, even within a political economy model, to consider what people do with media.

This, after all, was the point of audience research – to emphasise that consumption is a 'determinate moment' in the production of meaning through media texts (Hall 1980). The only problem was that audience research developed in an intellectual landscape in Britain decisively influenced by semiotics, so requiring that all questions about media start from the supposed structuring properties of the text itself. Although the connection of audience research (from fan practices to video use) to the moment of textual consumption was increasingly loosened until the audience become undecideable – undecideable, that is, in relation to the originary moment of textual consumption (Ang 1996: 70) – audience research remained constrained by its primary emphasis on people's relationships to texts.

It is to escape that constraint that my proposed paradigm starts not with media texts or media institutions, but with practice – not necessarily the practice of audiences (a point to which I will come back), but media-oriented practice, in all its looseness and openness. What, quite simply, are people doing in relation to media across a whole range of situations and contexts?

Like any new paradigm that seeks to resolve a crisis or contradiction in how a field of research is constructed, this paradigm was 'at least partially anticipated' (Kuhn 1970: 75) in the 1990s. First, there was important research into the whole range of domestic practices in which television viewing was inserted (Silverstone and Hirsch 1992; Silverstone 1994); this work developed a rich theoretical framework drawing on recent developments in the sociology of science and technology and encompassing the latest developments in the sociology of the family and social anthropology. The focus remained the home, as the primary site of media consumption, although there was a less noticed line of research on the public viewing of television (Lemish 1982; Krotz and Tyler Eastman 1999; McCarthy 2002).

The new paradigm was anticipated, secondly, by researchers who sought to move beyond the specific contexts of media consumption. Having concluded that 'television's meanings for audiences ... cannot be decided upon outside of the multidimensional intersubjective networks in which the object is inserted and made to mean in concrete contextual settings' (Ang 1996: 70), Ien Ang posed the different question of 'what it means, or what it is like, to live in a media-saturated world' (ibid.: 72). My own research inflected this general question from the perspective of power, asking 'what it means to live in a society dominated by large-scale media institutions' (Couldry 2000a: 6). The shift to a more widely focused research question was anticipated also by the emergence of the term 'mediation' (Silverstone 2005) to refer to the broad expanse of social processes focused around media, even if the first prominent use of that term (Martin-Barbero 1993) was concerned, still, with extending our understanding of media consumption to encompass a broader range of cultural participation. It is here that recent anthropological research into media processes, free as it is from any primary attachment to studying texts and their interpretation, has become a promising ally, while at the same time acquiring a higher profile in anthropology itself (Ginsburg, Abu-Lughod and Larkin 2002).

Important also were two explicit attempts to shift the paradigm of media research in the late 1990s. Coming from outside media studies, Abercrombie and Longhurst (1998) challenged what they saw as a paradigm of media research dominated by ideological questions (the 'incorporation/resistance' paradigm) and proposed to replace it by a 'spectacle/performance' paradigm that foregrounded the various levels of engagement people have with different aspects of media culture. While this proposal was valuable for drawing on a wider frame of historical, cultural and sociological reference than usual in media research, a problem (Couldry 2000a: 21) was its downgrading of questions of power, which itself made some contestable assumptions about how power works in media-saturated spaces. There was also the proposal that we were now entering the 'third generation' of audience research (Alasuutari 1999) in which the priority was to 'get a grasp on our contemporary "media culture"' (ibid.: 6), for example through an interest in the open-ended processes of identity construction linked to media (Hermes 1999). But this 'generational' formulation risked disguising the radical nature of the shift under way by holding onto the notion of 'audiences' as its central focus.

Perhaps, however, the definitive formulation of the paradigm shift under way comes from the media anthropologist Liz Bird, who announces a new approach 'beyond the audience', that aims to address 'the amorphous nature of media experience', arguing that: 'We cannot really isolate the role of media in culture, because the media are firmly anchored into the web of culture, although articulated by individuals in different ways ... The "audience" is everywhere and nowhere' (Bird 2003: 2–3).

It is worth noting, however, that Bird makes a crucial qualification: 'our culture may be "media-saturated", but *as individuals* we are not, or at least not in any predictable, uniform way' (ibid.: 3, emphasis added). There is the beginning of a separation here between our concern with a media-saturated 'culture' and our interest in the specificity of local experience. The term 'culture' has its own problems if implying a holistic notion of a distinct cultural system (Hannerz 1992). This suggests that, in formulating a new paradigm of media research, we should open our lens even wider to take in the whole range of practices in which media consumption and media-related talk is embedded, including practices of avoiding or selecting out media inputs (Hoover, Schofield Clark and Alters 2003). Such practices may not be part of what we normally refer to by 'media culture', but as practices oriented to media they are hardly trivial. This, it might seem, loosens the tie to media texts too much and plunges us into chaos. Fortunately, however, the recent emergence of a practice-based research paradigm in sociology ensures that we need not be left floating without theoretical moorings.

The Sociology of Practice

The recent shift towards practice in some social science has long philosophical roots (going back to, among others, Wittgenstein, Merleau-
Ponty) and is the latest in a series of attempts to overcome the old theoretical division between structure and agency.[3] These is no space to go
into this background here. The key question instead is what the notion
of 'practice' offers to media sociology. There are three important points
to be made.

First, as Ann Swidler (2001) explains, the aim of practice theory is to
replace an older notion of 'culture' as internal 'ideas' or 'meanings' with
a different analysis of culture in terms of two types of publicly observable
processes: first, practices themselves, particularly 'routine activities
(rather than consciously chosen actions) notable for their unconscious,
automatic, un-thought character' (ibid.: 74); and second, discourse,
which 'is not what anyone says, but the system of meanings that allows
them to say anything at all' (ibid.: 75). While we might query Swidler's
exclusive emphasis on routine activities (surely a concern with discourse
would lead us to be interested in practices that are associated with discourse – that is, which are self-reflexive) and, while we might also query
the term 'system' in the characterisation of discourse, it would be better,
perhaps, to refer to principles or ordering, without assuming that order
or system is necessarily achieved in discourse. Nonetheless, this represents a useful, pragmatic shift in the analysis of culture, including 'media
culture'. If recent media research has foregrounded media culture,
practice theory translates this into two concrete and related questions:
What types of things do people do in relation to media? And what types
of things do people say in relation to media?[4]

Second, practice research aims to be as open as possible in
analysing what practices are out there, which in turn depends on how
people understand what actions constitute a distinct practice – a complex question because actions are linked into a practice not just by
explicit understandings but also by being governed by common rules
and by sharing the common reference point of certain ends, projects
and beliefs (Schatzki 1996: 89). There undoubtedly are a whole mass of
media-oriented practices in contemporary societies, but how they are
divided up into specific practices, and how those practices are coordinated with each other, remains an open question.

We cannot resolve such questions here. What matters is taking this
question as our starting-point, since it distances us from the normal
media studies assumption that what audiences do ('audiencing') is a distinctive set of practices rather than an artificially chosen 'slice' through

daily life that cuts across how they actually understand the practices in which they are engaged. If we live in a media-saturated world, then it is reasonable to expect that how that world is carved up into recognisable practices may no longer correspond to categorisations formed in a 'pre-saturation' world (when audiencing could be assumed to be a discrete activity). But – and this is the point which practice theory makes clear – in order to establish what are the new principles by which practices orientated to media are demarcated, we cannot operate simply by our instinct as media researchers. We must look closely at the categorisations of practice that people make themselves.

Third, the space of practices is not as chaotic as might appear for the crucial reason that practices are organised among themselves. How this works is the fundamental question that Swidler addresses: 'how [do] some practices anchor, control, or organise others' (Swidler 2001: 79)? Put in these stark terms, this is a surprisingly difficult question. Swidler approaches it first from the point of view of definitional hierarchy: some practices are defined as part of a larger practice which provides their key reference points; so, for example, political marketing, lobbying and campaigning are part of the wider practice of politics. Secondly, she approaches it as a question of dynamic change: some practices 'anchor' others, because changes in the former automatically cause reformulation of the latter's aims. For the second case, Swidler makes an interesting suggestion that 'public ritual' has a crucial role to play in 'the visible, public enactment of new patterns so that "everyone can see" that everyone else has seen that things have been changed' (ibid.: 87). Some practices, in other words (although this is my gloss, not Swidler's) work to enact new forms of categorisation and distinction replied upon in other practices.

One of Swidler's examples is how the public performance of identity based on sexuality in San Francisco's Lesbian/Gay Freedom Day Parade (from 1971 onwards) changed the conditions in which sexual identity in San Francisco could be claimed and performed more generally. Swidler argues that anchoring practices are associated particularly with the management of conflict and difference, but that, once established, the principles enacted by those practices become part of the social 'structure' itself.

As Swidler herself makes clear, these suggestions are tentative, and much more work in this area is needed, but this practice-based approach is suggestive for how we might understand the relation of media-oriented practices to social practice as a whole. What if one of the main things media do is anchor other practices through the 'authoritative' representations and enactments of key terms and categories that they provide? A question, then, if we theorise media as practice, is; How, where and for whom does this anchoring role work and with what consequences for the organisation of social action as a whole?

Media as Practice: The Theoretical Challenges

Having now set the scene, I want to explore (inevitably schematically) what a theory of media-as-practice might be like, and what its key questions might be. As we have seen, this new paradigm is not fundamentally new, but it is distinctive in being formulated without any reliance on textual or political economy models and with enough generality to be open to wider developments in sociology and anthropology. As John Tulloch (2000: 19–32) has argued, media research and theory needs to be more closely integrated with the wider social sciences (although this requires some rapprochement on their part as well!). This is much more productive, I would add, than relying on the abstractions of philosophy or philosophically generated theories about media, whether in Scannell's (1996) use of Heidegger's philosophy of Being or the extensive use across media studies of Baudrillard's polemics or Deleuze and Guattari's conceptual explorations.[5] Media theory has no independent value as theory; it is only valuable when it helps us formulate better questions for empirical research.

To flesh out how a theory of media-as-practice affects the priorities of media research, I want to discuss three consequences of an emphasis on practice: anti-functionalism; openness to the variable and complex organisation of practice; and a concern to understand the principles whereby, and the mechanisms through which, practices are ordered. At this general level, media theory is no different from any other area of social theory, although media's role in representing the social world from which media are generated adds to the complexity of how their workings can be understood on a large scale. Media represent other practices and so have direct consequences for how those practices are defined and ordered.

Beyond Functionalism

I do not want to dwell long on this point, since I have covered it extensively elsewhere (Couldry 2005). Functionalism is so long dead in sociology and anthropology that it is embarrassing to find it alive and well in areas of media research. Functionalism is the idea that large regions of human activity ('societies', 'cultures' and so on) can best be understood as if they were self-sufficient, complex, functioning systems. Depending on taste, the metaphor of functioning can be biological (the natural organism, such as the human body) or technological (artificial systems, such as the machine). Societies, or cultures, are conceived in functionalist accounts as complex 'wholes' formed of a series of 'parts', each of which 'functions' by contributing to the successful working of the 'whole'. Action at the level of society's or culture's 'parts' has no unanticipated effects, and even if it does it is quickly absorbed back into the 'whole's' wider functioning through positive feedback loops.

There are many problems with functionalist attempts to model the multidimensionality of social and cultural practice, including media. Looking back from the beginning of the twenty-first century, one obvious problem is the difficulty of conceiving of any 'society' or 'culture' as a self-sufficient system, given the huge range of forces operating across societal and cultural borders.[6] The main problem, however, lies with functionalism's underlying claim that there are such totalities as 'societies' and 'cultures' which 'function' as working systems. The problem becomes clearer when this claim is applied in detail. We need go no further than Steven Lukes's (1975) classic deconstruction of functionalist accounts of political ritual, which analyses political rituals in terms of how they contribute to society's political 'stability' by affirming certain central beliefs and values. But even if there are such centrally held beliefs and values, which Lukes questions, this account begs deeper questions about 'whether, to what extent, and in what ways society *does* hold together' (ibid.: 297). Is there, Lukes asks, a functioning social 'whole' of which political rituals could be a 'part'?

Yet functionalist explanations continue to crop up in media research in some surprising places. The standard positions in debates about stardom and celebrity culture assume, at root, that the industrial production of celebrity discourse 'must' contribute to some wider social 'function', whether we call it identity-formation or social integration or both. Here, for example, is McKenzie Wark: 'we may not like the same celebrities, we may not like any of them at all, but it is the existence of a population of celebrities, about whom to disagree, that *makes it possible* to constitute a sense of belonging' (Wark 1999: 33, emphasis added). Where is the evidence that people 'identify' with celebrities in any simple way, or even that they regard 'celebrity culture' as important, rather than a temporary distraction, let alone that celebrities 'make possible' everyone's sense of belonging? The absence of empirical work here illustrates how functionalism blocks off routes to open-minded research.

An advantage of starting with practice – what types of things do people do, say and think that are oriented to media? – is that there is no intrinsic plausibility in the idea that what people do (across a whole range of practices and locations) should add up to a functioning 'whole'. Why should it? In the past, an apparent reason was that, without the ordering presence of 'society' as a functioning whole, the meanings and mutual relationships of practices could not themselves be understood, agency being incomprehensible without structure. Giddens's structuration theory (Giddens 1984), whatever detailed problems it raises, was a convincing move beyond that problem, since it showed how principles of order could both produce and be reproduced at the level of practice itself; social order, in other words, is 'recursively' present in practice and in the organisation of practice (Swidler 2001: 78). Practice theory, indeed, seeks to develop this insight by insisting that 'there is no reason to think that social life can exhibit [ordered] features only if it is a totality' (Schatzki 1996: 10) and by exploring other ways of thinking about social order.

One good reason, however, why functionalist ideas might still appear plausible at least in the area of media research is that media institutions, like governments, work hard to create the impression that they are at the 'centre' of the functioning whole of 'society', in the sense of a value centre (Shils 1975), not just as an administrative centre for practical purposes. Media studies (and incidentally also political science) must work hard to avoid, indeed to undermine, the pressures towards functionalism inherent in its topic. For the same reason, media studies (and political science) should resist the temptation to see the actual institutional centres of media (and political) culture as 'all there is': they must avoid the 'centrism' (Couldry 2005) which distorts the breadth of the actual field of media (and political) practice beyond these claimed 'centres'.[7] The simple starting point of practice (what is going on and where?) provides a useful counterweight to functionalist tendencies in media research.

The Varieties of Media Practice

The value of practice theory, as we have seen, is that it asks open questions about what people are doing and how they categorise what they are doing, avoiding the disciplinary or other preconceptions which would automatically read their actions as, say, 'consumption' or 'being an audience', whether or not that is how the actors see their actions. One possibility we need to be ready for – anticipated in the quotation from Ien Ang (1996: 70) already given – is that, in many cases, 'media consumption' or 'audiencing' can only be understood as part of a practice which is not itself 'about' media: what practice this is depends on who we are describing and when.

Watching a football game on television might for one person be best analysed as part of their intensely emotional practice as a football fan or fan of a particular football team; for another, perhaps that person's partner or child, it may be an obligation or pleasure of their relationship to share the first person's passion with them; for someone watching in a public space, it may be part of a practice of group solidarity; for a fourth, it may be something done to fill in time, instantly 'put-downable' (Hermes 1995) as soon as a friend rings the doorbell or the person gets the energy to go back to some work. Pointing this out is hardly new of course (see Bausinger 1984; Morley 1992). What it demonstrates, however, is that the main priorities for media research cannot be the varieties of how people read the text of this televised game (since 'watching football on TV' is not the practice we are interested in analysing) nor can it be the structure of the televised game's text considered in itself. It is more interesting to consider, first, the range of practices in which the act of watching this football game occurs and, second, the consequences of that common feature for the relationships between those practices. As to the first question, it will only be in the case of the football fan that the way they read the game's text is likely to be of research interest, since it is only here that the watching of the game forms a central, non-substitutable part of a wider practice. Political economy approaches are an important background in all these cases, but again probably only an important background in the case of the football fan, where economic pressures have had a major effect on both the places where televised games can be watched and the structure of the game itself. As to the second question, the fact that people performing a huge range of practices (from fandom to family interaction to group solidarity at a community centre or pub to just waiting for something else to do) should all be doing the same thing at the same time is, however, significant for our understanding of the time-space coordination of practices through media. Similar questions could be asked of watching a prime-time news bulletin, and here there might be more commonality around the practice of 'watching the news', an inherently general activity that is, perhaps, a distinct practice for many people. By contrast, if we took the activity of reading a celebrity magazine, this is much more ambiguous. Is it just passing time, a deliberate search for humour, or information seeking? The answer can only be given for particular individuals and groups in the contexts of their everyday practice, which must take into account the contexts, if any, where the contents of that celebrity magazine are later put to use.

Clearly this only begins to track the variety of media-oriented practices, and media-oriented actions that form part of other practices.

Large areas of this terrain have, of course, already been explored in media research, but there remain large areas that are still little known. To name a few: practices of using media sources in education; individuals' uses of media references in telling stories about themselves, their family or historical events; the uses of media in the legal system and indeed in work practices across the public world (so far, most research has focused on politics, but there are many other areas worth investigating). There is also the larger question of how media products and references to media are, over time, affecting practice in all production fields, which I have begun to explore elsewhere, drawing on Bourdieu's field theory (Couldry 2003b). Focusing on practice is a more radical adjustment to our research agendas than might at first appear. It is commonplace to study talk shows, for example, as texts, but much less common to study them as a social practice whereby particular groups of people are brought together to perform before each other in a studio.[8] The resulting text is only a facet of the overall practice.

At this descriptive level, media consumption at least (media production is different, since it is generally a rationalised work practice) may seem frustratingly heterogeneous rather than an ordered field. Its principles of order only derive, at least initially, from the order to be found in the various practices in which media consumption (and its uses) are inserted. But, as already suggested, media consumption (and production) may quite independently be important to understanding the commonalities between other practices. It is to questions of patterning and ordering that I wish to turn next.

The Ordering of Media Practice and the Media's Ordering of Other Practices

We return here to the difficult question posed by Ann Swidler: How do some practices anchor other practices, producing a hierarchy of practices and also contributing to the 'structure' within which those other practices occur and take on their meaning? The case of media-oriented practices, however, raises a specific question: Do media practices have a privileged role in anchoring other types of practice because of the privileged circulation of media representations and images of the social world? This is quite apart from questions about the internal hierarchies among media practices which, at least in forms such as the privileging of 'live' media coverage over other types of media coverage, are relatively familiar. Instead I am interested here in the more difficult question of the potential hierarchies between media practices and other sorts of practice. How can we investigate such a relationship and what concepts do we need to clarify it?

Here we need to draw on another area of (this time, classical) social theory: Durkheim's concept of social categories (Durkheim 1953). A social category for Durkheim is a concept which is involved in articulating a society's order, and these categories are put to work in formulating certain core understandings of how the social world works and of the values on which it is based. A fundamental difference between Durkheim's theoretical framework and practice theory is that Durkheim assumes 'society' as the fundamental entity underlying any sociological explanation, whereas practice theory does not. However, as I have shown elsewhere (Couldry 2003a), it is possible to draw on Durkheim's insights without subscribing to his functionalist assumptions in order to understand the categorical force of certain terms as they are mobilised in the rhetorics which media use to represent social 'reality' and their privileged role as communicators of it. A non-functionalist approach may be able to explain the binding authority of certain media practices in relation to other practices via the notion of 'ritual' (which, as we saw, Swidler herself introduces to explain how some practices anchor others, but does not explain). In ritual practices, wider patterns of meaning are recognised as being enacted, although not necessarily intended or articulated, by the performers (Rappaport 1999: 24). Indeed ritual is one important way in which the legitimacy of assumed wider values can be confirmed or communicated. Ritual practices are able to 'frame' those wider values and thereby reproduce them as follows:

1. The actions comprising rituals are structured around certain categories (often expressed through boundaries).
2. Those categories suggest, or stand in for, an underlying value.
3. This value captures our sense that 'the social' is 'at stake' in the ritual.

As a result (linking to Swidler) ritual practices may 'anchor' all sorts of other practices which deal in the same categories and values.

On what does the particular power of media-oriented rituals depend? There is no space to explain this in detail here, but it is based on the fundamental categorical distinction between what is 'in' the media and what is not 'in' the media, which enables media representations to be seen as standing in for, or speaking authoritatively about, the non-media practices they represent. The 'as seen on TV' label still used on some supermarket goods is just the simplest version of this distinction in use, but it illustrates the anchoring role of media practices at work. The pervasiveness of 'celebrity culture' (discourse about celebrity inside and outside media) is another example of such anchoring: even if, as already noted, it is uncertain how important celebrity discourse is in individuals' articulations of their identities, the idea that celebrity actions demand special attention is continuously reproduced. In that sense celebrity actions can be said to 'anchor' other practices by comprising a constant point of reference within them. These are just two examples of how the ritualised dimensions of media practice may have an ordering role in relation to other practices. The difficult question is how far this anchoring role extends across social practice in general.

Clearly, we are just at the start of a large area of research. The point is that these research questions only open up once we redefine the aim of media research as the analysis of media's consequences for social practice as a whole, studying the full range of practices oriented towards media (not just direct media consumption). It is important, however, to emphasise that, in researching the role of media practices and the products of media practices (images, representations, patterns of discourse) in ordering other practices across the social world, we are not giving up on the important concerns of historical media research with questions of representation because the study of how particular media texts embody claims about the social world in regular ways will remain important for our understanding of media's consequences for social practice generally. Similarly with the question of media 'effects' and media power: reorientating the media research paradigm as I am proposing does not mean abandoning such larger questions, but on the contrary attempting to answer them in more precise ways based on the details of everyday practice and its organisation. The aim then is not to abandon the interests of previous media research, but to displace and broaden its focus from questions based on the consideration of texts (and how texts are interpreted) to questions based on media practices' role in the ordering of social life more generally.

This of course is to put considerable weight on the term 'ordering' (or in Swidler's language 'anchoring'). I have already glossed this one way in terms of categories and rituals which are structured through categories. There are also other ways in which we might understand how certain practices order or 'anchor' others. First, we might look at the coordinated networks between agents and things that actor network theory analysed. Think of the practices which together make up the 'media profile' received by a major business corporation. They have an 'anchoring' role in relation to the business strategies of that corporation – because of the 'network' that links the actions of its executives, press office, key media contacts, major investors and so on – when an announcement of new strategy is made and the executives wait to see what media coverage it receives. Bad media coverage, because it is read

by investors as negatively affecting the corporation's value as an investment, will constrain the corporation's future actions. Such actor networks involving media practices with an anchoring role have been little
studied, but they are an important part of how many fields of practice
are ordered. This is just one example of how the detailed study of practice (including actor networks) might illuminate our understanding of
media's role in the ordering of social life more generally.

Other conceptual links might be made here, for example to
Bourdieu's concept of habitus which seeks to explain the underlying
determinants of the practices that are available to different agents
(Bourdieu 1977; McNay 1999). There are no doubt still other concepts
that might be useful for specifying how 'anchoring' might work that
draw on alternative theoretical perspectives – for instance Foucauldian
perpectives – but there is no space to pursue this here.

The point, rather, is that we need the perspective of practice to help
us address how media are embedded in the interlocking fabric of social
and cultural life. This question, as I have suggested, cuts deeper than
our sense of how it feels to live in a media-saturated world, since it covers both cognitive and emotional dimensions to how practices are
ordered; and in turn, through the link with cognitive questions (ways of
thinking and categorising the world), it links to the question of how
practices (possibilities of action) are differentially ordered for those
with ready access to media resources (whether as media producers or as
privileged media sources) and for those without. Through this, we can
perhaps hope to develop a different approach towards understanding
media's consequences for the distribution of social power.

Conclusion

I have tried to open up a direction for media theory, rather than map
anything definitively. I have been interested throughout in theory not
for its own sake but because it clarifies what questions are interesting
for media research and because of the structuring processes it can dis-
close. Much of my argument has involved contextualising a new
research paradigm that theorises media as practice, rather than as text
or production process: What range of practices are oriented to media
and what is the role of media-oriented practices in ordering other practices? This is, I believe, a more open and inclusive paradigm for media
research than previous ones.

It draws for its theoretical tools much more on general social science than on media research – unsurprisingly since it addresses ques-

tions that are no longer questions about media as such, or even about the direct consumption of media, but rather questions about the contributions media practices make to social practice more generally. No 'new' paradigm can, as I noted, be wholly new. Indeed we return here to the spirit of Lazarsfeld and Merton's (1969) exploratory remarks about mass media, made entirely within a social science perspective. For them the first, if the most difficult, question of media effects was: What are 'the effects of *the existence* of media in our society' (ibid.: 495, emphasis added)? This is the (admittedly vast) question to which we need to return with all our theoretical energies. Practice is perhaps the only concept broad enough to help us prise it open.

Notes

1. This article was originally published in the journal *Social Semiotics* 14(2): 115–32, 2004, and is republished here with permission. Thanks to Taylor and Francis for their consent to republish: the full version of the original article is available from http://www.informaworld.com.
2. A few years ago, I expressed this in terms of the study of 'the culture of media belief' but this now seems to me too limited in its selection from the wide field of media-oriented practices (Couldry 2000a, 2000b).
3. See, e.g., Bourdieu (1977), and for authoritative overviews of the term 'practice' as a whole, Schatzki (1996) and Reckwitz (2002).
4. Also implied here is studying what people believe and think, as evidenced by what they say and do.
5. *Editors' Note*: For a media studies introduction to Baudrillard, see Long and Wall (2009: 327–28); on (media) anthropological uses of Deleuze and Guattari, see Spitulnik (this volume) and Kapferer (2006: 135–37).
6. See Urry (2000) on 'society'.
7. The social 'centre' to which media implicitly claim connection is therefore doubly mythical: it is not a centre of value and it is not as much of a practical centre as media would like us to think (see Couldry 2003a: 37–54).
8. But see for examples of a practice-based approach: Gamson (1998) and Grindstaff (2002).

References

Abercrombie, N., S. Hill and B. Turner. 1981. *The Dominant Ideology Thesis*. London: Allen and Unwin.
Abercrombie, N. and B. Longhurst. 1998. *Audiences: A Sociological Theory of Performance and Imagination*. London: Sage.

Abu-Lughod, L. 1999. 'The Interpretation of Culture(s) After Television', in S. Ortner (ed.) *The Fate of 'Culture': Geertz and Beyond.* Berkeley: University of California Press, pp.110–35.

Alasuutari, P. (ed.) 1999. *Rethinking the Media Audience.* London: Sage.

Ang, I. 1996. *Living Room Wars.* London: Routledge.

Bausinger, H. 1984. 'Media, Technology and Daily Life', *Media, Culture and Society* 6(4): 343–52.

Bird, S.E. 2003. *The Audience in Everyday Life: Living in a Media World.* London: Routledge.

Bourdieu, P. 1977. *Outline of a Theory of Practice.* Cambridge: Cambridge University Press.

Couldry. 2000a. *The Place of Media Power: Pilgrims and Witnesses of the Media Age.* London: Routledge.

——— 2000b. 'Back to the Future? Rediscovering the Method in Audience Studies', unpublished paper delivered to Media Graduate Seminar, University of Sussex, February 2000.

——— 2003a. *Media Rituals: A Critical Approach.* London: Routledge.

——— 2003b. 'Media Meta-capital: Extending Bourdieu's Field Theory', *Theory and Society* 32(5/6): 653–77.

——— 2005. 'Transvaluing Media Studies: Or, Beyond the Myth of the Mediated Centre', in J. Curran and D. Morley (eds), *Media and Cultural Theory.* London: Routledge, pp.177–94.

De Tocqueville, A. 1994[1835–1840]. *Democracy in America.* London: David Campbell.

Du Gay, P. et al. 1997. *Production of Culture/Cultures of Production.* London: Sage.

Durkheim, E. 1953. 'Individual and Collective Representations', in *Sociology and Philosophy.* London: Cohen and West, pp.1–34.

Gamson, J. 1998. *Freaks Talk Back.* Chicago: University of Chicago Press.

Garnham, N. 1990. *Capitalism and Communication.* London: Sage.

——— 1995. 'Political Economy and Cultural Studies: Reconciliation or Divorce?', *Critical Studies in Mass Communication* 12(1): 62–71.

Giddens, A. 1984. *The Constitution of Society.* Cambridge: Polity.

Ginsburg, F. 1994. 'Culture/Media: A Mild Polemic', *Anthropology Today* 10(2): 5–15.

Ginsburg, F., L. Abu-Lughod and B. Larkin (eds). 2002. *Media Worlds.* Berkeley: University of California Press.

Grindstaff, L. 2002. *The Money Shot.* Chicago: University of Chicago Press.

Grossberg, L. 1995. 'Cultural Studies versus Political Economy: Is Anyone Else Bored with this Debate?', *Critical Studies in Mass Communication* 12(1): 72–81.

Hall, S. 1980. 'Encoding/Decoding', in S. Hall, D. Hobson, A. Lowe and P. Willis (eds), *Culture, Media, Language.* London: Unwin Hyman, pp.128–38.

Hannerz, U. 1992. *Cultural Complexity.* New York: Columbia University Press.

Hermes, J. 1995. *Reading Women's Magazines.* London: Sage.

——— 1999. 'Media Figures in Identity Construction', in P. Alasuutari (ed.), *Rethinking the Media Audience.* London: Sage, pp.69–85.

Hesmondhalgh, D. 2002. *The Cultural Industries.* London: Sage.

Hoover, S., L. Schofield Clark and D. Alters. 2003. *Media, Home and World.* London: Routledge.

Kapferer, B. 2006. 'Situations, Crisis and the Anthropology of the Concrete: The Contribution of Max Gluckman', in T.M.S Evens and D. Handelman (eds), *The Manchester School: Practice and Ethnographic Praxis in Anthropology.* Oxford: Berghahn, pp.118–55.

Kierkegaard, S. 1962[1946/7]. *The Present Age.* London: Fontana.

Krotz, F. and S. Tyler Eastman. 1999. 'Orientations Towards Television outside the Home', *Journal of Communication* 49(1): 5–27.

Kuhn, T. 1970. *The Structure of Scientific Revolutions*, 2nd edn. Chicago: University of Chicago Press.

Lazarsfeld, P. and R. Merton. 1969. 'Mass Communication, Popular Taste and Organised Social Action', in W. Schramm (ed.), *Mass Communications*, 2nd edn. Urbana: University of Illinois Press.

Lemish, D. 1982. 'The Rules of Viewing Television in Public Places', *Journal of Broadcasting* 26(4): 757–82.

Lewis, J. 1991. *The Ideological Octopus.* London: Routledge.

Long, P. and T. Wall. 2009. *Media Studies: Texts, Production and Context.* Edinburgh: Pearson.

Lukes, S. 1975. 'Political Ritual and Social Integration', *Sociology* 29: 289–305.

McCarthy, A. 2002. *Ambient Television: Visual Culture and Public Space.* Durham, NC: Duke University Press.

McNay, L. 1999. 'Gender, Habitus and Field: Pierre Bourdieu and the Limits of Reflexivity', *Theory Culture and Society* 16(1): 95–117.

Martin-Barbero, J. 1993. *Communication, Culture and Hegemony.* London: Sage.

Morley, D. 1980. 'Texts, Readers, Subjects', in S. Hall, D. Hobson, A. Lowe and P. Willis (eds), *Culture, Media, Language.* London: Unwin Hyman, pp.163–73.

——— 1992. *Television, Audiences and Cultural Studies.* London: Routledge.

Rappaport, R. 1999. *Ritual and Religion in the Making of Humanity.* Cambridge: Cambridge University Press.

Reckwitz, A. 2002. 'Toward a Theory of Social Practices', *European Journal Social Theory* 5(2): 243–63.

Scannell, P. 1996. *Radio, Television and Modern Life.* Oxford: Blackwell.

Schatzki, T. 1996. *Social Practices: A Wittgensteinian Approach to Human Activity and the Social.* Cambridge: Cambridge University Press.

Shils, E. 1975. *Center and Periphery.* Chicago: University of Chicago Press.

Signorielli, N. and D. Morgan (eds). 1990. *Cultivation Analysis: New Directions in Media Effects Research.* Newbury Park: Sage.

Silverstone, R. 1994. *Television and Everyday Life.* London: Routledge.

——— 2005. 'Media and Communication', in C. Calhoun, C. Rojek and B. Turner (eds), *The International Handbook of Sociology.* London: Sage, pp.188–207.

Silverstone, R. and E. Hirsch (eds). 1992. *Consuming Technologies.* London: Routledge.

Swidler, A. 2001. 'What Anchors Cultural Practices?' in T. Schatzki, K. Knorr Cetina and E. von Savigny (eds), *The Practice Turn in Contemporary Theory*. London: Routledge, pp.74–92.

Tarde, G. 1969[1922]. *Communication and Social Opinion*. Chicago: University of Chicago Press.

Tulloch, J. 2000. *Watching Television Audiences*. London: Arnold.

Turner, G. F. Bonner and D. Marshall. 2000. *Fame Games*. Cambridge: Cambridge University Press.

Urry, J. 2000. *Sociology Beyond Societies*. London: Sage.

Wark, M. 1999. *Celebrities, Culture and Cyberspace*. Sydney: Pluto.

CHAPTER 2

What Do We Mean by 'Media Practices'?

Mark Hobart

Who needs a collection on theorising media and practice, and why?[1] Except for the few malcontents who stray into academia, media practitioners and policy-makers are mostly too busy doing media to have time for scholars whose grasp of the intricacies of a fast-moving industry is often rudimentary. Have media and practice not been endlessly and largely repetitively theorised already? And has not the phrase 'media practices' been used so promiscuously as to be a cliché? Perhaps our time would be better spent doing something else.

The frequency with which media practice is invoked though suggests that it is an attempt to address a perceived difficulty. So I shall review the case for analysing the mass media in terms of practice. Such a review requires us to reconsider what is the object of study in media studies. Should it, for example, be media practices or media-related practices? Granted the prevailing naive realism (rather than empiricism) in media studies, what are the theoretical and philosophical implications of such a change? And how might a thoroughgoing account of practice affect what and how we research?

Existing Conditions Are Unlikely[2]

Most approaches to media studies, despite claims to the contrary, encounter two problems: how to address the relationship between academic models and actuality (whatever that is); and how to address the practices of which media production, distribution, reception and commentary arguably consist. So, is it possible to devise an account of practice that will meet the intellectual requirements of media studies and reflect recognisably the activities of practitioners? And, as Western scholars often imagine that their notional intellectual radicalism mysteriously frees them from potential Eurocentrism, does such an account make sense beyond the narrow confines of anglophone academia?

Here I argue that a critical appreciation of practice is as important as it will prove difficult. The reasons are historical and cultural. Since the Greek philosophers, the dominant approaches of European thought have been based on models, mostly ideal, that stress system, structure and coherence while downplaying or explaining away contingency, applicability and performance. Practice is generally defined in terms of, and invoked to address defects in, theories which have other concerns. In other words, its function is remedial, prosthetic or supplementary. And the gulf between the theorisers and theorised remains unbridged.[3] However, involving those whose practices are at issue requires not just turning our scholarly world upside down but reinventing our constitutive intellectual practices. A serious account of practice should be neither just another lurch of the juggernaut of theory nor, as is often the case, a strap-on.

There are two implications of the historical and cultural nature of theory which are immediately relevant. First, while the histories of science and social science may have obliged us to acknowledge that theoretical models are part of historical argument, we still have great difficulty recognising how far their presuppositions are also culturally specific. At its simplest, words have histories and accrete connotations. And the kinds of words we are talking about – like culture, media, meaning and practice – are singularly complex. They do not travel well outside the anglophone world. While apologists of globalisation might dismiss this as quaint difference shortly to be MacDonaldised or bombed into oblivion, how ironic were left-liberal media scholars to endorse approaches that reiterated a Eurocentric hegemony?[4] In principle at least, recognition of the complexity of the lived world is what anthropologists can contribute to media studies debates.

The second implication is less obvious. To what does an account of practice apply? Is it supplementary to existing approaches? If so, it is limited by the presuppositions of the model, the defects of which invoking practice is designed to ameliorate.[5] Or is it intended to replace them? To do so is difficult and challenging. Terms like mind, intention, understanding, meaning, have cultural histories which follow the theoretical ox like the cart it draws. Specification of what counts as practice similarly involves presuppositions. Now, the distinctive task of anthropologists is to recognise and work between incommensurate ways of imagining and engaging with the world without reducing one to the other.[6] To take just one example: does the account of practice include the researcher's own practices and milieux? Here old intellectual habits get in the way: the history of epistemological presuppositions, including the hierarchical relationship of the subject and object of study, the knower and the known. If we are to live in a postcolonial world, it is unacceptable to assume a priori that the practices of the researcher are of such a different and superior order that they can, or should, not be critically questioned or considered in relation to those of the subjects of research. Conventionally, sauce for the goose is emphatically not sauce for the gander.

Such a partial account naturalises the kinds of difference that I would argue analyses of practice should question. The purpose of invoking practice is precisely to eschew recourse to familiar epistemological and ontological systems and the conventional paraphernalia of theory. It also draws attention to the constitutive intellectual practices through which theory is replicated. Then the knower can no longer claim superiority to and separateness from the known but becomes part of the known with all the attendant problems.[7] So a theory of practice which fails to include the researcher and practices of theorising, research and writing as integral to it reiterates the presuppositions it claims to reject. A strong and workable account of practice is far more demanding than its proponents appreciate.

Where Are We?

What is the state of debate over practice in media studies? A thoughtful overview by Nick Couldry (this volume), is a convenient starting point. Couldry argues for a new paradigm which 'treats media as the open set of practices relating to, or oriented around, media' (p. 36). While, given the internal dissention in media studies, not everyone might agree with his analysis, his argument about the lack of attention to practice is strong and the case for redressing this compelling. Couldry sagely notes that 'focusing on practice is a more radical adjustment to our research agendas than might at first appear' (p. 47). And by bravely leaping into this shark-infested new paradigm,[8] Couldry reveals what a perilous venture this is.

For a framework Couldry looks to practice theory in sociology. Leaving aside how adequate this might be within sociology, it has evident problems as the general theoretical basis for media studies. How are yet more surveys and questionnaires going to add to a serious understanding of practices? It suggests a failure to appreciate what a study of practice entails. Detailed research into the interlocking phases of production in diverse media in different countries or how, say, different groups and kinds of viewers engage with television raises complex issues. It certainly invites ethnographic approaches and at least some recognition of the anthropological thinking behind such work. Waving sociological theory at anthropological problems tends to prove ungainly, incoherent and unworkable. How would it work? Do we use a sociological approach to deal with practices embracing large groups or populations and an anthropological approach to the relatively small groups where production and reception occur? And will the senses of practice designed for these different purposes be sufficiently commensurate as to avoid misunderstanding?

Couldry (this volume) spells out sensible considerations that need to be taken into account for a practice-based approach. However, when he attempts to use sociological practice theory to address the issues he has identified, the wheels start to come off. As Couldry notes, how to define practice is much more difficult than Swidler, on whom he relies, allows. She distinguishes 'routine activities (rather than consciously chosen actions) notable for their unconscious, automatic, un-thought character' from discourse as 'the system of meanings that allows them to say anything at all' (p. 41, citing Swidler 2001: 74–75). The former is so extensive as to be unknowable. And, if it includes the unconscious, on what authority is the researcher to infer the individual (or is it collective?) unconsciouses of large populations? Can we generalise a global theory of practice oblivious both to the research questions and their purposes, and also to people's self-understandings? Swidler's industrial seine-netting risks catching more seaweed and flotsam than anything. She defines discourse in terms of bounded systems of symbols and meanings (ibid.: 75). If an idealist, all-embracing model of culture can be made to become practice by prestidigitation, anything can, so making the notion entirely vacuous.

When Couldry addresses other aspects of practice, matters get more problematic still. The first is 'how people *understand* what actions constitute a distinct practice' (p. 41). Apart from explicit understandings, actions are supposedly 'governed by common rules and by sharing the common reference point of certain ends, projects and beliefs' (p. 41). The extent to which understandings are shared depends on how far away you are from the situatedness of daily argument. And, knowing what other people believe is deeply problematic (Needham 1972). This account of belief and rule-governed behaviour harps back to pre-Wittgensteinian models (cf. Schatzki 2001: 51–53). While the questions are admirably formulated, the proposed answers grow less convincing at each turn.

Couldry, citing Swidler, then asks 'how [do] some practices anchor, control, or organise others' (p. 42). Swidler's answer – and so Couldry's, with reservations – is in terms of a definitional hierarchy, to which Couldry adds that the media 'anchor other practices through the "authoritative" representations and enactments of key terms and categories that they provide' (p. 42). Now, hierarchy and authoritative representations are the familiar language of approaches which privilege the knower above the known from which Couldry wishes to distance himself. Among the difficulties, let me pick up two themes already introduced.

Does an analysis of practice not apply to the thinking of academics? If not, then we are back to the skewed account of practice which applies only to the object of study. If it does, then we cannot speak unproblematically of hierarchies or authoritative representations – whose, where and when? We would have to inquire critically into our own scholarly practices. We would have to consider who hierarchises practices and under what circumstances.[9] This in turn requires us to consider who does so as what, to whom, on what occasion, for what purpose. As Nelson Goodman has argued (Goodman 1968: 27–31), a pragmatist approach to reference entails not imposing correspondence theories, usually unthinkingly. It requires us to consider 'representation as' as a practice. Far from hierarchy solving the problem, it complicates the issue by posing entirely new sets of questions about who hierarchises whom on what occasions to what ends. Couldry is let down by his theoretical sources on practice. Similar confusions attend the idea of authoritative representations. Leaving aside who represents what as what to whom, according to whom and under what circumstances, are these representations considered to be authoritative? As with hierarchising, invoking the 'authoritative' merely compounds the problem.

What can we actually know about other people's practices, about their understandings of their practices and what underwrites our knowledge? There is a hidden presupposition about the psychic unity of humankind, usually modelled uncritically on academics' idealised self-imaginings or some fantasy of 'the everyday'. For a study of media in complex societies we have few grounds on which to presume transparency: for example, that the worlds of producers' and recipients' practices are mutually accessible. If translation is involved, as it is for most anthropologists, a whole further dimension appears.

I shall address only three obvious problems. How is the researcher to understand other people's practices? Implicit are a correspondence theory of reference, a universal hermeneutics and a direct access to other minds which assumes the researcher knows what is happening sufficiently to cover all reasonable eventualities, and has command both of available interpretive frameworks and what people are thinking. As A.F.C. Wallace noted, even in a dialogue between close interlocutors we have no grounds to presume that we understand someone else's utterances. All we can assume is that we can interrogate what they said in terms of our own frame of reference, which he calls 'equivalence structures' (Wallace 1961: 29–44). It remains unproven that our grounds for thinking that the frames of reference of an academic researcher, a film editor and a working class housewife watching television – far less media producers and viewers in other parts of the world – are likely to be similar.[10]

The second issue is translation. Quine argued that, outside the narrow confine of Western European languages, radical translation is an issue because there are always several alternative manuals by which we can translate any set of utterances (Quine 1960: 73–9). As Hesse (1978) has noted, Quine's argument about the under-determination of reference applies not only to translation but to the kinds of materials with which social scientists deal. We have to add the irrelevance of translation (or indeed interpretation) to the list of presuppositions required to launch this theory of practice.

Finally what grounds do we have for assuming the understandings of the subjects of study are commensurate with the researcher's, when anthropological research suggests this is usually not the case?[11] And how is the researcher to know the significance to participants of their practices?[12] Swidler's argument in terms of hierarchy and authority, and the failure to address the problems of understanding and translation, gives the answer. With breathtaking insouciance, this sociological practice theory objectivises, hierarchises and normalises Eurocentrically the subjects of study just as did its predecessors, except they made lesser claims. As a theory for a dialogic – or indeed any – understanding of other people's media practices, it is a non-starter. Couldry asks important questions but, in relying upon the sociology of practice, he ends up Swidled.

What Would an Account of Practice Involve?

This brief review shows how Couldry's argument is let down by the lack of appropriate theoretical resources on which to draw. So what would we need for a suitable account of practice? Indeed, is a single, coherent, acceptable account likely? I think not for several reasons. First, theory is best treated as a continuous argument between rival ways of understanding complex events and actions. The apparent consensus about the importance of practice results largely from discontent with existing theories, not with agreement about what practice is. Second, the use of theories and concepts depends on the purposes and objects of inquiry. Practice is particularly suited to detailed research of the kind anthropologists specialise in to address questions thrown up by previous research. It is inappropriate to the analysis of macro-processes, although it would be central to the overlooked questions about the constituent intellectual activities of researchers. Practice therefore, like culture or meaning, is likely to become a site of contestation. As one example, should we treat practices as 'the chief context of human activity – and of social orders'? Or should we treat practice as 'order-transforming activity' (Schatzki 2001: 46, reviewing Taylor's and Laclau and Mouffe's arguments respectively)? Which kind of approach will depend on the theoretical background and researchers' concerns. It cannot be settled by fiat. I happen to require an account which facilitates analysis of how practices transform groups, individuals and the conditions of their articulation. But that is just my personal preference determined partly by the research questions that interest me.

Attempting to formulate a definitive account of practice therefore would be premature. However, there are a range of issues and theoretical questions that need addressing. Because an account of practice aims to differentiate itself from previous approaches, it will presumably have to answer questions about the kinds of ontology, epistemology and politics entailed.[13]

Ontological Questions

What kind of thing is practice? What else inhabits the world, and what can we exclude? Is everything practice or to be redescribed as practice? Or are we, as many philosophers of practice are inclined, to allow other things such as skills, understandings, mind, intention, meaning, causation, language, logic, rules and much else besides? If the latter, as these concepts bring with them a long history of usage, how radical could such an account of practice ever be? It would land up as just another attempt to compensate for the shortcomings of existing theories. And how would such an account deal with lack, silencing and exclusion?

As an object of study, practice raises singular problems in that practices are not just historical and cultural but situated and so partly contingent.[14] They may be moments of slippage, change, openness. And what constitutes evidence of the existence of practices? The trap is naive realism. We may 'mistake features of discourse for features of the subject of discourse' (Goodman 1972: 24). Furthermore:

> If I ask about the world, you can offer to tell me how it is under one or more frames of reference; but if I insist that you tell me how it is apart from all frames, what can you say? We are confined to ways of describing whatever is described. Our universe, so to speak, consists of these ways rather than of a world or worlds. (Goodman 1978: 2–3)

Practice is not a natural object but a frame of reference that we use to interrogate a complex reality.

Practice therefore depends on it being identified as such. In other words, some agent or subject – be it the researcher, the media, local intellectuals or whatever – articulates some set of activities or events as a practice.[15] So researchers would be unwarranted naturalists to dismiss how their subjects of study imagine and articulate their practices. Among the practices in which we are likely to be especially interested are those which articulate, reflect upon, question and revise other practices. A strong account of practice requires us to work between two changing congeries of articulations – discourses if you will – a problem familiar to anthropologists.

Evidently different scholars will argue for different ontologies. Again, speaking personally, I prefer parsimony. Not least, each new element brings with it a far from innocent history of prior usage. Wherever possible I would aim to redescribe necessary concepts in terms of action or practice. So 'mind' is what mind has done on particular occasions.[16] Similarly the great icons of macro-analysis – structure, capitalism, the polity, economy – require rephrasing in terms of the constitutive practices of enunciating, invoking, reiterating and denying them on different occasions, without which they effectively remain transcendental (Laclau 1990a).[17] We can now see why media practices are so important: the mass media have become central to such articulation and its detailed study correspondingly important. If articulating other practices – by representing, mediating or commenting on them – is what gives the impression of ordering them, then our own and our interlocutors' analytical and commentary practices inescapably become part of the object of study.

On this account, practice is not supplementary to notions such as system, structure, order or individuals but replaces them. This is a radical move which will require time and argument to think through for anthropology and media studies.[18] Likewise, our assumptions about individual subjects require rethinking through the practices by which they are constituted, divided, addressed and learn to recognise themselves (Foucault 1982). And with this goes assumptions about individual agency.[19] The non-dualist approach I propose makes the articulatory role of the mass media much easier to think about. Unfortunately, old intellectual habits are so engrained that massive slippage is inevitable.

In the light of this, Schatzki's definition of practices as 'organised nexuses of activity' (Schatzki 2001: 48) fails to stress agency and articulation. I prefer to think of practices as those recognised, complex forms of social activity and articulation through which agents set out to maintain or change themselves, others and the world about them under varying conditions. Such a working account is deliberately open. Rather than attempt some universal definition which inevitably risks Eurocentrism and anticipating how other people imagine practice, I prefer to leave problematic for the time being what it is to articulate, to recognise as, or to ascribe agency and so on.[20]

How might practice be further circumscribed in a manner appropriate to the study of mass media? Couldry argues for 'media-oriented practice, in all its looseness and openness. What, quite simply, are people doing in relation to media across a whole range of situations and contexts?' (this volume: 39). He then specifies: 'do media practices have a privileged role in anchoring other types of practice because of the privileged circulation of media representations and images of the social world?' However, privileging the media this way begs the question, because it anticipates how media practices relate to other practices, or indeed what comprises a media-oriented practice. I prefer 'media-related practice', as it includes, say: women cooking meals so the family can view favourite programmes; family decisions about capital investment in radio, television or computers; preferences in dress or other consumer items shown in advertising or programmes.[21] It also allows for a consideration of absences: the refusal to read a particular newspaper, to watch soccer or whatever.

Epistemological Considerations

As the epistemological presuppositions of existing theories have been extensively criticised – for example, by Foucault and Derrida or, from a different background, Rorty (1979) – I would only note the legacy of naturalism in communication studies and the effective failure by cultural and media studies scholars to engage seriously with poststructuralist critiques (Chen 1996). I only have space to raise two questions: What is the relation between the knowledge or understanding of the researchers and the objects of study? And what are we actually doing when we research and write?[22] Specifically, how are we to represent other people's practices?

The work of Foucault enables us to go beyond the old divisions between the *Natur-* and *Geisteswissenschaften* and rethink scholarly inquiry and professional authority through which we 'authorise' our subjects (Asad 1986) and for whom. If we are critically to reconsider our own practices, then we need to rework the worn distinctions between describing, explaining and interpreting (Wittgenstein 1958). And interpreting has proven far less elegant and satisfactory than Clifford Geertz (1973) claimed. Interpreting, as a practice, is arguably endless and turns back on the interpreting subject:

> If interpretation can never be brought to an end, it is simply because there is nothing to interpret. There is nothing absolutely primary to interpret because at bottom everything is already interpretation ... one does not interpret what there is in the signified, but one interprets, fundamentally, *who* has posed the interpretation ... The second consequence is that interpretation always has to interpret itself. (Foucault 1990: 64, 66)

How we get from the gamut of people's intellectual practices, the attendant disagreements, misunderstandings and antagonisms to the neat, coherent expositions satisfying to the primary audience of Western academics remains largely mysterious. For example, Geertz's interpretations of Balinese culture notoriously titillate Western readers' fantasies about exotic Asia, but have precious little relation to the Balinese thinking they purport to interpret.[23]

Quite how researchers are supposed to understand other people's practices – media or otherwise – is likely to prove a vexing problem, even if the sociology of practice on offer, Eurocentrically, ignores it. As we do not have direct access to what other people think of their practices, we may require something like the method of re-enactment that Collingwood argued was distinctive of history and, by extension, anthropology, where we cannot assume shared experience, understanding or presuppositions. So the researcher has in effect to re-enact what the subject of study was up to through their own thinking. Collingwood outlined what this entailed for historical thinking (Collingwood 1946: 282–302), and it has a distinguished genealogy in British social anthropology, significantly in part through Evans-Pritchard's (largely unacknowledged) use of Collingwood.[24]

Understanding the circumstances of practices would presumably often require something resembling intensive ethnography by participant-observation, a quite different beast from what most media studies scholars imagine. Command of language and usage is a major issue because understanding what is said in newspapers, television and film demands not a Berlitz course but appreciation of endless and intricate references. Collingwood went further, however. To understand other people's practices requires recognition of the presuppositions implicit in their thoughts and actions, not in the abstract but as these are used in practice to evaluate their own and others' actions (Collingwood 1940). The researcher then brings their theory and training to bear critically on interrogating the evidence, which includes understanding gleaned from re-enactment.[25] The moment that media studies steps beyond the safe shores of the anglophone media, the world suddenly becomes a much more complicated place.

A stress upon practice requires us to rethink not just the object of study but the whole venture of media studies. If we are to reconsider media production, distribution, reception and commentary as practices, for example, the old issues of how structures of power work through media ideologies to perpetuate hegemony among individuals have to be recast – and not before time.[26] This is not to say that human subjects are not interpellated by, or implicated in, the mass media in various ways, but that what is happening is more complex and interesting than this framework allows. Media corporations are not omniscient, omnipotent agents (yet slaves to practical reason and ideology) because, on this account, they comprise congeries of practices, sometimes coherent, sometimes contradictory, sometimes unrelated, and largely uninvestigated. Similarly, the residual individualist/collectivism dichotomy implicit in the idea of interpellation, with its Lacanian genealogy,[27] prevents us considering the practices through which the media are brought to bear on people's lives. This potentially involves families, peer groups and friends as well as the complex circumstances of people's engagement and implication in the mass media. Quite simply, if we are to take practice seriously, we have more or less to rethink how we set about the study of media and mediation from scratch.

What Does it Look Like in Practice?

What can such a fine-grained, critical approach tell us about the media that we do not already know? The general case for ethnographic and anthropological studies of media has already been made (e.g., Ginsburg, Abu-Lughod and Larkin 2002; Bird 2003; Peterson 2003; Rothenbuhler and Coman 2005). As intensive ethnographies of production appear, surprising worlds open up that were inaccessible to other approaches, as they were never designed to address practice. At times the divergence is so stark that the reader wonders how they could possibly be talking about the same reality, as the brief examples below indicate, drawing on my research and that of some of my research students.

Much recent news coverage has been about the supposed threat of terrorism. As the chances of being involved in a terrorist attack are miniscule, what such 'masculine soap opera' (Fiske 1987: 308) obfuscates is the practices by which, on a daily basis, the media set about inculcating fear in their readers and audiences through articulating events in singular ways. This theme is explored in Angad Chowdhry's ethnography, which required him to research several different media organisations. To understand how newspapers engender a sense of immanent fear, he trained as a crime reporter for the Mumbai-based *Indian Express*. The training itself was an object lesson in learning practice. It involved not just how to write what is supposed to frighten the Indian middle classes, but how to represent the confusion, uncertainty, messiness and human suffering after the crime. Routine cannot entirely order the ambiguities and ambivalences of the journalist's own position between the newspaper, the police, relatives and parties wishing to use the media to various ends. To be a crime reporter is to be entangled in complicated sets of relationships and often murky political waters, to have an anomalous status and stand in a curious relationship with other reporters. Practice here is partly about survival. And much journalistic activity at that time in Mumbai had little to do with what might ever appear in print. Nor is past experience a simple guide to how to write future newspaper copy. New crimes may require new ways of coping with them as journalists struggle to transmogrify lived events into text. An analysis of practice is less about the much-publicised dilemmas and traumas of headline journalists reporting acts of terror and war than about managing social relationships and the daily practices of articulating fear.

How distinct are such media practices from media-related practices? Put another way, what on earth do mothers-in-law and weddings have to do with decisions about programming, especially in the highly industrialised, numerate and technophile climate of television production in Singapore? Ivan Kwek's detailed ethnography of media practice deftly undermines both practitioners' and media scholars' accounts. Executives of the Malay channel Suria in Singapore use sophisticated Taylor Nelson Sofres audience ratings to establish viewing figures and patterns. However, what actually happened at the crucial decision-making meetings between the station and the channel's advisory committee subverted executives' understandings of their own practices. Senior management fondly imagined that they exemplified state-of-the-art practical reason, driven by such considerations as viewer response, advertising revenue, and changing trends in the industry, the competition and government.

However, Kwek's study, which included boardroom practice, showed that quite different practices significantly affected decisions about commissioning programmes. In discussion executives would cite their relatives' opinions about programme quality, with mothers-in-law emerging as the most incontrovertible. Quite separately, weddings are an important, and frequent, social occasion among Malays. That was when television executives were actually confronted with members of their otherwise largely remote audiences. For media executives, such dialogue presented a more textured way of judging how programmes were received than disembodied viewing figures and so were taken seriously in board meetings.[28] This disjuncture between how people understand or represent themselves (for example, during interview) as against how their practices appear to the outside analyst, is arguably the *raison d'être* of anthropology. This difference cannot be reduced to either the participants' or the researcher's accounts alone without irremediable trivialisation. This example also highlights the shortcomings of an exclusive focus on media practices. What relatives, wedding guests and others have to say cannot be encompassed in an analysis of media practices without extending the notion to the point of meaninglessness. Equally significantly, for social action and decision-making it becomes difficult to distinguish media practices as an essential category from broader media-related practices.

That media practices might comprise a coherent object of study is only possible if researchers implicitly, but highly questionably, confine themselves to more or less institutionalised aspects of production and distribution.[29] In view of the myriad ways, sometimes unexpected, in which readers, audiences, mobile phone and internet users around the world engage with and make use of different media in their lives, are these to be excluded a priori? To collapse all these into media or media-oriented practice, what people are 'doing in relation to media' is to essentialise and prioritise the medium over all the other aspects of social action. By contrast, media-related practice is intended simply to provide an initial circumscription out of the whole range of identifiable practices in a society at any moment.

What are the implications of extending analysis to include media-related practices? Let me briefly draw upon my ethnography from Bali by way of answer. Among the most important media developments was the replacement of radios by television in the late 1970s, culminating in most households owning colour television sets by the early 1990s and being able to receive up to twelve terrestrial stations even without satellite dishes. The implications were far-reaching. Television viewing changed domestic and public activities in several ways. Some are familiar from studies of family viewing (e.g., Morley 1986; Lull 1990), like the impact of television watching on domestic routines including new kinds of power relations around choices of viewing. Village food stalls mostly went out of business except for the few that installed television, while public sets in village halls became the site for raucous humour and searing commentary on broadcast politics. Women's arduous daily routines were enlivened by listening, if not always watching, television, and new kinds of working relationships emerged. The number of witchcraft accusations plummeted, as people developed other concerns. The impact upon agricultural and industrial labour patterns was complex. Television viewing has come to affect many aspects of rural and urban social life.

The less direct implications of television and other mass media for practice are perhaps more interesting still. Access to commercial channels, then mobile phones and even computers, opened up new possibilities for consumerism, especially in the relatively affluent tourist regions, with major consequences for individual and family expenditure. Conspicuous consumption was redirected so that Balinese temple festivals came to resemble fashion shows. The implications for politics were also striking. Television and national and international news coverage (however sceptically the former was treated under the Suharto regime) transformed people's frames of reference and changed old relations of political patronage. The culmination was when the current president, Susilo Bambang Yudoyono, swept to victory over the political party machines because of his efficacy on television. These trends all depended upon intricately changing practices in which the mass media were implicated in all sorts of ways, although they were often not media-oriented practices.

It is far from the case that the mass media necessarily determine social practices. There is space for one only example. Theatre in Java and Bali has long been a form of popular entertainment. Audience studies widely presume viewers to be tabula rasa and so ignore complex cultural histories of viewing. The Indonesian audiences that television executives wish to attract widely have sophisticated prior understandings of narrative, rhetoric and reference which they share with actors, many of whom came originally from a theatrical background. Generally, television programmes emerge not *ex nihilo*, but from a discussion involving producers, viewers and others, in which commentary – commentative practices – from text messages to academic and newspaper reviews, to weddings and by mothers-in-law all play a part. While media practice might seem adequate, say, to analyse explicitly media-oriented activities like crime reporting, it has insuperable problems in addressing the complexity of social life of which media are part. In turning to practice, Couldry has inadvertently pulled the plug on media studies by showing that the media do not constitute a self-contained, discriminable class of phenomena.

Where to Now?

To recap: in this chapter I have examined the possibilities and problems of reconsidering the mass media and their social relations as practice. Couldry's proposal (see Chapter 1) provides an important starting point, which allows a long-overdue critical discussion of the philosophical pre-suppositions of media studies. However, in my view, even this account remains trapped within a Eurocentric and philosophically problematic frame of reference. While Couldry's proposed alternative object of study, media practices, is a great improvement, arguably it privileges a limited range of practices effectively centred around production and so fails to address the social context in which people engage with, use and argue over or ignore the media.

My own, more radical, account of practice is still exploratory. Its advantage is that potentially it avoids the ethnocentric closure which bedevils media studies. The disadvantage is that practices tend not to line up neatly. They exhibit sprawl, mutual contradiction, often unplanned originality, undecidability – in short they exemplify everything that undermines system. As Laclau pointed out, the genealogy of European thought from Aristotle has sidelined the contingent and unpredictable in favour of the essential and continuity (Laclau 1990a: 18–26). The episte-mological and political implications are obvious. However, it puts media studies scholars in a dilemma. To take on the full implications of a philosophy of practice wrecks most of the discipline. To carry on academic practice as usual by inoculating themselves occasionally with a judicious soupçon of practice-lite temporarily to ward off the more evident incoherencies makes a mockery of the whole purpose. We should not be too optimistic. As J.K. Galbraith remarked, 'Faced with the choice between changing one's mind and proving there is no need to do so, almost everyone gets busy on the proof' (Galbraith 1971: 50).

Notes

1. My thanks to Birgit Bräuchler and John Postill for their helpful comments on a draft of this chapter.
2. This subtitle is adapted from Peter Sellars's parody of political speechifying in which, as I recall, he declaims: 'I consider existing conditions unlikely and, if elected, would do everything in my power to change them'.
3. There has, of course, been a loyal opposition, whose genealogy is often traced most recently through Vico, Croce, Collingwood, Wittgenstein, Bakhtin and Volosinov and the philosophical pragmatists, notably Peirce,

Goodman and Quine. I find it useful to consider the work of Foucault, Baudrillard and Deleuze as part of this trend. Although it deals with problems more specific to analytical philosophy, granted how developed philosophical pragmatism (henceforth plain 'pragmatism') is, it is striking how marginal it has been to disciplines which involve, rather than theorise about, practice.

4. As an example, lecturing, as I do, on media and cultural studies in Indonesian is informative, because you end up giving side lectures on the background and history of the cultural usage of many of the key terms. And obviously Indonesian students relate ideas to their experience of the Indonesian mass media with fascinating, if unpredictable, results. Cultural translation consists in effect of everyone else having to learn the myths of the master race. Whether the rest of the world will continue to lie down quietly is questionable. For example, although statements of difference remain couched in the theoretical language of the hegemon, the proliferation of journals and collected volumes on Asian media and cultural studies suggests epistemological colonialism may be running its course.

5. This is the drawback of Bourdieu's approach which is, in the end, supplementary. While he made some steps in *Homo Academicus* (1988) towards recognising academic practices as an object of study, they are at such a level of generality as to ape the shortcomings of structure that practice was designed to redress.

6. How difficult it is to cross these divides is evident in the collection resulting from the Bielefeld conference on *Practices and Social Order* (Schatzki, Knorr Certina and von Savigny 2001) in which something purporting to be a coherent theory of practice is presented. This is only made possible by the authors' ingenious selection of examples which ignore most social life. Such armchair punditry not only reveals a profound Eurocentrism, but scholarly practices themselves remain conveniently unproblematised. This kind of theorising remains so trapped in its own world that it is part of the problem rather than a solution.

7. The political – and indeed imperial – implications of this hierarchical theory of knowledge are discussed by Inden (1990: 15). Significantly, he draws here upon the pragmatist philosopher, Richard Rorty (1979: 357), and more broadly upon that other pragmatist, Collingwood. For a more extended analysis of the colonial implications of power and knowledge, which is pertinent here, see Inden (1986).

8. Couldry frames his approach in terms of a new paradigm. If paradigm is not simply a synonym for approach or something similar, this is a strong claim because, from the debate following Kuhn's (1970) original argument (e.g., Lakatos and Musgrave 1970), a paradigm entails a rigorous ontology and epistemology, and specification of how the assumptions of the new paradigm differ from its predecessors.

9. The theorists in Schatzki, Knorr Certina and von Savigny (2001) refer simply to 'context', which ignores the circumstances of practice. To the question 'do

media practices have a privileged role in anchoring other types of practice because of the privileged circulation of media representations and images of the social world?' (Couldry this volume: 47), the answer is that the circumstances of privileging as a practice would have to come under scrutiny.

10. The assumption that media producers worldwide share frames of reference either because they have been trained in the same way or because of the dictates of technology is not supported by ethnographic studies.

11. This is the issue of radical metaphysics, which has been central to philosophical pragmatist concerns from Collingwood (1940) to Bakhtin (1986), Volosinov (1973) and Foucault (1986a, 1986b). The failure to recognise, let alone engage with, many streams of pragmatist thinking highlights we are dealing with a pre-theoretical theory of practice.

12. This problem is serious enough for well-articulated practices. How the researcher is supposed to know the unreflective or unconscious meanings of someone in another society boggles the mind.

13. I leave issues of power largely implicit here because I do not have space to develop them. Also, in the wake of Foucault's work, they are more obvious than before.

14. Contingency, a notoriously difficult problem to handle, can through practice be addressed by considering how it is articulated.

15. Whether some occurrence is construed as an action or an event depends on how it is articulated. Here the disjuncture between researcher's and participants' frames of reference comes in. Anthropologists are familiar with what we would call an event like disease being treated as the result of an action, such as witchcraft. 'Natural' calamities or great events may well be attributed with agency.

16. Collingwood put it succinctly. The sort of study of mind appropriate to historical and anthropological method, involves two renunciations. First, it renounces with Locke all 'science of substance'. It does not ask what mind is; it asks only what mind does ... Secondly, it renounces all attempt to discover what mind *always and everywhere does*, and asks only *what mind has done* on certain definite occasions. (Collingwood 1942: 60)

    Charles Taylor makes a related point about action and consciousness. Reflective 'awareness in our action is something we come to achieve. In achieving this, we also transform our activity' (Taylor 1985: 84).

17. Given my interest in how societies change, my short list of concepts to be redescribed in terms of practice include agency and subjecthood; structure and history; consciousness, meaning and the everyday. I have addressed each elsewhere.

18. Although the philosophical case has been argued through in some detail, how it would work for different human scientific disciplines is far from a matter of simply applying theory, not least because of the dual discursive nature of inquiry into practice.

19. Collingwood (1942) stressed how agency is widely complex or compound. Cf. Taylor: 'All action is not in the last analysis of individuals; there are irreducibly collective actions' (Taylor 1985: 93).

20. Recognising implies recognising as or representing as. Practices are not natural objects in the world. Articulation here is in the sense argued by Laclau and Mouffe (1985: 104–14). To develop Peirce, if actions are taken as primary, activities are sets of actions (that is 'Seconds'). Practices are more complex in that they involve the articulation of subjects, objects and purposes (and so are 'Thirds'). The categories are evidently overlapping and situational.

    In answer to the question 'Is television viewing a practice?' we cannot decide a priori, but must inquire about kinds and degrees of viewing, for what purposes and according to whom. I consider my flopping in front of the television after a hard day at work an activity, but a practice if I am critically watching an ethnographic film. So accounts of (usually) men watching news as part of making themselves informed citizens might be considered a practice in some situations, as might the couch-potato life of the British TV series, *The Royle Family*, where television watching is constitutive of their social life and roles.

21. It works nicely, for example, for domestic and industrial work patterns in Bali. Women frequently cook and make offerings with the radio or television on. And handicraft wood-carving often takes place in big sheds with several televisions sets tuned to different channels, so carvers can move around to watch their preferred channel.

22. I have attempted to address this question for ethnography in Hobart (1996).

23. See, e.g., Hobart (2000). I would adopt a harder line than readers may like. The abuses of interpretive power are so endemic that I would argue for avoiding interpreting altogether in favour of a critical analysis of others' commentaries on their own practices and productions (Hobart 2006).

24. It was Evans-Pritchard's secretary who told me that he had the collected works of Collingwood on his desk throughout his later years. The Collingwoodian tone is evident on a careful rereading.

25. This is therefore a version of the Baconian method (Collingwood 1946: 269–82). A key source of evidence is commentaries on practices by participants and others (Hobart 2006). For reasons which Collingwood, himself a philosopher, spelled out at length in his later work, debates about practice among analytical philosophers cannot offer a workable framework for the analysis of media practices, especially non-Western ones. Among other things, the object of study involves congeries of presuppositions which are both historical and culturally specific and so require historical or anthropological approaches. Insofar as philosophy presupposes its object, it is unsuited to this task. Insofar as practice requires recognition of the circumstances, purposes and outcomes of action, as Nigel Barley noted of a general theory of sexual intercourse, this kind of philosophy leads eventually to frustration, sterility and impotence.

26. It is not that issues of power are irrelevant, but the limitations of what were useful approaches and concepts in their day have become evident. You only have to think of the incoherencies in the notion of ideology (Laclau 1990b).

27. Althusserian accounts of interpellation look increasingly ropey anyway: see, e.g., Carroll (1988: 53–88) and Laclau and Mouffe (1985).
28. Precisely the same happened in the television stations in which I have worked in Indonesia. Here the recognition is effectively on the part of the researcher, which is why practice has to be defined between two frames of reference.
29. Whereas production relies on clearly-articulated practices in relatively small and highly organised groups, reception presents more problems. How useful it is to define as practice all the forms that reading and viewing of print and broadcast media alone may take is a moot point. As we are dealing with mass media, we are dealing with unknowably large populations. However, surveys, focus groups or interviews cannot access practices in the sense proposed. Here ethnography hits a problem too because, by synecdoche, a few examples have to stand for the whole. And looming over everything are two problems. What readers and viewers are making of what they read and watch remains largely undecidable. And it remains unclear exactly whether there is a coherent object of study.

References

Asad, T. 1986. 'The Concept of Cultural Translation in British Social Anthropology', in J. Clifford and G. Marcus (eds), *Writing Culture: The Poetics and Politics of Ethnography*. Berkeley: University of California Press, pp.141–64.

Bakhtin, M.M. 1986. *Speech Genres and other Late Essays*, trans. V.W. McGee, C. Emerson and M. Holquist (eds). Austin: University of Texas Press.

Bird, S.E. 2003. *The Audience in Everyday Life: Living in a Media World*. London: Routledge.

Bourdieu, P. 1988. *Homo Academicus*. Cambridge: Polity.

Carroll, N. 1988. *Mystifying Movies: Fads and Fallacies in Contemporary Film Theory*. New York: Columbia University Press.

Chen, K-H. 1996. 'Post-Marxism: Between/Beyond Critical Postmodernism and Cultural Studies', in D. Morley and K.H. Chen (eds), *Stuart Hall: Critical Dialogues in Cultural Studies*. London: Routledge, pp.309–23.

Collingwood, R.G. 1940. *An Essay on Metaphysics*. Oxford: Clarendon Press.

—— 1942. *The New Leviathan or Man, Society, Civilisation and Barbarism*. Oxford: Clarendon Press.

—— 1946. *The Idea of History*. Oxford: Clarendon Press.

Fiske, J. 1987. *Television Culture*. London: Methuen.

Foucault, M. 1982. 'The Subject and Power', in H.L. Dreyfus and P. Rabinow (eds), *Michel Foucault: Beyond Structuralism and Hermeneutics*. Brighton: Harvester, pp.208–26.

—— 1986a. *The Use of Pleasure: The History of Sexuality, Volume 2*. Harmondsworth: Viking.

——— 1986b. *The Care of the Self: The History of Sexuality, Volume 3*. New York: Pantheon.

——— 1990. 'Nietzsche, Freud, Marx', in G.L. Ormiston and A.D. Schrift (eds), *Transforming the Hermeneutic Context: From Nietzsche to Nancy*. Albany: State University of New York Press, pp.59–67.

Galbraith, J.K. 1971. *Economics, Peace and Laughter*. Boston Mass.: Houghton Mifflin.

Geertz, C. 1973. 'Thick Description: Towards an Interpretive Theory of Culture', in *The Interpretation of Cultures*. New York: Basic Books, pp.3–30.

Ginsburg, F., L. Abu-Lughod and B. Larkin (eds). 2002. *Media Worlds: Anthropology on New Terrain*. Berkeley: University of California Press.

Goodman, N. 1968. *Languages of Art*. Indianapolis: Bobbs-Merrill.

——— 1972. 'The Way the World Is', in *Problems and Projects*. Indianapolis: Bobbs-Merrill, pp.24–32.

——— 1978. *Ways of Worldmaking*. Hassocks: Harvester Press.

Hesse, M. 1978. 'Theory and Value in the Social Sciences', in C. Hookway and P. Pettit (eds), *Action and Interpretation: Studies in the Philosophy of the Social Sciences*. Cambridge: Cambridge University Press, pp.1–16.

Hobart, M. 1996. 'Ethnography as a Practice, or the Unimportance of Penguins', *Europaea* 2(1): 3–36.

——— 2000. *After Culture: Anthropology as Radical Metaphysical Critique*. Yogyakarta: Duta Wacana Press.

——— 2006. 'Just Talk? Anthropological Reflections on the Object of Media Studies in Indonesia', *Asian Journal of Social Science* 34(3): 492–519.

Inden, R. 1986. 'Orientalist Constructions of India', *Modern Asian Studies* 20(1): 401–46.

——— 1990. *Imagining India*. Oxford: Blackwell.

Kuhn, T.S. 1970. *The Structure of Scientific Revolutions*, 2nd edn. Chicago: University of Chicago Press.

Laclau, E. 1990a. 'New Reflections on the Revolution of Our Time', in *New Reflections on the Revolution of Our Time*. London: Verso, pp.3–85.

——— 1990b. 'The Impossibility of Society', in *New Reflections on the Revolution of Our Time*. London: Verso, pp.89–92.

Laclau, E. and Mouffe, C. 1985. *Hegemony and Socialist Strategy: Towards a Radical Democratic Politics*, trans. W. Moore and P. Cammack. London: Verso.

Lakatos, I. and A. Musgrave (eds). 1970. *Criticism and the Growth of Knowledge*. London: Cambridge University Press.

Lull, J. 1990. *Inside Family Viewing: Ethnographic Research on Television's Audiences*. London: Routledge.

Morley, D. 1986. *Family Television*. London: Routledge.

Needham, R. 1972. *Belief, Language, and Experience*. Oxford: Blackwell.

Peterson, M.A. 2003. *Anthropology and Mass Communication: Media and Myth in the New Millennium*. Oxford: Berghahn.

Quine, W.V.O. 1960. *Word and Object*. Cambridge, MA: MIT Press.

Rorty, R. 1979. *Philosophy and the Mirror of Nature.* Princeton, NJ: Princeton University Press.

Rothenbuhler, E. and M. Coman (eds). 2005. *Media Anthropology.* London: Sage.

Schatzki, T.R. 2001. 'Practice Mind-ed Orders', in T.R. Schatzki, K. Knorr Certina and E. von Savigny (eds), *The Practice Turn in Contemporary Theory.* London: Routledge, pp.42–55.

Schatzki, T.R., K. Knorr Certina and E. von Savigny (eds). 2001. *The Practice Turn in Contemporary Theory.* London: Routledge.

Swidler, A. 2001. 'What Anchors Cultural Practices', in T.R. Schatzki, K. Knorr Certina and E. von Savigny (eds), *The Practice Turn in Contemporary Theory.* London: Routledge, pp.74–92.

Taylor, C. 1985. 'Hegel's Philosophy of Mind', in *Human Agency and Language: Philosophical Papers 1.* Cambridge: Cambridge University Press, pp.77–96.

Volosinov, V.N. 1973. *Marxism and the Philosophy of Language,* trans. L. Matejka and I.R. Titunik. Cambridge, MA: Harvard University Press.

Wallace, A.F.C. 1961. *Culture and Personality.* New York: Random House.

Wittgenstein, L. 1958. *Philosophical Investigations.* Oxford: Blackwell.

CHAPTER 3

Media as Practice:
A Brief Exchange

Nick Couldry and Mark Hobart

Nick Couldry

Mark Hobart's comments greatly enrich the space of argument in which my original piece was situated. That piece, written in late 2003, was part polemic, part manifesto. I wrote it fast, because the then recent adoption of practice theory in sociology – in particular, social theory and the sociology of consumption – seemed to have urgent implications for the sociology of media, my own field. So while I was well aware of the deep philosophical currents swirling around the term 'practice', I deliberately stepped across them for my immediate purpose of disrupting current schemas for analysing 'media' and suggesting some new ones.

What emerges from our two pieces, written at different times and for different purposes, are two rather different ways of introducing practice theory to media research. The first, 'radical' approach (Hobart's) adopts practice as its key philosophical concept to ground a complete reorientation of our epistemology of social analysis. A second, 'instrumental' approach (my own) is more limited in scope and intent: it develops the analytical implications of certain debates and terms from practice theory to dislodge old habits in the specific field of media analysis. Underlying this difference, I suspect, is an underlying philosophical divergence between certain ontologies and epistemologies of the social which gives most weight to discourse and interpretation (for example, that of Ernesto Laclau, which Hobart applies to media research) and the rather different ontology and epistemology of so-called 'critical realism' (developed by Roy Bhaskar) which is concerned above all with the material bases of power. I have explored the implications of that divergence for understanding media power elsewhere (Couldry 2008).

The basic point, as I see it, is as follows: without denying for one moment the reconceptualisation by Foucault, Latour and others of power as dispersed (a fundamental shift in modern social thought), power is still an arrangement of people and things, actions and discourse, that involves coordination, sometimes over large scales, even if that coordination always must be enacted locally. My worry is that what at first seems radical in Hobart's reading of practice theory – and who could doubt him when, like Bourdieu, albeit within a very different language, he argues we must each be sceptical towards the power relations built into the analyst's pose – risks preventing us from grasping how contemporary power works, in part, through media and the stretched-out processes of mediation.[1] Here I welcome, incidentally, Hobart's suggestion of the term 'media-related' to replace my term 'media-oriented' practice, so as to emphasise that practices of interest in relation to media include many that are not oriented to media, indeed may be turned away from it. I could not agree more.

So there is a great deal of common ground between us which must be recognised. But it would be wrong equally to minimize the genuine philosophical divergences which shape our different perspectives on practice. It may be productive simply to list some of the philosophical choices involved here while leaving it to the writers of later chapters – and to readers – to form their own views about which, if either, of our epistemologies of practice is more useful for understanding media.

There are a number of major philosophical issues which it is clear (and here Hobart and I completely agree) need to be aired more widely within media research. There are broad philosophical debates:

- realism/anti-realism.
- the problems of incommensurability and translation – my view on this is shaped by Donald Davidson's (1984), I think, classic debunking of the apparently fundamental problems of radical incommensurability.
- the question of whether a notion of intersubjective understanding can be developed which avoids making transcendental assumptions. I believe it can, while Hobart doesn't (for a recent discussion of Davidson's contribution on this, see Grant 2007: 145–48).

Moving more towards the philosophy of social science, there is the question of:

- the ontology of social description – what entities do we suppose are fundamental to any description of the social world, and in particular how do we understand power and agency and their interrelations?

While in relation to media research, the main questions would seem to be:

- the consequences of genuinely internationalising media research (see here for some recent thoughts, Couldry 2007).
- the relative priority we give to problems of interpretation and translation versus the need to register regularity and hierarchy where it occurs in and between particular scales.
- our understanding of media power, and how and why that understanding is transformed as we increasingly compare research on media in different parts of the world.
- the legitimate role of philosophical argument in guiding, or laying rules for, empirical analysis in media research or in any other area (if legitimate, there is the further question of which philosophical debates and reference points are useful and which are not).

Hobart and I agree, I suspect, much more than might be immediately apparent, that these are the outstanding questions requiring clarification, but we draw on different philosophical and argumentative resources to address them.

A richer debate within media research will result, I believe, if we bring our philosophical premises out into the open and debate them. I look forward to more of this kind of debate and welcome Hobart's contribution in encouraging the debate about practice theory in media research in a more philosophically explicit direction.

Mark Hobart

Nick Couldry's response is important and constructive. A concern we share is that, with its empiricist, at times positivist, pedigree, media studies scholars prefer to get on with 'normal science' (Kuhn 1970) rather than reflect occasionally on quite what is involved in doing it. Ignoring, or being ignorant of, the philosophical presuppositions of any theory or practice condemns one endlessly to replicate the safe-looking, but ultimately sclerotic, certainties of moribund paradigms. Given the crisis that its practitioners are gradually recognizing media studies is in, Couldry and I agree that it is crucial that we start to question existing theoretical frameworks, and that is what our two pieces are about. So I welcome his drawing attention to the philosophical divergences between how we imagine practice. It is only out of such argument that the strengths and weaknesses of different approaches will emerge.

The philosophical debates that Couldry lists – realism, translation, intersubjectivity and the ontology of social description – do indeed need reconsidering urgently, most obviously for the study of non-Western media. The risk is of claiming to understand others using culturally specific frameworks which are imagined to be universal. Questions about translation and intersubjectivity, for example, may undermine taken-for-granted assumptions and threaten media studies as we know it.[2] I question, though, whether these complex epistemological and ontological questions boil down, as Couldry suggests, to the relative importance of interpretation and discourse as against the materiality of power. While we both reject the prevailing, but largely unthinking, empiricism, Couldry's choice of Bhaskar's critical realism as the route for an internationalised media studies presupposes a Kantian transcendentalism, which runs counter to the recognition of historical and cultural difference.[3]

When it comes to Couldry's account of what the main future research questions are, the differences between us become apparent – and informative. Our intellectual backgrounds, disciplinary training and what we understand as the purposes and limits of inquiry lead us to approach the issues in quite different ways. To what degree they are incompatible or incommensurate will, I trust, emerge out of further argument.[4] Couldry writes from the heartland of Euro-American media studies and is reasonably comfortable approaching it as a science, but he is concerned how genuinely to internationalise it. His suggestions for future research presuppose that normal science is working reasonably well but needs some updating and revision. Coming to media studies as an anthropologist, I am struck inter alia by the complacent Eurocentrism of media studies, reminiscent less of a self-critical discipline than a closed and self-confirming system of belief like Zande witchcraft (Winch 1970) or Nuer religion (Feyerabend 1975: 250–51). How, for instance, are we to determine that the scientific regularity which Couldry seeks to establish through research is not to a significant degree a product of the frame of reference?

Similarly, Couldry is concerned to establish hierarchy, but this applies not just to the object of study but to the relationship between media researchers and their subjects of study, who are knowable only in the terms designated by Western scholars. Anthropologists recognize this, sadly, as epistemological imperialism. In stressing the materiality of contemporary media power, Couldry is locked into a Western dichotomy of discourse versus materiality; and is also unable to recognize, let alone step outside, the formidable hegemony of Western academe. To me the materiality of power is only one of its modes. Phrased in other terms, historically, media and communication studies involve inter alia a tension between two substantive goals: servicing Western media industries and political activism. Anthropology by contrast, insofar as it can escape its colonial heritage, is, I think, of necessity critical. That is, its task is to challenge the hegemony of which it, like media studies, is part. For this reason I am much more sceptical than Couldry about how open the research agenda of media studies can ever be. Like the objectivity and impartiality of the news, I consider it a fiction necessary to the smooth running of academia, as news is of the polity.

We both recognize and appreciate that the differences between our approaches are not simply a matter of choosing philosophers who suit our taste but of drawing upon philosophical debate to try to articulate quite different ways of appreciating what knowledge does. It would be easy to put labels on what we are doing: naturalism versus humanism, conservatism versus radicalism, normal science versus trendy poststructuralist critique and so on. That misses the point and it enables people to carry on uncritically recycling tired, self-confirming and increasingly uninteresting work. To dwell on the differences is to miss the fact that Couldry and I both agree that media studies, and the study of media practice, without critical philosophical debate is sterile.

Notes

1. See Couldry (2000: 4–7) for a longer discussion on this point which draws on actor network theory.
2. I am grateful to Virginia Nightingale for pointing out to me how the object of study in most media studies is now defined around and reifies particular assumptions about media production. Similarly, treating communication as mechanical, and so largely unproblematic, neatly avoids how complex and uncertain a set of relationships communication comprises.
3. 'Only transcendental realism ... can sustain the idea of a law-governed world independent of man ... that is necessary to understand science' (Bhaskar 1978: 26).
4. For reasons of space, our original and much longer exchange had to be drastically shortened. The full version is available at http://www.criticalia.org/Debate_on_Media_Practices.htm.

References

Bhaskar, R. 1978. *A Realist Theory of Science*. Sussex: Harvester.
Couldry, N. 2000. *The Place of Media Power: Pilgrims and Witnesses of the Media Age*. London: Routledge.

———— 2007. 'Comparative Media Research as if We Really Meant it', *Global Media and Communication* 3(3): 247–50.

———— 2008. 'Form and Power in an Age of Continuous Spectacle' in D. Hesmondhalgh and J. Toynbee (eds), *Media and Social Theory*. London: Routledge, pp.161–76.

Davidson, D. 1984. 'On the Very Idea of a Conceptual Scheme', in *Truth and Interpretation*. Oxford: Oxford University Press, pp.183–96.

Feyerabend, P. 1975. *Against Method: Outline of an Anarchistic Theory of Knowledge*. London: Verso.

Grant, C. 2007. *Uncertainty and Communication: New Theoretical Investigations*. Basingstoke: Palgrave Macmillan.

Kuhn, T.S. 1970. *The Structure of Scientific Revolutions*, 2nd edn. Chicago: University of Chicago Press.

Winch, P. 1970. 'Understanding a Primitive Society', in B. Wilson (ed.), *Rationality*. Oxford: Blackwell, pp.78–111.

PART II

Media, Culture and Practice

From Fan Practice to Mediated Moments: The Value of Practice Theory in the Understanding of Media Audiences

S. Elizabeth Bird

In the last ten to fifteen years, ethnographically informed scholarship on media audiences has moved away from studies of direct engagement with texts toward a consideration of multiple articulations with media in everyday life (Bird 2003). In media studies, scholars have questioned the narrowness of studies based on the concept of 'audience response' to specific media, arguing that the complexity of media penetration in contemporary societies cannot be captured by such approaches (see Alasuutari 1999 for overview). At the same time, anthropologists have increasingly come to realise that cultures worldwide can no longer be understood without reference to the media. Many have turned to the media studies literature to address audience reception, while also arguing that more genuinely ethnographic approaches are needed to move beyond simple text–audience approaches (e.g., Abu-Lughod 1997; Mankekar 1999). Meanwhile, anthropologists have also been rethinking the anthropological idea of a defined field about which one can produce ethnographic accounts (e.g., Gupta and Ferguson 1997; Marcus 1998) and have called for multi-sited ethnography as a way to address complex cultural processes, such as the role of media.

Briefly put, it is the resulting interdisciplinary ferment that has led us to (re)discover practice as a guiding concept with which to conceptualise media audiences in the twenty-first century. Media scholars have strived to rethink what it means to live in a mediated world, and anthropologists have come to grips with why the reality of a mediated world matters to anthropology, both theoretically and methodologically (e.g., Askew and Wilk 2002; Ginsburg, Abu-Lughod and Larkin 2002;

Peterson 2003). Hobart, for example, describes his realisation that to understand the role of media in Balinese life, he needed to explore practices that 'only partly overlap with direct engagement in the medium (reading the newspapers, watching the box) and have as much to do with anticipating, chatting about, criticising, understanding and so on. Such practices also include Balinese commenting on their own practices' (Hobart 1999: 12).

My discussion, therefore, is situated in the context both of the exploding interest in media within anthropology and the turn toward a more anthropological approach to media audiences. As I have said elsewhere, '[w]e cannot really isolate the role of media in culture, because the media are firmly anchored into the web of culture, although articulated by individuals in different ways' (Bird 2003: 3). While Couldry (this volume) writes that my work represents the 'definitive formulation of the paradigm shift underway', I would rather suggest that my own work is positioned in this interdisciplinary context, represented by such scholars as Abu-Lughod (2000), Hoover et al. (2004), Gauntlett (2007), and of course Couldry himself.

Thus my interest in practice emerges from my long-standing commitment to understanding the media 'audience' in a more complex way than the 'audience response' approach allows, moving past both earlier 'effects' traditions and 'second-wave' (Alasuutari 1999) approaches, which are rooted in Hall's (1980) seminal 'encoding/decoding' model. The relevant questions about media are no longer 'What do media do to people and cultures?' or even 'What do people do in response to media?' As Couldry suggests, 'If recent media research has foregrounded 'media culture', practice theory translates this into two concrete and related questions: What types of things do people do in relation to media? And what types of things do people say in relation to media?' (this volume: 41). To this I would add: How are media incorporated into everyday communicative and cultural practices? This, I think, is a slightly different, if related, issue, one which I elaborate below in my discussion of mediated rituals such as weddings. However, I mean by this that in a mediated society existing conventions and practices are refracted through a mediated lens even if people are not consciously referencing the media. Thus, personal and cultural events (like weddings) are subtly changed by media models in a way that older 'media effects' research cannot capture.

Thus I align my work quite closely with the position taken by Couldry. I find that the focus on practices helps us conceptualise what to study in relation to the media in everyday life (beyond media texts themselves), and it also helps position anthropological ethnographic approaches at the centre of media audience study. It is a way to build on the already extensive, ethnographically inspired work that has been developing for several decades in audience studies, in which references to audience 'practices' abound. Such references begin as early as 1975, when Carey advocated a 'ritual' model of communication, drawing heavily on Geertz (1973) to deconstruct the 'transmission' model, arguing that much media consumption is less about the specifics of the media message and more about the activities surrounding reception. As he notes, 'culture must first be seen as a set of practices' (Carey 1975: 19), a point largely overlooked in the focus on the 'effective' transmission of meaning. The task of the researcher is to explore these practices and their interconnections with each other.

I see Couldry's 'instrumental' approach to media practices deriving from that tradition in communication study, which in turn drew heavily on anthropological models well before anthropologists themselves became greatly interested in the media. For me, the focus on practice is useful in helping me theorise the idea of 'the audience'; I am not especially interested in the much broader theoretical rethinking that Hobart (this volume) advocates. Defining this as 'radical', he argues for the need 'to consider all media and mediation as practice, root and branch' (Hobart, in reply to Couldry),[1] yet I am unclear where it takes us in terms of practical research. I find Couldry's most definitely non-radical approach more useful as a guide to studying the everyday role of media, although it does have some limitations.

The study of media practices maintains the focus on local, grounded activities, rather than theoretical (and possibly speculative) analyses of 'culture'. Nevertheless, as Ortner (1984, 1998) suggests, we must hold the constraints of structure and the power of audience agency together. The turn in media studies toward a conception of the 'active audience' gave agency back to those 'responding' to the media, in contrast to the transmission model of communication. However, the foregrounding of audience activity also downplayed the power of media producers to inscribe privileged representations of the world that place constraints on actual audience practices.[2]

Ortner's approach to practice is useful here. In 1984 she brought together disparate strands in anthropological theory to make the case for a 'practice' approach to culture, arguing that it fruitfully brings together several important perspectives in anthropology and sociology – such as Geertzian-inspired symbolic analysis, and the social drama approach of the British Manchester School. She argues that a central problem for anthropology, as it tries to make sense of culture in a world where bounded 'cultures' no longer exist, is the relationship between structure and individual agency. She effectively captures what has become a key problem for audience study: the tension between what she calls the 'cultural studies temptation: the fantasy that one can understand the workings of public cultural representations by interpreting/deconstructing the representations', contrasted with 'the ethnographic fantasy that doing fieldwork in and of itself provides the kind of "data" necessary to correct for the cultural studies illusion' (1998: 414–15).

As Ortner, Marcus (1998) and Gupta and Ferguson (1997) suggest, the imperative to develop a multi-dimensional, multi-sited ethnography requires us to dissolve still-current distinctions between interpretations derived from text-based rhetorical criticism (emanating mostly from cultural studies) and those derived from ethnographically based studies of audience response. At the same time, the still-relevant anthropological impulse toward holism and interconnection poses the significant challenge of how, in practical terms, to study practice.

Mediated Practices

From the above discussion, it should be clear that my understanding of 'practices' parallels that of Couldry and others who explore media audiences, such as Hoover et al. (2004), and Seiter (1999). It also connects to the work of Ardèvol et al. (this volume), who highlight 'play practices' made possible through the recent explosion in portable media technologies, or scholars such as Peterson (2009), in his study of Indian newspaper reading as cultural practice. Tracing my interest back to Carey (1975) my emphasis is on communicative practices – everyday talk and actions that in some way articulate with media. Some mediated practices involve direct interaction with texts (such as fan practices), while others are more accurately described as being inflected through media representation (such as how public social events have increasingly come to reflect mediated representations of what such events 'should' be). Then there are specific, often ephemeral, 'moments' of audience activity that point to the self-referentiality of media practices in a highly media-saturated culture, examples of which I describe below. I am not presenting developed ethnographic findings but rather suggesting how we might bring an anthropological sensibility to studies that must be both rooted in everyday interaction and located within multiple wider cultural discourses and power structures.

The Mediated Fan

The study of fan activities is booming as never before, and its relevance to the discussion of mediated practices (in terms of things people say and do that are related to or happen around media) is obvious. Fans engage in a huge variety of active, media-related practices that connect them, their chosen texts, and multiple other texts – such as media commentaries, web postings, fan fiction and so on – together in an articulation that is anything but static and linear. Inspired by the early work of Jenkins (1992), Bacon-Smith (1992) and the authors included in Lewis (1992), scholars have explored the world of fan practices, in which fans not only watch and talk but also create fan fiction, video mash-ups, conference events and so on (e.g., Gwenllian-Jones 2000; Bird 2003; Sandvoss 2005; Jenkins 2006). Such practices may create a genuine sense of community, in both the online and offline worlds. For instance, my work over an extended period of time with fans of the middle-brow TV show *Dr Quinn, Medicine Woman,* showed how fans carved out a strongly gendered online space, primarily through extended discussion on an e-mail list but also through fan-created websites and fan fictions sites, organised letter-writing campaigns, extending also to offline meetings. They used the primary text of the show as a springboard for richly nuanced discussions of everything from ethical behaviour and alternative lifestyles to Western history and Native American culture (Bird 2003). By now, scholarship has effectively dispensed with the idea that fan practices can be dismissed as the marginal activities of lunatics (Hills 2002).

Indeed, fans have come to epitomise a transformation of the media audience into a hotbed of activity, going far beyond 'response' to media texts. Ardèvol et al. (this volume) discuss this phenomenon as they explore the way fans have become producers of media texts, dissolving distinctions between producer, text and audience. Indeed, Jenkins argues that 'fandom represents ... the testing ground for the way media and culture industries are going to operate in the future' (Jenkins 2007: 361). He sees the new relationship between audience and producer as very complex, with a 'new kind of cultural power emerging as fans bond together within larger communities, pool their information, shape each other's opinions, and develop a greater self-consciousness about their shared agendas and common interests' (ibid.: 362–63). Media producers have been pushed to modify their products in response to fan demands: 'we might think of these new knowledge communities as collective bargaining units for consumers' (ibid.: 363). And while we may worry that fan activity is distracting people from significant, civic participation, Jenkins asserts its potential to lead to significant political action that may bring about cultural and social change by encouraging young people to see the internet as a way to organise politically (see, e.g., Dahlgren 2005). Gray echoes this possibility in his discussion of news fans, claiming that 'in many cases, [they] showed the ability for fan-like engagement and civic duty to work together' (Gray 2007: 85).

Thus fan activities provide a kind of locus in which we can explore media-related practices that take audience studies completely out of the realm of text/response. While fan studies originated in an interest in 'cult' media forms, further work has showed that these kind of active practices are now mainstream. The latest collection on 'fandom' (Gray, Sandvoss and Harrington 2007) presents an array of fan practices, sparked by everything from TV shows, news and movies to nineteenth-century concert halls, gaming and backyard wrestling. In a chapter on wrestling, for instance, McBride and myself describe inter-related practices around 'backyard' and 'indy' wrestling, practiced by young, white, middle-class men (McBride and Bird 2007). These practices are clearly mediated in that they are inspired by the spectacle of televised professional wrestling; fans who wrestle create their own characters and scripts, drawing on media examples. And the spectacle is also refracted through fans' own media constructions, as they film their events and distribute them on the internet, where others comment and construct new texts. Were we studying 'media audiences' or wrestlers? We argue that a key to the attraction of indy wrestling for its practitioners is a very real, bodily experience of often intense pain, which appears to alter consciousness. This is some distance from televised wrestling, often seen as the epitome of fake, inauthentic media. Yet, I would argue, it is indeed a mediated fan practice, which would not exist in the absence of the original media text. And this kind of analysis takes us far beyond an effects paradigm that might worry, for instance, whether violent wrestling on television 'causes' children to mimic the moves and become violent themselves.

Fan practices, then, represent a fruitful way to examine everyday life in a media world in which media texts, and discourse about texts, suffuse not only moments of actual media consumption but also people's world-views in a broad sense – for instance, their sense of ethics, emotions or gender identity. In that sense, I understand Couldry's assertions that media 'anchor' other practices, although I am wary of the way this term privileges media as the prime 'anchor' rather than as one connection among various cultural practices. At any given moment, another type of practice – for example, religious, political – might be considered the prime 'anchor' with which media might link. It is for that reason that I prefer the term 'articulation'. The study of fan practices shows us how individuals actively choose to articulate with media in a wide range of often unpredictable ways, moving us from a perception of 'the media' as a monolithic, even sinister force to an appreciation of individual choice and agency.

At the same time, I believe too heavy an emphasis on fan practices should be treated with caution. Jenkins argues that 'as fandom becomes part of the normal way that the creative industries operate, then fandom may cease to function as a meaningful category of cultural analysis' (Jenkins 2007: 364) since we will all behave like fans. However, I am not convinced that we all are (or could be) such active media practitioners. When I studied *Dr Quinn* fans, I was delighted with the creativity, enthusiasm and even erudition displayed by the online community. However, the show was being watched by several million people each week. Of those, a few thousand joined the listserv, and of those maybe two to three hundred participated regularly in the many fan activities. In our enthusiasm for the active fan we should not lose sight of the more mundane, even passive articulation with media that characterises a great deal of media consumption. The active media fan as the model of future media practice has other limits in that it tends to be quite ethnocentric, assuming a level of media saturation, affluence and access to technology that is not the norm worldwide. And finally, the current celebration of fan practices and local agency often ignores the power of media producers, who while they certainly respond to fan demands have also learned to co-opt fan activities in order to sell more effectively (see, e.g., McCourt and Burkart 2007).

Mediated Rituals

Fan studies take practices beyond the text, but we still see an articulation between text and practice. My second type of mediated practice does not show such clear articulation but rather represents everyday life refracted through a media lens. Many scholars have explored the idea of specific media events – such as the Superbowl, a state funeral, or a Royal wedding – functioning as community rituals (e.g., Scannell 1995; Couldry 2003; Kitch 2003; Lardellier 2005; Dayan and Katz 2006). Scholars have also described how activities surrounding certain media events take on a ritualistic form – for example, the way groups gather, talk and eat while viewing major televised sports events (Wenner 1989). More broadly, media practices, such as the daily routine of reading the newspaper or watching television, have also been seen as ritualistic (e.g., Thomas 2005). However, I believe we can also go in a slightly different direction by exploring ritual practices that are not ostensibly focused around the media but which are nevertheless mediated in subtle (and not-so-subtle) ways. Ortner invokes Turner (1969) and the Manchester School, arguing that, unlike the Geertzian-inspired analysis of 'culture as text', their explicitly practice-based approach added 'a sense of the pragmatics of symbols' as symbolic behaviour is acted out in observable events or 'social dramas' (Ortner 1984: 131). As Ortner puts it, this perspective 'wed[s] actors to the categories and norms of their society' by looking at the 'question of how symbols ... operate as active forces in the social process' (ibid.: 131). Ortner characterises 'modern versions of practice theory' as illuminating the fact that culture or society is a system, which although it is ideologically constraining is nevertheless constructed and reconstructed 'through human action and interaction' (ibid.: 159).

An important question for anthropology then becomes the need to simultaneously understand the ideological force of culture and the role of human agency. This conceptualisation fits well with the notion of understanding media 'audiences' as simultaneously creative and constrained. Ethnographic approaches to mediated practices should be framed in terms of how daily choices are limited not only by people's own social and economic circumstances but also by the power of inscription held by media producers. A good place to start might be everyday practices that in the most common sense are understood to be rituals – weddings, graduations, funerals – but are not normally considered primarily as sites of media consumption. Furthermore, by focusing comparatively on rituals across different cultures, and looking at the degree to which they integrate symbols and practices derived from media, we may be able to get a clearer sense of the different degrees to which cultures are media-saturated. Thus I am differentiating between 'media rituals' (as this term has been often used by other scholars) and 'mediated rituals'. With the first term, we start with the media: How does the reading of a newspaper become ritualised? With the second, we start with practices that are culturally understood to be rituals: How are wedding practices shaped by expectations generated through the media?

For example, marriage is universally a socially recognised ritual through which particular themes and values are enacted. According to Leeds-Hurwitz, 'marriage is the way in which a group perpetuates itself: within the family unit the way of life – language, religion, morals, customs – of the group is maintained and propagated' (Leeds-Hurwitz 2002: 53). In less media-saturated societies, most marriage ceremonies tend to follow a fairly standard, recognisable format, although offering individual choices and variations depending on affluence, status and so on. In many cultures those choices remain the domain of family members rather than the bridal couple themselves. Weddings are always public performances, as much or more about the community than about the bridal couple. And I would argue that the level of media sensibility is now a key factor in understanding the everyday practice of weddings. In media-saturated cultures, weddings are simultaneously about an extreme celebration of the individual, as well as being increasingly public performances that draw heavily on media scripts.[3] This change in the form of the wedding practice may in turn have much broader social and cultural implications.

At one level, we see the embeddedness of personal media like photography (including cell phones and other digital devices) in the event. At another level, which I am addressing here, is the cultural imperative that demands a choreographed performance, and a record of that performance that is as close to a media script as possible. In the West, especially in the United States, this has driven an industry of wedding planners and do-it-yourself counterparts – magazines, TV shows and websites – that take it for granted that a wedding must be developed, scripted and cast like a media production, with the bridal couple (especially the bride) as stars. For instance, brides.com, a site affiliated with a stable of bridal magazines and cable TV shows, invites its readers to 'follow these steps for an Oscar-worthy wedding video', explaining that for recording the event, 'letterboxing, split screens and picture-within-picture techniques are the new norm, as are DVDs that enable you to click on chapter stops like First Dance and Cutting the Cake ... Some innovative companies are using film instead of videotape to produce recordings with a Hollywood feel'.[4] One result is that the average U.S. couple now spends $28,800 on their wedding – a figure that excludes the honeymoon, engagement ring, bridal consultant and wedding planner.[5]

Contemporary idealisations of individual autonomy generally prevent people from explicitly acknowledging the media's role in personal decision-making (Alasuutari 1999). The rhetoric used throughout the industry, and by brides themselves (wedding work is still heavily gendered), speaks to the wedding as an opportunity to express one's unique identity. This is hard work, as brides sift through possible 'themes' or scripts that might be available. A member forum on brides.com presents an array of options that are discussed at great length by brides-to-be: What would it take to create a '1940s' theme, a 'Scottish highlands' theme, or a 'simple country' theme? A repeated motif in brides' postings is the need to be 'different', 'unique' or 'memorable', while not referencing media models explicitly (or even denying them). Thus, to achieve the 1940s look, a bride notes that the male attendants will wear 'zoot suits and my dress has a '40s feel ... [but] I'm not really wanting a "Hollywood" theme'. Others suggest 'gangster suits ... we're gonna use lots of glitz and sparkle'. A third directs participants to a site specialising in theme ideas, where she will find this advice: 'Close your eyes and imagine it's 1940. America's at war and you and the love of your life must get married before he ships off in two days ... this is as romantic as it gets ... With the country at war and most of our men enlisted, women could do nothing but sit at home waiting for their return'.[6]

For those who lived through the 1940s, the premise that they were defined by romanticism might be debatable; furthermore, the possible scripts for the bride are inconceivable without Hollywood imagery. Another popular wedding site, theknot.com, constantly presents the wedding as a movie: 'Your all-important I do's need an incredible soundtrack. The right music adds drama, enhances emotion, and keeps things moving'. Suggested engagement rings include 'unique settings, like Christina Aguilera's latticework diamond'. There are even ways to create a perfect performance around the proposal: 'Make her feel like a movie star and set your proposal to the scene of her favorite romantic movie. You could arrange your own *Pretty Woman* moment ... rent a white limo and climb through the moonroof with flowers in hand'.[7]

Thus the bride faces a smorgasbord of options, most saturated with the imagery of movies, television, celebrity discourse and advertising. She must create an event that expresses her uniqueness, yet is staged in a way that will be recognised and appreciated by her guests. The discourse on the multiple online forums conveys a sense of delirium, excitement and (understandably) panic. Very rarely does this discourse directly reference media imagery, yet the perfect wedding is understood to be a controlled but apparently effortless performance that comes as close as possible to replicating media imagery. Should one save money by having a friend take photos and video? No: only a professional understands the appropriate 'script' – capturing (and setting up) the right moments, producing a polished and coherent final product. Professional photographers, as Lewis (1998) writes, have a repertoire of poses and 'moments' that draw on the iconography of advertising, in which perfection is essential. Brides agonise about how to achieve this with real friends and family: Should one have equal numbers of blondes and brunettes? Is it unacceptable to exclude a friend who happens to be obese?

All this combines to create a picture of the ideal wedding as a highly mediated ritual, providing scripts, imagery and symbols that are often detached from the real personal lives of the people involved. The wedding speaks to the nature of a mobile, consumer-oriented society in which striving for unique identity is paramount, rather than the solidification of local, family or ethnic identity. Ethnic identity, for example, may be a style one can adopt for a day, or it may reflect a romanticised and mediated view of one's imagined or real ethnic heritage.

In addition to the ritual itself, the growth of the mediated event reaches out into the culture at large. At the most basic level, there is the economic impact of 'competitive weddings' in which couples drive themselves into debt to achieve the perfect experience.[8] Mediated practices are frequently also practices of commercial consumption. As Warde argues, 'Pursuit of variety ... results in continual expansion of the set of items conventionally defined as part of a decent and normal life ... [This] has potentially enormous economic consequences; getting people to dabble in everything offers splendid commercial opportunities' (Warde 2005: 142). The consequences of participating in such 'commercial opportunities' when one is not affluent may be quite dire; a full understanding of the power of mediated images can help us see real economic impacts.

We might also consider social impacts, such as the appearance of a new (if not yet professionally recognised) psychological disorder. This is post-wedding, or post-nuptial depression, covered recently by the *Observer* in the U.K. and *CBS News* in the U.S., and attributed to unrealistic expectations created by the wedding.[9] Forum discussions among brides stress the disjuncture between the 'event' as constructed on the beautiful video and the realities of everyday life. A study of such discourse, coupled with close engagement with actual people experiencing it (or not), could lead us into new insights not just about weddings as such, but about important issues in gender politics, cultural capital and economic disparities.

What I am presenting here is not, of course, a thorough, ethnographic study of the wedding as a mediated practice. Rather it is a snapshot of some of the questions that could be explored. Again, a full understanding of a cultural practice needs both rhetorical analysis and on-the-ground ethnography, providing an interpretation of both the power of media inscription and the role of individual agency, as Ortner advocates. Such a study would also investigate oppositional practices, which are often framed in the very same terms (expressing one's individuality and uniqueness) as those who buy into the mediated ideal. Brides who resist the ideal are not ignorant of it – their discourse is often framed defiantly as anti-materialist, 'authentic' and socially responsible. And then again, there are many people who are genuinely indifferent to the media discourse, whose main reference point for wedding planning may be family or ethnic traditions. Indeed, if we were to look cross-culturally, we might get a sense of the degree to which media frames have permeated particular societies. For example, extravagant spending and consumption at weddings has long been a tradition among affluent Indians. While traditionally this has had more to do with indigenous status distinctions than media models, could we profitably look at the framing roles of both Bollywood and Western media in offering new takes on tradition, and effectively mediating existing practices?

This kind of study does not abandon the anthropological claim of presence and direct engagement with people, nor does it deny individual agency, but it explores how that agency may be inexorably shaped by media. And it may help us move towards greater empirical understanding of questions that are assumed but not really proven. For instance Couldry (this volume) asks 'Where is the evidence that people "identify" with celebrities in any simple way, or even that they regard "celebrity culture" as important?' Perhaps a thorough look at the articulation of celebrity images and actual practice in such rituals as the wedding may help us with that question, although not in the narrow functional sense that Couldry rightly decries.

The Mediated Moment

Malkki (1997) argues that anthropology has built its theoretical and methodological foundation on the study of the mundane, with some exceptions, such as the Manchester School, whose focus was precisely on moments of discontinuity (Evens and Handelman 2006). Indeed, we can explore mediated culture through everyday practices like ritual performances. However, as Malkki also suggests, we might also learn through examining moments that break up the everyday flow and bring people together to marvel, laugh or discuss. Today's media audiences experience many of these 'mediated moments', ranging from the trivial to the significant, and these can be instructive in pointing to the nature of audience practices in a mediated society.

For instance, at the trivial end of the spectrum was the rather baffling saga of 'Turtle Boy', who entered media consciousness in June 2007. Ten-year-old Jonathon Ware visited the Rose Festival in Portland, Oregon, and had just left a face-painting booth, sporting an odd, white-painted look 'like Bart Simpson remade as a Dawn of the Dead flesh-eater' (Segal 2007). Following standard 'person-in-the street' style, Nancy Francis, a local television news correspondent, stopped him for an interview: 'Jonathon just got an awesome face paint job', she says to the camera, before asking: 'What do you think?' Jonathon answers in a flat, but definite voice: 'I like turtles'. Francis is briefly flummoxed but recovers brightly: 'All right! You're a great ... zombie ... Good times here at the Waterfront Village, open for the next 11 days!'

Until recently such moments passed, lost in the ephemeral world of familiar, though ever-changing, TV news. Someone in Portland might have muttered 'huh?' and then moved on. However, shortly afterwards, someone posted the seventeen-second clip on YouTube, where it caused a minor sensation with over a million views and multiple comments. Mainstream media covered the phenomenon, and entrepreneurs started marketing 'I like turtles' bags, hats and even ringtones. People posted remixes or 'mash-ups', setting the clip to music, in one case creating a video in which pugnacious Fox newsman Bill O'Reilly becomes increasingly frustrated as he receives the deadpan 'I like turtles', in reply to repeated questions about the Iraq War. Within a short time, the station aired the clip again, asking Turtle Boy to get in touch, which he did. Jonathon explained that he was caught off guard, and having just visited an exhibit of turtles, he blurted out the first thing he thought of. Jonathon's moment in the media sun was brief, and Turtle Boy's fame had dissipated by September.

Commentary on the incident was scathing. *Washington Post* humour columnist Gene Weingarten opined: 'If one applies any reasonable measure of critical thought to this ... video, one cannot escape the fact that it is entirely without humor' (Weingarten 2007). But Weingarten and others who used the incident to demonstrate the moronic nature of modern youth missed the point. As many YouTube comments noted, the humour lies not in Jonathon's words but in the incongruity of his response. In our mediated world, it seems many people are ready and able to respond 'appropriately' to a microphone thrust into their faces. Perhaps Jonathon should have pulled a scary face and mugged for the camera? As Fontana and Frey (2005) argue, we live in an 'interview culture' in which people are constantly being interviewed, off or on the media. The reporter here was not necessarily interested in what Jonathon had to say; these stories have a ritual feel to them – a minute or so of 'families having fun at the fair', before moving on. Jonathon's comments unexpectedly subverted the prepared frame, visibly disconcerting the reporter, who simply switches back into it. This is the point that most of the online comments made – praising the boy for a kind of subversion, intended or not. The Bill O'Reilly remix interview also comments on the ubiquity of media framing, suggesting that this kind of ritualistic questioning of government officials can only produce meaningless answers, speaking to the same parodic sensibility as John Stewart's *Daily Show*.

This is admittedly a trivial moment. However, a close look at such moments as they occur can show us something about the taken-for-granted sense of a world constructed by media. Jonathon's story is embedded in a much larger cultural discourse, which involves an awareness of the performed nature of 'reality' in media representations. And his moment of fame, during which his parents considered getting him an agent to manage his media appearances, speaks to the ever-present potential for regular 'audiences' to become celebrities. The practice of disseminating and responding to such moments is a new form of audience activity – related to the very active practices of the new media makers described by Ardèvol et al. (this volume), but from a perspective as critic, rather than performer.

A second such 'mediated moment' also speaks to the everyday practice and creation of celebrity, if in a more complex way. A media furore arose after a University of Florida student, Andrew Meyer, was shocked with a taser gun by university police officers towards the end of a speech by U.S. Senator John Kerry in Gainesville, Florida, on 17 September 2007. The incident was caught on video, immediately posted on YouTube, and viewed almost three million times over the next few weeks, in addition to extensive coverage on mainstream media. The basic facts were clear: Meyer rose to ask a rather rambling question, an officer eventually approached, handcuffed and then 'tased' him, as his cries of 'Don't tase me, bro!' are clearly heard.

The Meyer video was repeatedly shown and analysed. The incident raised significant issues about free speech and excessive police force, but also became emblematic of current, self-referential mediated audience culture. Today, media texts may spark chaotic cultural debates that involve not only personal interaction, but online, interactive comment boards and blogs, through which 'the story' takes shape. Meyer's story was initially framed as about the limits of free speech. For instance, viewer e-mails to CNN ranged from 'When a police officer tells you to do something, you do it ... This jerk was lucky he was only tased', to 'I think the police overreacted and violated this young man's right to free speech. They should be suspended'.[10] However, the story soon took other directions. It turned out that Meyer was an extremely media-savvy student journalist. He already had a personal website, where he liked to post facetious video clips, and which became a protest and promotional forum. Questions arose about whether he had instigated the incident, arranging to be filmed, his pleas being essentially an invitation to shock him. Others countered: So what? Does that change the outrageousness of what happened? University of Florida president, Bernie Machen, suspended the officers and ordered an investigation. The debate raged, with various interests weighing in, from the American Civil Liberties Union to pornographer Larry Flynt and radical journalist Greg Palast.

In October 2007, the University of Florida released a report concluding that Meyer provoked the incident and reinstated the officers

(Santiago 2007). Meyer eventually wrote letters of apology in return for charges being dropped. At year's end, the *St Petersburg Times* reported that the *Yale Book of Quotations* listed 'Don't tase me, bro' as the 'quote of the year', claiming it 'symbolises the influence and speed of popular culture'.[11] Indeed, such mediated moments are useful portals into the nature of a media-saturated culture, as the civil rights issue became submerged in a larger interrogation of how things become accepted as real. Was Meyer himself consciously engaging in a media practice or performance? If the video hadn't been made, would the arrest have become an issue? If the video had been made, but YouTube didn't exist, would the debate have remained in Florida? Without the internet, could any of this have happened? And has the important question of police overreaction been lost or trivialised? Do moments like these simply show how the proliferation of mediated practices may implode into a brief firestorm of self-referential discourse? A consideration of such moments, tracing them across the range of media, helps us see how complex the role of the audience has become.

Conclusion

For me, the focus on practice does not represent a radical rethinking of media audience studies. Audience researchers, interested in a more subtle understanding of the role of media in everyday life, are finding that ethnographic attempts to explore activities that happen around media are more helpful than the long-established focus on how people respond to specific media texts. I find Ortner's insistence on maintaining the relationship between structure and agency helpful in theorising the articulation between the undoubted ideological power of media representations and the actual practices of audiences, however broadly these audiences are conceived. Indeed, it is this point – the power of media structures and ideology – that I believe is neglected in Couldry's call to focus primarily on individual agency through audience practices.

My brief sketch above of various kinds of mediated practices suggests that one of the central challenges of this rethinking is practical: How does one carry out ethnographic research of such dispersed and multi-faceted practices? Abu-Lughod discusses what 'fieldwork' means in studying television audience practices in Egypt:

> I ... compare the fieldnotes and material I have for my television research with the small dog-eared notebooks and simple audio cassettes that resulted from my more localized research ... Now I have different sized

notebooks that are filled with notes taken in very different places …
observations and conversations with people are recorded alongside summaries of plots and bits of dialogue from … soap operas … I carry back
from Egypt video cassettes of television programs and piles of clippings
from newspapers and magazines, some with movie stars on the covers.
(Abu-Lughod 2000: 26)

Here, Abu-Lughod captures the apparently haphazard way in which we
almost have to explore mediated practices, because these practices 'happen' all around us. They may be more deliberative and conscious (such
as organised fan practices); they may become apparent in the unconscious performance of mediated scripts; or they may appear serendipi-
tously. As Couldry suggests, in studying practices, we must be open to the
ways practices are more or less organised and connected to each other.
This kind of consideration will help us determine how to approach practice ethnographically. For instance, research continues to involve direct
interaction with people, in terms of both what they say about media and
what they do with media. Hoover et al. (2004), for example, approach
the question of the role of the media in family life by exploring family
discourse about media. They suggest that many of us operate with 'public scripts' about how media affect us, for good or evil, and that this then
plays into conscious and unconscious practices around the media in the
home. To achieve this, they use a team approach in which individual
researchers work with families over extended time periods, bringing
back findings to be collaboratively analysed by the team. Markham and
Couldry (2007) approach the role of media, especially news, in everyday
life not only by examining news texts but by having participants write
self-generated diaries about their media practices. I have demonstrated
the use of various ethnographically inspired models to explore mediated practices, such as requiring participants to create collaboratively a television programme, through which I was able to show how media scripts
about Native Americans were articulated in ways that direct questioning
would not have elicited (Bird 2003). Similarly, Gauntlett (2007) asks participants to creatively visualise their identity through everything from
photographs, video and the building of lego models, then interpreting
how media-generated imagery may feed into these models of identity.
Such work, as Abu-Lughod suggests above, will involve attention to primary media texts (such as television programmes), but also discourse
about these texts, consideration of the political economy of media production and commodity consumption, as well as direct engagements
with the people we might still (for want of a better word) describe as
'audiences'.

For me, as for many working in cultural media studies, the focus on practice has for some years now been energising and productive, offering new ways to study media audiences. I do not see it as a radical theoretical break, either from the evolving tradition rooted in the exploration of the 'active audience' or from the rethinking of 'culture' in anthropology, represented by the move toward multi-sited ethnography and simultaneous consideration of both structure, ideology and local agency. However, it offers continuing potential for the more nuanced study of what it means to live in a mediated world. And if the study of mediated practices can move towards a genuinely comparative and intercultural perspective, the fields of media studies and anthropology will be mutually enriched.

Notes

1. *Editors' Note:* This quote refers to the extended version of the exchange between Couldry and Hobart available at: http://www.criticalia.org/ Debate_on_Media_Practices.htm.
2. For useful summaries and critiques of key works in audience studies, from 'effects' through 'active audience' to the recent 'ethnographic turn', see Brooker and Jermyn (2002).
3. For a discussion of media scripts and their role in cultural rituals, see Postill (2006).
4. Brides.com. 2007. 'Videography: The New Wedding Wave'. Retrieved 18 October 2007 from: http://www.brides.com/planning/photography/ feature/article/132049.
5. Source: www.theweddingreport.com. Retrieved 18 October 2007.
6. Wedding Decoration Idea. 2007. 'America's in Love: 1940s Theme Wedding'. Retrieved 16 October 2007 from: http://www.wedding-decoration-idea.com/wa_1940s_Theme_Wedding.aspx.
7. Source: www.theknot.com. Retrieved 18 October 2007.
8. See: 'Competitive Wedding Syndrome'. *Daily Mail* 29 May 2007. Retrieved 10 October 2007 from: http://www.dailymail.co.uk/pages/live/articles/ news/news.html?in_article_id=458419&in_page_id=1770.
9. See Hill (2003) and the forum postings at: http://www.mygroovywedding.com/ groovy-articles/17701-post-nuptial-depression.html. Retrieved 18 October 2007.
10. Source: http://www.cnn.com/2007/US/09/19/student.tasered/index .html?iref=newssearch. Retrieved 20 September 2007.
11. *St Petersburg Times*, 20 December 2007, 1B.

References

Abu-Lughod, L. 1997. 'The Interpretation of Culture(s) after Television', *Representations* 59: 109–34.
———— 2000, 'Locating Ethnography', *Ethnography* 1(2): 261–67.
Alasuutari, P. 1999. 'Three Phases of Reception Studies', in P. Alasuutari (ed.), *Rethinking the Media Audience*. London: Sage, pp.1–21.
Askew, K. and R.R. Wilk (eds). 2002. *The Anthropology of Media: A Reader*. New York: Blackwell.
Bacon-Smith, C. 1992. *Enterprising Women: Television Fandom and the Creation of Popular Myth*. Philadelphia: University of Pennsylvania Press.
Bird, S.E. 1992. 'Travels in Nowhere Land: Ethnography and the "Impossible Audience"', *Critical Studies in Mass Communication* 9(3): 250–60.
———— 2003. *The Audience in Everyday Life: Living in a Media World*. New York: Routledge.
Brooker, W. and D. Jermyn (eds). 2002. *The Audience Studies Reader*. London: Routledge.
Carey, J.W. 1975. 'A Cultural Approach to Communication', *Communication* 2: 1–10, 17–21.
Couldry, N. 2003. *Media Rituals: A Critical Approach*. London: Routledge.
Dahlgren, P. 2005. 'The Public Sphere: Linking the Media and Civic Cultures', in E.W. Rothenbuhler and M. Coman (eds), *Media Anthropology*. New York: Sage, pp.318–28.
Dayan, D. and E. Katz. 2006. *Media Events: The Live Broadcasting of History*. Cambridge, MA: Harvard University Press.
Evens, T.M.S and D. Handelman (eds). 2006. *The Manchester School: Practice and Ethnographic Praxis in Anthropology*. Oxford: Berghahn.
Fontana, A. and J.H. Frey. 2005. 'The Interview: From Neutral Stance to Political Involvement', in N. Denzin and and Y.S. Lincoln (eds), *Handbook of Qualitative Research*. New York: Sage, pp.695–727.
Gauntlett, D. 2007. *Creative Explorations: New Approaches to Identities and Audiences*. London: Routledge.
Geertz, C. 1973. *The Interpretation of Cultures: Selected Essays*. New York: Basic Books.
Ginsburg, F., L. Abu-Lughod and B. Larkin (eds). 2002. *Media Worlds: Anthropology on New Terrain*. Berkeley: University of California Press.
Gray, J. 2007. 'The News: You Gotta Love it', in J. Gray, C. Sandvoss and C.L. Harrington (eds), *Fandom: Identities and Communities in a Mediated World*. New York: New York University Press, pp.75–87.
Gray, J., C. Sandvoss and C.L. Harrington (eds). 2007. *Fandom: Identities and Communities in a Mediated World*. New York: New York University Press.
Gupta, A. and J. Ferguson (eds). 1997. *Anthropological Locations: Boundaries and Grounds of a Field Science*. Berkeley: University of California Press.
Gwenllian-Jones, S. 2000. 'Histories, Fictions, and *Xena Warrior Princess*', *Television and New Media* 1(4): 403–18.

Hall, S. 1980. 'Encoding/Decoding', in S. Hall, D. Hobson, A. Lowe and P. Willis (eds), *Culture, Media, Language*. London: Taylor and Francis, pp.197–208.

Hill, A. 2003, 'Brides Get the Blues as the Magic Wanes', *Observer*, 14 September 2003. Retrieved 20 October 2007 from: http://observer.guardian.co.uk/uk_news/story/0,6903,1041708,00.html.

Hills, M. 2002. *Fan Cultures*. London: Routledge.

Hobart, M. 1999. 'After Anthropology? A View from too Near'. Unpublished paper. Retrieved 2 October 2006 from: http://www.criticalia.org/Articles/After%20Anthropology.pdf.

Hoover, S., L.S. Clark, D.F. Alters, J.G. Champ, and L. Hood. 2004. *Media, Home and Family*. New York: Routledge.

Jenkins, H. 1992. *Textual Poachers: Television Fans and Participatory Culture*. New York: Routledge.

———— 2006. *Convergence Culture: Where Old and New Media Collide*. New York: New York University Press.

———— 2007. 'Afterword: The Future of Fandom', in J. Gray, C. Sandvoss and C.L. Harrington (eds), *Fandom: Identities and Communities in a Mediated World*. New York: New York University Press, pp.357–64.

Kitch, C. 2003. 'Mourning in America: Ritual, Redemption, and Recovery in News Narrative after September 11', *Journalism Studies* 4(2): 213–24.

Lardellier, P. 2005. 'Ritual Media: Historical Perspectives and Social Functions', in E.W. Rothenbuhler and M. Coman (eds), *Media Anthropology*. New York: Sage, pp.70–78.

Leeds-Hurwitz, W. 2002. *Wedding as Text: Communicating Cultural Identities through Ritual*. New York: Erlbaum.

Lewis, C. 1998. 'Working the Ritual: Professional Wedding Photography and the American Middle Class', *Journal of Communication Inquiry* 22(1): 72–92.

Lewis, L. (ed.) 1992. *The Adoring Audience: Fan Culture and Popular Media*. New York: Routledge.

McBride, L.B. and S.E. Bird. 2007. 'From Smart Fan to Backyard Wrestler: Ritual, Performance, and Pain', in J. Gray, C. Sandvoss and C.L. Harrington (eds), *Fandom: Identities and Communities in a Mediated World*. New York: New York University Press, pp.165–76.

McCourt, T. and P. Burkart. 2007. 'Customer Relationship Management: Automating Fandom in Music Communities', in J. Gray, C. Sandvoss and C.L. Harrington (eds), *Fandom: Identities and Communities in a Mediated World*. New York: New York University Press, pp.261–70.

Malkki, L. 1997. 'News and Culture: Transitory Phenomena and the Fieldwork Tradition', in A. Gupta and J. Ferguson (eds), *Anthropological Locations: Boundaries and Grounds of a Field Science*. Berkeley: University of California Press, pp.86–101.

Mankekar, P. 1999. *Screening Culture, Viewing Politics: An Ethnography of Television*. Durham, NC: Duke University Press.

Marcus, G.E. 1998. *Ethnography through Thick and Thin*. Princeton, NJ: Princeton University Press.

Markham, T. and N. Couldry. 2007, 'Tracking the Reflexivity of the (Dis)engaged Citizen: Some Methodological Reflections', *Qualitative Inquiry* 13(5): 675–95.

Ortner, S.B. 1984. 'Theory in Anthropology Since the Sixties', *Comparative Studies in Society and History* 26(1): 126–66.

———— 1998. 'Generation X: Anthropology in a Media-saturated World', *Cultural Anthropology* 13(3): 414–40.

Peterson, M.A. 2003. *Anthropology and Mass Communication: Media and Myth in the New Millennium*. Oxford: Berghahn.

———— 2009. 'Getting the News in New Delhi: Newspaper Literacies in an Indian Mediascape', in S.E. Bird (ed.) *The Anthropology of News of Journalism: A Global Perspective*. Indiana: Indiana University Press, pp.168–81.

Postill, J. 2006. *Media and Nation Building: How the Iban Became Malaysian*. Oxford: Berghahn.

Sandvoss, C. 2005. *Fans: The Mirror of Consumption*. Cambridge: Polity Press.

Santiago, R. 2007, 'UF Police Cleared in "Don't tase me, bro" Case', *Miami Herald*, 25 October. Retrieved 1 November 2007 from: http://www.miami herald.com/top_stories/story/283492.html.

Scannell, P. 1995. 'Media Events: A Review Essay', *Media, Culture and Society* 17(1): 151–60.

Segal, D. 2007. 'Meet Turtle Boy, Viral Video Star', *Scotsman*, 4 August. Retrieved 14 October 2007 from: http://news.scotsman.com/ topics.cfm?tid=864&id=1217902007.

Seiter, E. 1999. *Television and New Media Audiences*. New York: Oxford University Press.

Thomas, G. 2005. 'The Emergence of Religious Forms in Television', in E.W. Rothenbuhler and M. Coman (eds), *Media Anthropology*. New York: Sage, pp.79–90.

Turner, V. 1969. *The Ritual Process*. Chicago: Aldine.

Warde, A. 2005. 'Consumption and Theories of Practice', *Journal of Consumer Culture* 5(2): 131–53.

Weingarten, G. 2007. 'A Reptile Dysfunction', *Washington Post*, 26 August, W36.

Wenner, L. A. 1989. *Media, Sports, and Society*. New York: Sage.

CHAPTER 5

Thick Context, Deep Epistemology: A Meditation on Wide-Angle Lenses on Media, Knowledge Production and the Concept of Culture

Debra Spitulnik

For some time now, numerous scholars of media from diverse disciplines – such as anthropology, media studies, communication and sociology – have been conducting their work with a wide-angle lens on media and media's entanglements in people's lives, social worlds, political processes and so on. Much of this work has called for decentring media as the core object of study and for recentring research on wider fields of practices surrounding and intersecting media. More recently, there has been a call to theoretically (and practically) shift the study of media to the study of situated practice(s), as many of the chapters in this volume attest.

To a great degree, the epistemological strategies and stakes inherent in these moves have been underexamined. In this chapter I tackle epistemological issues head-on, asking what kinds of 'situating' are involved when one looks at media as situated practices? I connect this further to a problem common across qualitative social science knowledge practices more generally; namely, the recourse to ever broader and more complex arenas of context over the course of research and analysis. My overall aim here is to contribute to a wide-angle view of our own intellectual landscape, baggage and habits, and to suggest some ways that social science knowledge practices can be sharpened. For the case of this volume's theorisation of media and/as practice, there are also two more local aims: to generate explicit discussion about the epistemological practices connected with this move and to disrupt an artificial theory/method divide. As such this essay is at once a form of metacommentary, meditation and practical intervention.[1]

Wide-Angle Lenses on Media

Within media studies in the late 1980s and early 1990s, there were calls to extend research out to the furthest reaches of culture or context, to the point where researchers could engage in a form of 'radical contextualism' (Ang 1996) or reach 'a field without fences' (Hebdige 1988: 81). These arguments developed within media studies and cultural studies as scholars began doing more ethnographic work on popular culture and media culture, and they developed in tandem with scholarship in cultural studies and literary theory as scholars grappled with questions about the limits of 'the text', the locus of meaning production, and the wider field of variables that might explain a given social phenomenon. For the most part this work engaged theoretical arguments about the need to move from text to co-text and context. Grossberg, for example, argued that the media text is 'a mobile term ... located, not only intertextually, but in a range of apparatuses as well, defined technologically but also by other social relations and activities. One rarely just listens to the radio, watches TV, or even goes to the movies – one is studying, dating, driving somewhere else, partying, etc.' (Grossberg 1987: 34).

In addition, scholars in very different fields with very different kinds of research problems, such as the sociology of the home or family life, arrived at similarly expansive or context-rich approaches to media and made similar conclusions about the need to situate media within dynamic arenas of meaning, practice, habit, material culture and so on (see, e.g., Silverstone and Hirsch 1992; Silverstone 1994). Further, some might argue that the very best work in British cultural studies never lost sight of media's deep embeddedness in and entanglement with other systems of signification, power and practice (see Bennett 1982).[2]

In my own work, I have argued for 'widening the frame of reception studies to include the whole of culture – understood as the habitual practices, institutions, maps of meanings, and modes of meaning-making through which reality and lives themselves are made intelligible and compelling' (Spitulnik 2002b: 351).[3] Others have approached the study of media production in similar ways (e.g., Powdermaker 1950; Dornfeld 1998; Mazzarella 2003). Much recent work in media anthropology claims the wide-angle lens as a relatively distinctive orientation, and links this argument to claims that anthropology is particularly well suited for this given its bent towards both the holistic analysis of social facts and the ethnographic documentation of complex fields of everyday practice.[4] While these are very important contributions from media anthropology, one quickly gets into dangerous waters through such claims of distinction (Spitulnik 2005).

The more pressing issue, it seems to me, is not so much about disciplinary labels but about what happens epistemologically when we situate media practices and media phenomena within these wider fields. For example, how do we define units of analysis and how do we delimit objects of study? How do we determine which contextual field and which other practices are relevant for the media practice under consideration? And how do we model the observed and conjectured relations within contextual fields and fields of practice?

Thick Context and the Production of Knowledge

Asking such questions takes us away from debates about whether wide-angle lenses on media are 'better' or worse than 'narrow' ones, and refocuses attention on how we do our work and how we relate to our objects of study, as the study is being defined and as it is underway. Here, the core questions are about knowledge production, and particularly our relations to research design, evidentiality, discovery and argumentation. A whole host of issues are entailed here, and this is not the place to delve into them all. For the present, I focus specifically on what is at stake in the idea and practice of a wide-angle approach to media. At least two possible stances can be identified:

(a) a wide-angle approach is relevant to the central practice being studied and is crucial for developing explanations. It enables the researcher to make claims about typicality, variation and causality. It is used to situate and contextualise the observed practices and it is used to generate ethnographic texture.

(b) a wide-angle approach is necessary because it helps challenge and refine the initial definition of what the core practice being studied is. Not only does it achieve the goals of the first stance, it also pushes explanatory frameworks into potentially less predictable and more culturally specific directions.

These two stances are not necessarily mutually exclusive, and even within a single study there may be some alternation or merging of one with another. But for the sake of exposition here, I characterise them as distinct epistemological moments.

In (a), the epistemological focus is on branching out beyond the core object – such as a media text, direct moments of reception, or in-play practices of production – to add more richness, depth and texture to one's explanation. Additional details from the broader context may also be used to help explain variation in the particular practices or things under study. In (b), the epistemological focus is on operating with more open-ended analytical categories and being able to allow a possible shift in the ontological status of observed or conjectured processes, categories, and even objects, as the study proceeds. So to use a shorthand, (a) stresses an expanded research field for contextualisation and explanation; and, in addition to the goals of the first stance, (b) stresses an expanded and interrogated research field for critical verification of the field frame itself.

To flesh this out in more detail, let us consider an example from my fieldwork in Zambia. A group of young men are listening to the radio at a stand in the marketplace in the small town of Kasama. One of them is the vendor, the others are friends. A fairly narrow kind of qualitative media analysis would identify their activity here as 'listening to the radio' and would stick with predictable media-centered questions such as: What channel and program are they listening to? How long have they been listening? How often do they listen? What do they think about the program? What else do they listen to?

Under approach (a), 'listening to the radio' could also be used as the initial label for the central practice under consideration, but an attempt to document and analyse this as a situated practice would entail branching out beyond the predictable 'audience research' line of questioning. One might expand the research in any number of directions – for example, focusing more on the particular people involved in this scene, the particular program that is on air, the actual radio set itself, or the surrounding activities in the marketplace. Significantly, while pursuing these various routes, one may end up refining the label of just which practice is the core practice being investigated. For example it could be 'listening to radio in the marketplace' or 'listening to radio with friends,' or 'using a radio at a marketplace stand.'

A focus on people, for example, might ask a set of questions concerning the socio-centric nature of media use in this setting: How often do these young men get together and do this? Is the group composition fairly fluid, or are they all regulars? How do they know each other? How long do these kinds of gatherings last? What kinds of conversations and activities occur while the program is on? Who chose the program? What other activities do these young men do together? Do young men generally do this, or is this a unique group? A different line of person-centric questioning could explore a more biographical and subjective direction. For example, it might delve into the specific reactions of different individuals to the program, investigating how their own class levels or personal aspirations align or diverge with different messages in the radio program being listened to. Alternatively, it might investigate the particular media use patterns of the different individuals involved, and try to identify the salience of this particular listening experience in relation to their everyday lives and unique senses of self.

Research questions concerning media technologies and other commodities would go in a material culture direction. One could ask, for example: What kind of radio is it? What kind of condition is it in? Is there a particular status associated with this type of radio? What did it cost? Where is the radio placed on the stand? How loud is the sound? Is it there every day? Who owns it? Questions about surrounding context might ask: Are other vendors doing the same thing? What is being sold at this stand? Who are the clients and what do they do when they approach the stand? Why do people buy these particular goods? Is the vendor a relatively successful merchant? What do people say about this vendor and his goods? And so on.

While this may sound like a long list of things to investigate, they are fairly typical of the kinds of things media ethnographers explore as they situate the initially observed practice within a broader field of other practices (see Peterson 2003). Indeed, some are also very typical of the questions asked within cultural studies research on media use.[5] Under approach (a), these questions could be answered to provide a rich set of contextual details – for example, purely and simply more descriptive texture for the story of the radio in the marketplace – or they could serve a purpose beyond this, namely to generate a set of insights into the situated and culturally contingent nature of radio use and the unique positionality of particular social actors in this particular setting.

Doing the latter in my own work, I found that young men are almost always in groups when they are in public places, and that they often socialise around radios, particularly when there are soccer matches on or when they are visiting each other at home, but that radio listening in the marketplace is relatively rare (Spitulnik 2002b). Digging deeper, I discovered that radio use is rare in marketplaces due to the high price of batteries and the fact that continuous play exhausts a set of the locally-available batteries within a week. Unfortunately, it did not occur to me at the time to examine what made particular vendors exceptional in terms of bucking the trend when it came to battery purchases. So moving forward hypothetically with the scenario here (and placing it in the present), further research might reveal that this particular vendor is not supporting a household and that he is more of a free spender regarding personal expenditures, including media-related purchases. Taking a further step and asking 'why spend on radio batteries and not something else?' might open the research up into a different direction, for example into questions about consumption habits, personal biography or family status.

While I have presented this research scenario in a somewhat step-wise and perhaps overly simplified manner, it serves to lay bare what happens when ethnographic contexts of inquiry are progressively expanded from a single starting point, outwards to wider and wider fields of practice and culture. In actuality, researchers might not move progressively and methodically into wider and wider arenas of context or practice, but may they move in several directions at once, and per-haps operate with differing intensities in different directions, depend-ing on their interest, available opportunities, and what appears to be the fruitfulness or promise of the particular direction chosen. So rather than progressive expansion, this would be a more punctuated and uneven expansion of the research frame, one which might also be iter-ative, with various circling backs over the course of the research. The main motor in these movements is to explain typicality, variation and causality, along the lines of: 'practice b often occurs with practice c,' 'dif-ference f is related to feature g,' 'value x explains practice y,' 'personal trait p is a factor in practice q,' and so on. While some might find this shorthand positivistic, it reflects the general syntax of the kinds of state-ments interpretive cultural anthropologists make about typical behav-iours and cultural tendencies (see also van Maanen 1988).

Let us look now at this same research setting, using the epistemolog-ical stance of (b), which stresses the expanded and interrogated research field. I continue in a hypothetical vein here, using fieldwork insights. The aim is to model a process that can translate across situa-tions, but since I did not apply this approach to the particular case of the market vendor, I do not relate my own inductive process.

Research may start off similarly with an initial labelling of the core practice under consideration as 'listening to the radio,' and may also begin by documenting the various relevant local particulars such as those sought out by the questions itemised above for stance (a). These are typically the things that are easily observable and askable. They con-tribute greatly to the ethnographer's ability to speak about typicality and variation in the data, as well as about local cultural difference at a very descriptive level. But ultimately, such questions do not go far in answering deeper questions about what is going on from the perspec-tive of people's lived experiences and this unique sociocultural context. So to get to this, under approach (b) the researcher backs off from a more taken-for-granted, and perhaps more mainstream media theory identification of what the core practice under consideration is, and engages instead in the classic anthropological move of 'making things strange'. That is to say, the researcher tries to hold in suspension as much as possible any kind of assumption about the meaning of this scene. At the broadest level of 'meaning in suspension', the questions become: What kind of sense does this whole scene make? What are they doing? What kinds of cultural 'work' is accomplished by this behaviour? What kinds of cultural meanings are signalled by this behaviour? What do they think they are doing? What do they say they are doing?

Via this route, what is taken to be the core practice in need of investigation may then shift entirely away from 'listening to the radio' to any number of practices such as 'socialising with friends', 'being young men', 'competing for customers', 'attracting young women', 'having fun' or 'hanging out'. It is difficult to spell out the precise steps by which an ethnographer might arrive at one or several of these. This inductive process is not something that has been widely discussed in media anthropology, nor in anthropology more generally for that matter, outside of methods texts.[6] But it is something most of us do when we strive to work ethnographically from the ground up. Based on my own experience and conversations with other ethnographers I would describe it this way: The process of moving from one possible framing to an alternative one is driven of course by the weight of data and by the interpretations of local actors (see Peterson this volume), but it also involves what can be viewed as a kind of quiet reverse translation from what one knows about one's own culture, or jumping off from what one knows about other cultures, or an educated guess based on other research in the same ethnographic context. In all these respects, the impossibility of thoroughly being able to 'make things strange' is exposed, since one interprets 'the strange' while making comparisons with 'the known'. Still, what happens at least in part is a disruption of what is initially taken to be the practice under study. And this opens up a variety of other arenas for investigation. In this case, one might move research into the culturally specific meanings of masculinity and other practices related to young male identity, or into an exploration of how this scene relates to what has been identified as a culturally specific continuum of traditional versus cosmopolitan styles of status and performance in Zambia (Ferguson 1999). Other areas of expansion could be into the communication dynamics and soundscapes of sub-Saharan African marketplaces, or into a local phenomenology of entertainment, pleasure and aesthetic appreciation.

It is important to stress that as 'context' and 'situating' are potentially infinite, so too are the arenas of practice and cultural value that bear on this scene.[7] Obviously, within a single project one cannot go in all directions at once. There is no formula for how to choose which direction to go in, or how to avoid prejudging what one includes or excludes. It depends on the theoretical framework and the purpose of inquiry, and how fixed these are as the study gets underway.

So continuing in a hypothetical vein with the Kasama example, say the researcher asks the vendor why he has a radio at his stand. The fictional reply is: 'Because this makes mine the liveliest stand in the whole marketplace'. Initially, the media practice as situated practice might be identified here as 'competing to attract customers'. The researcher might go on to investigate a host of things such as culturally-specific logics of market psychology, what makes other stands 'lively', whether others share this impression of the vendor's stand, and how in general vendors try to attract customers. Perhaps very little pans out in helping to further explain the meaning of the vendor's remark, only some loose hints of what the concept 'lively' means and a range of unrelated data on how vendors attract customers through direct verbal hawking and established social networks. Going back to the scene the next day, the researcher in this hypothetical scenario notices a lot of dynamic interactions around the radio among both the friends who are hanging out with the vendor and the various customers who stop by. Styles of clothing, particular verbal idioms and even a certain kind of body language suddenly become more salient to the researcher. From here the analysis might take off: These stylistic things are operating to draw in customers. The radio might be a centre piece somehow, but it is this nexus of symbolic practices as a totality that is lending a certain value or prominence to the vendor's stand. Further, looking again at the particular idiom of 'lively', one discovers that there is a deep cultural history to this particular word in relation to Zambian concepts of modernity and the particular excitement surrounding modern media consumption (Spitulnik 1998). So just as much as the vendor is playing a radio, socialising with friends, and attracting customers, he is also displaying and being a certain kind of social persona in relation to modernity, style and consumption.

While there is more to say about how this hypothetical research in progress could continue, let us now take leave of the example to get back to a more direct discussion of epistemology. One of the starkest contrasts between the research scenario using (a) and the research scenario using (b) is in the way that the 'object of study' is situated. With (a), the central object is a very concrete practice: 'listening to radio in the marketplace'. Through a progressive set of inquiries in a wider contextual field that bears upon this central practice, the particular practice of radio listening is illuminated. With (b), situating the object of study actually shifts that object. By the end of the scenario above, the media practice of playing and listening to the radio is analytically embedded within, and in this case even subordinated to, other kinds of situated practices.

The contrasts between approaches (a) and (b) can also be high-lighted by considering the problem of naive realism or naturalism that Hobart writes of (this volume). Naive realism fits well with stance (a) but it is difficult to sustain within stance (b). As explained by Hobart, most of the kinds of things that fall under the purview of media prac-tices are not natural objects but ones that appear within a particular frame of reference. Proceeding as if the object is there independent of the reference frame is problematic, Hobart argues, since it erases the processes through which researchers are able to see and constitute research objects.[8] Position (b) allows more space for considering the constructed and potentially contingent nature of the frame of refer-ence and the categories which shape it.[9] It also leaves more room for reflexivity. Analytical categories can be open-ended and potentially revisable in relation to data collected 'on the ground'.

In a more extreme form, certain versions of (b) are more experi-mental and less 'normal' forms of knowledge production at this partic-ular moment in Western social science. The rhizomatic mode of knowl-edge production and discovery advocated by Deleuze and Guattari (1987) is one example of this. This method decentres the 'object' of study onto a multiplicity of dimensions, many or all of which are non-hierarchical or non-linear. Using the metaphor of the botanical rhi-zome – a plant which has horizontal stems that run along or below the ground, and which sends out shoots and roots from nodes on these run-ners[10] – Deleuze and Guattari's model prioritises a multiplicity of con-nections, entranceways, exits and directionalities. They write:

> [T]he rhizome connects any point to any other point, and its traits are not necessarily linked to traits of the same nature; it brings into play very different regimes of signs, and even nonsign states ... It is comprised, not of units but of dimensions, or rather directions in motion. It has neither beginning nor end, but always a middle (*milieu*) from which it grows and which it overspills. (ibid.: 21)

Taking the rhizome as a metaphor for the organisation of cultural value and 'the social', Deleuze and Guattari are thus suggesting, among other things, a de-privileging of linear causality and linear connection. Regarding the issue of context and the definition of fields of analysis, the implication is that the relevant question is not how big or wide the wide-angle is, or how far the outer reaches of context go, but what is done, analytically, inside the wider research frame. To the extent that a Deleuze and Guattari type of approach still embraces a modernist proj-ect of reasoned research and scholarship (and this might be debated), this would include producing an account of the rhizomatic organisation of context and the relationality across multiple dimensions within this context. In short, what I would call 'thick context'. Within this research frame, there is no a priori necessity for explanations and analyses to smoothly converge or make things more complex in a nested, or web-like fashion – as may be the case under (a) and more normative versions of (b) – but rather some may run counter to one another, or be more akin to loose ends or 'overspillage'.

Applying this to the Kasama fieldwork example, and simplifying greatly, one can picture a rhizomatic diagram with radio as a moderately large node that has relatively thin runners branching out to practices of market culture. In addition to this, the radio node has medium sized runners that connect with practices of friendship and male socialisation, and thick runners branching out into various meanings and practices related to modernity and cosmopolitanism. Some of the runners connecting to practices of market culture branch into nodes that are about business practices and others branch into nodes about merchandise. Further, some of the merchandise nodes have their own runners, some of which connect to some of the aforementioned runners related to modernity.

Significantly, what is held in critical suspension in this kind of approach is not only simple linearity but discreteness, as well as the value and necessity of analytic closure. Indeed, a core tension between stances (a) and (b) is about modes of knowledge production that prioritise discreteness versus those that do not. Discreteness – and all that comes with it in this particular moment of a post-Enlightenment Western mode of doing science versus art – is about isolating narrow units of study and discovering predictable relationships (causal, hierarchical, implicational, oppositional, and so forth) between these units. In this prevailing episteme,[11] more intellectual capital and economic capital tend to accrue to research paradigms that have neatly bounded objects of study, particularly ones that are measurable and that enter into measurable or computational relations.[12] Intellectual capital can be seen, for example, when labels like 'rigorous' and 'messy' are attached to scholarly arguments and explanations.[13] Economic capital manifests itself in salaries, grants, faculty sizes and so on. There is nothing natural or necessary about this. Rather, it is a historically contingent fact that modes of knowledge production tend to be organised along these lines right now and that rewards for certain modes of knowledge production tend to work this way.

Deep Epistemology: Beyond and Within the Wide Angle

So what is next? My suggestion here is that for the wide-angle study of media cultures and media practices one major challenge is to disrupt discreteness and still do science. This is difficult for all the reasons stated above, and more. On the list of things to contend with are not only a dominant episteme and reward structure, but the centripetal pull of everyday discourses about 'media effects', linear styles of writing and argumentation, and the contemporary relevance of measurement in the study of media in relation to market research and cultures of public opinion.

And with so much baggage and with so many lines drawn in the sand around the word 'science', why use the word at all? Then again, why not? Phrases such as 'human sciences' and 'social sciences' are already in our midst. To the extent that the word 'science' signals a relation to evidence, discovery and reason, it is important and useful. Is it possible to keep these connotations central while divesting the term of the baggage of positivism? Maybe the weight of history and our own language games have the lines too firmly drawn. But then again, something may shift if the term is reclaimed, not just verbally reclaimed but in coordination with a more articulated attention to our relations to evidence, discovery and argumentation.

So at the risk of stating the obvious, a wide angle is not enough by itself. Rather, it is a matter of not just attending to context but theorising context and attending to the discovery process itself. More than just wandering in 'a field without fences' (Hebdige 1988: 81), a more enriched or focused way of doing wide-angle media research might entail a series of dynamic moves such as carefully examining the lines of influence and connection within a context, looping back to the core research question, potentially shifting the question, and then taking a fresh look at the conjectured relations and objects within the wider context and revising them accordingly. This open-ended discovery procedure, with numerous back and forth movements between 'object of study', research questions and analysis is a familiar one.[14] The classic scientific method of hypothesis testing and revision, as well as the commonly termed 'funnel' method of progressive research inquiry (Johnstone 1999: 94) – that is, progressively narrowing down one's focus and analysis – certainly fit in here. So too do the typically more open and less hypothesis-driven approaches within much of cultural anthropology and cultural studies. For all of these there is ample room for the researcher to shift and refine questions as discovery is underway. Finer differences between these approaches lie in the degree to which researchers might be inclined to shift or modify core theoretical constructs and research objects, or how tightly they attribute analytical closure.

While most researchers closely attend to the various choices and trade offs as open-ended work proceeds – or at least hold this attentiveness as an ideal for research conduct – what is less common is that they relay some of the history of this open-ended process to their audience when work is presented.[15] One way to enrich wide-angle research is thus to more directly acknowledge the use of open-ended discovery procedures and walk readers through them. In Roger Sanjek's terms, this is about 'attention to ethnographic validity' (Sanjek 1990: 412). More generally, there is a need to create spaces for these kinds of discussions in our work beyond placing them in methodological introductions, appendices or footnotes, or in personalised research anecdotes or confessions.[16] This would be a way of doing what I would term 'deep epistemology', a mode of critically attending to knowledge practices in the doing and writing of research (see also Hobart this volume). Thus, to return to the field-without-fences metaphor, there are ways to wander (or better, move) not aimlessly or unboundedly but with rigor and accountability, and, in Marcus's terms, with 'innovative ways of bounding the potentially unbounded' (Marcus 1999: 9).[17]

Along these lines, in an earlier essay (Spitulnik 1998) I argued for explicit recognition and use of a conjectural method, building on and sharpening historian Carlo Ginzburg's (1980) conceptualisation of this method. Conjecture and clue hunting is nothing new in the interpretive social sciences, but a sharpened way of thinking about this type of intellectual work is sorely needed. In its fullest realisation I would describe and advocate it as a method which teases out resonances and connections between pieces of data across a wide range of domains, which takes a stand on the tenor and quality of conjectured links – for example as tight, loose, highly speculative, clearly causally driven and so on – and which, in the best of circumstances, also foregrounds its conjectural processes. For the particular research topic treated in that earlier piece – the cultural history of radio reception in Zambia – sifting through pieces of data of different orders and in different locations was at the forefront of the project. I argued there that doing a cultural history of the reception of new media technologies, and especially tracing the cultural associations that informed people's encounters with them, necessarily involves a straddling of several kinds of orders of data and it also requires an attentiveness to how the conjectural method is deployed, since the evidence is not all in one place or in one type of source. In the case of my study, the answers spanned across colonial documents, published accounts, listener interviews, linguistic structure, popular speech and visual representations.

A further way to sharpen knowledge practices is to be more explicit about angles of analysis and points of entry. This is of course related to discovery procedures but it merits separate consideration as well. Within anthropology, two of the most pervasively invoked frameworks for object construction and research-problem design are George Marcus's (1995) 'follow the *x*' formula and Arjun Appadurai's (1990) different 'scapes'.[18] Appadurai proposes that the new world system be interrogated in terms of ethnoscapes, mediascapes, technoscapes, financescapes and ideoscapes. Marcus (1995), meanwhile, proposes that, as a way to conceptualise multi-sited research, a selection be made from among one of the following strategies, so as to maintain focus and constancy with the research object and research labour: follow the people, follow the metaphor, follow the thing, follow the plot, follow the life, follow the conflict.

Significantly, both of these heuristic schemes are developed in the context of meditations on multi-sited research, yet their relevance lies beyond the question of new ways to carve out or track research objects in an increasingly globalised world. They both highlight, either indirectly in the case of Appadurai or directly in the case of Marcus, the challenges of navigating issues of context and object construction in general, regardless of a research problem's 'sitedness' or scope. That being said, there is still much more need for explicit discussion of the epistemological stakes of adopting a particular 'follow the *x*' formula or using a 'scape' metaphor to delineate a research topic and to conduct an investigation.[19] For example, a researcher might write about the relative pay off of one 'scape' or 'follow the *x*' technique over another, or argue for a multiply framed research project that shifts across more than one 'scape' or 'follow the *x*' framing. I would suggest further that a more radical epistemology along the lines of Deleuze and Guattari's could be envisioned and practised using these kinds of 'scape' and 'pathway' descriptors to concretely map out both the case-specific analysis and the knowledge practices that were used to achieve it: a 'thick context' rhizomatic map combined with a 'deep epistemology' rhizomatic map.

Where is 'Culture' in All of This?

My main concerns here have been to examine particular features of our prevailing epistemological landscapes and to suggest ways to sharpen knowledge practices. To characterise this as simply a discussion about methods would be misleading. Disrupting discreteness, attending to object construction and representing the various moves and paths taken during research are themselves stances that entail specific theoretical positions about the nature of social science and the social. At the same time, there are other areas of theory that remain underspecified here. For example, several contributions to this volume emphasise moving 'practice' to the centre of research on media and making a theory of practice central to a theory of media. One might also ask about the place of 'culture'. Is this understood to be part of practice, behind practice or out of the picture altogether?

Interestingly, the word 'culture' is used pervasively in media studies and cultural studies without it necessarily being tied to an explicit theoretical discussion of whether any particular culture concept is being used, if at all. Thus one hears of Bollywood culture, cassette culture, Walkman culture, remix culture and so on.[20] Implicitly it seems these coinages of types of 'media culture' and 'media cultures' are premised on the idea that modalities of media production and consumption are themselves akin to cultures or subcultures. That is, they might be considered historically contingent, place-specific ways of being-in-the-world that involve habitual practices and schemes of sense-making. In addition, they signal the important insight that a media technology itself can be seen as a locus for the production and crystallisation of culture. For example, du Gay et al. explain: 'The Sony Walkman is not only part of our culture. It has a distinct "culture" of its own. Around the Walkman there has developed a distinctive set of meanings and practices' (du Gay et al. 1997: 10).

While some might want to use the culture label in this generic 'set of meanings and practices' sense but dodge the culture concept to avoid all of its supposed baggage, I think there is much to gain by revisiting the concept of culture and by using it to develop richer and more complex analyses of what is going on within so called 'sets' of meanings and practices. One can ask, for example, how are these 'sets' or 'schemes' – and even tendencies towards habituality – organised? What kinds of themes, forces, linkages and so on structure them? And how might this comprise the tacit or unconscious knowledge that shapes the horizons of experience and action? A call to place practice at the centre of media studies might intersect this series of questions, but it does not necessarily supplant them. Moreover, it may risk missing (or needing to reinvent) theoretical frameworks that have already been developed within culture theory.

By arguing that we would be well served by revisiting some of these classic concerns of cultural anthropology – be they 'patterns' of culture, 'semiotic webs' or even a more 'culturally' nuanced version of habitus – I align myself with Brightman (1995) who contends that the rapid abandonment of the 'culture' concept in the late twentieth century, usually replaced by 'discourse' and 'practice,' in many corners of anthropology and cultural studies is more a story of 'relexification' and the objectification of straw men than one of a fundamental paradigm shift. As scholars such as de Certeau (1984), Hannerz (1992) and Brightman (1995) have argued, all in very different ways, the necessary critique of cultural holism does not leave us with just one option: to write against culture; that is, to dismiss the importance of culture and to abandon the culture concept.

That is not to say that all is rosy or clear on the side of 'culture'. Far from it. But by abandoning the culture concept – or, as is more often the case, by sneaking a minimalist and underspecified version of it through the back door – we might be selling ourselves short. Some basic ideas, which might be called 'classical' anthropological concepts – such as the idea of cultures as semiotic systems, involving hierarchical structures and relational idioms; systems of exchange and circulation; specific ways of constructing value, identities and communities through both mundane and ritual practice; ways of producing relationships through systems of exchange and communication; frameworks for personhood and subjectivity; all underlying the phenomenology of lived experience – can still be productively retained and worked through, theoretically. In fact, they might be made more explicit as analytical problems in research that already engages them implicitly. There are ways to engage these as problems of 'culture' or what might be termed 'cultural logics and their organisation', even if master-narrative social theories may no longer be tenable – particularly those built around deterministic models of structure and agency or system and practice, as well as the ethnographic ideal of neatly separating emic from etic – as Hobart, Couldry, and Helle-Valle all suggest (this volume).[21] Thus, for example, the rhizome system mapped out for the radio in the marketplace might be enriched not only by an additional mapping of the researcher's discovery procedures and conjectural weights, as suggested in the previous section, but also with some discussion about how dimensions of this particular rhizome system relates to social theory – for example, anthropological, Western, or Zambian-specific theories of value or theories of the self.

In this regard, as well as with respect to the epistemological points made earlier in this chapter, I diverge from Knauft's (2006) proposal that a 'post-paradigm' anthropology or cultural studies is desirable, or even an accurate characterisation of the present moment. While I agree with Knauft's genealogical review of dominant research trends, I prefer to think of the present moment as a kind of apparent paradigm avoidance and paradigm amnesia, which is a kind of paradigm itself. Further, as I suggest here and elsewhere (Spitulnik 2002a), there is a strong future (be it anthropology's or social science's in general) in what could be seen as an emergent paradigm centered on critical epistemology (also see Keane 2003).

Conclusion

In this chapter, I have argued for placing a critical epistemology at the centre of social science, whether it be media anthropology or any other approach to the social or to human experience. To a great extent the project of critical epistemology – regardless of whether the object or field is media – is about tracing out and interrogating relationships, relationality, framings and movements. Here, I have labelled this the joint problems of producing 'thick context' and doing 'deep epistemology', and have suggested that rhizomatic modes of analysis and knowledge production offer an alternative to the anti-foundational stalemate (or posturing of anti-foundationalism) that characterises much contemporary cultural research. To the extent that a critical epistemology can track its own knowledge practices and represent them, work that situates its objects within a field without fences can still be unbound but committed to identifying lines of influence, paths pursued and organising logics (including the researcher's) in a way that enriches both our understandings of people's worlds and what it means to do social science in general.

For the concrete project of media and/as practice signalled by this volume, some specific implications of engaging in this kind of critical epistemology can be spelled out as follows. If one of the new directives is to situate media practices, a critical epistemology invites us to wrap our minds around the 'hows' and 'whats' of this situating. The core proposal is that this situating needs to be done not just through or with an expanded research field, but through what I have called an expanded and interrogated and explicitly tracked research field. The implication is to disrupt naive realism assumptions about research frames and labels for practices under investigation, as well as to not confer automatic preference (or authenticity) to the frames and labels used from the metaculture or subjective end of things. Along such lines, I have carved out a path between the well-worn interpretivist/positivist divide. The point is to work with reflexivity, intuition and local categories, and at the same time to attend to and convey relationships to evidence and conjectural processes. Through a particular fieldwork case study I have shown how multiple avenues of inquiry apply to a single scenario, how research might proceed, how framings might shift, and how the even-tual choice of how to situate observed practices has consequences for which type of social theory and cultural analysis most directly illuminates the case. As a meditation on knowledge practices which also models some of them, it is hoped that this discussion both resonates with some of the greenest researchers – those in search of models and methods – and also opens up new conversations more broadly among the current practitioners of media practice research.

Notes

1. Special thanks go to the editors of this volume and to Nick Couldry, Tricia Fogarty, Mark Hobart, Bruce Knauft and Johanna Schoss for their very helpful comments on an earlier version of this essay. The direction I take here has also benefited greatly from engagements with undergraduate and graduate students in my ethnographic methods courses at Emory University. Epistemological stakes and analytical processes are rarely discussed in our how-to handbooks, but they are often on students' minds, from the most green to the more advanced. Fieldwork examples stem from Zambia research (1988–1990), which was supported by NSF and Fulbright-Hays grants. The chapter title is inspired in part by two famous pieces by Clifford Geertz.
2. That being said, what is relatively recent (within the last ten years or so) is work that considers the practical and ontological implications of the infinite regress of 'context' in relation to media's profound embeddedness in everyday life: see Ang (1996) and Hirsch (1998).
3. See also Mankekar (1999) and Abu-Lughod (2005), who orient their reception research in similar ways. For further discussion of this line of analysis on both the production and the reception ends, see Peterson (2003).
4. See, e.g., Askew and Wilk (2002) and Ginsburg, Abu-Lughod and Larkin (2002).
5. For a range of examples, see Morley (1992), Silverstone (1994) and Fisherkeller (2002).
6. For a general discussion of these methodological moves, see Emerson, Fretz and Shaw (1995), Fetterman (1998) and Bernard (2000). For more critical, reflective discussion, see Rabinow (1977) and Fletcher (2007).
7. For related discussions in linguistic anthropology and linguistic pragmatics, see Duranti and Goodwin (1992) and Silverstein (1992).
8. For extensive discussion of this problem in the interpretation of human experience and subjectivity, see Taylor (1971) and Geertz (1973).
9. Cf. Keane's rich discussion of epistemologies within American anthropology, which argues for 'sustaining the project of anthropology as an epistemological critique of received categories' (Keane 2003: 241). In addition, one might consider the analytical strategy that Marcus advocates for multi-sited research –

embedding arguments 'in the speculative, experimental aspect of ethnographic probing that is not as certain of the contextualising ground or space in
which it is working' (Marcus 1999: 10) – as equally valid for any inquiry that is
oriented along the lines of approach (b).

10. Examples of rhizome plants include potato, ginger and iris.
11. Coined by Foucault (1970), an episteme is a historically specific way of
knowing and of producing knowledge. For Foucault, these ways of ordering
relations of inquiry are tied to particular tropic formulations in language.
12. This is more the case in an inter-disciplinary sense than it is in an intra-dis-
ciplinary one. Differences in national disciplinary traditions also make
sweeping generalisation impossible. For example, within much of contemporary American socio-cultural anthropology, it has long been the case that
inquiry has been guided by a mistrust of 'techniques that give more scientific methods their illusory objectivity: their commitment to standardised,
a priori units of analysis, for example, or their reliance on a depersonalis-
ing gaze that separates subject from object' (Comaroff and Comaroff 1992:
8). See also note 8 above. But this is not the case for the U.S. academy more
generally. By contrast, in the U.K. there appears to be greater across-the-
board consensus among social scientists to attribute higher intellectual
capital to qualitative work. John Postill (personal communication) notes
that there is currently an acute shortage of social scientists with quantitative skills as most opt for qualitative approaches, to the chagrin of the gov-
ernment-funded research councils and those policy people who favour
quantitative research.
13. Other labels include 'hard' versus 'soft' science. See Taylor (1971) for an
important intervention in this debate.
14. Janesick's (2000) discussion of the choreography of qualitative research
and the iterative process of research inquiry provides a particularly useful
description of this process. Importantly, she also develops a compelling
epistemological argument that the scientific concept of 'triangulation' is
better understood as 'crystallization' in qualitative research.
15. One recent exception is Cerwonka and Malkki (2007).
16. See van Maanen's (1988) excellent discussion of different genre conventions in ethnographic writing and their relations to argumentation and
objectivity. Of particular interest are the performative and epistemological
implications of the long-standing convention within anthropological writing to separate discussion of research design and methods on the one hand
from data and analysis on the other hand. As van Maanen and others
(Clifford and Marcus 1986) have pointed out, this textual move reifies
methods and theory as separate moments of research and creates an
almost teleological relation between them.
17. A further dimension of this problem concerns the degree to which the
organisation of ethnographic knowledge can and should be modelled in
terms of local ontologies. A milder version of this position would seem to
align with the stance taken by Hobart (this volume), in which research and

analysis takes a cue from social actors themselves regarding the definition of bounded entities and 'units' of analysis. In a related vein, Hirsch (1998) argues that the local ontological status of 'bound entities' can shift to 'unbound entities' (and vice versa), as social actors apply culturally specific processes of systematisation and collation.

18. Another useful and widely used heuristic model is du Gay et al.'s (1997) 'circuit of culture' which identifies five major cultural processes: representation, identity, production, consumption and regulation. Du Gay et al. write, 'Taken together, they complete a sort of circuit – what we term the circuit of culture – through which any analysis of a cultural text or artefact must pass if it is to be adequately studied ... We have separated these parts of the circuit into distinct sections but in the real world they continually overlap and intertwine in complex and contingent ways' (ibid.: 3–4).

19. To date, these heuristics are applied rather uncritically, as if they were obvious, transparent and even natural. For example, Appadurai's 'scapes' have been widely adopted to identify zones of research and to justify research objects, in many cases irrespective of the theories put forth in his article. These 'scapes' seem to be taken as natural primitives, despite Appadurai's emphasis on them as 'perspectival constructs' (Appadurai 1990: 7).

20. See Manuel (1993), du Gay et al. (1997), Page and Crawley (2001), Nguyen and Nguyen Tu (2007) and Veal (2007), each on different 'cultures' respectively.

21. For example, see Strathern (2003).

References

Abu-Lughod, L. 2005. *Dramas of Nationhood: The Politics of Television in Egypt.* Chicago: University of Chicago Press.

Ang, I. 1996. 'Ethnography and Radical Contextualism in Audience Studies', in J. Hay, L. Grossberg and E. Wartella (eds), *The Audience and Its Landscape.* Boulder, CO: Westview, pp.247–62.

Appadurai, A. 1990. 'Disjuncture and Difference in the Global Cultural Economy', *Public Culture* 2(2): 1–24.

Askew, K. and R.R. Wilk (eds). 2002. *The Anthropology of Media: A Reader.* Malden, MA: Blackwell.

Bennett, T. 1982. 'Media, "Reality" and Signification', in M. Gurevitch, T. Bennett, J. Curran and J. Woollacott (eds), *Culture, Society and the Media.* London: Methuen, pp.287–308.

Bernard, H.R. (ed.) 2000. *Handbook of Methods in Cultural Anthropology.* Walnut Creek, CA: Altamira.

Brightman, R. 1995. 'Forget Culture: Replacement, Transcendence, Relexification', *Cultural Anthropology* 10 (4): 509–46.

Cerwonka, A. and L. Malkki. 2007. *Improvising Theory: Process and Temporality in Ethnographic Fieldwork.* Chicago: University of Chicago Press.

Clifford, J. and G.E. Marcus (eds). 1986. *Writing Culture: The Poetics and Politics of Ethnography*. Berkeley: University of California Press.

Comaroff, J.L. and J. Comaroff. 1992. 'Ethnography and the Historical Imagination', in *Ethnography and the Historical Imagination*. Boulder, CO: Westview, pp.3–48.

De Certeau, M. 1984. *The Practice of Everyday Life*. Berkeley: University of California Press.

Deleuze, G. and F. Guattari. 1987. *A Thousand Plateaus: Capitalism and Schizophrenia*. Minneapolis: University of Minnesota Press.

Dornfeld, B. 1998. *Producing Public Television*. Princeton, NJ: Princeton University Press.

Du Gay, P., S. Hall, L. James, H. Mackay and K. Negus. 1997. *Doing Cultural Studies: The Story of the Sony Walkman*. London: Sage.

Duranti, A. and C. Goodwin (eds). 1992. *Rethinking Context: Studies in the Social and Cultural Foundations of Language*. Cambridge: Cambridge University Press.

Emerson, R.M., R.I. Fretz and L.L. Shaw. 1995. *Writing Ethnographic Fieldnotes*. Chicago: University of Chicago Press.

Ferguson, J. 1999. *Expectations of Modernity: Myths and Meanings of Urban Life on the Zambian Copperbelt*. Berkeley: University of California Press.

Fetterman, D. 1998. *Ethnography: Step by Step*, 2nd edn. Thousand Oaks, CA: Sage.

Fisherkeller, J. 2002. *Growing up with Television: Everyday Learning among Young Adolescents*. Philadelphia, PA: Temple University Press.

Fletcher, R. 2007. 'The Fieldworker's Magic', *Anthropology News* 48(2): 19.

Foucault, M. 1970. *The Order of Things: An Archaeology of the Human Sciences*. New York: Vintage.

Geertz, C. 1973. 'Thick Description: Toward an Interpretive Theory of Culture', in *The Interpretation of Cultures*. New York: Basic Books, pp.3–30.

Ginsburg, F., L. Abu-Lughod and B. Larkin (eds). 2002. *Media Worlds: Anthropology on New Terrain*. Berkeley: University of California Press.

Ginzburg, C. 1980. 'Morelli, Freud and Sherlock Holmes: Clues and the Scientific Method', *History Workshop* 9: 5–36.

Grossberg, L. 1987. 'The In-difference of Television', *Screen* 28(2): 28–45.

Hannerz, U. 1992. *Cultural Complexity: Studies in the Social Organization of Meaning*. New York: Columbia University Press.

Hebdige, D. 1988. *Hiding in the Light: On Images and Things*. London: Comedia.

Hirsch, E. 1998. 'Bound and Unbound Entities: Reflections on the Ethnographic Perspectives of Anthropology vis-à-vis Media and Cultural Studies', in F. Hughes-Freeland (ed.), *Ritual, Performance, Media*. London: Routledge, pp.208–28.

Janesick, V. 2000. 'The Choreography of Qualitative Research Design: Minuets, Improvisations, and Crystallization', in N. Denzin and Y. Lincoln (eds), *Handbook of Qualitative Research*, 2nd edn. New York: Sage, pp.379–400.

Johnstone, B. 1999. *Qualitative Methods in Sociolinguistics*. Oxford: Oxford University Press.

Keane, W. 2003. 'Self-interpretation, Agency and the Objects of Anthropology: Reflections on a Genealogy', *Comparative Study of Society and History* 45(2): 222–48.

Knauft, B.M. 2006. 'Anthropology in the Middle', *Anthropological Theory* 6(4): 407–30.

Mankekar, P. 1999. *Screening Culture, Viewing Politics: An Ethnography of Television, Womanhood, and Nation in Postcolonial India*. Durham, NC: Duke University Press.

Manuel, P. 1993. *Cassette Culture: Popular Music and Technology in North India*. Chicago: University of Chicago Press.

Marcus, G.E. 1995. 'Ethnography in/of the World System: The Emergence of Multi-sited Ethnography', *Annual Review of Anthropology* 24: 95–117.

———— 1999. 'What Is at Stake – and Is Not – in the Idea and Practice of Multi-sited Ethnography', *Canberra Anthropology* 22(2): 6–14.

Mazzarella, W. 2003. *Shoveling Smoke: Advertising and Globalization in Contemporary India*. Durham, NC: Duke University Press.

Morley, D. 1992. *Television, Audiences and Cultural Studies*. London: Routledge.

Nguyen, M.T. and T.L. Nguyen Tu (eds). 2007. *Alien Encounters: Popular Culture in Asian America*. Durham, NC: Duke University Press.

Page, D. and W. Crawley. 2001. *Satellites over South Asia: Broadcasting, Culture and the Public Interest*. London: Sage.

Peterson, M.A. 2003. *Anthropology and Mass Communication: Media and Myth in the New Millennium*. Oxford: Berghahn.

Powdermaker, H. 1950. *Hollywood, the Dream Factory*, Boston: Little, Brown.

Rabinow, P. 1977. *Reflections on Fieldwork in Morocco*. Berkeley: University of California Press.

Rothenbuhler, E. and M. Coman (eds), 2005. *Media Anthropology*. London: Sage.

Sanjek, R. 1990. 'On Ethnographic Validity' in R. Sanjek (ed.), *Fieldnotes: The Makings of Anthropology*. Ithaca: Cornell University Press, pp.385–418.

Silverstein, M. 1992. 'The Indeterminacy of Contextualization: When is Enough Enough?' in P. Auer and A. Di Luzio (eds), *The Contextualization of Language*. Philadelphia, PA: John Benjamins, pp.55–76.

Silverstone, R. 1994. *Television and Everyday Life*. London: Routledge.

Silverstone, R. and E. Hirsch (eds). 1992. *Consuming Technologies*. London: Routledge.

Spitulnik, D. 1998. 'Mediated Modernities: Encounters with the Electronic in Zambia', *Visual Anthropology Review* 14(2): 63–84.

———— 2002a. 'Accessing "Local" Modernities: Reflections on the Place of Linguistic Evidence in Ethnography', in B. Knauft (ed.), *Critically Modern: Alterities, Alternatives, Anthropologies*. Bloomington: Indiana University Press, pp.194–219.

———— 2002b. 'Mobile Machines and Fluid Audiences: Rethinking Reception through Zambian Radio Culture', in F. Ginsburg, L. Abu-Lughod and B. Larkin (eds), *Media Worlds: Anthropology on New Terrain*. Berkeley: University of California Press, pp.337–54.

———— 2005. 'Claiming Media Anthropology: The Minefield of Disciplinary Essentialism and Scholarly Agenda-Setting'. European Association of Social Anthropologists Media Anthropology Network, e-Seminar. http://www.philbu.net/media-anthropology/spitulnik_comment.pdf.

Strathern, M. 2003[1991]. *Partial Connections*. Walnut Creek, CA: AltaMira Press.

Taylor, C. 1971. 'Interpretation and the Sciences of Man', *Review of Metaphysics* 25: 3–51.

Van Maanen, J. 1988. *Tales of the Field: On Writing Ethnography*. Chicago: University of Chicago Press.

Veal, M. 2007. *Dub: Soundscapes and Shattered Songs in Jamaican Reggae*. Middletown, CT: Wesleyan University Press.

CHAPTER 6

'But It Is My Habit to Read the *Times*': Metaculture and Practice in the Reading of Indian Newspapers

Mark A. Peterson

It is easier for a man to divorce his wife than to change his newspaper.
—Mr Suri, insurance administrator, Delhi

In January 1993 I interviewed Mr Kumar, a retired schoolteacher, about his newspaper reading habits. Mr Kumar had an extraordinary critical faculty. Not only was he keenly aware of every error of English grammar or spelling but he knew the names of numerous bylined reporters and correspondents and could rank them by the quality of their English and by what he saw as the related category of their 'reliability'. Our twenty-five-minute interview consisted largely of an extended critique of the *Times of India,* in which he outlined what he saw as its declining quality over the past decade and its failure to maintain political independence and impartiality.

When he had finished I asked him why he did not change to one of the many other daily newspapers available in New Delhi. I suppose I expected Mr Kumar to make some comment to the effect that the *Times* was the best of a bad bunch. He did not. Instead, he stared at me silently for a long time, then said: 'But young man, it is my habit to read *Times of India*'.

How shall we talk about the reading of newspapers, listening to radio, viewing movies and television, activity on the internet and the rest of the actions through which people engage with media texts? How shall we label these activities? Reading (like its cognates viewing and listening) carries with it a notion of the solitary individual engaged in a process of decoding or interpreting texts. It extracts the text and its reader from the rich matrix of social activities through which the text is obtained, as well as from those other activities within which reading may be embedded. To speak of reception is to endorse a broadcasting metaphor, in which messages from a sender are decoded by a receiver. This metaphor conceals more than it reveals, especially about the inter-textual play of media in everyday life. Mr Kumar did not merely receive the news in the *Times*. He considered it, evaluated it according to many criteria, some socially widespread among newspaper readers of his class and education, some idiosyncratic. He read stories aloud to others at the tea shop of which he was a habitué. Consumption is hardly a better term, dragging in as it does such metaphorical entailments as markets, value and other concepts inappropriate to many contexts in which media texts are apprehended. Mr Kumar never said he 'consumed' the *Times* or even that he 'bought' or 'subscribed to' it; he said he 'takes' it in some contexts, and that he 'reads' it in others. He did not speak of his newspaper as a consumer choice in a media market; he spoke of it as part of his life.

Certainly there is nothing wrong with these labels when we are speaking specifically and concretely of people engaged in these partic-ular activities – I will use 'reader' and 'consumer' below to refer to peo-ple reading and buying newspapers. But how do we speak more gener-ally about the full range of activities through which people engage with, and are engaged by, media in their everyday lives without pre-character-ising or pre-framing their activities?

Practice is a term employed to evade some of the problems posed by the terminologies of reading, reception and consumption. To speak of 'media practices' is to foreground activity without predefining the nature of the activities to be examined, other than that they involve media (Couldry this volume). Bourdieu developed his concept of prac-tice in part to help mediate between the tyranny of 'structure' – those approaches that treat social actors as merely carrying out their roles as components in a larger system – and the representation of social actors as relatively free agents inventing culture as they pursue their highly individual choices within a social milieu. In media research, we often see this tension played out between social theories that see 'readers and viewers as passive receivers of ideologically closed texts' (Carragee 1993: 336) versus gratification theory (Rosengren, Palmgreen and Wenner 1985), or theories of marketing research, in which social actors are rel-atively unconstrained consumers meeting wants and needs within the constraints of the market – itself presumably a product of consumer demand. Practice is useful because practices can be readily conceived as clusters of related actions. Mr Kumar was engaged in overlapping activ-ities of consumption, reception and reading. One of the crucial projects of a media-practices approach is to describe such activities and the ways in which they are ordered with regard to one another and with other practices, like making a living and maintaining friendships, with which they are linked.

Yet practice, too, has its critics. Many have argued that 'practice theory' is not, in fact, a theory at all but merely a shared conceptual vocabulary (Reckwitz 2002). The most carefully elaborated theory of practice, that of Pierre Bourdieu (1977, 1990), has come under considerable criticism for naturalising economic reason (the weighing of risk and reward by social actors) rather than recognising it as but one form of historically produced cultural logic (Dreyfus and Rabinow 1993). Anthropologists in particular have been critical of Bourdieu's tendency to overemphasise the importance of converting symbolic into economic capital rather than acknowledging that social and symbolic capital – such as strong kin bonds or deep religious faith – may be valued for themselves (Lash 1993; LiPuma 1993). Bourdieu has also been criticised for 'intellectualism' because of his Saussurean pursuit of structured oppositions to describe the organisation of social fields (Schatzki 1996: 140–42). While some of these charges may be overdrawn – Bourdieu charges his critics with a failure to recall that his works are not instances of a grand theory but evolving efforts in the development of one (Bourdieu 1993) – I want to note here that all of these criticisms are about the tendency of theory to overly focus on generalised patterns describing how practices operate at the expense of comprehending what they mean to the practical actors engaged in them.

For anthropologists, a classic way out of this conundrum is to read theoretical constructions about what people do against the conceptual lexicon of the people involved. This is part of the task bequeathed to anthropology by Malinowksi: the need for description and analysis to be true at once to empirical observation, and also to the 'natives' point[s] of view' (Malinowski 1922: 25). This is a particularly fraught project when, as usually turns out to be the case, 'the natives' are sophisticated media practitioners with complex understandings of their own practices and have well-articulated vocabularies for theorising about them.

In this chapter, I examine the concept of the newspaper-taking 'habit' as found in the discourse of media practitioners engaged with newspapers in New Delhi during fieldwork in 1992/3. I assess this indigenous concept of 'habits' against marketing theories of 'consumer loyalty', local metaphors of 'ritual' and 'addiction', and Bourdieu's habitus. I conclude that the best approach for dealing with the tensions of doing an anthropology of media practice is to recognise the analytical importance of metaculture, accounts by the people we study of their own cultural actions, which describe and guide, but do not fully explain, their media practices.

The Press in New Delhi

The Registrar of Newspapers for India (RNI) listed 116 daily newspapers for Delhi in 1992, including 37 English dailies, 53 Hindi dailies and 26 'other language' publications (primarily Urdu and Punjabi). The largest Hindi daily spot was contested between *Punjab Kesari* (340,000 subscribers) and *Nav Bharat Times* (300,000), distantly followed by *Hindustan* (125,000) and *Janasataa* (82,000). The largest English daily was *Hindustan Times* (317,000), followed by *Times of India* (170,000) and *Indian Express* (110,000). *Pratap* (25,000) and *Milap* (25,000) were the largest Urdu dailies, and *Jathedar* (15,000) was the leading Punjabi paper. RNI figures under-report newspapers that have ceased publication, but based on my own observations it is probably safe to say that there were between 40 and 60 daily newspapers in New Delhi serving a literate population of about 6,750,000. Even with only 10 per cent of publications providing audited circulation figures, the total readership of news publications (dailies, weeklies, fortnightlies and monthlies) surpassed the city's gross population, and readership of dailies, with only 25 per cent reporting audited figures, was over 1.5 million.[1]

These figures suggest a lively engagement between Delhi's literate population and myriad news publications, which was borne out by my fieldwork. Many people read more than one newspaper each day and more than a few bought multiple newspapers. People shared and exchanged newspapers and read them aloud in public reading rooms, tea shops and commuter buses (thus extending their reach beyond literate readers). When Mr Kumar spoke of 'taking' the *Times of India* he was employing a distinction made by many of my informants between newspapers they take and those they read. To read a newspaper as a social act merely signifies your interest in being informed; you might read almost any newspaper. To 'take' a particular newspaper is to use it as an emblem that says something about who you are in modern New Delhi. Taking a newspaper involves consumption, understood as 'the appropriation of objects as part of one's *personalia*' (Gell 1986: 112). As with other commodity signs, the consumer absorbs some of the characteristics associated with the newspaper. This distinction between newspapers one takes and those one merely reads was made possible by a complexly structured field of meanings in which what newspapers meant was determined in large part through their relationships with one another.

In New Delhi, the most important distinction was between the English press and the vernacular press, encompassing Hindi, Urdu and Punjabi. Although the big Hindi dailies often far surpassed the English newspapers in circulation, the English dailies were assumed to be the 'national' news-papers of the educated elites, focusing on business and national politics and offering a healthy dose of international news. Within each language niche, newspapers could be placed along a language continuum, from 'chaste' to vulgar. At one end, *Nav Bharat Times* positioned itself as an 'intelligent' newspaper by using a Sanskritised Hindi that sometimes varied from everyday spoken Hindi, while *Punjab Kesari* enshrined in print everyday words that did not appear in most dictionaries.

While nearly all newspapers derive a substantial portion of their revenue from advertising, the amount and quality of this was not directly determined by circulation figures. Medium circulation Hindi dailies with solid middle class readerships would often carry big advertisements that would elude mass circulation dailies, which often had to make do with movie and lottery advertising.

Newspapers often published multiple editions in several cities, yet they were associated with particular places. *Times of India* published editions in six cities but was associated in the popular imagination with Mumbai, as *Statesman* was with Calcutta and the *Hindu* with Madras. Some newspapers were associated with particular states or regions rather than cities, and a few are associated with groups of people.

In New Delhi, India's capital, most news was political news, especially in the dominant English and Hindi newspapers. Readers evaluated political content roughly as establishment or anti-establishment. Within these rubrics, a newspaper could be categorised as a party mouthpiece, a party-line newspaper or an independent newspaper. To speak of an 'establishment' or 'pro-establishment' newspaper was to refer to a newspaper's tendency to support the general status quo, while an independent newspaper was one that could support the establishment while still being critical of certain persons, events or activities performed by members of political institutions. Newspapers whose slant on the news seemed to consistently follow that of a given political party might be said to 'follow the party line'. To follow the party line was not, however, the same thing as being 'a party newspaper' or 'party mouthpiece'. A party newspaper was rarely critical of its affiliated party or what happened within it; they often had close financial links with the leaders of particular parties or were owned or run by party members.

Stories about who owned the press were also important in characterising newspapers. In the early 1990s, most newspapers were closely held companies owned by individuals or families. The Jain family owned *Times of India*, the Goenkas *Indian Express*, and *Rashtriya Sahara* was owned by the Roy brothers and so forth. Newspaper readers often told stories about newspaper owners which painted them as

Machiavellian schemers using their newspaper's power and influence to forward business goals. These morality tales were never only about the proprietors but said something about the newspapers themselves. A tale claiming that 'Samir Jain sells news like it was soap' could be told to indicate that the speaker does not regard *Times* as a responsible newspaper, while a tale about the failure of a proprietor to bend zoning laws could be used to suggest that the newspaper is losing its status if the government dares treat its proprietor in this way.

This field of distinctions that organises taste is elicited from stories newspaper readers told me about what they read, what they 'took' and why. When Indian readers began talking about newspapers they usually invoked two intertwined but distinct concepts: seriousness (as opposed to spiciness) and sincerity. Seriousness was an umbrella term that encompassed and integrated such issues as a newspaper's history, ownership and claims toward national significance. Informants occasionally defined it as 'respect in society' – as in '*Rashtriya Sahara* is not serious; it is selling many newspapers, but it has no respect in society' – or sobriety – 'The *Hindu* is a very sober paper. It is reassuring in its dullness'. Sincerity described perceptions of how newspapers dealt with their social responsibilities. An insincere newspaper might print news without regard to its possible effects on society whereas a sincere newspaper would weigh what it published and how it characterised potentially volatile news.

Finally, many readers referred to the 'spiciness' (*masala*) of news. Spice was indicated by a privileging of entertainment, crime and local news over national, political news, but was also indicated by signifiers such as large photographs or the use of colour. Newspapers have only limited space; newspapers that used only a few small black-and-white photographs were bland, but able to devote more space to news. Newspapers that ran large, five-column photographs and colour photographs were said to be sacrificing breadth and depth of coverage to spice up their newspaper and make it more palatable for the reader.

While it would be wrong to make too much of the food aspect of the 'spice' metaphor – my collaborators never extended it in any interviews with me – there is one important parallel. Like foodstuffs, newspapers generally have a short life. News is defined in large part by its newness, and old newspapers grow rapidly stale, degenerating into *raddi* (waste paper) once their news value has faded. Consuming a newspaper by merely reading it is like eating; the content quickly vanishes from the social field. Consuming a newspaper by 'taking' it, however, implies a link between the consumer and the newspaper that extends beyond the moment of consumption to produce pervasive social meaning. Like the comestibles described by Alfred Gell, these 'quite ephemeral items ... live on in the form of the social relations that they produce, and which are in turn responsible for reproducing [them]' (Gell 1986: 112).

Speaking of the News

This symbolic field of structured distinctions does not, of course, describe actual newspapers but rather serves as a repertoire on which actors draw to make use of newspapers in concrete social situations. Newspapers, like any other social good, serve as an idiom by which people socially construct themselves and through which they map themselves onto discourses of nation, family and world. Consider, for example, Sri Arora, the brass magnate and his family. I met Sri Arora when I went to one of his establishments to buy brass. Because I was an American I was quickly bumped up the ladder of employees to the owner himself. Sri Arora bought and sold old brass as his father had done before him, but he had expanded this into an import/export business. He employed twelve workers and had four sons, three of whom worked in the business. The second son attended 'a good English medium college' and no longer worked in the family business. Sri Arora took three papers: *Hindustan Times, Nav Bharat Times* and *Times of India*. He took *Hindustan Times,* because 'a businessman needs to read a newspaper with plenty of advertising, and also this is a newspaper about this city. It does not fill its columns so much with information about Bosnia and things I do not need to know about'. Sri Arora took *Nav Bharat Times* for his wife, who did not read English, and *Times of India* for his son, 'since that is what they read at his college. But I read them all'.

In his account of his newspaper consumption, Sri Arora positioned himself within a field framed by the distinctions described above. Sri Arora invoked place, as well as occupation – his immediate contextual 'need to know' – as his explanation for taking *Hindustan Times*. He also explained to me that it was the paper his father took for him when he was young, to help his English, and that he shares it with the three sons who remain with him in the business. Sri Arora thus situated himself simultaneously within his immediate social roles – family man, businessman, resident of Delhi – all by his choice of newspaper.

Taking *Times of India* 'for his son' marked his son's change of role. The first in the family to go to college, he found *Times of India* to be more prestigious among his peers than *Hindustan Times*. Changing newspapers was often a strategy for adapting to a new and unfamiliar social milieu. His father's taking the paper for him was a demonstration simultaneously of support but also of paternal control. The younger Arora had no qualms about asking his father to take the newspaper for him, he said, because he could rely on his father to do what was necessary for his success. He also said the general consensus in the family was that *Times of India* was a better journal for 'general knowledge', a crucial subject on school exams.

Sri Arora said he took *Nav Bharat Times* for his wife because it was the 'best' Hindi newspaper, but he made no effort to explain this term. The choice may have been a generational one: Sri Arora said he believed that was the newspaper her family had taken. He never offered the argument that she wanted that paper, and when I offered it to him in the form of a question, he repeated to me that he 'took the paper for her.'

Finally, Sri Arora also regularly bought the Hindi *Sandhya Times*, published in the evenings, but did not say so in our interview. I drew his attention to an issue lying on a chair in his office at the back of his shop. He waved his hand dismissively and said he did not 'take' it but that sometimes a vendor would come by and he would buy a copy. As we spoke about it, it became clear that in fact, while he did not subscribe to the paper, he bought one nearly every day and the vendor often made several trips to his office in order to catch him in. He said he bought it mostly for the jokes, which were useful to him as a businessman, and because men who came to see him in his office liked to pick it up and read it. The distinction between 'taking' (by which he meant subscribing) and occasionally 'buying' was an important distinction, distancing Sri Arora from the lower-status newspaper.

Sri Arora used his newspaper practices, and talk about them, to construct himself as a particular kind of man. He emphasised both his paternal authority and his role as a distributor of goods. He signified his comfort with the multiple languages of the papers (and hence his educated status), but also his encompassing authority and knowledge as head of the household. In addition, newspaper readership was a fundamental method through which Sri Arora established himself as a political being. One of the primary stated purposes of the newspapers was to provide him with material to talk about with his friends and business associates. His multiplicity of newspapers itself was a sign indicating him to be well-off financially and to be a man who followed politics and business closely. In his conversations, Sri Arora drew on the content of these multiple newspapers to construct a specific view of the nation, of where it was going and where it should go, which was not the vision of any one of those newspapers. These views were closely tied with his construction of himself as a father, husband, citizen and man of substance. Thus Sri Arora employed purchasing, reading, sharing and talking about newspapers as some of the many practices through which he constructed his day-to-day life.

At least in his interview with a foreign anthropologist, Sri Arora portrays his newspaper practices as partly reflexive, strategic consumer choices shaped by his perception of the links between particular newspapers and the gendered and age-patterned domains of family, education and work. It is thus tempting to conceptualise Sri Arora as mapping himself onto a pre-existing coherent system of symbols that is the property of some group. But the system of signification used by Sri Arora to construct himself through the idiom of his consumption is not really an encompassing set of shared norms and values because while these sets of structural continua – such as from chaste to vulgar – do in fact seem to under gird all of my informants' talk about news and consumption, they have different perspectives on these distinctions and hence exhibit different 'tastes' (Bourdieu 1984). Some articulated the Hindi of *Nav Bharat Times* as off-putting and pretentious, while others described it as educational and 'chaste'. Yet if the structures of signification organising newspapers in New Delhi cannot be reduced to a shared system of meanings, neither can they be reduced to a set of values structuring consumer choice. The idea that what one reads is the result of an appraisal of the value of one choice over another was implied in my question to Mr Kumar, which nonplussed him. Understanding the practice of 'taking' a newspaper as neither the expression of social order, implied by the media theories of Anderson (1991) and Habermas (1985), nor as a matter of consumer choice or gratification (Rosengren, Palmgreen and Wenner 1985), requires us to attend closely to Mr Kumar's own answer: habit.

Explaining Habit

'"Practice" brings into view activities which are situated, corporeal, and shaped by habits without reflection' (Thévenot 2001: 56). Indeed, Mr Kumar's practice of taking *Times of India* was situated within particular social spaces and deals with such corporeal objects as newspapers, chairs and glasses of tea, in interaction with Mr Kumar's body as well as those of fellow tea house habitués and newspaper delivery people. His activities in these settings with these objects are largely unreflexive.

Yet Mr Kumar can reflect on his practices, and does so – although generally not as part of these practices. One of the conundrums of ethnography is that it not only brings practices into view for the ethnographer but, through the ethnographer's questions, invites practitioners to reflect and comment on these practices. Schatzki calls the activities ethnographers encourage in their hosts – including 'describing … explaining, questioning, reporting, examining, and imagining' (Schatzki 1996: 91) – 'dispersed practices' because they can occur within and across many different domains of social life. The meanings and routines of these practices may shift from one social domain to another, and many forms of information may be practice specific – that is, there are certain kinds of information that emerge in certain kinds of practices, like interviews, and others that emerge in alternative practices, like shop talk (Briggs 1986).

Interestingly, Mr Kumar the social actor used the same term for his unreflexive practices as does Thévenot the theorist. For both, 'habit' describes this sense of actions performed automatically and unreflectively, which seem to actors to be natural and necessary – rather than cultural and symbolic – modes of behaviour. Mr Kumar was not alone in his terminology. Many Indians spoke to me in this way about their consumption of newspapers. To respond 'because it is my habit' or to answer 'because I have a long history of taking this newspaper' was usually considered to be an adequate explanation for a reading practice centred on a particular newspaper. As in the case of Mr Kumar, respondents often raised specific qualities of their newspaper in the course of our interviews but not as explanations as to why they chose these particular newspapers. As I sought to make sense of this, three key metaphors emerged from multiple interviews in which people sought to articulate the meaning of habit: brand loyalty, ritual and addiction.

Ranjan, a bureau chief for *Indian Express* in South India, laughed when I told him the story of Mr Kumar. It was all about brand loyalty, he told me. He offered the story that during one of *Indian Express*'s campaigns to expand its market in the South, a marketing research team came in. One of the target markets was that of the English-educated Nambutiri Brahmins of Kerala. Surveys showed that the political views of most members of this community were more in line with *Indian Express*'s political stance than that of South India's leading English newspaper, the *Hindu*. Indeed, Ranjan said, researchers found focus groups discussing the newspapers would sometimes grow outraged when discussing *Hindu* editorials. Yet when the researchers broached the idea of transferring to *Indian Express*, they were treated with incredulity. The *Hindu*, they were told, was the newspaper of the Brahmin community. Similarly in Kerala, Syrian Christians would refer to *Malayala Manorama*, and Catholics to *Deepika*, as the newspapers of their respective communities.

'Indians have the greatest brand loyalty of anybody in the world', a marketing executive at *Times of India* explained. 'And newspaper brand loyalty is greater than any other kind'. Brand loyalty is marketing jargon for the symbolic bond that can form between a consumer and a product such that, given a wide market selection, the consumer will consistently choose that product. Marketing research tends to assume that people are choice-makers moved primarily by perceptions of quality and by price; brand loyalty is the factor that accounts for a consumer being willing to consistently choose one brand over others regardless of minor shifts in price. The assumption is that having established that a particular brand is 'best' at a particular point in their consumption history, consumers will confidently continue to purchase this brand as a way to manage efficiently in a world of myriad and expanding choices. This is a logical and compelling argument but it does not really explain behaviour like that of Mr Kumar, or the community of Ranjan's story, who continue to take newspapers which they no longer see as being of the highest quality or which they admit no longer meet their needs.

Advertising executives explained this by reframing branding in terms of a product's 'secondary values'. In this view, the newspaper's brand serves in part as a commodity sign, an image possessing social and cultural value associated with a product such that it extends the meaning of the product beyond its use value (Goldman and Papson 1996). The brands *Times of India* or the *Hindu* stand for particular values quite aside from the content of the newspapers themselves. And some of these values indeed contribute to the consumption choices through which Sri Arora brings newspapers into his family and work spaces. Consumers buy the brand, not the product, both because of the ways the character of the brand prefigures the value of the product, but also because they hope to take on some of the character of the products they consume: they talk 'about themselves through the medium of the product' (Applbaum 2004: 43). But labelling it in this way begs the question of the nature of this supposed symbolic bond: What character is it Mr Kumar takes from *Times of India,* a newspaper whose content he criticizes? How does the *Hindu* have a Brahmin character if the Brahmins do not like its content?

People who buy and read newspapers are far less likely than newspaper producers to invoke rational choices and the logic of the marketplace in explaining their newspaper habits. Instead, habit was often spoken of in the sense of a personal routine; that is, a ritualised, repetitive behaviour associated with a particular time and place. Many informants, for example, described reading a newspaper as part of their morning routine. For example, after describing the 'ritual' of his own pre-commute breakfast-and-a-newspaper habit, Sunny, the marketing manager of the Delhi branch of a large Mumbai-based corporation, said:

This is how we Indians are about our newspapers. You will find it more so in rural areas. Those who can read will be taking their habits. Once I went to a town in Kerala. There was one taxi, and the fellow was reading his morning paper. He put it down and gave me tea and went back to his newspaper. This is how these people are. He wouldn't take me anywhere until he had finished his morning paper.

Ritual, as Couldry (2003) has argued, is of very little explanatory value if it merely refers to routine activity. Rather, we invoke the concept of ritual when 'ritual involves a pattern, form, or shape that gives meaning to the action'; the meaningfulness of these rituals often involves 'broad, even transcendent values' (Couldry 2005: 60). Lacking space to fully analyze Sunny's comments here, I will simply assert that Sunny is invoking a set of widespread cultural values that oppose ritual to rational, rural to urban and backward to modern. Just as Sunny insisted on his newspaper with breakfast every morning and lets disruption of this practice irrationally affect his moods, so the taxi driver is engaged in the irrational practice of putting his own habits above the needs of his customer (and putting the customer first is a cornerstone of Sunny's notions of rationality).

Informants also spoke of their habit in the manner of an addiction, like a drug habit. One informant, a lawyer, offered as one of the virtues of the press that 'it is an addiction which can be stuck to.' It is as compulsive as a drug addiction, he said, but is constructive rather than destructive. An advertising salesman at *Times of India* in Delhi told me that although he was employed by the *Times*, and recognised the *Times* as the better paper, he was 'addicted' to the *Statesman*. 'Since I was twelve I have read that paper', he said. '*Times* is now the better paper but the *Statesman* is my habit I cannot give up'. Similarly, an insurance administrator named Mr Suri explained that he had begun doing the crossword puzzle in *Mid-Day*, an English eveninger, at a period in his life when it was convenient to buy it from a vendor on his way home and his status in his company was so low that it would not matter if people saw him carrying it. Once he had risen to an executive position he did not want to be seen with such a journal; yet he was 'hooked.' He therefore clipped the crossword puzzles from *Mid-Day* and carried them in his briefcase to do in instalments as time permitted.

The metaphor of addiction not only stresses again the notion that one's newspaper practices are beyond rational choice but also raises the important notion of pleasure. Addiction implies pleasure – indeed, a pleasure that becomes a need. Foucault (1978, 1984) emphasises the role of pleasure in establishing the agent's subject position within a social order, arguing that pleasure derives from regulation and self-control rather than indulgence and excess. Furthermore, pleasure can be experienced as a resistance to power. But as Pasternak has pointed out, Foucault tends to fall into 'the conflation of state power with social power' (Pasternak 1987: 97). I read Foucault in light of Bourdieu's tripartite division of power into orthodox, heterodox and doxa. In Foucault, orthodox power is represented as 'the king' or 'the law'. Here, orthodox power refers to the normative power of the dominant group in a given social field. For Mr Suri, and the salesman from Calcutta, these 'addictions' serve as little heterodoxies that resist orthodox claims to define valuable forms of symbolic capital in favour of nostalgia, indexes of place and other significations. To successfully do so, they must still draw on a common underlying and uncontested doxa, in this case the field of newspaper distinctions discussed above. In these examples, 'addiction' excuses resistance to the social pressures that manage status or require capitulation to a group norm within a particular field by referring back to prior social fields in which the newspaper was more valued.

Habit and Practice

Drawing on his crossword experience, Mr Suri, the insurance administrator, offered an ingenious explanation of how newspaper habits work:

> In every newspaper there must be a crossword puzzle. You begin doing it and you come to understand the thinking of the persons who are writing it. The way they put the clues together, the way they organise ... And if later you try to do a crossword puzzle in another newspaper, it is not quite the same. You can do it but you have not developed the habit for doing it. You are eager to go back to the paper you are familiar with.

Habit, Mr Suri suggested, was a capitulation to the comfort – the pleasure, the meaningfulness, the ritual – of doing again what one has done before. The more one engages with a newspaper, both mental engagement with content and physical engagement with the activities of reading and consuming, the more one is likely to repeat those engagements. Warde (2005) suggests that in addition to the internal pleasure derived from the social consequences of the practice – in this case, the pleasure of asserting one's self in the context of conformist pressure – there may be intrinsic rewards in a practice like Mr Suri's involving the psychological balance between competence and challenge that Cziksentmihalyi

(1991) calls 'flow'. When something interrupts the comfort of this habitual engagement with news, like the arrival of a customer or a promotion to a better position, one may act creatively to salvage one's habit as much as possible in the transformed context.

Mr Suri's theory of habit is remarkably like that of Bourdieu's habitus, 'a system of lasting, transposable dispositions which, integrating past experiences, functions at every moment as a matrix of perceptions, appreciations, and actions and makes possible the achievement of infinitely diversified tasks, thanks to analogical transfers of schemes permitting the solution of similarly shaped problems' (Bourdieu 1977: 83). Learned as part of growing up in a society but continually reshaped by ongoing experiences of social life, habitus reflects the tendency of people to employ the same practical solutions when faced with decisions to be made both in familiar and unfamiliar environments.

Bourdieu begins by assuming that distinctions such as those people make between newspapers are arbitrary rather than reflecting real objective conditions (such as the actual 'nature' of the respective newspapers) but that people generally misrecognise this 'cultural arbitrary' (Bourdieu and Passeron 1996: 32). Social life is a constant struggle to construct a life out of the cultural resources one's social experience offers, in the face of formidable social constraints. By living in a society structured by such constraints, and organised by the successful practices of those around you, one develops predispositions to act in certain ways. One develops not rules for reading newspapers but a sense of how one might read newspapers that allows the individual to improvise endlessly without ever straying too far from what those living their lives in similar circumstances would recognise as meaningful behaviour. Culture is thus reproduced through habitus, since it is 'productive of practices conforming with … [the] cultural arbitrary' (ibid.: 32). Actors brought up in a specific environment learn to feel comfortable doing particular kinds of activities; they in turn shape the environment of others (especially children) and therefore create cultural continuities.

Habitus involves a practical knowledge which is neither theory nor rules nor value nor strategy but a continuous assessment of situations and an improvisation of action on the basis of one's sense of what will work. This practical knowledge – of the distinctions between newspapers and hence how to buy them, interpret them and talk about them and their content – is neither entirely automatic nor consciously strategised, for it includes deeply embodied habits – such as recognising and decoding English or Devanagiri scripts – and complex semi-reflexive activities – such as carrying on a conversation about the news. Clearly, '[t]he concept of habitus has a lot of work to do in Bourdieu's concep-

tual scheme. It is something of an overburdened concept whose meaning tends to slip, slide and even disappear, as it is deployed in different
contexts' (Shilling 1993: 149). Teasing out the kinds of habitus involved
in a practice like reading the news thus becomes an important component of analysis. Wainwright, Williams and Turner (2007) suggest that
it is important to tease out different forms of habitus, such as those that
are individual to a particular person's body, those that express institutional character, and those that are the results of specific forms of training. In Mr Kumar's case, this might refer to his need for glasses to physically engage in the act of reading, his training as an English teacher
which gives him the capacity and confidence to critique the use of
English by *Times* writers and editors, and the habits that give any urban
Indian the character of 'educated', so that even though he is fluent in
Hindi it would not occur to him to pick up a Hindi newspaper, even if
he wanted to read the news and no English newspapers were at hand.
Teasing out levels of habitus is a first step; as Schatzki (1996) and
Couldry (this volume) argue, it must be followed by attention to how
multiple levels of habitus are linked into habitual actions, and how multiple actions – buying the newspaper, reading the newspaper alone or
aloud to an audience, talking about the news – are aggregated into
practices.

Metaculture and Interpretive Practice

Not every activity is a practice, of course. Practice, whether partly strategised as in Sri Arora's case or mostly unreflexive as in Mr Suri's case, has
the characteristic of being customary or habitual. Practices are also
strongly linked to contexts that give them meaning. Indeed, Giddens
argues that institutions are but 'practices which are deeply sedimented
in time-space' (Giddens 1979: 80). For Bourdieu, practice is defined by
a dialectical relationship between a structured context and the habituated dispositions people have for acting in those contexts. Bourdieu's
work has tended to focus on the way in which people reproduce environments (even in transformed ways) as contexts and habits mutually
(re)construct one another. Since habitual actions are learned, though,
new practices must also emerge when social actors find themselves in
new contexts and must modify their practices as their habitual actions
cannot fully accommodate to the new social field. Giddens refers to this
when he describes socialisation as part of 'a double-contingency of
interaction' producing a progressive 'involvement with society'
throughout the life trajectory of social actors (ibid.: 129). As actors

enter into unfamiliar situations they draw on their knowledge of similar social fields and associated habitual actions but must use these to accommodate the demands of the situation at hand. Perhaps still the best work on this 'interpretive practice' (Beeman and Peterson 2001) – the dialectical process of redefining social contexts and redefining actions to suit them – is that of Erving Goffman (1974), whose language of habitual interpretive 'frames' which can be 'broken' and 'repaired' in order to negotiate mutually interpretable behaviour has much in common with practice theories.

These issues are important because the situated knowledge we derive from ethnographic work – whether participant observation, surveys, interviews or other techniques – often involves an intervention into practice by the act of our asking our hosts to reflect on their practices. The presence of an ethnographer asking questions about practices provokes metacultural activities that produce discourses through which people reflect on, define and redefine cultural action. Metaculture refers to the reflexive aspects of culture that has effects on practices (Urban 2001). These requests require creative work on the part of our informants as they interpret our requests and formulate responses. A full understanding of what our informants are trying to tell us therefore requires us to recognise how they are responding to us and to our requests. As Bourdieu insists, 'the effort of reflexivity ... seems to me to be the fundamental condition for the progress of scientificity in the social sciences' (Bourdieu 1993: 274). In the cases I have presented here, my position in 1992/3 as a white, male American scholar from an Ivy League university, my affiliations with Delhi and Jawaharlal Nehru universities, my modest facility with Hindi and Urdu and fluency in English, and my prior work as a journalist in Washington, D.C., all shaped the nature of my interviews and the strategies through which my hosts reflected on their practices.

For example, Sunny, with his MBA and marketing focus, was making a distinction here between rational people like himself (and me), and ritualistic people like the village taxi driver. In so doing, he drew on a deeply rooted discursive structure in India that situates people on a continuum of modernity from irrational, rural, illiterate masses to rational, educated, urban professionals. While the taxi driver was literate, he was nonetheless described as ritualistic rather than rational, and did not proceed as Sunny knows a good entrepreneur should by putting the customer's needs ahead of his own in order to maximise profits. Sunny could ironically link himself to the taxi driver as a fellow Indian who indulges in these silly, ritualistic actions, while at the same time establishing his own fundamental modernity (and hence superiority) by noting that he never lets his own breakfast rituals interfere with business. Likewise, Sri Arora used his interview to position himself as both modern and traditional: he read English and Hindi, situated himself as a traditional Delhi businessman and a traditional parent. Yet he distanced himself from both Hindi-language newspapers when talking with me, a Western, English-speaking scholar. For me, he emphasised his English skills, his English newspapers and his son's education while downplaying his Hindi newspapers, and even his Hindi-speaking customers.

What is hidden from me in my observations of newspaper practices and interviews about newspapers becomes apparent as I come to recognise the interpretive frames that guide my informants' interviews with me. My Indian hosts assume a continuum between modernity and the not-yet-modern. They are constructing themselves and India as much through their interview performances as through their newspaper reading practices. Their invocation of habit, and their effort to locate metaphors to explain habit, happened because I asked them to explain their practices. What's more, their answers draw my attention to the extent to which this whole process was engendered by the implications present in my first question to Mr Kumar, and my subsequent repetition of this story to them as cultural consultants: the assumption that in a market people will choose the best product for the best price. Where, after all, did my question come from if it was not stimulated by my own culturally situated assumption that newspapers competed against one another in a marketplace and consumers bought the newspapers they deemed 'best'? Their answers, in turn, offer me elements of an indigenous theory of practice that turns on contrasts between the comforts of ritual and the status of modernity.

Conclusion

'One cannot grasp the most profound logic of the social world unless one becomes immersed in the specificity of an empirical reality, historically situated and dated, but only in order to construct it as an instance … in a finite universe of possible configurations', writes Bourdieu (1993: 274). In this case, I have been using Mr Kumar, Sri Arora, Mr Suri and stories told by newspaper editors about Nambutiri Brahmins as instances in a particular universe of practices. While describing consumption practices that resist simple market choice explanations in New Delhi in 1992/3, I have also been considering implications of these instances for the analysis of media practice. My argument is that the tendencies of practice theory to abstraction and generalisation are best countered by careful attention to the metacultural discourses through which those engaged in these practices account for their own practices, and that this in turn can be accomplished only through careful reflexive attention to our own ethnographic practices.

Notes

1. The significance of newspapers in the early 1990s was rooted in part in the fact that India's electronic news media were under government control and hence usually regarded as substantively different from newspapers, which were uncensored. Since then, the rise of independent television news, the emergence of new information technologies and the lifting of restrictions on foreign direct investment in print and broadcasting have transformed many of the structures of the fields within which people engage in media practices.

References

Anderson, B. 1991. *Imagined Communities: Reflections on the Origins and Spread of Nationalism*, rev. edn. London: Verso.

Applbaum, K. 2004. *The Marketing Era: From Professional Practice to Global Positioning*. London: Routledge.

Beeman, W.O. and M.A. Peterson. 2001. 'Situations and Interpretations: Explorations in Interpretive Practice', *Anthropological Quarterly* 74(4): 159–62.

Bourdieu, P. 1977. *Outline of a Theory of Practice*. Cambridge: Cambridge University Press.

——— 1984. *Distinction: A Social Critique of the Judgment of Taste*. Cambridge, MA: Harvard University Press.

——— 1990. *The Logic of Practice*. Stanford, CA: Stanford University Press.

——— 1993. 'Concluding Remarks: For a Sociogenetic Understanding of Intellectual Works', in C. Calhoun, E. LiPuma and M. Postone (eds), *Bourdieu: Critical Perspectives*. Chicago: University of Chicago Press, pp.263–75.

Bourdieu, P. and J.C. Passeron. 1996. *Reproduction*. London: Sage.

Briggs, C. 1986. *Learning How to Ask: A Sociolinguistic Appraisal of the Role of the Interview in Social Science*. Cambridge: Cambridge University Press.

Carragee, K.M. 1993. 'A Critical Evaluation of Debates Examining the Media Hegemony Thesis', *Western Journal of Communication* 57: 330–48.

Couldry, N. 2003. *Media Rituals: A Critical Approach*. London: Routledge.

——— 2005. 'Media Rituals: Beyond Functionalism', in E.W. Rothenbuhler and M. Coman (eds), *Media Anthropology*. London: Sage, pp.59–69.

Cziksentmihalyi, M. 1991. *Flow: The Psychology of Optimal Experience*. New York: Harper Perennial.

Dreyfus, H. and P. Rabinow. 1993. 'Can There Be a Science of Existential Structure and Social Meaning?' in C. Calhoun, E. LiPuma and M. Postone (eds), *Bourdieu: Critical Perspectives*. Chicago: University of Chicago Press, pp.35–44.

Foucault, M. 1978. *The Use of Pleasure: The History of Sexuality, Vol. 2*. New York: Pantheon Books.

———— 1984. 'Truth and Power', in P. Rabinow (ed.), *The Foucault Reader*. New York: Pantheon, pp.51–75.

Gell, A. 1986. 'Newcomers to the World of Goods: Consumption among the Muria Gonds', in A. Appadurai (ed.), *The Social Life of Things: Commodities in Cultural Perspective*. Cambridge: Cambridge University Press, pp.110–38.

Giddens, A. 1979. *Central Problems in Social Theory: Action, Structure and Contradiction in Social Analysis*. Berkeley: University of California Press.

Goffman, E. 1974. *Frame Analysis: An Essay on the Organisation of Experience*. New York: Harper Colophon.

Goldman, R. and S. Papson. 1996. *Sign Wars: The Cluttered Landscapes of Advertising*. New York: Guilford Press.

Habermas, J. 1985. *A Theory of Communicative Action, Vol. I: Reason and the Rationalization of Society*. Boston: Beacon Press.

Lash, S. 1993. 'Pierre Bourdieu, Cultural Economy and Social Change', in C. Calhoun, E. LiPuma and M. Postone (eds), *Bourdieu: Critical Perspectives*. Chicago: University of Chicago Press, pp.193–211.

LiPuma, E. 1993. 'Culture and the Concept of Culture in a Theory of Practice', in C. Calhoun, E. LiPuma and M. Postone (eds), *Bourdieu: Critical Perspectives*. Chicago: University of Chicago Press, pp.14–34.

Malinowski, B. 1922. *Argonauts of the Western Pacific*. New York : Dutton.

Pasternak, M. 1987. 'Norms and Normalization: Michel Foucault's Overextended Panoptic Machine', *Human Sciences* 10: 97–121.

Reckwitz, A. 2002. 'Toward a Theory of Social Practices: A Development in Culturalist Thinking', *European Journal of Social Theory* 5: 243–63.

Rosengren, K.E.P. Palmgreen and L.A. Wenner (eds). 1985. *Media Gratification Research: Current Perspectives*. London: Sage.

Schatzki, T. 1996. *Social Practices: A Wittgensteinian Approach to Human Activity and the Social*. Cambridge: Cambridge University Press.

Shilling, C. 1993. *The Body and Social Theory*. London: Sage.

Thévenot, L. 2001. 'Pragmatic Regimes: Governing Engagement with the World', in T. Schatzki, K. Knorr Cetina and E. von Savigny (eds), *The Practice Turn in Contemporary Theory*. London: Routledge, pp.56–73.

Urban, G. 2001. *Metaculture*. Minneapolis: University of Minnesota Press.

Wainwright, S.P., C. Williams and B.S. Turner. 2007. 'Globalization, Habitus and the Balletic Body'. *Cultural Studies – Critical Methodologies* 7(3): 308–25.

Warde, A. 2005. 'Consumption and the Theory of Practice', *Journal of Consumer Culture* 5(2): 131–53.

CHAPTER 7

Embedded/Embedding Media Practices and Cultural Production

Ursula Rao

Introduction

This chapter investigates an emerging culture of local news production in India. It is set against the background of a profound transformation of the Indian news-making business that among other things has led to a rapid expansion of local news-making since the 1990s (Jeffrey 2000; Rao 2010a). The growing availability of space for local information is welcomed by citizens who actively engage with editorial personnel and push their concerns, hopes and achievements into newspapers. In this chapter I will focus specifically on the way aspiring local leaders appropriate news production in order to create fame. In this process a politics of importance traditionally associated with the public arena and realised in public performances is carried into newsprint through news that displays importance rather than giving information. The multiplication of such news creates a public sphere of a particular character: a collage of competitive expressions of alliances, connections and eminence, rather than a rational debate of public concerns.

My interpretation draws on recent debates about the performativity of practice. I focus on the doing of culture as a process of rearticulation, in which accumulated cultural memory and habitus undergo transformation. More specifically, I explore how variable sets of repositioned political practices and cultural imaginaries[1] contribute to shaping local news and create a flexible hybrid of news as political display. Culture appears as a process. Not only do traits and traditions progressively change, but so too do the relations of these traits and traditions. It is an argument against an overemphasis of order within cultural operations. Structure, order, function are in themselves insufficient tools for explaining social relations. A theory of practice can serve as a counterweight by focusing also on drama, contingency and change. Interpreting media as practice means to focus on the complex workings of media in a net of culture in flux.

The chapter begins with a comparative introduction of selected practice theories. This provides the theoretical grounding for the analysis of the media activities that accompanied the controversy over the shooting of the film *Water* (dir. Deepa Mehta) in the North Indian holy city of Banaras.[2] The excessive focus on individual leaders in the media during the anti-*Water* campaign struck me as significant and motivated me to investigate the connection between performative politics and (local) news-making practices. I demonstrate how the cooperation between journalists and leaders reinstates techniques of political persuasion in a media context. My conclusion discusses the connection between reflective practice and cultural change. I introduce ideologies pertaining to the public sphere (mass media) and social arenas (performative politics) and show how the doing of politics, the writing of news and the (academic) interpretation of practice interactively contribute to the remaking of culture.

Analysing Media as Practice

In Chapter 1, Nick Couldry calls for a new paradigm in media studies taking media practice as the 'epicentre of new research questions' (p. 36). The new approach should decentre an older obsession with media text and look at a broader context of social activities that are related to mass media's presence in the world. This demand builds on two recent developments. Firstly, since the late 1980s a significant shift has occurred in the study of production and reception. Scholars have moved from seeing production and reception as determined by structure, text or technology to emphasise the contested nature of engagements with media (e.g., Ericson, Baranek and Chan 1989; Mazzarella 2003). Secondly, there has been a continuous expansion of the range of social contexts analysed in relation to media. Production and reception are less often looked at in isolation but instead as part of changing political landscapes, community relations, family structures or cultural imaginaries (e.g., Brosius and Butcher 1999; Ginsburg, Abu-Lughod and Larkin 2002).

Elizabeth Bird sums up this development in her critical discussion of audience research, where she suggests we analyse not only media cultures but 'media *as* culture' (Bird 2003: 2). In contemporary (Western) society, media have become an inseparable part of the 'web of culture' (ibid.: 3). In a media-saturated world, the term 'audience' does not denote any specific group but is a position adopted routinely by all members of society. The way people inhabit this position has consequences for social relations and cultural perceptions (see also Abu-Lughod 1995; Peterson this volume). Couldry extends this perspective in a theoretical and more encompassing model for the future of media studies. Media analysis, he suggests, should focus on media-related practices and the way they inform the very substance of culture. Couldry's guiding research question assumes a hierarchy: What is the structuring role of media practices in society and how do media-related practices 'anchor' other practices?[3]

While I fully agree that practice theory can serve to overcome the limits of functionalist interpretation, Couldry's reduced version of it is trapped in a static model. Two assumptions inform his approach: firstly, practices are ordered; and secondly, this order is transparent and can be understood through (academic) reflection. This is in line with a structuralist interpretation of practice, a prominent example of which is Bourdieu's (1977, 1987) interpretation of the logic of practice. Bourdieu introduced habitus and fields as the two mutually constitutive structuring devices of society. A social field is constituted through objective conditions favouring the development of a particular type of habitus (that has individual variations but produces astonishingly similar biographies within any particular field) as optimally adjusted sets of predispositions for practice. People structure unravelling events by applying to them a determinate set of practical solutions. These habitually employed practices act as structuring devices, which order events and eventually reproduce the field and the habitus.

Different fields within modern society – professions or classes[4] – are entangled with one another. Like actors in fields, fields acquire positions within a universe of relations in which dominant fields imprint their logic onto other fields (e.g., Bourdieu 1992). In his work on French journalism, Bourdieu (1998) asserts that media professionals and their activities constitute a social field, which produces knowledge that has become extremely powerful and heavily influences all fields of cultural production, such as art and science. Within the field of media production, Bourdieu sees television as occupying the most important position. He insists that only an internal analysis of the embodied practices of media professionals and their relationships to each other can open up an understanding of the way the social is constituted in the contemporary world.

While Couldry does not talk of fields or habitus, he assumes demarcated sets of ordered practices that influence each other in a domino style, with media practices in the pole position. Couldry offers no justification for this a priori assumption about the centrality of media. As an anthropologist, I read it as an almost ironic reversal of a typical anthropological perspective. The novelty of media technology in remote areas has inspired anthropologists to look at the way local practices shape the position of media within different cultural settings. Here, it is a particular set of cultural practices first, which imprint on the way people use media. Both perspectives are fraudulent, since they are forced to assume a particular cultural given from which influence is derived.

However, hierarchy is only a minor concern. There is the crucial question of order. Mark Hobart (this volume) criticises Couldry for reintroducing culture as structure via one particular theory of practice. Once the hallmark of anthropology, the notion of culture as structure, organism or system has been under continuous attack for the last twenty years. It is unable to explain cultural change, to deal with the heterogeneity of cultural universes and to capture the contingency of everyday life.[5]

Change, drama and contingency are the focal points of an intellectual tradition exploring performance.[6] Performance, or the doing of practice, is never fully determined by accumulated history but is the reappropriation of a habitus and a cultural repertoire in a new and uncertain situation. It is a moment of conjuncture between the prescriptive and the spontaneous, the structure and the event, the habitus and its realisation (see Sahlins 1987: xiv). It is not only a case of models structuring events but also events recasting models (Handelman 1998). In a way Bourdieu's theory allows for this dynamic, even though he himself does not exploit this potential in his mostly conservative analysis of the social world.[7] In *The Logic of Practice*, Bourdieu introduces the term 'regulated improvisations' (Bourdieu 1987: 107), capturing the two sides of practice: reproduction and invention.

Thus, the alternative to structure is not chaos. The question is: How are order and contingency related? An analysis of practice must consider continuation and variation as two elements that re-regulate practice. Derrida (1978) has addressed this concern in a theory of iterability. In a debate with Austin (1990), he critiques the assumption that the affectivity of performative speech acts is a result of language conventions. Speech acts, Derrida asserts, are 'quotations' that while drawing on identifiable models take on a different connotation according to context. Reiteration creates a slippage in meaning. The model enters as trace not as a fixed entity. Judith Butler (1993) has applied this theory to the analysis of gender construction, where she acknowledges the possibility for social change accomplished through reactualisation in performance. Gender categories are subverted when variations afford shifts in meaning. Practices in these theories are not accomplices of structure. They reappropriate structured universes and change them in a process of adaptation.

Such restructuring is at the centre of my argument in this chapter. I focus on political practices and how they are reinstated in a media context. It is not a microhistory of slippages but an analysis of how a particular political register is used in shaping emerging news-making practices which again reshape political practices and the public sphere. For the sake of clarity I suggest an analytical distinction between two public fields: news writing (public sphere) and political performances (public arena).[8] Political performances are played out in public spaces where political rituals serve to produce and demonstrate social hierarchies, promote particular leaders and disseminate ideological positions. They centre on individuals and are efforts in persuading the public to believe in the benevolence of the host. The public sphere created by the newspapers belongs to a different cultural order. The press is part of the project of 'modernisation', an instrument for popular education and 'rational' debate. It is supposed to deliver political scrutiny and inform readers about significant social developments. In sum, the notions that inform the making of the public sphere and the public arena are radically different, even incongruent. However, what appears as separate in a moral economy is entangled in practice. Political staging and media writing are entwined in the field of local reporting. In this chapter I will analyse in detail this process of rearticulating traditions of ritualised public politics in a media context. Politicised media create innovative combinations of cultural traits that experience repositioning.

My interpretation makes use of de Certeau's distinction between 'tactics' and 'strategies' (de Certau 1984: xix). Like Bourdieu, Michel de Certeau addresses the question of how practice is generated. However, he opposes the statist approach taken by Bourdieu and Foucault (1977) and directs attention toward that which escapes structure, which grows and exists beneath it and at its margins. Tactics are cunning combinations of possible practices, an opportunity that is seized upon to create an advantage. It is the act itself, ephemeral and situational, which is not in line with a dominant order. When accumulated, such acts may render structure ineffective. They are the fuzziness of everyday life that carries the potential for transformation.

The following description of the way ambitious personalities utilise the newspaper boom to create personal advantages is an analysis of tactics. Local leaders seize emerging opportunities to 'abduct' the authority of the press and turn it into a resource of power. Multiple copying leads to an accumulation of this tactic and thus creates a force to be reckoned with. The question then arises whether accumulation turns tactics into strategies, models that follow an accepted rationality used in calculated relationships. I will address this question below, when I discuss how academic reasoning – as well as reflections by the elite – creates its own spin and thus is one factor in recasting practice.

Troubled Waters

When Deepa Mehta came to Banaras in 2000 to shoot *Water* – the third film in a trilogy of *Fire, Earth, Water* – she encountered protests from the local Hindu Right, whose members rejected her script about the plight of widows in 1930s Banaras as an insulting misrepresentation of Indian womanhood. Over a period of two months these protests became more and more vociferous, and although there were also vehement supporters of Mehta's project in the end the film crew had to succumb to Hindu nationalist interests and give up the plan to shoot *Water* in Banaras.[9] Between mid January and March 2000, newspapers reported extensively about the developments in Banaras. They painted the image of a city in turmoil. This was in contrast to the experience of direct observers. Protests in Banaras were highly localised and enacted by a clearly defined group. Members of the film crew were particularly upset about the dust a 'few protesters' kicked up and speculated about who could have had an interest in discrediting the film. Journalists also saw anti-*Water* protests as a publicity stunt of a selected few: 'They all meet at Papu's tea stall at Assi Ghat [the place where the shooting was supposed to take place], where they *make* all the news!'[10] Yet, in spite of this cynical interpretation, newspapers continued to report on the events, driven by competition for coverage and demands from the state office. News personnel adopted what Pedelty calls 'pack-reporting' (Pedelty 1995: 31–32), when all reporters stay and move together, ensuring that they get the same news and share perceptions. What Pedelty describes for the particular situation of foreign correspondents during a war is in Bourdieu's (1998) terms a general characteristic of the 'journalistic field'. Market competition drives reporting towards homogenisation (and banality).

I do not intend to replicate these findings but wish instead to investigate the local scene to discuss the reasons for the specific character of press writing. The starting point is the connection local observers make between political ambition and media hype. Digging deeper, I shall discuss the relation between media, civil society and leadership that is created and expressed here. I contend that the controversy served as a platform for the display of leadership, negotiations of images and the communication of moral issues. It flourished at the conjuncture of a particular publishing policy and a culturally moulded style of leadership competition. In order to show the connection I will first uncover the personalised style of much of the reporting about the *Water* affair. I will then summarise some characteristics of performative politics before drawing a comparison and concluding about the links.

For two months the press was full of reports concerning *Water*, with two to five long articles daily in all regional newspapers.[11] Articles narrated the initial efforts of the film crew to start shooting, the destruction of the set by violent protesters, the introduction of security measures, and the ban on shooting imposed by local administrators, who saw law and order as endangered. Reports about the fate of the film project were complemented by comments from actors in civil society. It is not surprising that we encounter almost daily explications by major political leaders. High standing members of the Hindu Right were quick to realise the potential for publicity here and made a ready appearance before the press.

What is of interest to me is the attention given to local speakers – particularly in the Hindi press – whose activities and statements informed many news texts. An article published in the *Hindustan* demonstrates the style of such reporting. The article begins with a summary of the day's events, and in its second part reproduces the public statements of various local speakers, who are introduced with their organisational affiliations and the position they occupy in civil society. In the following I paraphrase the content of this second part of the article.

Binda Pandey (former member of the Legislative Assembly representing the BJP,[12] and an active woman leader) said that the film would insult the culture and women of Kashi[13] and thus should not be made nor allowed to be shown anywhere. Sudhakar Pandey (president of the City Progress Committee and a famous writer) elaborated on the history of widow ashrams in the city and complained that Deepa Mehta wanted to make money by inventing an incident that does not reflect the general situation of widows in 1930s Banaras. Five scholars of Sanskrit and the Vedas threatened to drown themselves in the Ganges if the film was made. Dr Vijay Karn (state assistant secretary of the local section of the Hindu nationalist organisation, Sanskar Bharti) is quoted saying that Mehta will not be given a chance to attack the dignity of the city. Jitendre Kumar (state president of Sanskar Bharti) saw the need to protect Indian culture from the attacks of foreign media. Dr Kalmeshvar Upadhyaya (working president of the city unit of the World Hindu Council[14]) met the district magistrate and demanded that shooting be stopped. In a petition to the authorities, the Kashi Scholar's Association[15] demanded the right to approve the script before shooting be allowed at a sacred place like the *ghat.*[16] The petition was signed by fourteen men of local eminence who are all listed in the article. The text then continues that Suhel Akhtar (national secretary of the National Hero Abdul Hamid Foundation) is said to have commented that a film-maker who made insulting films like *Fire* and *Earth* should not be allowed to continue. A petition to this end was sent by the local sections of two Hindu nationalist organisations: the World Hindu Council and Shiv Sena[17] to the government and the city administration.[18]

This text is remarkable for its redundancy. It adds little substance to a debate about the quality of the film but acts as a guideline to who contested the shooting. It gives the protest a face. Such a list of participants could be expected to be of interest particularly to residents of Banaras, who are eager to keep track of (upcoming) leaders. The article also directly meets the desire of local personalities to spread word of their activities, toward which (vernacular) newspapers appeared to be sympathetic. Throughout the two months the list of speakers quoted in the newspapers continued to grow rapidly. Through innumerable quotes, journalists duplicated what was communicated to them in a flood of press notes, a proliferating number of (miniature) press conferences, small protest marches and suicide threats. The English-language press ignored most of these local voices, following general policy guidelines to focus on major events and statements by decision-makers.[19] In contrast, Hindi journalists were pushed to publish about these grassroots activities. A visit to the local office of the Hindu newspaper *Dainik Jagaran* was revealing. During the controversy all eleven reporters – who normally have different beats – worked on the same story, responding to a flood of *Water*-related events and announcements. *Dainik Jagaran* here followed what has become a guiding principle in much vernacular news writing today: to provide a ready outlet to as many local voices as possible.

The development of this imperative is tied to changes in the newspaper market of post-liberalisation India (Jeffrey 2000). Rapid economic growth, the ready availability of advertisements, increasing literacy rates and growing political awareness stimulated continuous swift growth of the newspaper market in India that took off in the mid-1980s. Hindi newspapers have done well in terms of circulation figures, which today by far outnumber those of English-language publications (Jeffrey 1993, 2000).[20] In a profitable but also increasingly competitive news market, vernacular papers have exploited their close association with the locality and have expanded local reporting in an unprecedented way. The guiding principle is that people want to read about their immediate environment and about themselves in the newspaper (Ninan 2007).

In order to fill the increasing number of local pages with stories of interest to readers, Hindi newspapers have adopted what I have called an 'open-door policy' (Rao 2010a, b). Editorial teams working for the local pages are open to the influx of concerns formulated by citizens of all strata. They reach the newspaper through three channels of communication. Local people have mastered the skill of writing press releases, which Hindu newspapers tend to accept with very little editing. There is an extensive network of informants who contribute articles from all localities and major communities. Finally, a particular writing style is adopted that acknowledges individuals' contributions through long lists of participants and the quoting of many opinions. Urban dwellers use these channels extensively to launch complaints, share grievances, express opinions, inform about their 'social work', give identity to a local community and compete for eminence (Rao 2010a, b).

Reporting on the *Water* story opened a window to this policy. The emerging controversy turned into a media event also because countless people came forward to offer their comments and invest in publicity. By giving credential to all these voices the Hindi press gives voice to public opinion. It does not mediate a balanced debate but rather confronts the reader with an overkill of voices, set within the dichotomous framework of the 'protection of culture' versus 'artistic freedom'. There are few elaborate statements designed to gain an intellectual edge, but there are many populist expressions pursuing public attention, eminence and status. The movement gained speed also because more and more activists pushed their voices into the media, using the event as a stepping stone for status and recognition through visibility.

The connection between visibility, leadership ambition and media policy is well illustrated by the activities of Kaushal Kishor Mishra, one of the figures who emerged as a leader during the controversy. Mishra entered the conflict relatively late, weeks after the local Hindu nationalist organisations had made their opening moves. He remembers that his interest in the protest was stimulated when he got hold of a copy of the script and suddenly saw a possibility to 'prove' the anti-Hindu bias of the film. From this moment on, he claims, the attitude of the press changed and now turned against the film. When he realised the potential for a successful fight, Mishra grabbed the opportunity, founded the Organization for the Defence of the Culture of Kashi (KSRSS, Kashi Sanskriti Raksha Sangharsh Samiti) and elevated it to the status of a coordinator and leader of the protest activities. He created and cultivated this image through investment in publicity, sending daily press releases and organising made-for-media events. His efforts bore fruit. During the peak of the movement the KSRSS and Mishra were mentioned in several newspapers every day for ten days. Such a boost in popularity, Mishra hoped, would turn him into an obvious candidate for the BJP during the next state election.[21]

Charismatic Leadership: Fusing Performative Politics and Media Discourse

Mishra's appreciation of the importance of newspapers in disseminating a name and creating fame is part of an approach that recreates the typical 'leader centeredness' of Indian politics. Charismatic leadership is at the heart of the Indian political system, in which electoral success is tied to the ability of individuals to stand out through a popular image and a network of relations (Brass 1983, 1998; Jaffrelot 2003). A leader typically builds a following by patronising a well-defined social group – caste, ethnicity, class – or set of social groups – other backward classes, scheduled castes, Muslims. They trade patronage and favours for the loyalty of followers who in turn participate in creating a benevolent public image of them. The political field consists of an elaborate hierarchy of leaders, with national politicians depending on local leaders for sustaining their power through communication with the grassroots. Local leaders are indispensable for the circulation of a positive image, the mobilisation of votes, the initiation of public protests as well as the communication of political ideologies and parliamentary decisions. Supporting those in power, local leaders can negotiate advantages for themselves and their clients, which in turn increases their own fame and may help them to climb further up the ladder of political power (Brass 1965, 1998; Price 1989; Dickey 1993b; Mines 1996; Eckert 2003).

The making of leaders is closely tied to public arenas.[22] Official functions, rituals and festivals offer a plethora of occasions for the public display of status, social engagement and eminence by selected individuals. The connection between political power and performative politics reaches across several historical periods (Price 1989). There is ethnohistorical evidence for the role of temple rituals for royal authority (Eschmann, Kulke and Tripathi 1978; Stein 1978; Dirks 1987) while in colonial society festivals bore a whole new set of leaders engaged in the independence movement (Cashman 1970; Freitag 1989). Today, meanwhile, party leaders invoke deities, undertake pilgrimages, attend temple festivals or organise devotional events as part of their (electoral) campaigns (Davis 1996; Kaur 2003; Rao 2003; Schnepel 2006). The central element of all these events is the creation of visibility. Organisers, sponsors and special guests crowd the stage to perform rituals, give speeches, be thanked and garlanded. Names of eminent persons are disseminated through announcements, pamphlets and banners. The order of appearance and the role of individuals in the performances communicate information about their status, their networks and position in social and political hierarchies.

While this display of leadership is regularly part of religious celebrations, there are also secular occasions for the ritualised production of status – like Ambedkar's or Gandhi's birthday, laying the foundations of new buildings, anniversaries of public institutions, annual functions at schools or universities, and the opening of conferences and fairs. Films and film clubs also offer political opportunities. From the 1960s onwards a set of political leaders in South India have been recruited from the film industry (Hardgrave and Neidhart 1975; Dickey 1993b; Agnihotri 1998). The ascent of actors and actresses to power is tied to the activity of fan clubs, widely active in the urban landscape. Fan clubs are founded mostly by lower-class males, who organise around a movie star to celebrate them, watch their films and organise social activities in their name. The self-declared reason for such activity is the desire to participate in social advancement and thus add to the fame and positive image of the hero. However, engaging in 'altruistic' social activities, young men also create a platform for expressing social distinction. Activists stand out in the crowd and build in the shadow of their star their own fame and reputation. Such fan activity blurs the borders between media reception and political activism, which is fully transcended when fan clubs are recruited as part of the cadre of an actor-turned-politician (Dickey 1993a, 1993b, 2001).

The intimate connection between image making and political ascent as a pertinent form of Indian political leadership has given mass media a strong role in the design of political careers. What some big stars practice at the top end of the political hierarchy is replicated by 'small people' at the local level since the opening up of the news media for the influx of local news. At this level ambitious personalities create an image and spread their fame not through the embodiment of archetypical characters in fictional genres but through continuous investment in the making of a heroic real life image, disseminated through the press and stabilised through personalised networks.

The connection is very clear in Mishra's case. His political ambitions energise him to continuously invest in a strong position as institutional big man in a cosmos of organisations (Mines 1996). His social engagement connects him to the university elite of the region, the main religious authorities in Banaras, the cadre organisations of the Hindu Right and its parliamentary wing. Ideologically he acts as a fighter for the preservation of a 'pure' Hindu culture in an emerging 'clash of civilisations' – explicitly referring to Huntington's (1998) book. Mishra regularly speaks up as a representative of these organisations in the press and thus continuously floats his name in the public sphere.[23] Struggling to build up an image as an efficient leader, Mishra joins in a competition that is acted out not only in the public arena but more and more in the media. This was obvious in the case of the *Water* controversy where the hectic media activity was at odds with the rather limited commotion in the public arena. While direct observers dismissed the event as media hype, local leaders purposefully directed their activity more at the press than the observing public, thereby acknowledging the influence of the press and appropriating it for their own purposes.

The *Water* controversy is not an isolated event but is part of a new form of local reporting that developed following increased competition in the local news market (Rao 2010a; b). Evidence of this new style of personalised reporting at the local level is also provided by Rajagopal (2001), who analyses the press coverage of the Hindu nationalist campaign for the making of a Ram Temple at the mythical birthplace of the god Ram. The movement was directed against the Babri Mosque, situated at the site claimed by Hindu fundamentalists and which was illegally destroyed by fanatics in 1991. This violent destruction led to pogroms against Muslims and widespread religious riots. Rajagopal (ibid.: 151–211) notes that the Hindi press – unlike the English-language press – actively engaged with the movement, bringing it close to the people and making it intelligible through extensive reporting from the grassroots. He writes that reporting in Hindi newspapers was 'subjective' (ibid.:167), by which he also means involved extensive quoting of statements from leaders and the printing of direct propaganda. Rajagopal explains this style of reporting with reference to the greater familiarity of Hindi journalists with the symbols of the movement, sympathy for the movement and the economic interests of proprietors. My analysis of production provides another angle. The open-door policy promotes the newspaper as a place for leadership competition. City reporters are thankful for ready-made statements, a sentiment that resonates with ambitious personalities who have learned how to hit the headlines.

The mutual entanglement of local news-making practices with public leadership competition carries performative politics into the written domain. A cultural technique developed in the public arena appears in new attire as news. Innumerable people communicate through news by appropriating the cultural capital of the press in order to become recognisable individuals in the public domain. The attractiveness of the news medium is not only a corollary of its wide circulation but a result of its function as an authorising institution. Expected to communicate accurately about issues of social importance and to act as political watchdogs, newspapers lend credibility to statements disseminated through their pages. This authorising function is comparable to that of other institutions that carry weight, for example in the religious domain. Religious rituals, the institutions connected to them and the beliefs invested in them lend authority to those who make a special appearance here (Appadurai and Breckenridge 1976). Invested with the notion of the fourth estate, the written word of the newspaper carries weight. News writing makes things real and creates the 'facts' of social life. Activated by the desire to exploit the media for creating fame, local leaders mimic the activities of PR institutions, spin doctors and corporate advertisement.[24] By doing so, they create the public sphere as a practice which is quite distinct from the idealised notion of the press as an organ for 'rational' deliberation.

The Interpretation of Media Practice

Habermas's study of the transformation of the public sphere in Europe has profoundly influenced the way media generated publics are conceptualised. Most prominent is his notion of the bourgeois public sphere – located between the thirteenth and nineteenth centuries. He describes the bourgeois public sphere as a debate maintained by private people who criticise and control political power through rational argument. Newspapers facilitated this exchange by articulating and circulating opinions within a larger community, thus functioning as 'mediators' and 'intensifiers' of public concerns (Habermas 1992: 285; 2001: 105). While Habermas's description of the bourgeois public sphere as historical condition has been variously criticised,[25] it continues to invigorate a shared ideal. The notion of the press as an instrument for interest-free deliberations that control state power is a normative standard in contemporary democracies. It is inscribed in the institutional set-up of modern states, has pride of place in the educational material for new media elites, and is part of a standard rhetoric in the public sphere itself (e.g., Gripsrund 1999; Johnson 2006). This is also true for India, where the concept of the press as a fourth estate is routinely invoked by journalists as a justification and guideline for their work (e.g., Padhy 1994; Peterson 1996).

A quite different public forum is created through leader-centred performances in the public arena. Public performances are not idealised as providing 'objective' information or critical evaluation. They are the doing of politics. They introduce and create powerful individuals and highlight their position within political hierarchies. As such they communicate valuable information, making power networks transparent to the urban public while crafting them. However, what is constructed as distinct in a moral economy is entangled in practice. News writing, as I have shown in this chapter, can become a function of performative politics. Leaders at times substitute activity in the public arena for the production of news texts (press releases that become news texts). These initiate public recognition, advertise individual's activities and allow conclusions about social networks. Where performative politics is retained, it is proliferated through mass media. Able organisers ensure that their performances catch the attention of the press along with that of the viewing public. Furthermore, organisers actively influence public memory of performances by issuing elaborate press releases which express the importance of the event, interpret its messages and list organisers and special guests. The sheer quantity of such news items as well as the fact that press releases are today often very well written, tempts journalists to print them without further research. News articles are then a direct extension of self-presentation in public performances.

This interpretation reverses an argument made by Ramindar Kaur (2001, 2003) in her study of the Ganapati festival in Mumbai, which constitutes another instance of the intersection between public sphere and public arena. In the 1980s newspapers in Mumbai began to sponsor competitions between different temporary shrines – dedicated to the Hindu god Ganesha – set up during the festival. Prizes were given for decoration, artistic style, educational message, social engagement of committee members, and cleanliness and discipline at the shrines. As a corollary of these competitions, social messages and patriotic themes became hugely popular. More and more Ganesha shrines commented on ongoing political events and thus turned into a medium for the negotiation of national values. Kaur concludes that these changes inserted rational debate – associated with the public sphere – into the festival. The Ganapati festival began to connect the political debate of the literate – in the newspaper – with rationalisations in the religious domain, consumed by the masses. Kaur calls this sector in which public sphere and public arena overlap the 'public field' (Kaur 2001: 25).

My conclusions about the intersection between the public sphere and public arena are quite different. I conceive of a cacophony of voices that enter the news medium through an extension of performative politics, rather than the promotion of 'rational' debate by the news media outside its own domain. However, I agree with Kaur about the need to comprehend practices as simultaneously situated in different social contexts. I worked with an analytical separation between the public sphere and public performances that was based on two criteria: a difference in medium (public performance versus media text) and a cultural imaginary ('objective' press versus 'subjective' public performances). It is this analytical separation that allows for the identification of a border violation. However, arguing from the position of practice this separation is artificial. Ambitious individuals use various registers and a range of expressive traditions to maximise outcome. It is only against an ideal construction that legitimises self-promotion in public performances and delegitimises it in the press that the same act appears as two. And it is only then that an argument can be made about performative traditions being carried over into the domain of news-making.

This act of academic classification is not without consequences. Demystifying the press as an organ for the 'mere' expression of leadership competition provides fodder to those who lament the loss of quality in contemporary journalism. It furthermore strengthens the image of the vernacular press as being of low quality, promoting fundamentalism and spreading the excitable speech of ego-centred leaders.[26] Such theories lend clarity to an intricate practice. They reduce the complexity of a cultural motion by exclusively emphasising a particular strategic moment as part of a combination of tactics.

In this chapter I have described tactical operations of aspiring local leaders working from outside established institutions, using all possible public platforms to produce recognition and ascend institutionalised positions. These activities ignore an ideological distinction between different public domains. Local leaders seized an opportunity as it arose to produce cunning combinations of different techniques of recognition. Thereby they subverted the state (the national government approved the shooting of *Water* twice but could not or would not ensure implementation) and an idea of the press as an organ for 'objective' reporting. Using the term 'subversion' I obviously do not intend to justify these activities or claim that they are benevolent; rather, I wish to unravel the logic of practice that operates from the margins.

The tactics used by local individuals to spread their fame coincides with the long-term strategy of the newspapers to expand their local market. De Certeau defines strategy as 'the calculus of force-relationships which becomes possible when a subject of will and power … can be isolated from an "environment." A strategy assumes a place that can be circumscribed as *proper* and thus serve as a basis for generating relations with an exterior distinct from it' (de Certeau 1984: xix).

Hindu nationalism can be described as such an agent. It is a highly visible institutionalised force with a well-developed ideology. Its representatives act to replace a secular political order with a culturalist model of the state (Jaffrelot 1996; Ludden 1996). Protesters of the anti-*Water* front utilised this framework. Desiring fame and recognition (mixed possibly with conviction), they expressed their views in the rhetoric of a recognised ideology. They rarely spoke as individuals but as representatives of identifiable organisations within civil society, like the World Hindu Council, Shiv Sena or the BJP. These institutions acted as authorising and legitimising contexts, just like the press and the adoption of ritualised forms of protest. In this sense the aspiring leaders operated not from the margins but re-enacted institutions that are at the heart of modern India. It is this dimension that is highlighted by observers who warn against ideological closure that follows the Hinduisation of Indian society, towards which news reporting contributes (Nanda 2003).

In an analysis of practice, the ideological struggle between Hindu nationalism and secularism appears as only one dimension that feeds reporting. There is also ceremonial politics exploited in an economy of (local) eminence that meets the desire of proprietors to offer the newspaper as a medium of local people to local people. The conjuncture of these different motions disturbs order by reassembling traditions in unprecedented ways. This movement is not captured sufficiently by fixing it in a hierarchy of ordering practices. News writing does not anchor a political practice that celebrates the leader, or the other way round. Negotiations between media strategies and local desires for recognition fuel an open-ended process of social change. The analysis of practice generates an appreciation for the context that pushes cultural change, identifies models that inform the process and analyses dynamics that structure the outcome.

This analysis of practice blurs the boundaries between social categories like politics and media as well as producers and consumers of newspapers. Agents belonging to various idealised fields meet in a shared arena, reshuffling the way elements in civil society relate to each other. An analysis of 'border crossings' questions the clarity produced in structuralist accounts of practices in which we find demarcated fields (Bourdieu) or sets of ordered practices (Couldry). The doing of politics and the writing of news subvert the neat order of analytical classification. It brings into view the various layers of cultural activities that together contribute towards forging a 'new' order that relies heavily on inherited structures and concepts, but is yet not determined by them. The task of practice analysis is to come to terms with this process of recursive recombination and its relevance for the remaking of a culture in flux. Praxis analysis here is not the identification of regulated and demarcated universes but an investigation into the process of replaying cultural elements in new contexts. It is an analysis of restructuration as an ongoing process of creating meaningful contexts for acting and knowing within a cultural universe.

Notes

1. I am referencing here specifically cultural notions of the press as an organ for the dissemination of social 'facts' and 'rational' debate.
2. The analysis is based on material collected during ten months of fieldwork in Lucknow and other parts of Uttar Pradesh, undertaken during the years 1999, 2000 and 2002. Conclusions about news-making practices are based on my fieldwork in the following four news companies: the English-language newspapers the *Hindustan Times* and *Times of India*, and the Hindi language newspapers *Dainik Jagaran* and *Hindustan*.
3. See also Hobart (this volume).
4. Bourdieu's theory of field includes a critique of the Marxist notion of class. He argues that a theory that explains class merely through economic factors is too narrow. In turn, he suggests that class needs to be understood as a complex set of ideas and practices which produces and reproduces a particular habitus that serves as the criteria of inclusion and exclusion. Classes exist in competition and also use – besides political and economic power – cultural capital and habitus as a justification for their dominance (Bourdieu 1984, 1995).
5. For useful summaries, see Jenks (1993) and Kuper (1999).
6. For an excellent summary of performance theories in social sciences, see Carlson (2004).
7. Bourdieu's social activism though speaks a different language, as Calhoun (1993) points out. His scholarly and political engagement was driven by the belief that reflection bears the potential for change.
8. See also Kaur (2001).
9. Deepa Mehta finally produced the film in 2004, shooting it in Sri Lanka without any publicity; it opened the Toronto film festival in 2005. See: http://www.rediff.com/movies/2005/sep/02ajp1.htm. Retrieved 5 September 2005.
10. *Hindustan Times*, 8 March 2000.
11. The following summary of news discourse is based on the coverage in the Lucknow editions of the *Hindustan Times, Times of India, Hindustan, Dainik Jagaran* as well as *Pioneer* (English) and *Amar Ujala* (Hindi) between 30 January and 9 February 2000.
12. Bhartiya Janta Party (Indian People's Party) acts as the parliamentary wing of the Hindu nationalist movement.
13. Kashi is another, more traditional, name for Banaras. It carries a religious connotation and refers to Banaras as an abode of the god Shiva and a place for his worship.

14. Vishva Hindu Parishad (VHP) was founded in 1964. The organisation is active across the globe and has established a worldwide net of people supporting Hindu nationalist ideals.
15. Kashi Vidwat Parishad.
16. The *ghats* are stairs leading down to the Ganges River. They are – among other things – used for religious rituals and are considered part of the sacred territory which is marked by the holy river.
17. Shiv Sena promotes aggressive assertions of Hindu nationalist ideals within and outside parliament. It was founded and is most successful in Mumbai but has sister organisations in many places in North India.
18. *Hindustan*, 31 January 2000.
19. When I visited the local office of the English-language paper the *Hindustan Times* the correspondent pointed at a huge pile of press notes. With a dismissive tone in his voice he commented: 'It is a fashion to give press notes of every small event. I ignore most of them!' (8 March 2000).
20. The year 1979 is one watershed in the Indian newspaper business. It marks the end of direct censorship imposed by Indira Gandhi on the press for nineteen months. Subsequently, newspaper sales grew steadily, which is also attributed to the thirst of people for critical political information after the suppressive years of emergency.
21. Source: interview with Mishra, 8 March 2000. Today Mishra is vice-president of the Uttar Pradesh BJP (Intellectual Cell) and continues to create arguments about the need to protect Hindu culture in the press.
22. Sandria Freitag (1989) introduces the term 'public arenas' in her study of colonial India to capture the character of performative politics acted out in public places. An increasing number of public political performances promoted the development of an alternative realm of politics outside the colonial state during the late nineteenth and early twentieth century. Public arenas became the rallying ground for the independence movement.
23. A recent publicity stunt was a staged fight for the right of state employees (here: university teachers) to join the Hindu nationalist cadre organisation RSS. See: http://www.secularindia.com/news/2006/11/30SANGH %20LINK.htm or http://news.oneindia.in/2006/11/30/bjp-mulls-national-movement-on-bhu-rss-issue-1164961134.html. Retrieved 15 July 2007.
24. I do not wish to imply that there are no critical reading practices. In fact I found that many readers were appalled by leaders' practices of self-promotion through the press and made assumptions about the political leaning of various newspapers (on reading practices in India, see Peterson this volume). Yet people continue to believe in the importance of the newspaper as social organ. In spite of the fact that actual newspapers fail to live up to expectations, readers hold on to the view that the press is a significant organ for public debate and an essential part of democracy. Pushing their voice into the newspaper, leaders hope to cash in on the social capital the newspaper has as authorised medium.

25. Habermas has been criticised for overstating the difference between the various forms of the public sphere, as well as for his clear-cut distinction between the state and civil society. Objections have also been raised concerning his concept of rational debate, his idea of media-manipulated masses and his singular emphasis on the role of the media that ignores other forms of social communication like gatherings, festivals, rituals and so on (see, e.g., Dahlgren and Sparks 1991: 5–6; Hartley 1996; Jeffrey 2000: 11–19; Kaur 2001: 25–26).
26. For the description of such positions, see Stahlberg (2002) and Peterson (this volume).

References

Abu-Ludghod, L. 1995. 'The Objects of Soap Opera: Egyptian Television and the Cultural Politics of Modernity', in D. Miller (ed.) *Worlds Apart*. London: Routledge, pp.190–210.

Agnihotri, R.A. 1998. *Film Stars in Indian Politics*. Delhi: Commonwealth Publisher.

Appadurai, A. and C.A. Breckenridge. 1976. 'The South Indian Temple: Authority, Honour and Redistribution', *Contribution to Indian Sociology* 10: 187–211.

Austin, J.L. 1990[1962]. *How to Do Things with Words*. Oxford: Oxford University Press.

Bailey, F.G. 1996. 'Cultural Performances, Authenticity and Second Nature', in D. Parkin, L. Caplan and H. Fisher (eds), *The Politics of Cultural Performance*. Oxford: Berghahn, pp.1–17.

Bird, S.E. 2003. *The Audience in Everyday Life: Living in a Media World*. London: Routledge.

Bourdieu, P. 1977. *Outline of a Theory of Practice*. Cambridge: Cambridge University Press.

────── 1984. *Distinction: A Social Critique of the Judgment of Taste*. Cambridge, MA: Harvard University Press.

────── 1987. *Sozialer Sinn*. Frankfurt: Suhrkamp.

────── 1992. *The Rules of Art: Genesis and Structure of the Literary Field*. Cambridge: Polity Press.

────── 1995. *Sozialer Raum und 'Klassen' und Leçon sur la leçon*. Frankfurt: Suhrkamp.

────── 1998. *On Television and Journalism*. London: Pluto.

Brass, P.R. 1965. *Factional Politics in an Indian State: The Congress Party in Uttar Pradesh*. Berkeley: University of California Press.

────── 1983. *Caste, Faction and Party in Indian Politics*. Delhi: Chanakya Publications.

────── 1998. *Theft of an Idol: Text and Context in the Representation of Collective Violence*. Calcutta: Seagull.

Brosius, C. and M. Butcher (eds). 1999. *Image Journeys: Audio-Visual Media and Cultural Change in India.* Delhi: Sage.

Butler, J. 1993. *Bodies that Matter: On the Discursive Limits of 'Sex'.* New York: Routledge.

Calhoun, C. 1993. 'Habitus, Field, and Capital: The Question of Historical Specificity', C. Calhoun, E. LiPuma and M. Potone (eds), *Bourdieu: Critical Perspectives.* Chicago: University of Chicago Press, pp.61–88.

Carlson, M. 2004[1996]. *Performance: A Critical Introduction.* London: Routledge.

Cashman, R. 1970. 'The Political Recruitment of God Ganapati', *Indian Economic and Social History* 7: 347–73.

Dahlgren, P. and C. Sparks (eds). 1991. *Communication and Citizenship: Journalism and the Public Sphere in the New Media Age.* London: Routledge.

Davis, R.H. 1996. 'The Iconography of Rama's Chariot', in D. Ludden (ed.), *Making India Hindu.* Delhi: Oxford University Press, pp.27–54.

De Certeau, M. 1984. *The Practice of Everyday Life.* Berkeley: University of California Press.

Derrida, J. 1978. 'Structure, Sign, and Play in the Discourse of the Human Science', in *Writing and Difference.* Chicago: University of Chicago Press, pp.278–94.

Dickey, S. 1993a. *Cinema and the Urban Poor in South India.* Cambridge: Cambridge University Press.

——— 1993b. 'The Politics of Adulation: Cinema and the Production of Politicians in South India', *Journal of Asian Studies* 52(2): 340–72.

——— 2001. 'Opposing Faces: Film Star Fan Clubs and the Construction of Class Identities in South India', in R. Dwyer and C. Pinney (eds), *Pleasure and the Nation.* Delhi: Oxford University Press, pp.212–46.

Dirks, N. 1987. *The Hollow Crown: Ethnohistory of an Indian Kingdom.* Cambridge: Cambridge University Press.

Eckert, J. 2003. *The Charisma of Direct Action: Power, Politics, and the Shiv Sena.* Delhi: Oxford University Press.

Ericson, R.V., P.M. Baranek and J.B.C. Chan. 1989. *Negotiating Control: A Study of News Sources.* Toronto. University of Toronto Press.

Eschmann, A., H. Kulke and G.C. Tripathi (eds). 1978. *The Cult of Jagannath and the Regional Tradition of Orissa.* Delhi: Manohar.

Foucault, M. 1977. *Discipline and Punish: The Birth of the Prison.* London: Allen Lane.

Freitag, S.B. 1989. *Collective Action and Community: Public Areas and the Emergence of Communalism in North India.* Berkeley: University of California Press.

Ginsburg, F.D., L. Abu-Ludghod and B. Larkin (eds). 2002. *Media Worlds. Anthropology on New Terrain.* Berkeley: University of California Press.

Gripsrund, J. 1999. *Understanding Media Culture.* London: Arnold.

Habermas, J. 1992. *The Structural Transformation of the Public Sphere: An Enquiry into a Category of Bourgeois Society.* Cambridge: Cambridge University Press.

——— 2001. 'The Public Sphere: An Encyclopaedia Article', in M.G. Durham and D.M. Keller (eds), *Media and Cultural Studies Keywords.* Oxford: Blackwell, pp.102–7.

Handelman, D. 1998. *Models and Mirrors: Towards an Anthropology of Public Events.* Oxford: Berghahn.

Hansen, T.B. 2001. *Urban Violence in India: Identity Politics, 'Mumbai', and the Postcolonial City.* Delhi: Permanent Black.

Hardgrave, R.L.J. and A.C. Neidhart. 1975. 'Films and Political Consciousness in Tamil Nadu', *Economic and Political Weekly* 101(2): 27–35.

Hartley, J. 1996. *Popular Reality: Journalism, Modernity, Popular Culture.* London: Arnold.

Huntington, S.P. 1998. *The Clash of Civilizations and the Remaking of World Order.* London: Touchstone.

Jaffrelot, C. 1996. *The Hindu Nationalist Movement and Indian Politics, 1925 to the 1990s: Strategies of Identity-building, Implantation and Mobilisation.* Delhi: Viking.

——— 1998. 'The Politics of Processions and Hindu–Muslim Riots', in A. Basu and A. Kohli (eds), *Community Conflicts and the State in India.* Delhi: Oxford University Press, pp.58–92.

——— 2003. *India's Silent Revolution. The Rise of the Lower Castes in Indian Politics.* Delhi: Permanent Black.

Jeffrey, R. 1993. 'Indian-language Newspapers and Why They Grow', *Economic and Political Weekly* 28(38): 2004–11.

——— 2000. *India's Newspaper Revolution: Capitalism, Politics and the Indian Language Press, 1977–1999.* Delhi: Oxford University Press.

Jenks, C. 1993. *Culture.* London: Routledge.

Johnson, P. 2006. *Habermas. Rescuing the Public Sphere.* London: Routledge.

Kaur, R. 2001. 'Rethinking the Public Sphere: The Ganpati Festival and Media Competitions in Mumbai', *South Asia Research* 21(1): 23–50.

——— 2003. *Performative Politics and the Cultures of Hinduism: Public Uses of Religion in Western India.* Delhi: Permanent Black.

Köpping, K.-P. and U. Rao (eds). 2000. *Im Rausch des Rituals: Gestaltung und Transformation der Wirklichkeit in körperlicher Performanz.* Münster. Lit.

Kuper, A. 1999. *Culture: The Anthropologists' Account.* Cambridge, MA: Harvard University Press.

Ludden, D. (ed.) 1996. *Making India Hindu: Religion, Community, and the Politics of Democracy in India.* Delhi: Oxford University Press.

Mazzarella, W. 2003. *Shoveling Smoke: Advertising and Globalization in Contemporary India.* Durham, NC: Duke University Press.

Mines, M. 1996. *Public Faces, Private Voices: Community and Individuality in South India.* Delhi: Oxford University Press.

Nanda, M. 2003. *Prophets Facing Backward: Postmodern Critiques of Science and Hindu Nationalism in India.* New Brunswick, NJ: Rutgers University Press.

Ninan, S. 2007. *Headlines from the Heartland.* Delhi: Sage.

Padhy, K.S. 1994. *The Muzzled Press: Introspect and Retrospect.* Delhi: Kanishka.

Pedelty, M. 1995. *War Stories: The Culture of Foreign Correspondents.* New York: Routledge.

Peterson, M.A. 1996. 'Writing the Indian Story: Press, Politics and Symbolic Power in India', Ph.D. thesis. Providence: Brown University.

Price, P.G. 1989. 'Kingly Models in Indian Political Behavior', *Asian Survey* 296: 559–72.

Rajagopal, A. 2001. *Politics after Television: Hindu Nationalism and the Changing of Indian Public*. Cambridge: Cambridge University Press.

Rao, U. 2003. *Negotiating the Divine: Temple Religion and Temple Politics in Contemporary Urban India*. Delhi: Manohar.

——— 2010a. *News as Cultures: Journalistic Practices and the Remaking of Leadership Traditions in India*. Oxford: Berghahn.

——— 2010b. 'Empowerment through Local News-making: Studying the Media–Public Interface in India', in E. Bird (ed.), *Anthropology of News and Journalism*. Indiana: Indiana University Press, pp.100–15.

Sahlins, M. 1987. *Islands of History*. London: Tavistock.

Schnepel, B. 2006. 'Jagannath: Eine ostindische Gottheit im Spannungsfeld politisch-ritueller Machtkämpfe', in U. Rao (ed.), *Kulturelle VerWandlungen. Die Gestaltung sozialer Welten in der Performanz*. Frankfurt: Peter Lang, pp.269–84.

Stahlberg, P. 2002. *Lucknow Daily: How a Hindi Newspaper Constructs Society*. Stockholm: Almqvist and Wiksell.

Stein, B. (ed.) 1978. *South Indian Temples: An Analytical Reconsideration*. Delhi: Vikas.

PART III

Media Practices in Context

Communication, Cognition and Usage: Epistemological Considerations of Media Practices and Processes

Guido Ipsen

Media as Semiotic Practices and Processes

This chapter focuses on media practices and processes as two aspects of the same sphere, namely the domain that encompasses human cognition and communication by making use of technical means. In doing so, I concentrate on epistemological questions concerning the meaning of media. How can semiotics, as a discipline concerned with the processes of cognizing and interpreting signs (Nöth 2000), contribute to the questions raised by Couldry (this volume) about media practice as a new research paradigm? Semiotic theory, as understood in its pragmatist tradition on which I shall focus here,[1] is a fundamental approach to studying the 'formation of belief', as formulated by Charles Sanders Peirce (CP 5.538).[2] In using the term 'formation', Peirce already presupposes that belief is not only the result of some process that precedes our here and now. Neither does he see belief as some a priori category to be reconstructed in the mind. Rather, belief is immersed in a continuous phase of becoming. Its life cycle never ends, just as the mind is continuously subjected to cognition. Peirce calls this process 'semiosis'; that is, the process in which signs change and emerge, and the highest order of signs – symbols – come into existence:

> Symbols grow. They come into being by development out of other signs, particularly from icons, or from mixed signs partaking of the nature of icons and symbols. We think only in signs. These mental signs are of mixed nature; the symbol-parts of them are called concepts. If a man makes a new symbol, it is by thoughts involving concepts. So it is only out

of symbols that a new symbol can grow. Omne symbolum de symbolo. A symbol, once in being, spreads among the peoples. In use and in experience, its meaning grows. Such words as force, law, wealth, marriage, bear for us very different meanings from those they bore to our barbarous ancestors. The symbol may, with Emerson's sphynx, say to man, 'Of thine eye I am eyebeam'. (CP 2.302)

The famous sphinx, mocking her human counterpart, refers to her mystery as the very product of the human mind – the riddle is in the mind of the beholder. So too are symbols: they are the product of the mind. Symbols change as do the minds that produce them. This notion transcends Peircean semiotics and has recently been formulated anew by the Finnish semiotician Eero Tarasti in his theory of 'existential semiotics', in which he defines signs as being 'in the flux of becoming' (Tarasti 2000: 7). We may perceive 'media' as carriers of symbols. The agent of symbol generation and change is the human mind.

I suggest that the idea of signs being involved in this phase, or flux, of becoming may contribute to the general issue of this volume as an epistemological background that is provided by semiotics as a bridging discipline par excellence, in that it encompasses media studies, sociology and philosophy. A flux is a concept of process, and as we will see in the discussion of semiotic theory the process of sign formation is initiated and maintained by social exchange and practice. Hence the usability of the semiotic paradigm for our present discourse on media practice.

The process of semiosis covers all aspects of sensation, cognition and communication. Pragmatist semiotics investigates every part of this process in which signs are perceived, processed and passed on to other sign users. It may seem awkward to turn to these basic concepts – concerned with the workings of the human mind and the exchange of meaning between diverse minds – when beginning a chapter on media, which have for the most part been defined as means quite detached from the human body, let alone the brain as the seat of mind. If scholars explore media, they tend to focus on technology. Those perceptions brought to media users via technology are declared the 'signs' transported or processed by the media in superficial assessment of what a sign and a sign carrier is. Such is sometimes even a viewpoint taken by applied semioticians who choose individual media such as TV, radio, newspapers or stamps as their research focus.[3]

Semiotics has been quite successful in its endeavours to explore artefacts called 'media'.[4] In this context, media artefacts are difficult to define. Semiotics considers a stamp a medium as it does computers. Still, both differ considerably. Whereas the first is a 'passive' artefact which 'changes' only in respect of its interpretation – similar to books, paintings, statues, monuments, architecture and so on[5] – the computer is an 'active' medium that changes as a result of being used. Still, the computer in itself does not represent much: it depends on processing data in order to represent (Winograd and Flores 1986: 86–87). A computer mediates only whatever it is given to store or process.

In creating this vagueness in subject matter, media semiotics generates a problem already apparent in traditional media studies, namely the creation of the myth that technological entities called media are agents creating, or carrying, meaning independently of the involvement of human actors. Yet, as Peirce reminds us, 'nothing is a sign unless it is interpreted as a sign' (CP 2.308),[6] by which he refers to the general essence of meaning, namely that it is existent in the mind only.

If we follow the paradigm of media studies, though, whatever is a media process is necessarily a process guided by the delimitations of technology. Whatever is a media practice then is an activity defined by the opportunities provided by technology instead of mind. However, there are two imperative reasons to abandon this paradigm. The first reason is that meaning is not being generated within or by technology. Whatever the capabilities of a machine, semiotically speaking it will never generate meaning autonomously in the way that the human mind does. Unless we believe that human intellectual abilities have been implanted by some higher entity – a stance I shall not be adopting here – the human intellect is the result of an evolutionary process in which our species adapted to the necessities provided by its *Umwelt*, or exterior lifeworld (von Uexküll and Kriszat 1970: 6–14).[7] Machines, however, are products of the human intellect and as such are at best capable of mimicking human thought. This proposition, as trivial as it may seem, is fundamental to my present argument. Media as such may serve to store, transport or in any other possible way convey semiotic units that may serve to generate meaning. However, meaning as such cannot be found in the media; that is, semiotic units within the media are but items that may in the end be represented as signs in the mind. Meaning is hence exclusively rooted in the minds of humans. Humans naturally engage themselves in media processes and practices, but these should be viewed as being determined by cognitive experience not vice versa. Cognitive experience is generated in personal and social activities of many kinds. This semiotic turn in media studies which I suggest here in the wake of Couldry's proposal denies a series of fundamentals – one might call them myths – that have been adopted as true in media studies, starting from the writings of McLuhan (1967), who put media technology at the very core of what he understood as the 'message' until the arrival of hype about computer technology in the 1990s, when text networks called hypertexts[8] were imagined to represent actual processes of interpretation and association (Bolter 1991: 195; Landow 1992: 4).

There is a second reason for abandoning the technology-centred point of view of media studies which, despite the modern focus on the social environment of media usage, represents the very basis of this discipline. Admittedly, contemporary media studies may even be perceived as being sociocentric,[9] but the social aspect is mostly grounded in technology research. I do not attempt to replace technology by sociology in this chapter. Even the social aspect of media usage is nothing but a window on individual and communicated cognition. Whatever a medium means should be defined by and within the process and practice of its usage. Let us take two examples.[10] First, the telephone. Originally, telephones were devices used for communicating messages. Initially, they were not even considered for bilateral communication. Telephones served as a substitute for the radio and public parlours made telephones accessible for listening to music broadcasts. The result of introducing the phone to the economic sphere was a facilitation of communication, albeit with social stratification. Only leading executives had access to phones and therefore the devices were used as social markers. The history of the telephone is one of the most illustrative examples for defining media by usage, and the ensuing technological evolution that strives to fulfil the requirements ever better. Second, the computer. The computer can be seen as both a machine, a tool and a (communication) medium. Information science first developed digital processing technology for the calculation of missile trajectories in the Second World War. Only later did it become a central technology for the storage and processing of data of all kinds. Essentially, the computer today can be seen as a machine for generating or preserving social spheres, a creative tool for designing technology and society, and only finally as a medium for the transfer of information. Both the telephone and computer have experienced deep changes in usage. If asked to define the telephone or the computer, audiences of the early twentieth century, or the 1950s respectively, might have well resorted to the facts of practices of their times.

Hence, appropriateness in media usage is absolutely secondary; ingenuity and context must come first. As soon as we let ourselves be guided by ideas such as 'this medium *y* is exclusively designed to be used for *x*', we delimit ourselves to looking at only part of the story, namely the realm of intentionalism.[11] As I hope to have shown in the examples above, media practices do not emerge from the appropriateness of artefacts alone. They emerge from necessity: we cannot deal with media without 'processing' them. In order to understand this concept of making media mean what they are used for, we need to clarify what we understand by these facets of the media sphere (Debray 1996: 26) which we call 'necessity', 'process' and 'practice'. Let us clarify again: We argue that media practice is an activity that constitutes media meaning. This is the domain of production and interpretation. Whatever we understand by 'media' is not a given, static meaning constituted by some technology but by humans using devices. At the same time, media devices and the engineering, economic, cultural and ideological spheres that surround them are not isolated from practice, which encompasses the entire domain of cultural communication.

The constitution of media processes is not exclusively related to individual usage. Media processes are phases of activity which change media but which are rooted in everyday media practice. We must understand that this cannot be isolated from other fields. Collateral experience (CP 8.178) – that is, experience not directly concerned with the handling of devices but with multiple practices related to media – defines how humans make use of media, which again constitutes the processes to which media are subjected.[12] This chapter therefore explores processes of making sense of media, as in practices of usage. Media studies' socio-technocentrism is hence countered by the semiotically inspired idea of sign processes, or semiosis, as conceived by Peirce (CP 5.484).[13] In the present context this may be summarized by the proposition that whatever a medium means only becomes real within the practice of its immediate usage, as this is relevant alone to it being understood, and it is from here that processes emerge again which offer potential for divergent practice in the future. In order to show in greater detail this semiotically inspired idea for a perspective on media, this chapter will present some key thoughts from philosophers and semioticians. Towards the end of the chapter I will summarise these ideas in a newly shaped semiotic paradigm for understanding media as artefacts of everyday human usage.

Peirce's Concepts of Mediation, Actuality and Potentiality

What is a medium? For a classical media scholar it may be a means to transfer or store messages (see Jensen 2002). The main challenge to this traditional definition is the paradigm erected by critical media studies and reception theory, which developed more active perspectives on media. The former asks for responsibility in media processes, the latter investigates the effects of media. With the change of study paradigms came more definitions of 'media'. The number of definitions of the term media today seems to equal the number of their authors, and it is close to impossible to track them all, let alone list and discuss them in the scope of this chapter. Why then decide to return to a scholar such as Charles Sanders Peirce and begin with philosophical reflection? Peirce is celebrated as the founder of modern semiotics. But where is the connection to media except for the obvious fact that signs are somehow connected to the meanings transported by media?

Peirce had a very well developed notion of what the essence of mediation in cognition is. In his theorising, mediation does not occur on the level of communication first. Rather, it is already an essential part in creating thought as such. In a famous quote often used by contemporary authors (see Nöth 1998: 57) writing on media semiotics today, he replaces the term sign, which is at the core of semiotic theory, with medium: 'All my notions are too narrow; instead of sign, ought I not to say medium?' (MS 339; cf. Parmentier 1985: 23). What did Peirce intend to infer by this paraphrasing of the terms medium and sign? We need to keep in mind that in 1906, when these words were written, no media studies existed. Hence, the term medium has to be taken as bearing a more fundamental quality of something 'in between', this being a quality which Peirce attributed to the sign itself. But then, if we are to transfer Peirce's historical understanding of mediation at the sign level to our modern conceptions of media in media studies – that is, as means of representation, transformation, transfer and processing of knowledge – do we arrive at a possible amalgamation of the terms? Or is this an unnecessary confusion of terms resulting in a melange of semiotics and media studies that will take us nowhere? Nöth makes clear that despite the gulf of time between 1906 and now, Peirce's dictum 'reminds us of the fact that the investigation of signs, as well as of the media, is identical to the investigation of mediating processes between the world we live in and our cognition in which this world is reflected, or perhaps constructed' (Nöth 1998: 57).

The semiotic term 'medium' as conceived by Peirce is much more fundamental than any conception of medium subsequently generated by media studies. We might understand it as such: Peirce's medium, as a shorthand for 'mediating force', is situated at the core of everything we might perceive as a medium today. The mediating force which is a general aspect of sign-ness is all present. Any object carries with it the mediating force of 'telling' something which it is not in itself due to its sheer presence, in the manner a rose mediates 'beauty'. Media artefacts are, however, more directed in 'mediating': like all signs, they mediate something that they are not. On top of that, they mediate signs which we might say they carry with them, as a TV set carries images and sound.

These signs are not associated with the original signs in the sense beauty is attributed to a rose. In this sense, media are meta-signs. The meaning of a TV programme transcends the immediate presence of the TV set; yet it does not exist independently of the TV as an artefact.

What does mediation mean in the context of Peircean semiotics? Peirce conceptualised the sign as a threefold entity. There is nothing beyond the third, he claimed, and based all concepts he developed in the course of his long writing life on this idea. The sign as such is composed of three components: the representamen; the object; and the interpretant. Let us assume that a thing is to be perceived by an interpreting mind such as yours or mine. Perception requires representation in the mind, which is achieved by either processing stimuli by sensor organs or producing the virtual analogy within the mind. The result is the representation of a thing as a sign in the mind. A sign, in semiotic reasoning, is hence a fictive, real, figurative or ideal unit which stands in some capacity, mode or fashion for something else to somebody's mind in some situation – just as this text creates signs in your mind in this reading situation. This instance of representation is called the representamen. As can be easily understood, the representamen is an entity of absolute actuality. It is ever-present. Whatever you perceive, you perceive it now – and now – and now again – just as you continuously perceive mental imprints of the words you read on this page.

Peirce calls the representamen the 'first' in his conception of the sign. 'Second' is the object. This term does not refer to an actual, quasi-real object as a 'thing' of the real world but the object of representation. Whatever you have in your memory of what you read before is no longer presented to you by your senses; it is already processed by your mind and therefore beyond absolute actuality. What is a representamen referring to, what does it call up in your interpreting mind? Nothing else than whatever you recognize as previously cognized, or as having similarity to, or as in any way being associated to, the representamen from your experience in the past. This means that whenever you see a 'door', you immediately know that it leads to some other space than the one you are situated in, and that it should allow for passage from one space to another. There is no other possibility of interpreting the sign of 'door' once you have experienced, and thus learned, what doors are all about. The object is our collective and individual experience space.

Alas, the sign as such also contains a third component, namely the interpretant. Here lies Peirce's great achievement: to include the element of change and progress in his conception of the sign. The interpretant equals the 'effect' of the sign. Naturally, an interpreting mind is not capable of grasping all there is to know about a thing in one moment. Neither do we have omniscient powers over the things of the world. In order to create a non-stagnating world-view we depend on progress in our knowledge in order to advance it through cognition. Hence, signs must be fallible, as they must be prone to replacement by more advanced signs.[14] Reality, which Peirce dubs 'brute force', may through its unpredictability have a sudden impact on our understanding of certain signs, which is a truth we can neither prevent nor deny. Such is the nature of semiosis. All of the incalculable effects that a sensation of reality may have on the formation of interpretants will become part and parcel of the essence of the sign in the future. Hence, Peirce makes a difference between the past, the present and the future of a sign. Whereas the object of the sign, resembling the experience horizon, is set in the past of the interpreting mind, the representamen in set in the immediate present. The interpretant is then set in the future, without ever being fully realised in the present. Hence, the sign always bears a potential which is situated in the future, or as Peirce puts it, the sign is 'esse in futuro' (CP: 2.184).

If this is valid for signs in general, it is especially important for the concept of mediation in signs, to which we shall now return. If there is a past and a future in signs, as represented by the past experience comprised by the object and the sign's future effect in the interpretant, then the immediate present of the representamen mediates between the two. However, the immediate, also called 'firstness' by Peirce, cannot hold meaning as such; it is dependent on connecting itself to object and interpretant in order to create the full sign. Let us now translate Peircean terminology into media terms. Confronted with a media device, a user cannot possibly contrive any meaning directly from the device as such – neither from the mere syntax of the messages, or the semantics of the parts of the code presented by the medium. The device – and the sounds, images, or whatever the device may be capable of reproducing – represent nothing else than representamina, that is immediate firstness, to the user's interpreting mind. The message transported by the device is therefore by no means 'the medium', as McLuhan argued. The message is a nothing without the creative force set in the user's minds. In order to decipher the meaning behind the message, the users must draw on their knowledge, which is the experience basis, or – again in Peircean terms – the object connected to the experience about the medium artefact, and the code of the message. Only thus will meaning be decoded and interpreted. But will it also be generated as easily? Naturally, a message contains no precoded meaning that will be recognised in a one-to-one relationship by users. The effect of the sign will only come about as a correlation of the past and present of the medium. Whatever the medium 'is' according to the object in the interpreter's mind is actuality. Whatever may come about by interpretation in the user's mind is potentiality, as it cannot be pre-defined to its full extent.

We are thus now approaching a closer understanding of what a medium process is in Peircean terms. It is, in itself, the semiotic turn through which any artefact must necessarily pass as a result of its inclusion in human cognition. As such, a medium can only introduce to the process of semiosis the objective meaning that was accumulated in its co-text and context in the past, and it shall mean in the future whatever interpretative effects the actual usage will have. Hence, the processes of usage are a semiotically necessary component of discussing what a medium is. It can never be anything 'as such' but only whatever it may represent to the human beings who actually use it under specific circumstances in specific contexts. This semiotic fundamental supports Couldry's call for a new media studies paradigm rooted in media practice, 'in all its looseness and openness' (this volume: 39).

So far, I have explored Peircean semiotics in order to sketch the epistemology of the semiotic process in which media artefacts are involved. It is now time to turn to practice. In order to illustrate the direct impact of practice on media meaning from the semiotic viewpoint, it is imperative to fully grasp the social nature of the sign itself. Hitherto, we have seen that signs, rephrased media by Peirce, are subject to constant change, which renders stability of meaning somewhat temporary. Peirce suggests that the effect of the sign, or the interpretant, is in itself divided into three levels of interpretant, namely the immediate interpretant, the dynamical interpretant and the final interpretant. The immediate interpretant is the direct, momentary quality of an effect a sign may cause – for example, in sensing a radio, an interpreter may be surprised, delighted or angry. The dynamical interpretant then is the actual effect caused in a specific situation. For example, a radio in a retro design of the 1930s situated in an all-new loft in Paris causes some effect quite distinct from a radio of utilitarian design used in a São Paulo slum. I turn to the visual appearance of the radio device here on purpose. In order to understand what media are, it is not enough to study messages or institutions: media practice research needs to focus on sensations in situations. In the radio example, the usage of a radio as a design element has some influence on the importance of the messages transmitted via radio for the owner of that device, which can be easily seen from a variety of daily media practices.

One option, as research on conspicuous consumption argues (see Veblen 1902: 68–101), is a reduced focus on the usability of products. Regard the following tagline from an internet test: 'What a fantastic accomplishment! In these days of conspicuous consumption, the Dualit DAB Kitchen Radio is the Humvee of digital radios. It may not brim with features, but you could drop it off a cliff and it would still be home in time for tea'.[15] In this case, design outweighs the media-intrinsic needs of a device, which means – at least from the advertiser's perspective – that the owner need pay little heed to the actual messages conveyed by the device. Another option, of course, is that the radio is such an important part of the consumer's daily life that they spend considerable funds on the device. In case of the person depending on the radio as an information source, design is of secondary importance in the first place.[16]

This takes us directly to the final interpretant. Finality here is the quality of something being relatively stable in meaning. Eventually, a 'rule' may govern the effect of signs, rendering the latter more regular. Such a rule is then a form of habit. The necessary step from dynamical to final interpretation then is the creation of regular, habitual or conventional interpretation that transcends the individual mind. It is hence indispensable to understand the importance of social communication for pragmatist semiotics. How can a sign attain the status of a 'rule' in the effects it causes on being perceived or imagined? Obviously, it is not enough that a single person interprets the sign in an isolated manner to achieve the creation of such a rule. How easily such isolated interpretation might result in imagining reality completely at odds to the interpretation of reality as a socially agreed and thus empirically tested result! Finality must be approached through communicating signs. Communication is an empirically measurable process of exchanging beliefs among sign users. We may also call this process, which is an inherent part of semiosis, discourse.

In social discourse, our own beliefs concerning the meaning of signs are at times challenged and at other times strengthened. In discourse, communities of sign users form by collectively attributing the same meaning to signs, which, in semiotic terminology, means that they share the same interpretation. Nevertheless, as mentioned above, collateral individual experience may deviate from the communally shared belief. Thus, innovation may be introduced into discourse, and finality, as stable as it may have become in years of unchallenged usage, is rendered relative and fallible. Such fallibility is the essence of the sign as related to its meaning. Whatever a sign means at present, it may still gain another meaning in the future. The change to a present meaning from a past meaning is only possible through the sign actions of interpreters – in other words, by their practising on signs. Hence, any impression that the meaning of signs may inherently reside within the signs themselves is utterly wrong. The same is true for media; it is the very practice of using them, of changing the interpretative value of the media, which creates new meanings around them. This can be made transparent by the actual history of individual media and the value attributed to them in a historically coherent society, such as the usage of the telephone in the United States. From the initial idea of the inventor to the usage as a mass medium, many stages of usage were experienced. It is especially the case that in the contemporary age of the hybridisation of media, we may understand that media practice continuously shapes people's understanding of what media are.

Cassirer: Symbolic Forms and the Binary Relation of Culture and Technology

The twentieth century was the structuralist century. Structuralism as a trend in linguistic and semiological thinking was one of its most prominent features. The paradigm of thinking in structures, not processes, has been so paramount throughout the past century that the formulation of structures in thinking, perception, language, politics, culture and so on may be seen as a necessary result of a zeitgeist that emerged from the formation of nations and distinctly structured sciences in the nineteenth century rather than a true model of social or scientific reality.

It is no surprise that certain structuralist – or, for that matter, poststructuralist – trends in philosophy have been of defining importance in the study of media. One of the prime examples is the impact of socalled mass culture on media discourse, originated by one of the best-known modern critical thinkers, Walter Benjamin (Benjamin 1936; cf. Couldry this volume: 35). Benjamin argued that 'mass production' has a direct influence on the quality of artefacts. In the case of art objects, the uniqueness and aesthetic quality is lost, according to Benjamin. A mass-produced *Mona Lisa* is not a thing of beauty to be admired. It might actually be thrown away if not wanted any more. As an effect on mediation processes, mass media have certain effects Benjamin identified as potentially negative. In regard to propaganda and the ensuing practices of the totalitarian regimes of the twentieth century, he was doubtlessly correct. However, the stigma of mass culture being of 'less' value persisted until the 1970s when scholars such as Umberto Eco (1984) developed new perspectives on culture and developed the concept of levels of culture.

Interestingly enough, the trend of favouring structure over process persisted throughout the twentieth century and resulted in, among other things, the parallel trends of structuralist semiology versus pragmatist semiotics – the first being oriented towards code and structure, and dominating sign discourse; the latter being focused on sign processes and the development of rules and meaning embedded therein, and unfortunately suffering from a shadowy existence. The dominance of structuralist discourse hindered the recognition of thinkers such as Peirce, who was only reintroduced into semiotic discourse by Sebeok in the last third of the century (see Sebeok 1991). For the same reason, Benjamin's ideas on media have dominated in media discourse and have superseded the ideas of another major philosopher of the same period, namely Ernst Cassirer. In his *Philosophie der symbolischen Formen* (Cassirer 1997[1923–1931]), Cassirer lays the foundations for understanding technological artefacts as symbolic forms – that is, as utterances of culture as such. In the essay 'Form und Technik' (Cassirer 1985[1930]),[17] which is an extension of the *Philosophie der symbolischen Formen*, Cassirer (ibid.: 46) specifies that the form of technology does not rest on it being technology as such but on being effective, on its activity.[18] Cassirer continues, dubbing technological progress 'human activity':

> The real, the deeper advantage [in human activity] rests in the gaining of 'form': the fact that the *expansion* of effort at the same time changes its qualitative *meaning*, and in doing so creates the possibility of a new world-aspect. Activity would truly prove in vain in the end in its continuous increase, its expansion and growth, if there were not concurrently an intrinsic alteration, a continuous change of meaning in preparation and in effect. (ibid.: 53)

According to Cassirer, cultural activity as such creates meaning. Human activity in itself is responsible for the change that its own meaning is subjected to. This is a natural movement of the dynamic mind (ibid.: 55). But if we project this notion of activity onto media practice, are we then on the path of positivism? Is media practice, in the words of Cassirer, automatically creating an ever-better understanding and usage of media as part of the 'technics', that is the 'form' of culture created in the activity? Cassirer does not fall into the positivist trap; neither does he evade the question about the value of artefacts and activity. He refrains from assessing the positive and negative consequences of human activity against one another. Rather, Cassirer emphasises that form is a necessary function of culture. It is a fact, whether we approve of the outcome or not (ibid.: 69).

The inherent connection of media processes and practices is also anticipated by Cassirer to some extent. After defining form he investigates the interrelation of cultural change and technological innovation.

The key to understanding how media as artefacts correlate to media action as practice rests in understanding the potential that is harvested from innovation as a necessary outcome in the progress of time. Cassirer proposes an opposition between the 'spirit of the tool' and the 'tool of the spirit' (ibid.: 74). In making a comparison with language, he emphasises that in reaching the status of symbolic communication language only gained the potential that it still offers us today. In such a way, every symbolic tool represents a potential that may be harvested in the continuous practice of its usage. However, the symbolic value of the tool exists only in reference to the minds of its users, as symbols are imprints on minds, and never quasi-real artefacts in themselves. By following Cassirer in our approach to media we therefore arrive again at the social sphere of media users, on which we must concentrate our analytic efforts, as the symbolic form of the media rests on the awareness of the community and the individuals who exercise media practice.

Barthes: Text and Work

Arguably the most important approach to media analysis that Couldry argues we take is the concentration on practice as a creative force in media usage. In doing so, he regrets the ongoing concentration on the cultural text, and suggests another strategy: 'The aim ... can be stated directly: to decentre media research from the study of media texts or production structures (important though these are) and to redirect it onto the study of the open-ended range of practices focused directly or indirectly on media (Couldry this volume: 36–37). Even though we have so far focused on semiotic and philosophical ideas that are quite contrary to structuralism, the final thinker to be presented in this epistemological review is one of the great minds of the Saussurean tradition, Roland Barthes. In his later writings, Barthes took an intellectual turn and tried to lighten the burden of 'structure' that had prevailed in the major part of his early work. One of the key ideas about texts that originated from Barthes is the difference between 'work' and 'text' in the programmatic essay 'From Work to Text' (Barthes 1977). Even before questioning fundamentally the power of the text in this piece, Barthes had laid the foundation of text as practice, as we may call it for our present purposes. As early as 1970, Barthes sketched the qualities of an 'ideal text', which represented a revolutionary concept, hardly to be realized in the form of paper-based books (Barthes 1974). Barthes was therefore simultaneously attacking the traditional notion of text and postulating a new paradigm when saying that in this ideal text the networks are many and interact, without any one of them being able to surpass the rest; this text is a galaxy of signifiers, not a structure of signifieds; it has no beginning; it is reversible; we gain access to it by several entrances, none of which can be authoritatively declared to be the main one; the codes it mobilizes extend *as far as the eye can reach*, they are indeterminable. (ibid.: 5–6)

It seems we may call the technical realization of media only the carrier of Barthean textuality, which is the equivalent of the concept of practice rather than the artefact. This theory of text remains influential. Landow (1992: 3) even took this definition of text as a starting point to formulate an entire hypertext theory based on poststructuralist notions, thus transforming Barthes into a quasi-protagonist of the hyped discourse on electronic text that emerged with the rise of hypertext in the mid-1990s.

Regardless of such attempts at monopolising him to justify poststructuralist literary theory, Barthes did create one of the most revolutionary concepts of text. This concept rests on the notion that 'text' is not static. This absence of stasis is seen by Barthes both in text as a web of signs and in text as carrying meaning. Text, in Barthes' perspective, is a practice, or rather, a process of producing meaning in the practice of making use of signs. The only rather static element in this process is the so-called 'work' – that is, the material carriers of textuality, such as a book that may be found on a shelf. The text, on the other hand, is seen at both ends of the transmission of signs; namely, the production and the reception side of making use of a book, for example. Both the author and the reader are included in such practice: the former as a gatherer of signs, a knitter of the network of textuality; the latter as an interpreter of signs. However, such production of text does not result in the transmission of text as an artefact carrying meaning similar to a messenger. All that is transmitted is the work; it represents merely a framework of signs that must be given meaning again by the reader. It is the reader who must rely on their own knowledge, their experience being the basis of interpreting the text. Hence the independence of reader from author, and hence, in our context, the independence of media practices from media artefacts.

Media as technological artefacts may direct their usage, or the overall media practice concerned with them, to some extent. However, by no means do they dictate meaning generation in practice at a general level. The latter exclusively rests with the users. Although media scholars have shared this perspective, it seems that the obvious presence of technology dominates research even today. In German media studies, the research paradigms are ever more organised according to the patterns of technology (Faulstich 2003, 2004), thereby transcending the borders between critical theory and media studies (Tholen, Coy and Warnke 2005). This emphasises the need for the paradigm shift called for by Couldry.

Conclusion

Three independent semiotic and philosophical sources allow us to support the proposal that we focus on media practice for media research. These sources contain three epistemological approaches: the first, regarding interpretation; the second, regarding the relationship between technology and culture; and the third, regarding practice as meaning production in cultural texts. Each of them supports us in our endeavour. All of these sources originate from diverse scholars working in different periods. Such is the result of a theoretical semiotic investigation into the subject matter of media practice as based in signs and sign processes.

One argument against the semiotically defined primacy of practice research at the end of this chapter may be that the semiotic musing presented here is exclusively based on theory. There is, after all, no immediate empirical proof involved. But is this in fact the case? Semiotics, as Peirce conceived of it, is an exclusively empirical science. How so? The reason is that experience can only be taken for granted in research if it is to be measured, both individually and in a group. Peirce provides the theoretical basis for approaching this kind of empiricism.

Furthermore, wherever we go from here in doing practice-oriented research into media, we shall need an epistemological basis for grounding our research. Media studies has so far been a field where theory has been borrowed from other disciplines. Semiotics, however, according to Nöth, is a 'media study *par excellence*' (Nöth 1997: 5), and in following him we may conclude that the theoretical concepts of semiotics are a serious enough foundation for media practice research. Any further criticism of this theoretical approach is easily deconstructed by focusing on research that has already been done on the development of various media. Regardless of which technology we look at, a brief glance at media histories – such as that of the computer, the telephone or the cinema – shows that technological history is always immediately connected to social history, and thus the history of practice (see Ipsen 2004). I believe that it is not only time for 'theorising media as practice' (Couldry this volume) in our current research. It is equally important to review former media studies in this new light, to finally accept the facts of semiotic processes as inherent parts of media practice. In doing so, the individual and social reality of producing meaning in and by using media may be finally embraced as a research paradigm.

Notes

1. With the somewhat overt emphasis on pragmatist semiotics I seek to avoid the impression that this chapter was written in the tradition of structuralist semiology. The latter, as already pointed out by Couldry (this volume), has been the major paradigm for studies of the sign in the twentieth century. However, the pragmatist tradition, as founded by Charles Sanders Peirce and carried on by scholars such as William James, John Dewey and George Herbert Mead, has from the beginning been concerned with the effects of cognitive processes. From this some of the finest traditions in semiotics, psychology, pedagogy and sociology have emerged. It is time to reunite these with the study of media as cultural processes.

2. References to Charles Sanders Peirce's writings are to the *Collected Papers* (CP) (Peirce 1931–1958), which are commonly quoted by a scheme giving numbers for volumes and paragraphs – i.e., 1.332 would refer to Volume 1, paragraph 332. Peirce's unpublished manuscripts are referred to by the abbreviation MS plus the number of the manuscript (Peirce 1967).

3. One example of this perspective on signs to be found within media studies is Bignell (2002: 7), who neglects the aspect of process altogether.

4. See the volume edited by Nöth (1997) for a general overview.

5. I neglect here temporal change, such as deterioration, weathering, etc. These do have significant influence, but they are subject to interpretation on another level.

6. Indeed, the fact of the necessity of mind transcends the actual presence of a mindful being. Peirce also uses the term 'quasi-mind' (e.g., CP 4.536) to illustrate this. In this sense, whatever can be a sign has the potential for being so due to the fact that a perceiving mind would make a sign from it. The quality remains the same in the absence of a mind. But no sign exists beyond cognition. In actual discussion, the point loses weight since whatever we discuss as a 'potential sign' has already gained the quality of an actual sign. Otherwise, how could we discuss it?

7. The German term 'Umwelt' has been adopted into international usage. According to von Uexküll, it does not equal 'environment' (which is its literal translation), but is the sum of sensory perceptions, cognitions, and other subliminal effects that emanate from the physical environment. Hence, even though they live in the same 'environment', a human being and a spider experience it as a completely different 'Umwelt'.

8. The term 'hypertext' is most fascinating. Originating from information organisation theory, it was first coined by Ted Nelson (1981), going back to a concept of networked information units devised by Vannevar Bush in 1945. The original idea of hypertext was that all available knowledge should be available in one networked resource pool. Whereas both the originators as well as the propagators of the hypertext principle maintained that 'true' hypertexts are text networks that are more or less 'liberal' – i.e., text networks in which the roles of authors and readers blur – con-

temporary reality has outdated this purist concept. Text networks such as the World Wide Web, in which authorship is held almost exclusively by actors maintaining sites, are also called hypertexts today. In the early 1990s, the internet, or World Wide Web as one of its growing services, was not discussed as an option for hypertext. For a more detailed overview, see Ipsen (2001). The hypertext concept is another illustrative example of how media practice changes our ideas about media. In this case, the commercial dimension of the internet made isolated hypertext solutions, which were true to the original conception of hypertext, obsolete. Today, globally networked information webs are hypertext.

9. The social aspect of media usage is a major focus of contemporary media studies. Still, the outcome of these researches is that technology as such has a certain 'effect' on humans, which can be measured subsequently. In my perspective, media are a cognitive construction in the first place.

10. In the following passage, I shall rely extensively on Hopper (1990) and Höflich (1998) for the telephone and Schelhove (1997) for the computer.

11. Intentionalism in literary theory refers to the idea that a text means whatever the author intends it to refer to, regardless of the interpretation of the reader.

12. In this regard, the usage of radio makes for an excellent example. Listening to the radio while having breakfast, reading a newspaper or while not occupied with another activity creates different modes of media usage, from strictly monomedial to consequently intermedial practice. Also, the radio may merely serve to create 'background noise', which again creates a different aspect of usage. The realms of collateral experience are hence imperative.

13. 'It is important to understand what I mean by semiosis. All dynamical action, or action of brute force, physical or psychical, either takes place between two subjects [whether they react equally upon each other, or one is agent and the other patient, entirely or partially] or at any rate is a resultant of such actions between pairs. But by 'semiosis' I mean, on the contrary, an action, or influence, which is, or involves, a coöperation of three subjects, such as a sign, its object, and its interpretant, this tri-relative influence not being in any way resolvable into actions between pairs' (CP 5.484).

14. This idea of signs always continuing to progress towards 'more' knowledge seems over-positivist; here we do not mention processes of forgetting, either collectively or individually. However, the continuous process of change in signs in Peircean terms does not resemble an alteration between the states of 'knowing' and 'forgetting', as knowledge itself is something relative. Rather, the reality represented by signs is subjected to shifts in its interpretation – which is, in short, shifting between what is interpreted as 'necessary being', 'actual being' or 'possible being' (CP 5.454). To not know the meaning of an artefact, for example, from an ancient civilization, then shifts the interpretation towards imagining the possible. The actual being of the artefact, however, cannot be put into question.

15. CNET Networks. 2008. 'Dualit DAB Kitchen Radio Review'. Retrieved 7 May 2008 from: http://reviews.cnet.co.uk/digitalradio/0,39030009, 49283111,00.htm.
16. See, e.g., Skuse (1999) on radio use in Afghanistan.
17. This essay is unfortunately not available in English.
18. This notion of 'form' must not be confused with the structuralist idea of form as a set of rules, as in Hjelmslev's (1961: 58) stratum of form from which is produced substance – i.e., formed signs from the matter of unformed sign potential. In this model, form is not a process but a structure.

References

Barthes, R. 1974[1970]. *S/Z*, trans. R. Miller. New York: Hill and Wang.
——— 1977. 'From Work to Text', in *Image – Music – Text.* New York: Hill and Wang.
Benjamin, W. 1936. *Das Kunstwerk im Zeitalter seiner technischen Reproduzierbarkeit.* Frankfurt am Main: Suhrkamp.
Bignell, J. 2002. *Media Semiotics: An Introduction.* Manchester: Manchester University Press.
Bolter, J.D. 1991. *Writing Space: The Computer, Hypertext, and the History of Writing.* Hillsdale, NJ: Lawrence Erlbaum.
Cassirer, E. 1985[1930]. 'Form und Technik', in *Symbol, Technik, Sprache. Aufsätze aus den Jahren 1927–1933.* Hamburg: Meiner, pp. 39–91.
——— 1997 [1923–1931]. *Philosophie der symbolischen Formen.* Vols. 1–5. Darmstadt: Primus.
Debray, R. 1996. *Media Manifestos.* London: Verso.
Eco, U. 1984. 'Massenkultur und "Kultur-Niveaus"', in *Apokalyptiker und Integrierte: Zur kritischen Kritik der assenkultur.* Frankfurt am Main: Fischer, pp.37–58.
Faulstich, W. 2003. *Einführung in die Medienwissenschaft.* Stuttgart: UTB.
——— 2004. *Grundwissen Medien.* Stuttgart: UTB.
Hjelmslev, L. 1961. *Prolegomena to a Theory of Language.* Madison: University of Wisconsin Press.
Höflich, J.R. 1998. 'Telefon: Medienwege – Von der einseitigen Kommunikation zu mediatisierten und medial konstruierten Beziehungen', in W.R. Halbach and M. Faßler (eds), *Geschichte der Medien.* Munich: Fink (UTB), pp.187–225.
Hopper, R. 1990. *Telephone Conversation.* Bloomington: Indiana University Press.
Ipsen, G. 2001. 'HybridHyperSigns: Semiotische Parameter von Skriptstrukturen WWW-gebundener Hypertexte', Ph.D. thesis. Kassel: Kassel University.
——— 2003. 'The Crisis of Cognition in Hypermedia', *Semiotica* 143(1–4): 185–97.

———— 2004. 'The Interdependence of Cultural Evolution and Medial Development', in M. Bax, B. van Heusden and W. Wildgen (eds), *Semiotic Evolution and the Dynamics of Culture*. Bern: Peter Lang, pp.35–52.

Jensen, K.B. 2002. *A Handbook of Media and Communication Research*. London: Routledge.

Landow, G.P. 1992. *Hypertext: The Convergence of Contemporary Critical Theory and Technology*. Baltimore, MD: Johns Hopkins University Press.

McLuhan, M. 1967. *The Medium is the Message*. New York: Bantam.

Nelson, T.H. 1981. *Literary Machines*. Swarthmore, PA: Self-published.

Nöth, W. 1997. 'Introduction', in W. Nöth (ed.), *Semiotics of the Media*. Berlin: Mouton de Gruyter, pp.1–11.

———— 1998. 'Die Semiotik als Medienwissenschaft', in W. Nöth and K. Wenz (eds), *Medientheorie und die digitalen Medien*. Kassel: Kassel University Press, pp.47–60.

———— 2000. *Handbuch der Semiotik*. Stuttgart: Metzler.

Nöth, W. (ed.). 1997. *Semiotics of the Media*. Berlin: Mouton de Gruyter.

Parmentier, R.J. 1985. 'Signs' Place in Medias Res: Peirce's Concept of Semiotic Mediation', in E. Mertz and R.J. Parmentier (eds), *Semiotic Mediation*. Orlando, FL: Academic Press, pp.23–48.

Peirce, C.S. 1931–1958. *Collected Papers*. Vols. 1–6, C. Hartshorne and P. Weiss (eds); Vols. 7–8, A.W. Burks (ed.), Cambridge, MA: Harvard University Press.

———— 1967. *The Peirce manuscripts (MS)*. Microfilm edition following the Annotated Catalogue of the Papers of Charles S. Peirce by Richard S. Robin. Amherst/Mass.: University of Massachusetts Press.

Schelhove, H. 1997. *Das Medium aus der Maschine: Zur Metamorphose des Computers*. Frankfurt: Campus.

Sebeok, T.A. 1991. *A Sign is Just a Sign*. Bloomington: Indiana University Press.

Skuse, A. 1999. 'Negotiated Outcomes: An Ethnography of the Production and Consumption of a BBC World Service Soap Opera for Afghanistan', Ph.D thesis. London: University of London.

Tarasti, E. 2000. *Existential Semiotics*. Bloomington: Indiana University Press.

Tholen, G.C., W. Coy and M. Warnke (eds). 2005. *Zur Ortsbestimmung analoger und digitaler Medien*. Bielefeld: Transcript.

Veblen, T. 1902. *The Theory of the Leisure Class: An Economic Study of Institutions*. New York: Macmillan.

Von Uexküll, J. and G. Kriszat. 1970. *Streifzüge durch die Umwelten von Tieren und Menschen*. Frankfurt am Main: Fischer.

Winograd, T. and F. Flores. 1986. *Understanding Computers and Cognition*. Norwood, NJ: Ablex.

CHAPTER 9

Language-games, In/dividuals and Media Uses: What a Practice Perspective Should Imply for Media Studies

Jo Helle-Valle

no course of action could be determined by a rule, because every course of action can be made out to accord with the rule ... hence also obeying a rule is a practice.

—Ludwig Wittgenstein

persons emerge precisely from that tension between dividual and individual aspects/relations.

—Edward LiPuma

Introduction

'Practice' has been a buzzword in social theory for more than thirty years (see, e.g., Bourdieu 1977; Ortner 1984). But despite this relatively long history we are far from anything that might be called a paradigm of practice theory. As several commentators have noted, 'practice theory' covers a wide array of perspectives (Warde 2005: 132). This can be seen from reading the works of theorists that are often mentioned in connection to practice theory: Bourdieu, Garfinkel, Latour, Butler (Reckwitz 2002: 144). This variation in theory need not bother us if we argue that the term can serve as something 'good to think with' – a guideline pointing us vaguely in one direction – and that there is really no need for a more precise term. However, in this chapter I take the opposite stance and argue that we should strive for more precision. There is, I contend, a crucially important ontological – and therefore also an analytical – point that a proper treatment of practice theory can bring to the fore. In this chapter[1] I argue that we should approach practice theory in a way that brings out what I believe is its most important theoretical point, namely that we should rid ourselves of any idea of *langue*. Saussure's *langue* is, as we know, based on the idea that in studies of language observable expressions of meaning are only 'surface phenomenon' – they belong to *parole*, or 'speech' – and that underneath this surface lies that 'real thing' – the logical, consistent system of meaning that 'guides' or determines the often imperfect expressions that we can hear and see.

The idea that 'beneath', 'above' or 'parallel to' the visible world there is some sort of reality that explains the one we have access to through our senses has haunted Western thought at least since Plato's forms (*ideai*). This idea has taken many forms but in the social sciences and humanities it has perhaps acquired its most explicit and clear expression in structuralism. Now, critiques of structuralism have been so forceful and convincing that hardly anyone dares to call themselves a structuralist nowadays, but I contend that the idea that we need to uncover some kind of underlying structure is so ingrained in us that variants of this idea pop up in various guises again and again. It is less an issue of researchers who knowingly advocate and use (post)structuralist models as it is of others who unwittingly make use of perspectives that directly or indirectly draw on various forms of *langue*. This tendency manifests itself in a variety of ways (see, e.g., Helle-Valle 1997: 47–48) but in media anthropology the most common form is perhaps to essentialise media content – a point I will return to below.

Thus, practice theory's main task should be to help us get rid of what, ontologically speaking, is a totally ungrounded idea. What it can do – dealt with in the proper manner – is provide us with a different foundation for explaining regularity and order within various realms of social life, including media-related practices. And this alternative foundation is practice itself. Most importantly, an appropriate application of practice theory would help us move beyond the structure/agency dualism that haunts analyses in the social sciences because it will embed structuring forces in mundane, everyday practices – not as some external, more or less transcendental power.

What does 'practice itself' mean? In my view 'practice' is everything that is done; activities in one form or another. Of course, observable actions are practices but so are 'mental' acts like speaking and even thinking.[2] But if anything that goes on in the field that we study is practice, then what isn't practice? From the point of view of social science, researchers' abstractions are not practices. Or more precisely, such abstractions are practices of and for the researcher but they are not practices belonging to that which we study. Ontologically speaking it is crucial to keep the researcher's abstractions apart from that which we study. Terms like rule, structure and the like are such abstractions and we should be wary of using them as causative forces for the realm we study. What we are left with is practice itself: *Im Anfang war die Tat*, 'In the beginning was the deed' (Goethe, in Wittgenstein 1979: §402).

This approach to practice theory raises two issues: An ontological one that centres on why explanations of social phenomena must come from the realm of practices, and one that deals with the analytical challenge of how practice can be used as a starting point for a positive science – positive in the sense of making order out of chaos, not being content with deconstruction. The first issue has to do with what is entailed in avoiding ways of thinking that rest on some kind of *langue*. I dwell on this issue because I claim that it is a tricky issue – almost everybody agrees about the virtues of practice-based non-dualist approaches but *langue*-like elements tend to sneak into analyses nevertheless. Thus, my critique is not directed against (media) anthropologists advocating some kind of structuralist position; rather, it is that our language, our academic tradition and insufficient reflections on what we in our academic practices do, easily lead us in such a direction. Hence a proper reflection on this ontological point is necessary.

The second issue concerns what kind of ordering principles can be used by researchers as means of creating a structured and ordered understanding of a practical world – in general as well as in media anthropology. Leaning on late Wittgensteinian philosophy I suggest that 'language-game' – as a designation of the practically formed communicative contexts that provide statements with meaning – should be fundamental to forming our understanding of social life. I furthermore argue that embodiment and consumption as analytic foci are in line with this reasoning.

By giving the contextualisation of practice precedence for practice theory the complexity that comes from attempting to incorporate a wide array of factors into a holistic analytical perspective is reduced. I suggest that this is a better kind of analytical 'anchorage' than Couldry advocates when he – inspired by Swidler – suggests that some media practices anchor other practices. An example of such analytic anchorage is domestication research. This perspective focuses on the home as a communicative context that is needed in order to understand how media are used.

Finally, I hold that practice theory is at odds with conventional ways the social sciences handle persons and agency. I present the unfamiliar concept of 'in/dividual' as a necessary analytic element in a practice theory that emphasises the centrality of language-games.

Praxis

A suitable starting point for this discussion is the distinction Reckwitz makes between practice (*Praxis*) and practices (*Praktiken*), whereby the former 'represents merely an emphatic term to describe the whole of human action (in contrast to "theory" and mere thinking)', while *Praktik* 'is a routinised type of behaviour which consists of several elements, interconnected with one other: forms of bodily activities, forms of mental activities, "things" and their use, a background knowledge in the form of understanding, know-how, states of emotion and motivational knowledge' (Reckwitz 2002: 249). While Reckwitz 'dismisses' the former as 'merely an emphatic term', I hold that it is praxis – 'in the singular' (ibid.: 249) – that points to the crucial ontological and epistemological foundation for what makes practice theory radical and different. In my opinion it is Wittgenstein's late philosophy[3] that explains this most convincingly.

According to Wittgenstein, the trouble with language and meaning is that:

> it may come to look as if there were something like a final analysis of our forms of language, and so a single completely resolved form of every expression ... This finds expression in questions as to the essence of language, of propositions, of thought ... Something that lies within, which we see when we look into the thing, and which an analysis digs out ... [T]hought is surrounded by a halo ... We are under the illusion that ... [there] is a *super*-order between – so to speak – *super*-concepts. Whereas, of course, if words like "language", "experience", "world", have a use, it must be as humble a one as that of the words "table", "lamp", "door" (Wittgenstein 1968: §§91–92, §97).

Instead, Wittgenstein argues, 'we must stick to the subjects of our everyday thinking, and not go astray and imagine that we have to describe extreme subtleties ... We are talking about the spatial and temporal phenomenon of language, not about some non-spatial, non-temporal phantasm' (ibid.: §§106, 108). This is so because naming and meanings are not mere reflections of reality but conventions created for certain purposes. Therefore, one must turn to real language enacted in real life. This 'Copernican turn' provides Wittgenstein with a very different understanding of language and meaning than the conventional philosophical ones. Briefly stated, his view is not only that meaning lies in use but that meaning *is* use – there are no essential, context-independent meanings that can be extracted from the uses and still be said to 'represent' the term (e.g., ibid.: §§120, 197). This reflects a point

Malinowski once made: 'the conception of meaning as *contained* in an utterance is false and futile. A statement, spoken in real life, is never detached from the situation in which it has been uttered' (Malinowski 1974: 307; cf. Malinowski 1935: 52–58; Gellner 1998: 151–54). The fundamental point here is to rid ourselves of the idea that meaning – as a reality within the field we study – can exist outside specific uses.

To substantiate this radical stance Wittgenstein argues that if there exists some kind of 'super-order' then we would have to account for some kind of causal link between this 'langue' and practices – between what is purportedly ordering (a 'structure') and that which is ordered (everyday life). If there was no such causality the structure would not have any impact, and hence be irrelevant, to the sociality we study. For this connection Wittgenstein uses the term 'rule' to designate the alleged link between structure and practice. As long as we do not believe that the subjects we study respond automatically to some kind of hidden, structuring force, it follows that rules must be interpreted in order to be put to use. By way of example Wittgenstein demonstrates that we have to abandon the idea of a 'master script' that informs our understanding of words and deeds. The explanation can be summed up as follows: 'no course of action could be determined by a rule, because every course of action can be made out to accord with the rule ... hence also obeying a rule is a practice' (Wittgenstein 1968: §§201–2). The problem is that if we were to spell out the coded representations that structure language with new coded representations we face an infinite regression (ibid.: §§201–2; see also Searle 1980: 228; Taylor 1993). Hence, rules cannot by themselves explain practice since the necessary interpretations of rules do not determine the rule's content, and therefore a rule cannot provide us with the causal link between structure and action. What is left of the term then is only what we give as explanations of regularity within a given field of practice. This is analogous to saying that although we can construct grammars in language grammar does not explain how people use language. A rule must therefore be 'as humble a one as that of the words "table", "lamp", "door"'. Consequently, if obeying a rule 'is not a question about causes, then it is about the justification for my following the rule in the way I do' (Wittgenstein 1968: §217). Thus, 'rule' is not some transcendental or immanent force that explains action but is either a verbalised statement done by the subjects we study ('the children shall not watch television before they have done their homework'), or our naming of regularities that can be observed ('based on our observations we can state that as a rule the children in the families we have studied do their homework before they watch television').[4]

To see this more clearly we need to remind ourselves of the simple, but yet often hidden, distinction between two ontological realms: that which we study (observable practices, including talk, ideas, perspectives and values) and our tools for studying a social reality. Our 'toolbox' contains logical rules (about validity), paradigm(s) (theories, models, methodologies), and concepts we use in order to give meaning to what we study. As the metaphor suggests, our tools are not part of the material we work on. But because many of the analytic terms we use are also in operation among those we study it is in practice often difficult to keep the ontological realms apart. Thus, the first type of rule-following belongs to the field we study (the researched subjects' justifications of practices) while the latter (regularities) is an inference by the researcher and hence not part of what we study. Thus, as long as we can observe that those we study present a rule as an explanation for what they do, or don't do, it is undoubtedly part of our field of study.[5] The latter type of rule – the researcher's inference – is, however, a contention about the field we study but the contention itself is not part of the studied field.

Failing to be aware of this distinction can lead to invalid analytic conclusions because we might endow our constructed (analytic) concepts with causal powers – which implies a form of concept fetishism: this amounts to 'the fallacy of treating the objects constructed by science, whether "culture", "structure", or "modes of production", as realities endowed with a social efficacy, capable of acting as agents responsible for historical actions or as a power capable of constraining practices' (Bourdieu 1977: 27). Thus, the fallacy lies in constructing concepts that one afterwards reintroduces as causative parts of what is studied, hence invalidly creating ordering principles that do not belong to the reality we study. 'To slip from regularity, i.e. from what recurs with a certain statistically measurable frequency ... to a consciously laid down and consciously respected ruling ... or to unconscious regulating by a mysterious cerebral or social mechanism, are the two commonest ways of sliding from the model or reality to the reality of the model' (Bourdieu 1990: 39).[6]

There is no fallacy involved in referring to the expressed rules informants present, nor in observing regularities. The fallacy lies in using either of them as explanations for practices. In the first type of rule the problem is flawed epistemology: motives are not reducible to linguistic utterances but are contextualised and embodied practices (see below). Thus, using verbally stated rules as an explanation is at best a restricted, partial truth.[7] In the second type of rule, the fallacy would lie in invalid changes in the meaning of 'rule'. Pointing to a statistical regularity is entirely different from presenting it as a cause. If it should serve as a cause we would have to give plausible explanations for how such regularities influence people's behaviour: Is it a norm, a compulsion or some mechanical mechanism that regulates behaviour?

What this amounts to is that observed practices must be explained by pointing to the field of practice, which implies that there is no valid place for a model that relies on some sort of *langue*. Wittgenstein's work thus represents a powerful rejection of various types of Platonist transcendentalism that is so often present in various disguised forms, also in modern social analyses. And most importantly, it also suggests, I argue, a valid way out of the problem. For while it is one thing to deconstruct beautiful academic constructions that base themselves on ordering principles of this type, it is another altogether to present an alternative that can actually function as a valid form of understanding, systematisation and explanation.

Praktiken

Turning from the ontological to the analytical, from praxis to practices – to what Reckwitz (2002) considers being the prime area of attention – we need to find sources of order in practice itself. As I mentioned earlier, for Reckwitz practices (*Praktiken*) are routinised types of behaviour consisting of forms of bodily and mental activities, things and their uses and background knowledge. As a consequence of this view, the 'single individual – as a bodily and mental agent – then acts as the "carrier" (*Träger*) of a practice' (ibid.: 250). Thus, Reckwitz, along with most other advocates of practice theory, turns to forms of 'material phenomenology' in an effort to bring together the various aspects of human action that too easily become separated in our handling of the matter: analytic distinctions tend to turn into substantive divisions – mind becomes separated from body, the social from the individual, and so on. The problem with such a strategy, however, is that 'everything' is lumped together and the models that are developed are almost as complex as life itself and serve badly as tools for academic labour.

Couldry (this volume) – following Swidler (2001) – suggests a way out of this complexity by asking whether some practices anchor, control or organise others. If so, it would be possible to reduce the complexity by highlighting these anchoring practices. Couldry suggests that certain media-related practices serve as such an anchor due to the dominant position media have in late-modern Western societies. There can be various objections to this contention (see Couldry and Hobart this volume) but to me the two main objections are that it smacks of ethnocentrism and it is insensitive to the issues studied – not all research topics suggest a prioritising of the media field. For instance, it is difficult to think that the prioritised role of ritualised media practices (Couldry this volume) holds if one's research theme is alcohol use in an isolated village in Papua New Guinea.

I propose that instead of searching for anchoring elements within the social fields we should instead turn to the analytic apparatus and ask whether there are some analytic elements that anchor others. With Wittgenstein I hold that the language-games moulded in forms of life serve this analytic function – they constitute the analytic bedrock of explaining meaning and hence social life. As I have argued in the previous section, there is nothing 'behind' practices. Text is formed by context: meanings vary in relation to the practical contexts that the meanings appear in. This is the background for Wittgenstein's term 'family resemblance': the meanings of a term constitute 'a complicated network of similarities overlapping and criss-crossing'; they are like 'various resemblances between members of a family' (Wittgenstein 1968: §§66–7). In other words, different practical situations affect meanings in ways that make meanings resemble one another without having an essential core (Needham 1975). However, some situations are more alike than others and hence we find that meanings overlap more in some cases than in others. Wittgenstein terms such similar situations language-games and forms of life: The 'term "language-*game*" is meant to bring into prominence the fact that the *speaking* of language is part of an activity, or of a form of life' (Wittgenstein 1968: §23). Hence, to study meaning is to study uses of language within forms of life.

It follows from the ontological argument about the logical prominence of practice that 'language-game' is the term for how meaning is embedded in fields of practice – and that it is such anchored meaningfulness that provides artefacts (including media artefacts) and actions with social significance. Hence, it is reasonable to consider this as fundamental for an understanding of social practices, and giving language-game such a prioritised position would lessen the analytic complexity. It is important to acknowledge that the concept of 'language-game' is not restricted to linguistic practices – bodily and mental activities and the uses of objects are ingrained parts of language-games. Let me briefly outline some of the consequences of this, and start with the body–mind–society knot.

Many of the issues underlying the idea of embodiment seem to be similar to those of practice theory – a dissatisfaction with an overly formalised and dissected type of understanding of social phenomena, where analytic distinctions turn into separate realities. So in this area of theorising we also find frequent attempts at theoretical and analytic synthesis; thus there is talk about the individual, the social, the cultural, the physical body. And the theorising seems to produce methodological tools which are so complex to apply to data that it does not really bring us a long way. However, if we turn to Ian Burkitt's book *Bodies of Thought* (Burkitt 1999) there are some cues that can simplify matters in the way I suggest here. He makes oft-stated points about how mind and body, thought and emotions, the individual and the social are intertwined, and then, in discussing the body–mind issue in relation to emotions, he writes that:

> in Wittgenstein's [1968] account of feeling joyful, he claims that we recognize this emotion through behaving and thinking in a joyful manner, not by reflecting on an inner state or attitude of joy. The emotion then … is *a bodily expression within a situation* that gives us joy. Wittgenstein says that "joy designates nothing at all. Neither something inner, nor something outer" … by which I take him to mean that joy is not the expression of an inner or outer cause; instead, the expression *is* the joyful feeling … Furthermore, these conditions are not found inside a person but are aspects of the conditions of life within which a person exists … Emotional conflict, then, does not arise from internal states of ambivalence; instead, it emerges within social contexts which are themselves inherently ambivalent or filled with conflict. People in such situations may choose not to express a bodily felt emotion, but that does not necessarily make the affect an "inner" experience. In such circumstances, a person may think of the emotion in that way, and yet it has been created within relations to others and has a meaning for the person only in that context; otherwise, the emotion would not be identifiable or intelligible. (ibid.: 117–18)

Several things are worth dwelling on here. Firstly, the parallel with Wittgenstein's argument about the meaning of words: meaning is use, and emotion is expression – there is nothing behind or hidden that is expressed through practice. More important is the emphasis on context: emotions, as embodied knowledge and competence in general, are made relevant only within given practical contexts – that is, within language-games and forms of life. This suggests some important methodological directions and therefore also some analytic simplification. It tells us, first, that we should direct our attention to the specific settings in which a practice takes place and, secondly, that we should resist the temptation to extrapolate our findings to other contexts. We must concentrate on identifying contexts in which a given practice unfolds and see how practices (including linguistic ones) get their meanings from that language-game. When this has been done we can take the next step, searching for the ways that mind, body and objects together contribute to and are formed within the given language-game.

The same analytic process is of course relevant for media-related practices. The obvious point is that the 'text' – the mediated content – by itself is insufficient for determining how people relate to it. This was of course the point Stuart Hall (1980) made with his concepts of encoding and decoding. The encoding – the creation of a text by some author – sets certain frames for how it can be interpreted but it can never narrow the possibilities down to one. The reading of a text – the decoding – is always open to several interpretations. More importantly, however, is that this perspective on media practice also implies that we cannot assume that audience reactions to a given media content will be consistent across contexts or language-games. Thus, instead of thinking that we are disclosing aspects of a culture, or other group-related attitudes, we are revealing context-specific perspectives. I am not saying that this is a point media anthropologists are unaware of; what I claim is that analyses are often conducted and conclusions are drawn in ways that ignore the context-specificity of media reception, and hence violate the point I argue here. Let me provide two short examples.

In a recent media anthropology anthology, Rothenbuhler (2005) discusses 'the symbolic patterns that appear across media coverage, public talk, interpersonal talk, and the symbolic aspects of behaviour in public places' that emerged in the USA in the aftermath of the 9/11 attacks on the World Trade Centre in 2001. These patterns 'can be read as reflections … of communicative and cognitive structures' (ibid.: 177). Although he is careful to point out the 'multi-facted' nature of symbols, Rothenbuhler's conclusions are fairly clear in the sense that there is one interpretation of the event that is presented: 'The Firemen as represented on TV, in newspapers and magazines, in talk and imagination were powerful symbols of paradox'; they 'were rescuer-victims, citizen-soldiers, inside-outsiders, sentimental-officials, masculine men who cry' (ibid.: 177). Thus, although the polysemy of symbols is emphasised the analysis is not only insensitive to the fact that the USA is made up of various ethnicities, religious and political views, and hence no doubt countless interpretations of 9/11 and its aftermath, but the analysis must by necessity analytically ignore the fact that the same event – and hence its media coverage – can be understood in various ways depending on the context in which it is interpreted. I hold that it is extremely tricky to conduct an analysis of a national interpretation of such an event. Either one would have to restrict oneself to analysing the media's presentation of the event – and not go into how people themselves interpret the media – or one would need to conduct a thorough investigation of how different groups of people interpret the event in different settings. Such an investigation would obviously require solid data – and methodology-triangulation – and a host of analytical reservations or a very modest conclusion about what is actually revealed through the analysis.

Another example is an article on how Ghanaian audiences relate to and interpret a certain type of domestic film genre (Meyer 2003). Many of these films focus on the relationship between men and women, on women's greed for material goods and the consequences of such greed. One film in particular is analysed in detail and the author is careful to point to the importance of including audiences' reactions to the film. But again the actual analysis of what the film conveys in terms of meaning is fairly specific in its interpretation and very general in its audience relevance. With some reservations there is one interpretation that is presented as the 'real' Ghanaian one. The very idea that there is one authoritative way to interpret media content such as a specific film must either be based on some kind of *langue*-like idea about a cultural logic, or it must be based on very well-researched material that must include solid information about how people say they understand a film (which might not be synonymous with how they in fact interpret it), which categories of people understand in it what ways, and whether communicative contexts alter their understandings of the film.[8]

Thus, the analytical importance of communicative contexts requires sensitivity not only to shifting audiences but also to how the same subjects might change their views depending on the setting in which they consume media content. And this is indeed the viewpoint around which the domestication research perspective is built. Developed in Britain in the 1980s, and inspired by cultural studies, anthropology and consumption theory, its basic contention was that we cannot know how media users take in media content and media technology without taking the context of media use into consideration. This perspective stresses the necessity of making media consumption compatible with the cultural (and hence moral) frameworks it is part of. This accords nicely with Wittgenstein's insistence about the crucial role of language-games. Moreover, its understanding of the domestic sphere – as a central sphere for media consumption – is valuable in that it describes and analyses the routinised and ritualised practices (*Praktiken*) that media consumption in this institutionalised social context is part of. In addition, the perspective also stresses the significance of media consumption not only in terms of content but also in terms of technology, as physical objects as well. We are thus faced with the double articulation of information and communication technologies (ICTs), which must be accepted by their users as integral parts of the language-games they become parts of both in terms of mediated content and objects (see, e.g., Morley 1986; Hirsch 1992; Silverstone 1994).

However, as Dag Slettemeås and I have argued elsewhere (Helle-Valle and Slettemeås 2008), there are inconsistencies in the analytic apparatus of domestication research that have unfortunate effects. Most important in the context of the present chapter is that 'domestication' is sometimes treated in a general manner as the act of 'taming' and sometimes as that which belongs to the domestic sphere. We argue that the term should be definitionally restricted to the first meaning – taming – because the latter connection not only leaves out instances of media use in non-domestic settings (like workplace or gaming halls) but most importantly it tends to reify and essentialise the domestic as a setting, fixed and set apart from the rest of society. It is crucial to keep an open mind as to what goes on in domestic settings. Homes are many things: from conventional, middle-class nuclear families to gay couples or communes. Moreover, within the same home many different communicative contexts (language-games) are formed (and dissolved) depending on who is present and what kind of practices unfold. A home might accommodate not only children's movies but also erotic films. In other words, we need to be aware of the many language-games that can be found within what we conventionally call the domestic sphere.

Thus, the proposed revision of the domestication research perspective would privilege language-games. With such a focus we achieve a simplification that turns the virtually unmanageable complexity of practice theory into an analytically and methodologically manageable perspective. Moreover, it gives 'practice' precedence, and does not reach out for analytical help from a structuralist *langue.*

In/dividual

The practice theory I have advocated here implies a radical shift in perspective. One important implication is that we need to see media use as part of a wider array of interconnected practices, which again has important methodological consequences. Studying media practices entails gathering data from a wide fan of events and processes (Ang 1996; Couldry this volume). Yet we should not hastily conclude that we can reveal a seamless cultural totality that encompasses a group's media practices. The ontological argument demands that we restrain our generalising ambitions: an observed response to media (as content as well as technology) is not an indication of a group's general attitudes other than within the setting in which consumption takes place. This not only calls for caution when making inferences from data, it also questions widely held ideas about how to treat analytically the subjects we study. In short, since all perspectives are context-specific, since there is no unifying common langue, and since subjects move in and out of various language-games, it follows that people act and think differently in different language-games.[9] This means that in a sense subjects are different persons in different settings (Helle-Valle 2004, 2007). No doubt such a view clashes with our conventional terminology and thinking about individuals in the social sciences. Hence I suggest supplementing the term 'individual' with 'dividual' so that we can analytically conceive persons as in/dividuals.[10]

There is general agreement that Western (late) modernity contains a strong focus on the individual. In an economic system based on individualised incomes and a socio-political system in which people are free and equal in a qualitatively new sense it is no wonder that it is of crucial importance to construct oneself as an individual. It is necessary in a practical sense but it has also become an ideological project – individualism (see, e.g., Giddens 1991). At the centre of individualism is the issue of identity. This is a concern for each and every one of us: we need to come to terms with, and display, what and who we are. Basic to this perpetual project is the idea of having an essence, that we are something unique and that this individual core is consistent in time and space: we are who we are irrespective of the social constellations we are parts of. Of course, we play roles and adjust our conduct to fit situations (Goffman 1971) but the general idea is that 'beneath' these roles we are one, consistent and whole. The very term individual reflects this view, we are indivisible.

'Individual' and 'identity' are concepts that are also widely used in research and it is my contention that the ways these terms are understood and used are unduly affected by the ideology of individualism. These terms carry with them biases about consistency in thought, attitude and mores that are more reflections of Western ideology than of observed conduct. We are, in the words of Katherine Ewing, blinded in our academic efforts by an 'illusion of wholeness' (Ewing 1990) and if we were able to see through this illusion we would observe that 'people can be observed to project multiple, inconsistent self-representations that are context-dependent and might shift rapidly' (ibid.: 251). The problem is that the ideological connotations of the terms unintentionally become part of our analyses and therefore affect our academic results.

If we take seriously the context-dependent practical reality of everyday life, a conventional view on individuals and identity is misleading.

What we need is a conceptual apparatus that grasps the changes that take place in persons as they move in and out of various language-games. For this reason, the perspective that persons emerge from the tension between dividual and individual aspects or relations (LiPuma 1998: 57) can be analytically fertile. The 'dividual' points to the embodied state of mind that is linked to a specific language-game, hence the practice-bound part of a person. We can similarly think that the sum of these dividualities together constitutes a person. However, there are also forces and situations that encourage a person to envision themselves as one consistent whole – an individual. As mentioned, the very ideology of individualism is obviously one such factor but as LiPuma (ibid.: 56) points out individual aspects of persons are especially salient in language (the 'I') and in the physicality of the body. These 'synthesising' forces impress on the person an urge to appear as an essential, seamless unity. I would also suggest that the degree of individuality is a result of the issue at hand, the language-game one is engaged in: engulfing activities like for instance playing a video game are highly dividual while a situation where the player is discussing with a parent how much video gaming they can do, and when to do it, is a communicative context that necessarily involves more perspectives and views (immediate fun versus sensible uses of time, education, future life, obligations, morality and so on). This amounts to attempting to bring several communicative contexts together in one situation. We might call it a language-game complex – that is, a complex formed in order to integrate several language-games (see Storm-Mathisen 2007). Dividual and individual are hence not opposites but should be seen as extremes along a continuum. Let me briefly illustrate some of the possible advantages of this point of view.

In 2003 some colleagues and I interviewed three adults that had lived for two weeks in a Future House (a 'laboratory' built as an apartment that is used for developing and testing new domestic ICTs) outside Oslo. We showed them the pilot of an interactive gaming service that a major betting company in Norway had designed. The basic idea was that one could play sports online and bet on anything from the game's outcome to the result of a penalty kick. A year earlier we had shown the same pilot to four nuclear families in the same Future House. The strikingly uniform reaction from the adults in these families was that this was immoral. It was literally out of context – sitting in front of the TV at home together with one's children was not the right setting in which gambling should take place (Helle-Valle 2003; Helle-Valle and Slettemeås 2008). We were now curious as to what reactions we would get by showing the same pilot to the three adults, who had stated that during the two weeks they had lived together that they had developed a sense of being a commune. Would they have the same reaction as the parents from nuclear families? Interestingly enough they were totally devoid of moral reservations. They were captivated by it and wanted to know when it might be available. Although we tried in our interview to elicit an objection to the game, we had no success until we asked them to imagine that they were parents with their small children present while they used it in their living room. Then the moral reaction was both immediate and strong, not unlike the reactions from the parents we had previously interviewed: it was, they said, a dangerous and immoral product that should not be part of family life (Helle-Valle 2007; Helle-Valle and Slettemeås 2008).

To explain this case in terms of conventional ideas about individuals and consistent identities is not fruitful. We would perhaps have to say that what took place in the minds of the commune members was that they revealed their 'true' liking of online gambling but that when we forced them to relate it to family life their moral concerns kicked in. And we could similarly say about the parents in the first interviews that they 'really' liked the pilot but that the presence of their children made them repress the feeling and focus on the negative sides of things.

This might be true but my first point is that it would be analytically more rewarding to see these cases in light of a context-bound perspective. When the three adults of the commune watched the pilot they entered into a language-game that included no thoughts about being a household or what negative consequences the gaming service might have for children – markedly different to the immediate communicative context in which the parents framed their watching. The three adults of the commune were clearly so deeply into their own perspective that hints at negative sides of this service did not appear – at least not until we explicitly asked them to envision this service in a prototypical household. Then an immediate, visible change to how the experience was framed took place – our question resulted in an instant change of language-game, and hence also attitude. It is more rewarding to understand this change as a change from one dividuality to another rather than to see it as a change of role or 'letting in' some concern.[11] Such a view will more effortlessly bring forth the way that language-games provide frames for perception and evaluation. What was detectable in the three adults' response after the changed framing of the game was that they operated with both perspectives at the same time after the first, initial change of perspective. The discussions afterwards in various ways displayed both the concerned parent's perspective and that of the independent adult in a non-family setting. Thus, in terms of the terminology I have introduced they changed first from one relatively simple language-game to another and then, as they had time to reflect on the change itself, they changed to a more complex language-game – one that incorporated the perspectives of both the previous ones. This change entailed a change from a relatively dividual towards a more individual position.

So far my argument has been purely analytical in the sense that I do not claim that people are dividual but that it is analytically fruitful to see persons as emerging from the tension between dividual and individual aspects. However, I wish to go one step further and suggest that it is reasonable to consider the substantial sides of the contention. If we take seriously the claim that thinking, feeling, perceiving and so on are embodied processes that are anchored in concrete practices, it follows that in/dividuality is much more than an analytical stance and a question of playing roles. For example: I still recall a horrid experience I had as a fourteen-year-old when I was watching a film on television with my parents and it turned out to verge on pornography. I felt the situation to be extremely embarrassing, and the reaction was highly embodied, a feeling of nausea. Needless to say, as with most teenagers there were other embodied emotions that dominated when watching erotic images alone or with friends. What this exemplifies is the point Burkitt made (see above) about emotions and contextualised embodiment; it also exemplifies the concepts habitus and hexis, as Bourdieu uses them, dispositions that are inculcated in the person from early on and which constitute a practical sense, a 'feel for the game'. These dispositions are not mental structures but embodied habits that at the same time constitute specific structured and structuring social forces. For Bourdieu, habitus comprises the link between society and subjectivity – and hence the bridge between objectivism and subjectivism. In short, it is his way of merging action and structure within a theory of practice (see Bourdieu 1977: 82–83; Calhoun 1993; see also Connerton 1989).

Conclusion

The aim of this chapter has been to argue for a certain view of what practice theory should entail. The ontological argument is that what should characterise practice theory is abstaining from evoking *langue*-like explanations of regularity and order, which I contend is much more common than might be expected because many authors unwittingly revert to such analytic tactics. The second concern has been to draw out some of the implications of this ontological argument. Like many others I suggest that embodiment and consumption are salient features of practice theory. Moreover, I argue that Wittgenstein's concept of 'language-game' provides an anchorage that makes the analytic apparatus manageable. In addition I draw attention to what I consider to be a missing piece in the development of practice theory: if we agree that practice is situated and we accept that meanings, and hence also persons' perspectives, change with changing contexts, it follows that the ideological view of the person as an individual, as consistent in their outlook and conduct, is flawed and unfortunate. Therefore we need to rectify our bias and approach the person as a composite of dividual as well as individual aspects. In this way we heed the analytic point of giving practice itself precedence and at the same time give analytic space to the actor by not reducing the subject to a mere *Träger*, a passive carrier, of practices. An additional advantage to this is that by focusing on how the person – and hence the actor – is always embedded in a communicative-practical framework this conceptual tool box provides us with the means to avoid ending up in the perpetual dualism of structure versus agency. Instead of positing these as opposed to each other, as often happens in academic practice, we are in a position where agency simply cannot be considered outside the concrete, practical circumstances the agent is situated in; hence agency always unfolds within a structure.

My proposed approach has ontological, analytical and methodological implications for research in media anthropology. First, it requires sensitivity to ontological issues: we need to be aware of how we use our analytic concepts, and we especially need to avoid treating such concepts as belonging to that which we study. Secondly, we must lower our ambition to generalise by not only acknowledging that media content is differently received by different groups within a population but also that the same persons might interpret a given message differently depending on the communicative context that media consumption is taking place in. Finally, since the communicative context affects the ways media are consumed it follows that we need to reach wider in our methodological efforts than conventional media research has done, and include ethnographic field methods (see, e.g., Ang 1996; Askew 2002; Hartmann 2006). However, since determining what constitutes the relevant context for media consumption cannot be done a priori such a methodological turn also implies a problem (Schlecker and Hirsch 2001). Latour's (1993) advice to 'follow the networks' inductively and empirically is probably the best answer. The practice turn in media anthropology thus constitutes challenges but the reward will be better, more holistic and realistic studies.

Notes

1. I am deeply indebted to my colleague Ardis Storm-Mathisen for fruitful dialogues and insightful comments. I also wish to thank the volume editors for their constructive feedback.
2. Mere thinking is an activity but if the thinking does not have social consequences of some sort it is sociologically uninteresting. I am aware that this wide understanding of practice is at odds with leading scholars in the field: cf., e.g., Reckwitz (2002: 249), Schatzki (2002: 70–78), Couldry (2004) and Hobart (this volume). My deviant use of the word is due to my emphasis on the ontological aspect of practice theory, in which a crucial point is to distinguish between what is studied and the tools researchers use. In addition, one might object to the more conventional view of practice as routinised types of activities that constitute a 'field' of practice, as what counts as 'routinised' might be hard to determine. Such a distinction between activities and practices might also easily lead to analytical biases.
3. As many know, Wittgenstein changed his views on language and meaning fundamentally during his philosophical career. After having been the central inspiration of the Vienna school, he dismissed his former views during the 1930s. His original view was based on a positivist idea about reaching accurate and certain knowledge, while his latter perspective implied a fundamental rejection of this idea. Not only did he reject the idea that it was possible to reach such insight, he dismissed it as misguided and uninteresting (Wittgenstein 1968; Monk 1990).
4. This understanding of Wittgenstein's treatment of rule-following is similar to that presented by Bloor (2001), although Bloor's and my arguments differ significantly.
5. Whether or not this can be said to be the real reason for some (non-)action is another matter. This relates to the distinction between saying and doing and is a methodological issue. It is worth noting, however, that the simple distinction between saying and doing is quite misleading since from a practice point of view saying is doing. Nevertheless, when language is used referentially – in this case as explaining why something was done – it is meaningful to distinguish between what has been done and what informants say has been done.
6. Thus, Bourdieu's advice is pertinent: 'any scientific objectification ought to be preceded by a sign indicating "everything takes place as if ...", which, functioning in the same way as quantifiers in logic, would constantly remind us of the epistemological status of the constructed concepts of objective science' (Bourdieu 1977: 203, n.49).
7. This is relevant if one objects to my discussion here by arguing that rules might point to habits. It is not in itself wrong to substitute 'habit' for 'rule' but the former suggests an embodied – and hence at least partly non-linguistic – disposition while the latter is conventionally linked to a linguistic phenomenon. Hence, if one uncritically refers to the habit as a rule and

uses it as an explanation for observed practices it is at best a misleading shorthand for a complex practice involving embodied elements.

8. With my knowledge of new gender relations in Africa I find it extremely unlikely that men and women would interpret such films more or less in similar fashion, and that so-called independent women would take to them in the same way as older, married women (see Helle-Valle 2004).

9. See the Wittgenstein/Burkitt argument above.

10. Most anthropologists know the concept of the dividual from South Asian and Melanesian ethnography: e.g., Marriot (1976) and Strathern (1988). A focus in this tradition is on how different dividuals in a person are connected to different relational networks. Emphasis is on how this fits into a cultural holistic logic, not as elements in concrete language-games. Moreover, the term is used as a contrast to their understanding of the Western conceptualisation of personhood. The way I use the concept here differs in significant ways from this tradition. I take an eclectic approach because I believe it has great evocative potential in the context I use it here. In tandem with 'individual', 'dividual' provides a more balanced understanding of human beings in that the conceptual pair highlights how perspectives are always contextual.

11. It seems to me that conventional uses of Goffman's perspective (role play, front and back stage, etc.) involve ideas about strategies of pretending, hence hiding or modifying, 'real' feelings, dispositions and strategies. This is analytically unfortunate because, first, it ignores Goffman's emphasis on the importance of framing (Goffman 1974) and, secondly, it is highly problematic – both analytically and methodologically – to assume that subjects lie or pretend.

References

Ang, I. 1996. *Living Room Wars: Rethinking Media Audiences for a Postmodern World.* London: Routledge.

Askew, K. 2002. 'Introduction', in K. Askew and R.R. Wilk (eds), *The Anthropology of Media: A Reader.* Oxford: Blackwell, pp.1–12.

Bloor, D. 2001. 'Wittgenstein and the Priority of Practice', in T.R. Schatzki, K. Knorr Cetina and E. von Savigny (eds), *The Practice Turn in Contemporary Theory.* London: Routledge, pp.95–106.

Bourdieu, P. 1977. *Outline of a Theory of Practice.* Cambridge: Cambridge University Press.

——— 1990. *The Logic of Practice.* Cambridge: Polity Press.

Burkitt, I. 1999. *Bodies of Thought: Embodiment, Identity and Modernity.* London: Sage.

Calhoun, C. 1993. 'Habitus, Field, and Capital: The Question of Historical Specifity', in C. Calhoun, E. LiPuma and M. Postone (eds), *Bourdieu: Critical Perspectives.* Cambridge: Polity Press, pp.61–88.

Connerton, P. 1989. *How Societies Remember*. Cambridge: Cambridge University Press.

Couldry, N. 2004. 'Theorising Media as Practice', *Social Semiotics* 14(2): 115–32.

Ewing, K.P. 1990. 'The Illusion of Wholeness: Culture, Self, and the Experience of Inconsistency', *Ethos* 18: 251–78.

Gellner, E. 1998. *Language and Solitude: Wittgenstein, Malinowski and the Habsburg Dilemma*. Cambridge: Cambridge University Press.

Giddens, A. 1991. *Modernity and Self-Identity: Self and Society in the Late Modern Age*. Cambridge: Polity Press.

Goffman, E. 1971. *The Presentation of Self in Everyday Life*. Harmondsworth: Penguin.

———— 1974. *Frame Analysis*. New York: Harper.

Hall, S. 1980. 'Encoding/Decoding', in S. Hall (ed.), *Culture, Media, Language: Working Papers in Cultural Studies*. London: Huchinson, pp.128–38.

Hartmann, M. 2006. 'The Triple Articulation of ICTs: Media as Technological Objects, Symbolic Environments and Individual Texts', in T. Berker, M. Hartmann, Y. Punie and K.J. Ward (eds), *Domestication of Media and Technology*. London: Open University Press, pp.80–102.

Helle-Valle, J. 1997. *Change and Diversity in a Kgalagadi Village, Botswana*. Oslo: SUM (Centre for Development and the Environment), University of Oslo.

———— 2003. 'Familiens Trojanske Hester? En Kvalitativ Undersøkelse av Bruk av Digitale Medier i Norske Hjem', Research Report. Oslo: SIFO (National Institute for Consumer Research).

———— 2004. 'Understanding Sexuality in Africa: Diversity and Contextualised Dividuality', in S. Arnfred (ed.), *Re-Thinking Sexualities in Africa*. Uppsala: NAI (Nordic Africa Institute), pp.195–207.

———— 2007. 'Kontekstualiserte Medier, Kontekstualiserte Mennesker – Et Annet Blikk På Mediebruk', in M. Lüders, L. Prøitz and T. Rasmussen (eds), *Personlige Medier: Livet Mellom Skjermene*. Oslo: Gyldendal, pp.16–35.

Helle-Valle, J. and D. Slettemeås. 2008. 'ICTs, Domestication and Language-Games: A Wittgensteinian Approach to Media Uses', *New Media and Society* 10(1): 165–86.

Hirsch, E. 1992. 'The Long Term and the Short Term of Domestic Consumption: An Ethnographic Case Study', in R. Silverstone and E. Hirsch (eds), *Consuming Technologies: Media and Information in Domestic Space*. London: Routledge, pp.208–26.

Latour, B. 1993. *We Have Never Been Modern*. London: Longman.

LiPuma, E. 1998. 'Modernity and Forms of Personhood in Melanesia', in M. Lambek and A. Strathern (eds), *Bodies and Persons: Comparative Perspectives from Africa and Melanesia*. Cambridge: Cambridge University Press, pp.53–79.

Malinowski, B. 1935. *Coral Gardens and Their Magic*. London: Allen and Unwin.

———— 1974. 'The Problem of Meaning in Primitive Languages', in C.K. Ogden and I.A. Richards (eds), *The Meaning of Meaning*. New York: Harcourt, Brace and World, pp.296–336.

Marriot, M. 1976. 'Hindu Transactions: Diversity without Dualism', in B. Kapferer (ed.), *Transaction and Meaning*. Philadelphia: Institute for the Study of Human Issues Publications, pp.109–42.

Meyer, B. 2003. 'Visions of Blood, Sex and Money: Fantasy Spaces in Popular Ghanaian Cinema', *Visual Anthropology* 16(1): 15–41.

Monk, R. 1990. *Wittgenstein: The Duty of Genius*. London: Vintage.

Morley, D. 1986. *Family Television: Cultural Power and Domestic Leisure*. London: Comedia.

Needham, R. 1975. 'Polythetic Classification: Convergence and Consequences', *Man* 10: 349–69.

Ortner, S. 1984. 'Theory in Anthropology since the Sixties', *Comparative Studies in Society and History* 26: 126–66.

Reckwitz, A. 2002. 'Toward a Theory of Social Practices: A Development in Culturalist Theorizing', *European Journal of Social Theory* 5(2): 243–63.

Rothenbuhler, E.W. 2005. 'Ground Zero, the Firemen, and the Symbolics of Touch on 9-11 and After', in E.W. Rothenbuhler and M. Coman (eds), *Media Anthropology*. London: Sage, pp.176–87.

Schatzki, T.R. 2002. *The Site of the Social: A Philosophical Account of the Constitution of Social Life and Change*. University Park: Pennsylvania State University Press.

Schlecker, M. and E. Hirsch. 2001. 'Incomplete Knowledge: Ethnography and the Crisis of Context in Studies of Media, Science and Technology', *History of the Human Sciences* 14(1): 69–87.

Searle, J. 1980. 'The Background of Meaning', in J. Searle, F. Kiefer and M. Bierwisch (eds), *Speech Act Theory and Pragmatics*. Dordrecht: Reidel, pp. 233–46.

Silverstone, R. 1994. *Television and Everyday Life*. London: Taylor and Francis.

Storm-Mathisen, A. 2007. 'Kontekstualisert Mening. Teoretiske og metodologiske betraktninger fra en empirisk undersøkelse av 13-åringers utsagn om klær i identitetsrelaterte språkspill', PhD. thesis. Oslo: University of Oslo.

Strathern, M. 1988. *The Gender of the Gift*. Berkeley: University of California Press.

Swidler, A. 2001. 'What Anchors Cultural Practices?' in T.R. Schatzki, K. Knorr Cetina and E. von Savigny (eds), *The Practice Turn in Contemporary Theory*. London: Routledge, pp.74–92.

Taylor, C. 1993. 'To Follow a Rule', in C. Calhoun, E. LiPuma and M. Postone (eds), *Bourdieu: Critical Perspectives*. Cambridge: Polity Press, pp.45–60.

Warde, A. 2005. 'Consumption and Theories of Practice', *Journal of Consumer Culture* 5(2): 131–53.

Wittgenstein, L. 1968. *Philosophical Investigations*. Oxford: Blackwell.

———— 1979. *On Certainty*. Oxford: Blackwell.

CHAPTER 10

A Barthian Approach to Practice and Media: Internet Engagements among Teleworkers in Rural Denmark

Jens Kjaerulff

Barth has not, perhaps, had the recognition he deserves. Compared to stars such as Bourdieu or Geertz, his work remains little known outside anthropology. This may be a consequence of being based in Oslo, rather than Princeton or Paris; it may be a consequence of intellectual fad and fashion. Whatever the reasons, however, Barth's body of work is one of the richest and most imaginative in anthropology. He is a social theorist of greater significance than his lack of wider reputation might suggest.

—Richard Jenkins

The Norwegian anthropologist Fredrik Barth is not widely recognised as a proponent of practice theory. His most famous publications are without question his contributions to *Ethnic Groups and Boundaries* (Barth 1969) and the essays collectively known as *Models of Social Organization* (Barth 1966). In wider circles at least, these writings have probably earned Barth more of a reputation as a proponent of transactionalism (and, in a more derogatory tenor, of methodological individualism and economism) than of theorising practice. However, much of Barth's oeuvre has emerged during the forty years since *Ethnic Groups and Boundaries* was published, and while Barth's wider reputation largely remains based on his early work, his approach has developed significantly since this time.[1] Convention notwithstanding, Barth's work clearly has a focus in common with what has become known as 'practice theory'. Ortner (1984) summarised this focus in a famous essay where she situates practice theory against other directions of thought in anthropology. Referring to Peter Berger and Thomas Luckmann's epigram –

'Society is a human product. Society is an objective reality. Man is a social product' (Berger and Luckmann 1967: 61, quoted in Ortner 1984: 158) – Ortner states that while earlier anthropology emphasised the second and third components of this set, the focus in practice theory is on the first component in conjunction with the two others; that is, on 'understanding how society and culture themselves are produced and reproduced through human intention and action ... while at the same time maintaining – ideally – a sense of the truths of the two other perspectives' (Ortner 1984: 158). The place of human intention and action in social and cultural reproduction has remained a central focus of Barth's work since the 1960s and his consistent pursuit of this has continued to develop and mature through extensive empirical work in highly diverse settings.[2]

In this chapter I draw on aspects of Barth's more recent work to suggest that the media practices I consider, commonly known as 'telework', are culturally underdetermined. I will argue that this illuminates patterns of internet-related engagements which are otherwise hard to account for, and that this in turn may explain an attraction of internet[3] as a novel medium and means of social action. However, this point extends from a wider argument I will advance: namely, that practice theory should be empirically committed to practice in the rather encompassing and colloquial sense of 'what people actually do', as the basis for developing theory.

As the term has come to be embraced in social sciences, 'practice' is often used in a narrower and somewhat scholastic sense. For example, Ortner distinguished 'modern practice theory' from other attempts to 'put human agency back in the picture', stating that the latter yielded 'either too much or too little to the systems/structures perspective' (Ortner 1984: 159). Although this understanding of practice thus implies an ostensibly balanced systems/structures perspective, it retains notions of 'system/structure' as being central to practice theory all the same, and so restricts the meaning of the concept. More recently, in an article that Couldry (this volume) considers an authoritative overview in this regard, Reckwitz has similarly pointed to a more restricted sense of the term when used in social science:

> Practice (*Praxis*) in the singular represents merely an emphatic term to describe the whole of human action (in contrast to theory and mere thinking). "Practices" in the sense of the theory of social sciences, however, is something else. A "practice" (*Praktik*) is a routinized type of behavior which consists of several elements, interconnected to one another: forms of bodily activities, forms of mental activities, "things" and their

use, a background knowledge in the form of understanding, know-how, states of emotion and motivational knowledge. A practice – [for example,] a way of cooking, of consuming, of working … – forms so to speak a "block" whose existence necessarily depends on the existence and specific interconnectedness of these elements, and which cannot be reduced to any one of these single elements (Reckwitz 2002: 249–50).

I have various reservations regarding such narrower usages. Most obviously perhaps, the two senses of 'practice' distinguished in the quote are sometimes used interchangeably, so that the second sense is confounded with the first. Such implicit double usage effectively enables a fallacy familiar to anthropology, that of elevating theoretical constructs to the empirical level of ethnographic description.[4] But even where the term is used only (and explicitly) in the second more restricted sense, conceptualising human practice in terms of 'blocks' comprising at once 'forms' of bodily and mental activities, seems to entail questionable assumptions of integration and shared premises within such entities. In short, routinisation may indeed be a matter of degree and apparently similar routines may be variously informed, as I will discuss in more detail below. Confounding the physical appearance of behaviour with whatever ideational schemes might inform such behaviour seems a dubious starting point for furthering insights into such complexities. Moreover, human action not readily captured in terms of such a conceptual scheme effectively falls outside the scope of investigation and is thus of no theoretical consequence.

Such problems strike me as major fault lines in the exchange between Couldry and Hobart that frames this volume (see Chapter 3), though perhaps in all fairness this reflects issues pertaining to practice theory on a wider canvass. Hobart justly reacts by asking 'what do we mean by media practices?' and by raising a range of reservations regarding the ontological and epistemological assumptions entailed by Couldry's vision of practice. I agree with Hobart's call for a more radical approach. However, where Hobart's leverage to this end is philosophy my inclination is to strive in the first instance for a greater measure of humility towards the empirical phenomena we seek to understand and depict (Barth 1989: 121, 1995: 66). A first step in this direction must be to think of practice in a more open and colloquial sense of the term. Striving towards developing theory based on empirical studies of 'what people actually do' remains a worthwhile objective if we are prepared to be surprised in the field and heed what we in fact find.

Drawing on fieldwork among people working from their homes in rural Denmark by means of internet – an engagement broadly known as 'telework' – I suggest that much human action variously involving internet does not readily lend itself to being classified with reifying terms such as 'types' of behaviour or 'routines'. This may strike the reader as trivial. However, my point is not that this finding is particularly exotic but rather that it should be taken seriously. A more sustained attempt is needed to theorise these empirical states of affairs. What a Barthian perspective contributes here is a theory of cultural process rather than cultural forms. This has been at the heart of Barth's 'generative approach' throughout, which insists on anthropology as an empirical mode of enquiry, reflected in Barth's 'ideal of naturalism', likewise a hallmark of his work. I will expand on both later in the chapter.

Regarding media engagements, my approach is in line with Couldry's suggestion elsewhere in this volume that an aim should be to broaden the focus to questions of media's role in 'the ordering of social life more generally'. This direction of research has gained momentum in recent years. Miller and Slater's (2000) landmark study of internet is one example, though it is also suggestive of the challenge involved in pursuing this direction of research. Situating their internet study in Trinidad, Miller and Slater see a need to remark in their introduction that 'paradoxically perhaps – this is not just a study of Trinidad but … it really is an ethnographic approach to "the Internet"' (ibid.: 2). Arguing that a deeper understanding of cultural and social life in Trinidad is a prerequisite for understanding what internet 'is' there, they suggest the apparent paradox is sidestepped by also acknowledging that social and cultural life in Trinidad (as elsewhere) is 'constantly being redefined through engagements with forces such as the internet' (ibid.: 1–2). This is in line with the perspective I will advance, where cultural process is seen as situated in terms of particulars, such as media among other things.

In what follows I first provide a truncated account of the fieldwork that is the focus of my discussion. I then outline some components in Barth's work and apply them to the material in developing my arguments. This progression is in part intended to convey a sense of how I came to appreciate Barth's perspectives. I was not familiar with his more recent publications when I embarked on this research. Indeed, at that time I pursued analytic schemes more in line with the conception of practice I have here briefly criticised. It was only in the course of my empirical pursuits, wrestling with 'what was there' in the field, and coming to terms with abandoning 'what was not there', that I gradually discovered the relevance of Barth's work for what I had at hand.

Telework in Practice

'Telework' and 'telecommuting' are terms which designate the capability and practice of working from home via computer network technology. The terms are used in academic literature on the topic and at large, both about self-employed people and company employees who use network technology to work from their homes in different ways (Armstrong 1999; Ellison 1999; Haddon 1999). My research into telework was prompted by an interest in cultural and social change and the place of media in it, and a simultaneous interest in how to approach such issues empirically and theoretically.[5] A partial inspiration was my critical reading of Anderson's famous argument about the significance of print media in the emergence of national consciousness (Anderson 1983). What I missed in Anderson's historical study of change was attention to micro processes of cultural transition, as experienced in and resulting from the course of everyday life. For good reason this may be hard to enquire about empirically in historical retrospect. But the problem I sensed seemed to point to wider ontological and epistemological issues entailed in inquiring about change, i.e. (briefly) in terms of 'what' changes, and what constitutes a 'change' in the first place (Kjaerulff 2006). While change is most commonly approached in terms of wider scales, it must logically unfold in particulars. I was interested in what a close-up analysis of change would uncover, and the context of internet seemed to be an exciting opportunity for approaching this through anthropological fieldwork.

My focus on telework came about by happenstance. I was watching a news story on TV one evening that focused on a group of teleworkers in a Danish village. Backed by statistical research conducted on behalf of a Danish ministry, it was claimed that telework would become much more prevalent in the not too distant future. The group of teleworkers portrayed was taken to suggest how 'working life' and 'village life' would change as a result. In contrast with a prevailing view of village life as something that has been deteriorating since the agrarian revolution – and perhaps well before (see Williams 1973) – the story suggested how social life in the village had already become reinvigorated as a result of the increasing number of people now present there during the working week.

The group portrayed on TV had emerged between teleworking neighbours who routinely met once a week, for 'work lunches' as they called these events. Anyone from the village working from home was welcome to join, and new social relations within the village were allegedly taking shape this way. More than that, new sources of professional inspiration were allegedly emerging among these teleworking vil-

lagers of very different professional backgrounds. Concretely, the story
indicated how, while having lunch, these people were 'discussing each
others projects', as one put it. On TV, the group was depicted studying
the drafts of an architect who was a member of the group. His drafts
were spread out on top of the lunch table, as the group's members commented on and eagerly enquired about this work in progress.
Meanwhile, another member of the group, a psychologist, said how discussions with a fellow teleworker who was a journalist had given him
entirely new perspectives on certain aspects of his own work. Thus, not
only village life but also working life was seemingly changing as the
practice of telework became more prevalent. Indeed, this was the claim
made not only on the TV programme but also in the research reports
that the story referred to.

What in part intrigued me about this story was the contrast it provided to another vision of change related to flexible work which had
just been published at the time, Richard Sennett's study of the personal consequences of work under 'new capitalism' (Sennett 1998).[6]
Sennett suggests that flexible work is detrimental to social life and identity, and in passing he elevates working from home to 'the most flexible
of flextimes' (ibid.: 58). Inspired in part by the work of Giddens, a practice theorist of some standing (see Ortner 2006: 2), Sennett points to
'the primary value of habit in both social practices and self-understand-
ing' (ibid.: 44) as part of his argument. In a historical context, Sennett
discusses how the emergence of novel industrial work habits or 'routines' as he puts it – for example, related to time-measurement –
became endowed with cultural and social significances different to
those intended by the managers who introduced such routines in a spirit of 'scientific management' (ibid.: 32–44). Among workers, such routines became culturally appropriated and associated with social resistance and pride (ibid.). In this way Sennett shows how the practice of
novel industrial routines led to novel cultural meanings apart from
what was imposed from above, and so remained important micro factors in how cultural change came about. Sennett's historical account
may thus be seen as a practice-oriented account of change.[7] However,
Sennett's main argument in the book is that present-day practices of
flexibility annihilate habits and routines in the domain of work, with
social identity being consequently at stake.

From this perspective the lunch group portrayed on TV was particularly interesting. On the one hand the group seemed at odds with
Sennett's vision of change and routines under contemporary 'flexible'
circumstances, while on the other it seemed in line with the perspective
on change and routines that Sennett outlines historically. The members

of the group had seemingly developed some new 'habits' or 'routines' that suited their novel ways of practising flexible work, and effected various 'changes' in the course, speaking as they did of their neighbours as 'colleagues' and developing their 'projects' in collaboration with them. I was also attracted by the idea advanced in the TV programme of the lunch group and the village as concrete 'windows' through which to study wider questions about changes related to media use, all the more since the group was a spontaneous rather than a formally imposed arrangement, and so very much an affair of 'practice'.[8]

I ended up doing sixteen months of fieldwork (between 1999 and 2000) in the village portrayed in the TV programme with the lunch group as my point of departure. When I embarked on this fieldwork I simply envisioned developing analytic perspectives outlined in Sennett's historical discussion and using them to focus on the novel work routines these teleworkers had developed. As it turned out, these ambitions were frustrated as I gradually found many discrepancies between the story I had seen on TV and that which I could observe as I participated in the group's lunches on a weekly basis. For one thing, I was surprised by the extent to which the lunches seemed in practice not to be much about 'work'. I certainly never saw the architect's drawings on the lunch table, nor anyone else's projects. In the course of my informal interaction with the group some members of it indicated that the story on TV had been an exaggeration, that they in fact did not consider each other 'colleagues', and that the group involved just 'commonplace socialising' (*almindeligt menneskeligt samvær*). At other times, however, the very same individuals would point out that the group was occasionally and in some ways about 'work' after all, in the sense that they could exchange occasional tips – about such things as tax issues and IT troubleshooting – and meet up with like-minded people in the middle of the working day.[9] Not only was I confused, so it appeared were they. For example, they occasionally reprimanded one another for serving food that was too lavish rather than being affordable and 'work-like', and for inviting fellow villagers to the lunches who were unemployed (and so ostensibly did not 'belong' there). While the lunches clearly comprised elements of routinised behaviour – in terms of such things as timing and the consumption of food – their routinisation seemed at best a matter of degree, and the cultural significance of the lunches as a 'work' routine was certainly less than straightforward, as even my informants effectively acknowledged. In short, the concept of 'routine' as a main analytic category began to appear increasingly questionable, no less so than when it came to thinking in terms of 'types' of routines, which my original argument about change hinged on.

However, my intention had never been to focus exclusively on this lunch group – indeed, the story on TV had concerned the village as a whole, in a sense of 'society writ large'. But my frustrations with the lunch group probably pushed me towards pursuing a more open inquiry on wider empirical grounds, and more eagerly and sooner than I might have otherwise done. As part of this effort, I carried out a survey of all the households in the village and the area immediately surrounding it in which I enquired about 'work via internet from home' rather than 'telework'. One result of this was that I found that the extent of such engagements was already considerably greater than what had been forecast by the TV programme as the likely scenario ten years in the future, based on the aforementioned statistical research. Although a main purpose of my survey had been to create a starting point for contact with a broader range of informants, it underscored telework as 'practice' in the sense of 'what people actually do', regardless of how such behaviour is labelled. Of the entire stock of respondents, only two had a teleworking arrangement formally designated as such, in the sense of a written agreement with their workplace, which is really quite remarkable given the extent of written regulations and contracts in the world of work otherwise. As I pursued more intensive fieldwork among more of these 'informal' teleworkers, I found not only a staggering diversity in terms of how telework was practised,[10] but I also found that behavioural flux across time was a prevalent feature of the teleworking practices I became familiar with, reflecting the complex circumstances which informed them.

Let me provide a more concrete sense of this by referring to some circumstances of just one individual. When I first encountered Edward, he informed me that he had had an informal agreement for three years with his workplace to take care of frequent overtime by way of teleworking, but that he had made a firm decision to abandon this arrangement half a year prior to my arrival as it had intruded unduly on his family life. Edward and his wife explained how work, and even just the potential of engaging in work-related matters, had preoccupied him more often than not due to the internet connection he had with his workplace. The family had allegedly had difficulties 'reading his behaviour' at home and had never been quite sure whether he was really 'mentally present', as they put it. This way of practising parenting and partnering was not one they really wanted to subscribe to.

As I gradually became more intimate with this family, it emerged that Edward had never informed his workplace of his firm decision to end the teleworking arrangement as a means of handling overtime. Indeed, it turned out that he was at pains to maintain his teleworking status as far as his workplace was concerned, because, as he put it, of its 'flex-flex' dimension. On formal grounds he did nothing wrong but he felt uncertain and somewhat anxious about whether his colleagues might interpret his decision to end teleworking as 'slack' in terms of the work hours they thought he continued to deliver from home, and so set social dynamics in motion with tangible and unfortunate consequences for his career. Hence the relative secrecy regarding his decision to terminate his active teleworking as far as his workplace was concerned. In a real sense then – a social sense – he could still be perceived as 'teleworking' – that is, working in part from home to take care of overtime issues. As I became yet more familiar with this household through frequent informal interaction, I gradually found that he also still actively teleworked in the conventional sense on an occasional basis (e.g. to handle overtime, or when he or his children got sick), despite his prior stated rejection of this option. These engagements fluctuated and were mostly carefully negotiated with his wife as a matter of 'making exceptions to the rule', as they put it. But Edward would sometimes also telework when his significant others were not at home. He downplayed this, and above all saw his continued teleworking arrangement as a way of dealing with a wider and continuous problem he struggled with, of making things 'work out' (*få det til at gå op*), as he put it.

In less spectacular fashion, similar instances of behavioural flux and struggles to 'work things out' were readily detectable across a broad spectrum of the lives that I followed. Telework aside, such things are perhaps inherent in living a life with multiple, simultaneous, and at times conflicting, agendas. In the course of practical living, people try to work things out through twists and turns and by embracing various and shifting means. They may indeed be partially successful in some endeavours, but most successes are limited in duration and people may change their outlook, agenda and course of action. Practices of telework may variously reflect this, but to appreciate what informs them we must go beyond the context of internet. A theory of practices such as these should be able to reflect flux in behaviour and uncertainties and multiple concerns that simultaneously informs it, as an integral part of cultural process. It was in such regards that I found Barth's work increasingly compelling.

A Barthian Approach

In general terms, two connected aspects of Barth's work may be said to stand out through his oeuvre: his analytic approach of creating what he calls 'generative models' of what confronts him in the field; and his commitment to what he has called 'an ideal of naturalism'. He has characterised the latter in part as 'a struggle to *get [his] ontological assumptions right*: to ascribe to our object of study only those properties and capabilities that we have reasonable grounds to believe it to possess' (Barth 1987: 8). In line with this, a basic assumption in Barth's work is that social and cultural order reflects the result of process. This would appear similar to many others who study social and cultural construction (see, e.g., Wuthnow et al. 1984; cf. Barth 1989: 123). The difference may be concisely stated as being that Barth attempts to depict 'construction' (for example, of cultural 'order') in the sense of a verb (ordering, for example), where many others effectively depict it in the sense of a noun (an order). Barth articulates this by saying that his theoretical work concerns process rather than form. Generative models 'provide a kind of understanding and explanation which a model of form, however meticulous and adequate, can never give. To explain form, one needs to discover and describe the processes that generate the form' (Barth 1981: 33).

But his naturalism goes further, in that he demands that 'analytical operations … should model or mirror significant, identifiable processes that can be shown to take place among the phenomena they seek to depict' (Barth 1987: 8); that is, the phenomena we concretely confront when doing fieldwork. In Barth's view it is this naturalist component which makes the analytic approach of constructing generative models 'subservient to the objectives of an empirical science' (Barth 1981: 33). Stated differently, Barth's generative models are analytic constructs that aim at accounting for – that is, 'generating' the phenomena we confront during fieldwork as processes through which the degree of cultural and behavioural order(ing) which can be observed emerges. If such order(ing) is only 'partial' – the work lunches I described above being a point in case, in so far as they were indeed partially 'about work' – this should be reflected in the model so that it only generates that degree of order(ing). In turn, it should of course also provide grounds for reflection in terms of the wider implications of this for the model and its components as theoretical constructs. In line with the latter, Barth has modified and further developed his theoretical constructs considerably over the years, but the basic ideas of the generative approach and the ideal of naturalism as a corrective have distinguished Barth's work throughout.[11]

Barth's work is considerably richer than I can convey here while also developing my more specific arguments, but a highly accessible and concise starting point for my present purpose is his study of the Omani town of Sohar, in particular the introduction to a discussion of the reproduction of cultural diversity (Barth 1983: 191–96). Here Barth argues for the importance of distinguishing between 'behaviour' on the one hand and the cultural 'ideas' which may variously inform such behaviour on the other. For my purposes the distinction allows me to account for the fact that the lunches were simultaneously informed by various cultural ideas – for example, the interaction to varying degrees concerned both work and village (among other things); different group members interpreted the lunches somewhat differently (as did the same individuals at different times); there were occasional disagreements about what food it was appropriate to serve, and who 'really' belonged to the group; there was also my own bewilderment (in part anthropologically informed) regarding what was going on. Barth's objective with this distinction is to account for the reproduction of cultural diversity in Sohar, where people of various cultural backgrounds – ethnicity, religion – have interacted on a daily basis for centuries. Such diversely informed interactions compromise the notion of culture as an analytic term. Barth brings this out by asking:[12]

> [H]ow much meaning must be conveyed between them for us to be able to regard two persons as participating in the same culture? Or, obversely, how little shared meaning should there be for us to be justified in saying that two persons participate in two different cultures? … How full of meaning must the acts of another be; must the meanings be identical with those entertained by the other, need they be only compatible; or can they indeed be contradictory and still justify the view that the two persons 'share a culture'? (ibid.: 192).

In developing his model of cultural reproduction in this setting, Barth argues that we should strive towards naturalism in terms of how such reproduction takes place. He proposes that we think of cultural reproduction as 'experience-induced': 'The meanings, understandings and values that we hold have developed and assumed their nuances in experienced contexts … This implies that the ideas that compose a culture must develop in each separate person as a precipitate of continuing experience through life' (ibid.: 194). Stated differently, if we take 'experience' seriously as an idiom for thinking about cultural reproduction, we need to attend to how experience actually unfolds empirically; that is, at the level of concrete human beings 'experiencing' living a life.[13] This in turn implies that experience, in the nature of things, must be concretely situated, and this brings me back to the model under consideration. Barth argues that cultural ideas do not shape behaviour alone; other factors impinge as well (in the work I here refer to he lists things such as resources, material environment, social organisation and interactionally predicated strategic factors), while shaping the experience of action and events accordingly (ibid.: 191–96). Barth suggests this perspective may account for the prevalence of different 'nuances in meanings, understandings and values' which he examines as eventuating through differently situated, and so differently experienced, action. Barth introduces a distinction between 'recognizing' and 'embracing' cultural ideas to suggest the span of such nuances (ibid.: 192–93). These pespectives allow him to account for interaction as informed by partially shared meanings. They also form the basis of a model of partial cultural reproduction of various traditions in Sohar, and the place of various material and social changes in this over the past century. In the Sohar study he seeks to articulate this partiality on both accounts with the idiom 'streams' of culture and tradition (e.g., ibid.: 84–85, 1989: 130–31), which he interrogates in terms of their coherence and differing conditions of persistence.[14]

It is important to appreciate that while this, of course, is only a model of situated action, in turn applied to theorise cultural reproduction, its strength lies in the empirical approach to theorising cultural process as something unfolding in quite concrete terms, accessible through fieldwork, in the 'here and now'. The approach sees social action as informed by various traditions 'already' reproduced, and indeed in the process of further ongoing reproduction.[15] It is in this light I suggest that the lunches which formed my starting point are less trivial than they may at first seem.

Working from home via internet, rather than at a workplace among conventional colleagues, clearly comprises a significant change in terms of the material and other contextual factors impinging on teleworkers' behaviour and experience of working, and in this regard the lunch group's members presumably shared similar circumstances of working, which they objectified as such themselves. But given their highly different professional experience and the lack of a formal, institutional frame for their lunches, the conditions for the persistence of work as a 'cultural stream' was, hardly surprisingly, not very uniform, and what they in fact shared in terms of work was rather limited. Yet, the lunches were clearly not formless. They were indeed a recurrent event, to a degree routinised on various accounts, and recognised as such by participants, in part in terms of 'work'. In this way the lunches may be modelled as partially structured by work as a cultural 'stream' among other factors – that is, in terms of ideas about timing (it happened during the 'work day'), who could participate, what food it was appropriate to serve, and what subjects of conversation were suitable. But the partiality of this, reflected in the variety of other perspectives apart from 'work' that the group's participants quite randomly engaged in the course of the lunches, was a salient feature in practice.

As I said earlier, my contribution should be judged less in terms of the field material I present than the manner in which I theorise it. The need for this becomes all the more apparent if we turn from the limited context of the lunches as an (internet-related) routine towards the larger issue of everyday life as reflected in my truncated account of Edward's experience with teleworking. In his more recent work, Barth has developed the perspectives I have outlined and I will summarise a few key points which I consider of particular significance to my argument here.

Barth introduces a model of social action where he distinguishes between 'events' and 'acts'. The concept of 'event' refers to 'the outwards appearance of behaviour', while 'act' refers to 'the intended and interpreted meaning of that behaviour' (Barth 1992: 21–24, 1993a: 158–60 et passim). In some ways, this distinction resembles that between behaviour and ideas introduced above, and may be deployed for similar explanatory purposes. The same event – such as telework – may be interpreted differently, as an act, by different individuals – for example, by Edward, his wife, or by Edward's colleagues. But the distinction allows for a more dynamic model of events as subject to and shaped in part by continuous (re)thinking and (re)action. Barth suggests that events are underdetermined (Barth 1993a: 5) and highlights this by observing that events are often 'at variance with the intentions of individual actors' (Barth 1989: 134), a point he has developed at some length.[16] It is notable that his predicament goes some way towards accounting for the momentum of ongoing (re)action and reflection, and so indeed of cultural 'development' or partial cultural reproduction. Barth in turn develops his perspective on the latter, proposing 'knowledge' as an alternative conceptual prototype to what anthropologists have conventionally thought of as 'culture'. This has been a main project in much of Barth's later work, which he has described as an effort to develop an 'anthropology of knowledge' (see, e.g., Barth 1993a: 160, 1995, 2002) and it would exceed my purpose here to embark on a more detailed account of what this perspective entails.[17] Of particular relevance to the argument I want to advance, however, and tying in with the aforementioned predicament, is the fact that Barth sees knowledge ('culture') as one of our most basic means to cope in a life that is inherently somewhat underdetermined and uncertain (see, e.g., Barth 1987, 1993a: 3–8, 305–23).[18] Barth has even suggested that people's (including academics') inclinations to represent their circumstances as 'belonging in larger classes and interlinked in chains of recurrence and predictability' – that is, the way 'culture' is often conceived of and portrayed – may be seen in part as a way of countering such uncertainty (Barth 1993a: 5–6, 319–20).

I highlight these things, since this predicament strikes me as salient in Edward's unfolding engagements with internet and his telework arrangement. Indeed, Edward pointed out that the 'struggle to work things out' was ongoing. He and his wife originally envisioned the arrangement as an attractive way of meeting simultaneous requirements and desires in terms of work and family. In the course of events they both got to know this way of working better, but it also turned out to be different from what they had hoped. At the same time Edward got to know what he called the 'flex-flex' potential of the arrangement. Based on the knowledge he acquired from the experience of teleworking he then decided to terminate the arrangement. But despite no formal wrong–doing, Edward was uncertain about how this act might be interpreted by his colleagues, and the 'flex-flex' dimension became more important to him. As it turned out, contrary to what he stated and presumably intended, he also continued to work from home on an occasional basis despite his decision, something that was a potential source of disagreement and uncertainty in the domestic context.

While the perspectives I have briefly outlined go some way to conceptualising and accounting for the actual trajectory and development of Edward's reflections and actions, I want to concentrate here on how they might also provide insights in terms of the attractiveness of internet as a novel medium and means of action. If we accept that a momentum of ongoing (re)action and reflection may arise from a predicament where events are underdetermined and partially at variance with the intentions of individual actors, internet may indeed appear as a potentially powerful resource for 'making a difference' in this regard, on a range of counts. By embracing telework, Edward was able to leave his office when the formal work day was over, despite the need for overtime, and so in theory at least he was able to improve matters with regards to his ideals of family life by spending the remainder of the day 'with' his family. At the same time, in his professional capacity as a branch manager supervising the work of more than forty employees, the potential for increased productivity entailed in telework was not lost on him. Presumably there was also room for improvement and ongoing innovative action when it came to his culturally informed ideals of economic performance, and Edward encouraged telework among employees within his own branch for this reason.[19] As it turned out, teleworking did make a difference on both counts, but neither outcomes were quite what Edward had envisioned.

The significance of internet I want to point to in this context is brought out by Edward's 'flex-flex' practice of telework. As his circumstances in this regard suggest, social dimensions of events can be at variance with the intentions of individual actors. That Edward's teleworking arrangement turned out to work differently from what he himself had envisioned was one thing. The assessment of this turn of events by others was a different, but not insignificant matter, potentially with quite tangible consequences. The 'flex-flex' dimension of the arrangement points to the potential internet affords in terms of entertaining cultural ideals at the level of representation, despite deviation from these ideals when it comes to actual practice.

Other scholars have highlighted findings that to a degree resonate with what I here point to. Miller and Slater, for instance, write that internet engagements in Trinidad are informed in part by a quest for what they call 'expansive realization'. Here 'internet is viewed as a means through which one can enact – often in highly idealized form ... what one thinks one really is ... [C]ontradictions concerning one's ability, in practical life, to be who one thinks one is seem capable of being resolved on the expanded scale and terrain of the internet' (Miller and Slater 2000: 10–11). However, I believe the attraction of internet in this account only truly emerges once we appreciate the wider circumstances of social action and culturally informed reflection to which I have here sought to link it.

Conclusion

The main argument of this chapter has concerned the notion of 'practice', which I understand to be that which 'people actually do'. I have argued that practice theory should above all amount to an empirically based inquiry among people living a life. This may appear simple-minded, and not quite in line with Hobart's (this volume) call for a 'radical' approach, with which I sided in the introduction. I concede that my approach is less radical than Hobart's in terms of the attention I devote to discursive and interpretive practice, scholarly as well as 'out there', and to the intricate relation between these domains. But 'practice', from the naturalist perspective inspired by Barth that I have outlined above, is situated on a wider canvas than that of cultural discourse. As I hope to have shown, 'other factors' apart from cultural ideas also impinge on the particulars of human life to such an extent that lived reality may be at odds with cultural ideals. This is so whether or not we anticipate or understand it, but in practical terms we are often forced to try and actually do something in response. This puts our cultural ideals and their relation to human intention and action into perspective, and importantly our experience and culturally informed outlooks are shaped accordingly. For this reason, as Barth has put it, 'it is insufficient to delimit the object of anthropological study to … ideas, collective representations, or cultural forms: we need to locate them in a system wider than that which culture itself encompasses, so as to be able to record the praxis of a way of life and ask what people do in the world they inhabit' (Barth 1987: 87).

It is from this wider canvas that I have proposed that Barth offers a 'radical' empirical approach to enquiring about and theorising practice. On these grounds, and with examples from my fieldwork among teleworkers, I have proposed a model of cultural process as underdetermined, which I argue goes some way to account not only for the internet-related engagements that confronted me in the course of my research, but also for the attraction of internet as a means to engage with the world, which only truly emerges from this wider theoretical perspective. In this regard, my effort to theorise telework as media practice would appear in line with Couldry's (and others') call for a broader scope in media research. As media may become ever more obtrusive in the worlds we inhabit, it is – perhaps paradoxically – all the more important not to be deceived by this obtrusiveness and to retain a wider picture.

Notes

1. See Barth (1981: 76–104) for a response to some of these criticisms.
2. There are various other strands of anthropology which anticipated dimensions of what became known as practice theory: see, e.g., Evens and Handelman (2006).
3. In keeping with the case I am arguing in this chapter, I use the term 'internet' without the definite article 'the' throughout the chapter as I do not believe in the existence of a single, monolithic internet.
4. See also Jo Helle-Valle's discussion of this problem (this volume).
5. For a fuller account of this study, see Kjaerulff (2010).
6. In brief, the project I envisioned involved focusing on 'work' as a distinct cultural phenomenon (see, e.g., Dumont 1977; Wallman 1979; Joyce 1987; Otto 2004). It was in this context that I read Sennett and took a particular interest in this TV programme.
7. Analytically, the general idea here of a dialectic between actions and their conceptualisation is of course not particularly novel. Marx (1973) pursued a similar line of thought regarding the emergence of a generic concept of work, as preceded by an increased practice in the use of money as a generic means of exchange.

8. Indeed, backed by statistical research, this village was portrayed as representative of future trends at a national (Danish) level in a not-too-distant future.
9. The lunches were usually at 12 noon on Wednesdays, for which reason they were known among members as 'the Wednesday lunches'.
10. This is an issue which I must leave aside here for lack of space.
11. It deserves mention here that the notion of 'models' may be confusing, given its figurative ring. In practice Barth's models comprise prose rather than diagrams – that is, they are conceptual constructs intended to reflect the dynamic nature of the various phenomena he tries to depict. In this way Barth spoke of, for example, 'transactions' and 'values' in his early work, while in later years he developed 'experience', 'concerns' and especially 'knowledge' as key analytic terms (see, e.g., Barth 1993a, 1993b, 1995, 2002). For an exception in this regard, see Barth diagram depicting a generative model (1993a: 159).
12. The problems Barth raises here regarding the concept of culture strongly resemble some of the problems I pointed to earlier regarding a narrower concept of 'practice'. To appreciate this in the context of the following quote, substitute the word 'culture' for 'practice' when reading the quote.
13. Barth's focus on individuals has been subjected to considerable criticism. I believe this criticism is misguided as it is rooted in two different uses of the term 'individual'. Bruce Kapferer, who was one of the more prominent critical readers of Barth's early work, concisely brings out these different uses in a work published more than a decade after the peak of the critique of Barth in this regard. Following Dumont, Kapferer distinguishes between 'the individual as an empirical unit' and 'the individual as culturally or ideologically valued' (Kapferer 1988: 12). He observes: 'The empirical statement that all societies are composed of individuals, separate biologically integrated behaving units, is generally unproblematic. It becomes problematic when it is stated as a cultural value or it is assumed that all societies, for example, carry dominant conceptions of the primacy of the individual in society or of the autonomy of the individual in society that are essentially the same despite superficial cultural differences' (ibid.: 12–13). In accordance with this distinction, Barth uses the phrase 'each separate person' in the quotation cited in the sense of an empirical unit, whereas Barth's critics have taken him to task for speaking of 'individuals' in the latter, ideological sense of the term.
14. This has also been a main project in Barth's later works, set in different places, and modelled in different ways.
15. This is another point where Barth's critics have gone wrong. In brief, because Barth focuses on concretely situated cultural processes in the 'here and now', he has been taken to task for ignoring wider cultural schemes as they may impinge on social action, and for assuming that people could construct their worlds afresh or by free will, irrespective of wider cultural schemes.

16. See Barth (1993a: 286–304) for the development of this issue in relation to his research in Bali. Somewhat similar ideas have recently been developed by Anna Tsing (2005) using a different analytic vocabulary.
17. See the literature just cited in this regard, and Kjaerulff (2010) for an application of it.
18. This idea is of course not entirely novel. Berger and Luckmann (1967) make a similar point, but largely relegate uncertainty to a past when 'the construction of society' presumably began. Meanwhile Dewey (1929) pursued a related idea (see also Whyte 2002: 174).
19. Details of the results of this are beyond the scope of this chapter.

References

Anderson, B. 1983. *Imagined Communities: Reflections on the Origin and Spread of Nationalism*. London: Verso.

Armstrong, N. 1999. 'Flexible Work in the Virtual Workplace: Discourses and Implications of Teleworking', in A. Felstead and N. Jewson (eds), *Global Trends in Flexible Labour*. Basingstoke: Macmillan, pp.43–61.

Barth, F. 1966. 'Models of Social Organization', Royal Anthropological Institute Occasional Paper. London: Royal Anthropological Institute.

——— 1969. *Ethnic Groups and Boundaries*. Oslo: Universitetsforlaget.

——— 1981. *Process and Form in Social Life: Selected essays of Fredrik Barth, Volume I*. London: Routledge and Kegan Paul.

——— 1983. *Sohar: Culture and Society in an Omani Town*. Baltimore, MD: John Hopkins University Press.

——— 1987. *Cosmologies in the Making: A Generative Approach to Cultural Variation in Inner New Guinea*. Cambridge: Cambridge University Press.

——— 1989. 'The Analysis of Culture in Complex Societies', *Ethnos* 54(3/4): 120–42.

——— 1992. 'Towards a Greater Naturalism in Conceptualizing Societies', in A. Kuper (ed.) *Conceptualizing Society*. London: Routledge, pp.17–33.

——— 1993a. *Balinese Worlds*. Chicago: University of Chicago Press.

——— 1993b. 'Are Values Real? The Enigma of Naturalism in the Anthropological Imputation of Values', in M. Hecter et al. (eds), *The Origin of Values*. New York: de Gruyter, pp.31–46.

——— 1995. 'Other Knowledge and Other Ways of Knowing', *Journal of Anthropological Research* 51: 65–68.

——— 2002. 'An Anthropology of Knowledge', *Current Anthropology* 43(1): 1–18.

Berger, P. and T. Luckmann. 1967. *The Social Construction of Reality: A Treatise in the Sociology of Knowledge*. New York: Doubleday.

Dewey, J. 1929. *The Quest for Certainty: A Study of the Relation of Knowledge and Action*. New York: Minton, Balch and Company.

Dumont, L. 1977. *From Mandeville to Marx: The Genesis and Triumph of Economic Ideology*. Chicago: University of Chicago Press.

Ellison, N.B. 1999. 'Social Impacts – New Perspectives on Telework', *Social Science Computer Review* 17(3): 338–56.

Evens, T.M.S. and D. Handelman (eds). 2006. *The Manchester School: Practice and Ethnographic Praxis in Anthropology*. Oxford: Berghahn Books.

Haddon, L. 1999. 'Approaches to Understanding Teleworking', *Telektronikk* 4: 29–38.

Jenkins, R. 1996. *Social Identity*. London: Routledge.

Joyce, P. (ed.). 1987. *The Historical Meanings of Work*. Cambridge: Cambridge University Press.

Kapferer, B. 1988. *Legends of People, Myths of State. Violence, Intolerance, and Political Culture in Sri Lanka and Australia*. Washington, DC: Smithsonian Institution Press.

Kjaerulff, J. 2006. 'Internet and the Change of What? Complexities and Flexibilities among Teleworkers in a Danish Village'. Paper presented at the Biennial Conference of the European Association of Social Anthropologists, Bristol.

——— 2010. *Internet and Change: An Anthropology of Knowledge and Flexible Work*. Hojbjerg: Intervention Press.

Marx, K. 1973. *Grundrisse*. London: Penguin.

Miller, D. and D. Slater. 2000. *The Internet: An Ethnographic Approach*. Oxford: Berg.

Ortner, S.B. 1984. 'Theory in Anthropology Since the Sixties', *Comparative Studies in Society and History* 26(1): 126–66.

——— 2006. *Anthropology and Social Theory. Culture, Power and the Acting Subject*. Durham and London: Duke University Press.

Otto, T. 2004. 'Work, Wealth and Knowledge: Enigmas of Cargoist Identifications', in H. Jebens (ed.), *Cargo, Cult and Culture Critique*. Honolulu: University of Hawaii Press, pp.209–26.

Reckwitz, A. 2002. 'Toward a Theory of Social Practices: A Development in Culturalist Theorizing', *European Journal of Sociology* 5(2): 243–63.

Sennett, R. 1998. *The Corrosion of Character: The Personal Consequences of Work in the New Capitalism*. New York: Norton.

Tsing, A.L. 2005. *Friction: An Ethnography of Global Connection*. Princeton, NJ: Princeton University Press.

Wallman, S. (ed.). 1979. *Social Anthropology of Work*. London: Academic Press.

Whyte, S.R. 2002. 'Subjectivity and Subjunctivity: Hope for Health in Eastern Uganda', in R. Werbner (ed.), *Postcolonial Subjectivities in Africa*. London: Zed Books, pp.171–88.

Williams, R. 1973. *The Country and the City*. London: Hogarth Press.

Wuthnow, R., J.D. Hunter, A. Bergesen and E. Kurzweil. 1984. *Cultural Analysis: The Work of Peter L. Berger, Mary Douglas, Michel Foucault and Jürgen Habermas*. London: Routledge and Kegan Paul.

CHAPTER 11

Can Practice Theory Inspire Studies of ICTs in Everyday Life?

Toke H. Christensen and Inge Røpke

Introduction

In recent years, rich countries have witnessed a proliferation of information and communication technologies (ICTs) in everyday life. The mobile phone has been adopted by almost all age groups, computers are found in most households (often more than one), 'old' analogue television and radio equipment is being replaced by digital equipment, and the stock of music centres, videos, camcorders, answering machines, digital cameras, printers and so forth is exploding. ICT equipment is thus one of the fastest growing categories of consumer goods. In addition, microprocessors are increasingly integrated in many other categories of consumer goods, giving rise to the expression 'pervasive computing'. The widespread adoption of ICT equipment can be seen as an element in constructing a new 'normality' in everyday life: the expectations and conventions regarding a normal home's necessary 'infrastructure' and the ordinary gear for a normal way of life are changing, and the changes are proceeding rapidly.

This chapter takes a closer look at the construction of a new normality in everyday life – following up on Shove's (2003) work on the social organisation of normality in relation to comfort, cleanliness and convenience – and discusses how this development can be studied from the perspective of practice theory. In the following, we show how a practice theory approach shifts the analytic focus away from the consumption of ICT as such and toward the practices that integrate ICT as one element among many others. Thereby, a practice theory approach helps us to avoid the risk of ending up with a 'media-centric' understanding of the use of new media (see Couldry this volume) and adds interesting details and subtleties to the study of the construction of a new normality in everyday life. Our application of practice theory in the study of the normalisation process shows how ICTs have become integrated into a wide range of practices of everyday life and thus may contribute to the increasing 'materialisation' of everyday practices.[1] Finally, our attempts to apply practice theory in empirical studies reveal some theoretical and methodological issues that need more consideration, including how social interaction may contribute to change and problems concerning how to delimit practices.

The increasing consumption of ICT products can be analysed as resulting from various general consumption drivers identified by economic, sociological and anthropological theories, which focus on the interplay between the rapid innovation and renewal of ICT goods on the one hand, and the driving forces behind consumption growth emanating from individual motivations and the conditions of everyday life on the other (see Røpke 1999, 2001). Examples of general consumption dynamics encouraging ICT consumption include the search for individual independence (everyone needs their own computer to avoid the need for coordination with other users), the use of goods as social markers (the rapid renewal of ICTs provides ample material for identity formation), the interest in time saving and time shifting in a busy life (video, internet and podcasts allow the user to be entertained and informed when they have the time), the need for real-time coordination and for keeping up contacts with important others in a fragmented and spatially dispersed everyday life (mobile phones increase accessibility), and the need for keeping everyone in the family up to date in relation to a competitive labour market (training in using computers is a 'must').[2] This approach is useful when the intention is to highlight the potential for general consumption growth in relation to ICTs.

However, we wonder whether a deeper understanding of both the development of a new normality in everyday life and related consumption growth is possible through studying the social practices of which consumption is an integral part. It might be useful to deal with particular practices instead of just looking at driving forces in general because the focus on specific practices can highlight dynamics and changing patterns of everyday life that are not so obvious when focusing on general explanations of consumption growth. A related argument for turning towards practices is that when people use goods and services they do not consider their activities to be about 'consumption' but rather to be about doing things like cooking, travelling or cleaning (Warde 2005: 150, n.6). Consumption is, so to speak, 'derived' from practices.

In the following, we first introduce practice theory very briefly with the main intention of providing a framework for our empirical analysis.

The framework is then applied to identify and analyse practices involving the use of ICTs, including both computer use as a dispersed practice and some examples of integrative practices. Finally, we summarise our empirical work and point out issues and questions that need further consideration.

Practice Theory

Elements of practice theories can be found in the work of several philosophers and sociologists, and there is no generally accepted account of core concepts and relations. Our outline leans heavily on a review article by Andreas Reckwitz (2002), an article by Alan Warde (2005) where he explores the potential of practice theories for the study of consumption, and a case study by Elizabeth Shove and Mika Pantzar (2005). As we said above, our main interest is to discuss how practice theory can be formulated in ways that can inform and support empirical work. The philosophical account of practice is not so easy to apply in empirical analysis (Warde 2005: 135–36) so we intend to discuss some of the issues brought up by its practical application.

The ambition of Reckwitz is to outline an 'ideal-type' model of practice theory based largely on common elements from several authors, in particular Bourdieu, Giddens and Schatzki (Reckwitz 2002: 244). Reckwitz starts by characterising practice theory as an example of what he calls 'cultural theories' (ibid.: 245). In contrast to classical economic and sociological perspectives, a cultural perspective introduces collective cognitive and symbolic structures – a shared knowledge that enables and constrains agents in their interpretation of the world and in their behaviour. The socially shared way of ascribing meaning to the world influences what is regarded desirable and which norms are considered legitimate, so action is explained and understood by reconstructing the cognitive-symbolic structures, and social order is seen as embedded in these structures. Reckwitz identifies four versions of 'cultural theories' – one of them being practice theory (ibid.: 246–50). The versions differ with regard to where they 'locate' the social and, accordingly, what the 'smallest unit' of social analysis is. The social – collective cognitive and symbolic structures – can be located in the human mind, in chains of signs, symbols, discourses or 'texts', in interactions between human agents, or in practices as suggested by practice theory. These practices are thus the smallest unit of social analysis.

The concept of practice is used in different senses. Sometimes it is used only in the singular to describe action in contrast to theory and pure thinking. In the theory of practice, the concept also refers, first, to a coordinated entity (a more or less coherent entity formed around a particular activity) and, second, a performance (the carrying out of some action). Focusing on practice as a coordinated entity, Reckwitz defines the concept as follows:

> A "practice" ... is a routinized type of behaviour which consists of several elements, interconnected to one another: forms of bodily activities, forms of mental activities, "things" and their use, a background knowledge in the form of understanding, know-how, states of emotion and motivational knowledge. A practice ... forms so to speak a "block" whose existence necessarily depends on the existence and specific interconnectedness of these elements. (ibid.: 249–50)

Schatzki defines practice as a coordinated entity as follows:

> a temporally unfolding and spatially dispersed nexus of doings and sayings.... To say that the doings and sayings forming a practice constitute a nexus is to say that they are linked in certain ways. Three major linkages are involved: (1) through understandings, for example, of what to say and do; (2) through explicit rules, principles, precepts and instructions; and (3) through what I will call "teleoaffective" structures embracing ends, projects, tasks, purposes, beliefs, emotions and moods. (Schatzki 1996: 89)

Warde summarises the three components forming a 'nexus' as understandings, procedures and engagements. Schatzki emphasises that practices have to be enacted to reproduce the nexus. As Warde puts it: 'Practices are thus coordinated entities but also require performance for their existence. A performance presupposes a practice' (Warde 2005: 134). The performance is carried out by individuals who are thus seen as 'carriers' of the practice. This perspective implies that both the patterns of bodily behaviour and the mental activities of understanding and desiring inherent in a practice are seen as elements and qualities of the practice, not as qualities of the individual (Reckwitz 2002: 250). As a basis for closer inspection of the practice concept, we apply Reckwitz's conceptualisation of a practice as an entity of routinised activities that includes different components. The routinised activities are both bodily and mental – so integrated that they are often referred to as bodily-mental routines. Routinisation is reflected in the fact that practices become embedded within the body: 'when we learn a practice, we learn to be bodies in a certain way.... The body is not a mere "instrument" which the agent must "use" in order to "act"' (ibid.: 251).

The mental aspect of activities is conceived very broadly and includes a certain know-how, particular ways of interpretation, certain aims and emotional levels. Again, it is emphasised that these mental patterns are not the possession of the individual but part of social practice, and if an individual carries out a practice, they 'must take over both the bodily and mental patterns that constitute the practice' (ibid.: 252).

Bodily-mental routines involve different components. Objects are necessary components of many practices and enter into stable relations with agents carrying out a given practice. Objects are thus constitutive elements of practices, and they can both enable and limit certain bodily-mental activities. Knowledge is also mentioned as a constitutive element of practices, and – as in relation to mental activities – broadness is emphasised: a way of understanding, know-how and a certain way of wanting and feeling (ibid.: 253–54). In general, Reckwitz argues as if practices are carried out by individuals more or less in isolation. Of course, he is well aware that many practices involve social interaction, but this is not really visible in his discussion. This omission is probably due to the importance he attaches to demonstrating that in practice theory the social is not placed in social interaction as such but in practices and their constitutive components. Furthermore, social interaction can seem so obvious that it does not need to be mentioned. However, to provide a useful concept for empirical analysis we find it relevant to bring social interaction more to the fore as constitutive for practices. Reckwitz only comments on this indirectly, when he deals with objects: 'The stable relation between agents (body/minds) and things within certain practices reproduces the social, as does the "mutually" stable relation between several agents in other practices' (ibid.: 253). To make social interaction more visible in relation to practices, it is necessary to include it in the description of the bodily-mental activities constituting a practice.

For empirical studies, the delimitation of practices is an important issue: When do we deal with a coordinated entity? Reckwitz mentions a broad variety of examples: 'a way of cooking, of consuming, of working, of investigating, of taking care of oneself or of others, etc.' (ibid.: 249–50). However, these examples are too vague and unclear for analytic purposes. Schatzki contributes more to analytic clarity by distinguishing between two forms of practices: 'Dispersed practices' are general and appear in many different contexts, for example describing, explaining, reporting and imagining (Schatzki 1996: 91).[3] 'Integrative practices' are 'the more complex practices found in and constitutive of particular domains of social life' (ibid.: 98), for example farming practices, teaching practices, cooking practices, voting practices and religious practices. Integrative practices often include dispersed practices, sometimes in a specialised form. In relation to empirical studies of ICT, both forms of practices could be relevant as ICTs can influence general ways of finding and storing information, for instance, as well as particular practices belonging to different social domains such as shopping and cooking. In the empirical part of this chapter we concentrate on integrative practices since our empirical material is most relevant for identifying such practices.

By arguing that integrative practices are constitutive of particular social domains, Schatzki suggests that practices belong to a kind of micro level that constitutes domains at a middle-range or macro level. This fits well with the idea of individuals as carriers of practices. But how can practices be identified and distinguished from other practices? Based on the outline above, the core criteria for the identification of a practice are that:

1) bodily-mental activities (individual and social interactions) are routinised and repetitive;
2) activities incorporate components such as understanding, know-how, states of emotion, motivational knowledge, and usually also objects, which are all interconnected;
3) interconnected activities and components are perceived as meaningful entities in a given society or culture.

Obviously, a key problem in applying this approach to empirical studies is to specify the meaning of 'interconnectedness' or, in Warde's summary of Schatzki, the nexus based on the linkages formed by understandings, procedures and engagements (Warde 2005). The same issue reappears at the level of social domains, which are also defined by some kind of interconnectedness. The 'translation' of this abstract concept into empirically workable delimitations is not an easy task. Empirical studies applying a practice theory approach have been carried out, for example by Elizabeth Shove together with various collaborators.[4] In one of the first in this series of contributions, Shove and Pantzar (2005) analyse the case of Nordic walking, involving the use of walking sticks. In their account of the approach, they emphasise the material dimension of practice, which, they argue, has been under-theorised by such social theorists as Bourdieu, Giddens and de Certeau (ibid.: 44). Shove and Pantzar 'work with the notion that practices involve the active integration of materials, meanings and forms of competence' (ibid.: 45), or in other terms, equipment, images and skills. Whereas Warde rationalises Schatzki's list of linkages to understandings, procedures and engagements, Shove and Pantzar incorporate Warde's three components into two – images (meanings) and skills (competence) – and bring a third component – equipment (materials) – more to the fore by emphasising the centrality of materials. Like Reckwitz, they do not explicitly include social interaction in the description of the bodily-mental activities that constitute a practice. In general, Shove and Pantzar reduce the complexity of the philosophical account of practices and lose some of the subtleties. Furthermore, in the case of Nordic walking, the problem of interconnectedness delimiting the practice is not pressing due to the centrality of walking sticks, which are mainly used for one purpose.

Warde points out that 'philosophical descriptions of practices often seem to presume an unlikely degree of shared understanding and common conventions' (Warde 2005: 136), and this makes them open to the criticism that it is difficult to account for change. However, in sociological applications, both inertia and change are in focus. The routine character of practices and their bodily-mental embeddedness implies that they tend to be carried out in the same way; but not all practitioners perform them in the same way (adding to the complexity of identifying a practice), and sometimes practitioners improvise and experiment, so established conventions are challenged. In addition to internal seeds of change, practices are also influenced by changes that are external to the specific practice under study, such as changes in adjacent practices, institutional arrangements, the economic situation and technological innovations. Shove and Pantzar highlight 'how new practices emerge through and as a result of specific forms of consumer–producer interaction' (Shove and Pantzar 2005: 45). The case of Nordic walking illustrates how already familiar elements of competence, image and equipment are integrated in new ways to create a new practice, how producers and consumers interact in this process, how the practice becomes institutionalised, and how different national conditions influence the uptake of the new practice. The approach demonstrates the need, which tends to disappear in philosophical discussions, for highlighting agency in accounts of the social construction of practices (see also Hobart this volume), and the importance of studying the social, economic and technological framework of a particular practice. Simultaneously, the dynamic character of the formation of practices is stressed.

To support the empirical analysis, we summarise our conception of practices in Figure 11.1 below. We place the bodily-mental activities at the core of practice, and these activities integrate the three components identified by Shove and Pantzar. By exposing the activities, and not only the components, the importance of social interaction as a defining characteristic of a practice can be made explicit. The distinction between the two components – skills/know-how and meaning/emotions – is not a reflection of the dualism between body and mind, since both components include bodily and mental aspects. Skills and know-how comprise acquired movements of the body as well as knowledge of procedures, and the meaning/emotions component includes not only symbolic images but also the physio-chemical processes in the body related to emotions (or, in Schatzki's terms, to teleoaffective structures). A practice is embedded in an ever-changing social, economic, cultural and technological context that we visualise as an outer circle. In the conclusion, we return to some of the problems that occur in the empirical application of these ideas.

The aim of the following sections is to make a preliminary evaluation of the applicability of the theory of practice discussed above by using the theoretical concepts to identify and analyse practices involving the use of ICTs. The analysis also highlights some of the dynamics behind changes in normal standards in everyday life. As ICT has become integrated into a wide range of domestic and family-related practices – an interesting observation in itself – we limit our analysis and discussion to

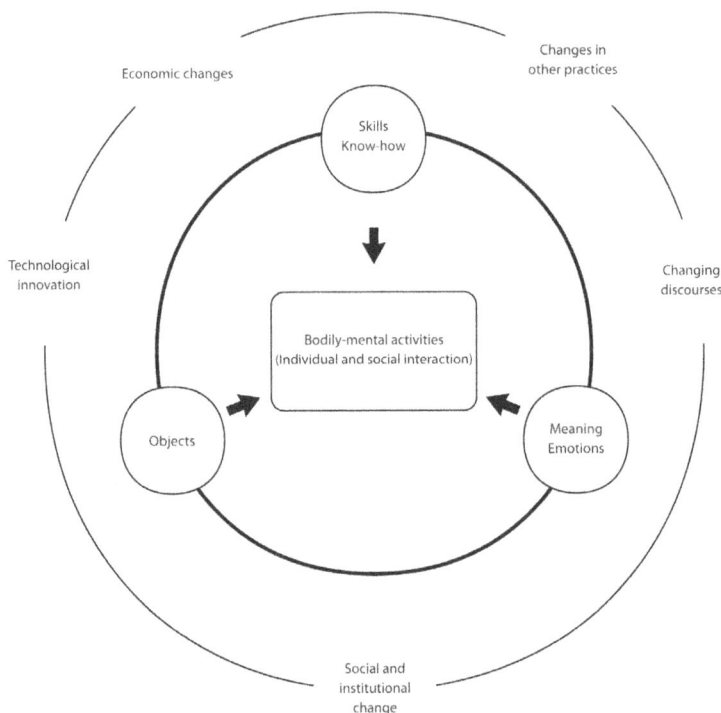

Figure 11.1 A practice-theoretical model that places bodily-mental activities at the core of a given practice and highlights social interaction as a defining characteristic of that practice.

a few practices that involve the integration of computers, the internet and mobile phones. Qualitative interviews with nine Danish families make up the empirical material (each family was interviewed twice). The interviews were carried out between 2004 and 2006 and focused on the use of ICTs by family members (primarily the parents) and how this was situated in the complex of meanings and practices that made up every-day life (see Christensen 2008). In addition, we draw on a number of interviews carried out in 2007–8 as part of a study of ICT use and residential energy consumption (see Røpke, Christensen and Jensen 2010) and insights from other ICT studies.

The Use of ICT: Dispersed and Integrative Practices

Before going into details of a number of distinct and integrative practices involving the use of ICTs we make a few comments on the practice of using a computer and ask whether it might be adequate to view this practice as a dispersed practice comparable to the general practices of describing, explaining and imaging.

Although it is difficult for many of us to remember it, there was a time when the computer was a new and revolutionary invention – an astonishing device that did amazing things such as calculating very fast or creating 'virtual environments' for games. And since we were used to typewriters, it took most of us a considerable amount of time to get used to new word processing programs such as Word Perfect. It called for intense concentration to learn such 'simple' operations as deleting words 'on the screen', to 'copy and paste' blocks of text and to 'save' documents on the 'floppy disk' or the 'hard disk'. All these words and operations were difficult to understand on the basis of our prior experiences and knowledge from the time before the computer. Similar experiences followed with the introduction of the internet. At a more general level, we had to learn to 'navigate' in 'virtual environments' on the screen; learn to coordinate movements of hands and fingers using the 'mouse' or keyboard with cursor positions on the screen. We also had to learn to open and close programs, to change 'default settings', to choose between several options on the program menus, to search for software updates, to 'shut down' the computer in a proper way and to handle digital threats such as viruses, Trojan horses, spyware and hackers.

Today, most people feel comfortable using a computer. We have become 'trained users' of the computer and its software and find few difficulties in navigating in the 'virtual environment' of the computer and the internet. The practice of computer use is a mental-bodily routinised practice involving components like things (the computer and its accessories) as well as meanings and skills. It is a practice similar to dispersed practices in that we regularly meet situations in our everyday life calling for the use of the same understandings and competences that are involved in computer use. Think, for instance, of the programming of video recorders, the interface of mobile phones, withdrawing money from cash dispensers, changing the settings on television sets or using DVD players. All these activities have clear similarities with the use of computers and draw on the same understandings and skills. Although the practice of computer use does not have the same degree of ubiquity as the dispersed practices mentioned by Schatzki (describing, explaining and imaging), the meanings and skills related to human–computer interaction have a generic character; the same meanings and skills are integrated elements of a variety of different practices, including those presented and discussed in the following sections. This makes it reasonable to understand basic computer use as similar to dispersed practices.

The list of everyday practices that integrate modern ICTs is almost endless and includes shopping, home banking, photographing, getting the news, maintaining social relations, coordinating and planning family-related activities and working from home (just to name a few examples from our research). The length of the list alone illustrates how deeply ingrained new ICTs have become in modern everyday life and across a wide range of everyday practices. In the following, we discuss a number of integrative practices that involve the use of modern ICTs: shopping, 'holding things together', 'maintaining social networks', entertainment and personal documentation. For each practice, we delineate the bodily-mental activities involved and describe some of the components that hold the practice together – that is, the objects, meanings and skills. A short description of the practice is followed by examples of how the use of ICT is integrated into the practice and how this might change the practice itself.

Shopping

Most people will probably recognise shopping as a meaningful entity, as something we do often and in similar ways, with many common features. This is not to say that the practice of shopping does not involve many variants. Obviously, there is a big difference between daily grocery shopping and a monthly stroll in a shopping centre looking for new clothes. But in both cases it makes sense to people to think of themselves as 'going shopping', an activity that involves distinct roles (purchasers versus salespersons) and distinct behaviours ('ways of doing').

With regard to bodily-mental routines, shopping involves such embodied movements as walking down the aisles of the shopping centre while glancing over hundreds of products to search for a specific product or group of products (such as household cleaners). In fact, shopping involves a high number of routinised activities, such as writing shopping lists, parking close to the shop entrance, grabbing a basket or trolley at the entrance, choosing between different products, standing in line at the checkout and paying either by cash or credit card. Shopping also involves a curious mixture of self-discipline and desire, of allowing oneself to indulge in the world of consumer products while at the same time bearing in mind the financial or normative limits to one's consumer behaviour. Thus, the ability to handle both self-discipline and desire is probably one of the most significant skills related to shopping as a practice. In relation to this, it is important to note that according to a practice theory perspective, the desire and need for consumer goods are themselves an outcome of practices; most practices 'need' appropriation and the use of goods, services and ambience in order to be carried out successfully (Warde 2005).

Shopping integrates a number of skills and meanings. These include: skills, such as the ability to search and critically assess information about the price and quality of products, to choose between alternatives and to combine desire and self-discipline in the successful performance of shopping; and they include meanings, like the idea of being a responsible political consumer, the ideal of getting a 'good bargain', and the understanding that you have to pay before you can have a product (ownership). The practice of shopping also integrates a number of objects, ranging from the products, of course, to shopping baskets and trolleys, credit cards, cash and shopping lists. All these things act as components of the social practice and play an important role for the performance of the practice. However, how to define and limit the list of things related to the practice of shopping is an open question. Like most integrative practices, shopping is embedded in and dependent on larger systems of objects, knowledge and economic and social institutions. Shopping in large shopping centres would have been inconceivable if it were not for the car and the infrastructure it involves (roads, petrol stations, traffic regulations and so on). And payment by credit card would have been impossible without permanent data connections between local terminals and central computers. And shopping, in itself, can only be a meaningful practice in a society based on industrial production and with a market economy. Therefore, the question is: What kind of objects (or material infrastructures) should be included on the list of 'things' connected to a certain practice (in this case shopping)? And what kind of objects should not? Similar questions could be posed concerning skills and meanings.

Living in a modern society – where social life and daily reproduction are highly dependent on large technological systems and diversified social systems – the attempt to map all the components related to a specific practice would be a 'neverending story'. Therefore, for practice theory to be applicable it is necessary to determine empirically and analytically what is 'inside' and what is 'outside' the practice in focus. One example could be to restrict 'things' related to a social practice to the material objects directly involved in the practice – things that are present at the moment when a practice is performed by a person or a group of persons. In relation to shopping, 'things' would thus include the shopping trolley or basket, the shopping list, the credit card or cash and even the checkout. In this perspective, private motoring (cars, roads and so on), the credit card system, adverts, shopping centres and the modern market economy – just to name some of the most important – form the material, social, economic, political and cultural institutions that 'surround' shopping as a practice and in which it is embedded. These institutions are themselves constituted by practices.

Mobile phones and the internet are becoming integrated more and more into aspects of the practice of shopping. In order to understand the diversified use of ICT in relation to shopping, it is helpful to distinguish between 'daily' shopping, which is closely related to the day-to-day reproduction of the household, and the more irregular purchase of consumer durables (such as televisions, refrigerators and cars) or other forms of 'extraordinary' services (such as holidays). Daily shopping is often done in the afternoon (after work) and consists of a short trip to a local supermarket for consumables like milk, food, detergents and toilet paper. In relation to daily shopping, our interviews show an extensive use of the mobile phone and text messaging for communication between family members in order to coordinate shopping – for example, to sort out who is going to do the shopping and what to buy. More rarely, the internet is used for daily shopping. In fact, using mobile phones to coordinate daily shopping is one of the most frequent uses of the mobile phone among parents. But has the use of mobile phones 'changed' the practice of daily shopping *per se*? This question cannot be answered in a simple way. On the one hand, the bodily-mental activities related to shopping are unchanged: shoppers still walk down the aisles of the supermarket and form a queue at the checkout. On the other hand, there have been some important changes in who does the shopping and how it is planned, changes that to some degree can be ascribed to the interplay between the new possibilities of the mobile phone and more general changes in modern family life, including gender relations.

Perhaps the most visible changes can be seen in the practice of preparing dinner. This is closely related to the practice of daily shopping, and our interviews indicate that the use of mobile phones has contributed to making the planning and organisation of dinner more fluid and short-term. In the Danish context, up to the 1980s preparing dinner was a much more gendered practice than it is today. Then, it was predominantly women (mothers or housewives) who prepared dinners and were responsible for doing the shopping related to this. Although women still bear the main responsibility for domestic work, the situation has changed regarding dinner and men share a larger part of cooking today (Bonke 2002). This change is part of a more general loosening of the gender structures of domestic work and changed gender relations in the family. Some sociologists use the concept of 'the negotiating family' (Jørgensen 1999) to describe how the distribution of domestic work has become the subject of daily discussion and negotiation between parents in modern family life. The loosening of gender structures involves the need for a continual negotiation and coordination of daily activities, and our interviews with Danish families show that the mobile phone in particular is used for short-term coordination. Thus, phone calls between partners during the daytime often involve questions like: What are we having? Who is going to prepare dinner? Who is going to do the shopping? What should I buy? In sum, the example of daily shopping illustrates how a practice is changed through contextual changes (in this case changed gender relations) in combination with the integration of a new technology.

With regard to the purchase of durable goods and 'extraordinary' services, several of those interviewed make use of the internet. In particular, one of the interviewed families uses the internet extensively to find information on a wide range of products (like a new car, furniture, fittings for their bathroom and different kinds of wooden floor), and they also purchase products over the internet regularly. Often, the parents sit in front of a computer in the late evening (after the kids have gone to bed) and spend a few hours searching the internet for information while sharing a bottle of wine. This example is interesting in that it shows how parents create a cosy and relaxed feeling around the activity of shopping – a feeling similar to the situation of watching television. In fact, the husband explicitly compared the situation of sitting together and searching the internet with watching television together. Thus, the internet has brought shopping into the frame of the home and has created a new possibility for situations of 'togetherness' that draws on some of the same elements as the practice of watching television. A more general conclusion would be that the use of the internet is integrated into the practice of shopping along with more 'traditional' activities such as reading brochures, visiting shops or talking with friends about their experiences with particular products.

Holding Things Together

Daily planning and coordination are important elements in modern families' attempts to 'hold things together' and to manage the temporal and spatial dispersion of family members. For instance, organising dinner involves much communication (mediated as well as non-mediated) between parents as well as between parents and their children. But 'holding things together' includes more than coordination and planning. To some families (and notably to parents), 'holding things together' also involves a particular time awareness in relation to most domestic activities such as preparing dinner and doing the dishes or the laundry. All these daily chores (and practices) are often so tightly planned that even small delays or unexpected changes in the schedule cause problems and experiences of time pressure and stress. This is a common experience of dual-income families and has been compared to a 'house of cards' (Frissen 2000).

Daily experiences of time pressure or busyness are closely related to a concern with 'holding things together', as illustrated by an excerpt from an interview with a 38-year-old mother, who lives with her husband and three children in Copenhagen:

> What makes us feel busy? Well, we have to go to work. And [in the afternoon] do some shopping, pick up the children [from school and day care], prepare dinner. And then it's time for [helping the children with their] homework and putting the children to bed. And then it is time for doing the washing up and cleaning. And doing the laundry. And then the time is – sometimes it is ten or half past ten [in the evening]. And then we have a bit of leisure time ... if you have not fallen asleep ... [T]here are a lot of duties in normal everyday life which might not sound like much, but when putting it all together it turns out to be a lot, right ... Well, sometimes I feel – I have to take care that I do not sit down, because [if I do] I become really tired. It is better to do something, right – walk around.

'Holding things together' (*holde sammen på det hele*) seems to be a meaningful category to several of the interviewed families. But it is more than 'just' a meaningful cultural category; a number of actions and routinised activities are related to parents' daily struggle to 'stay on top of things', which makes it reasonable to characterise 'holding things together' as a social practice.

The interviews show that 'holding things together' involves both bodily and mental elements. As the 38-year-old mother said in the excerpt above, she avoids sitting down in the evenings before she has finished her daily chores. If she sits down and relaxes she fears that she would be overcome by fatigue and would not be able to finish the domestic work. Therefore, she carries on until 'everything is done'. This – and other interviews – points out an interesting bodily component of the practice of 'holding things together' – namely the bodily self-discipline that is manifested in the common understanding of keeping your body or head busy in order to avoid being overcome by exhaustion. Closely related to this component is a mental component expressed by the idea that one has to finish the domestic work ('clear everything away') in the evening before one can feel truly relaxed. When the dishes are done and the kitchen is cleaned, one is ready to begin a new day and can finally calm down and relax. This is comparable to the notions of hot and cold spots mentioned by Southerton (2003) and the notions of 'rush' and 'calm' mentioned by Shove (2003); people often distinguish between periods of intense busyness (rush) and periods of relaxation (calm), and they deliberately create periods of rush in order to generate protected pockets of 'quality time'.

'Holding things together' as a practice comprises a number of different activities and some of these involve the use of ICT. The following list, which is based on our interviews, shows some of the variety of activities related to the practice of 'holding things together':

- list making (e.g., 'to do' lists);
- using a diary (to write down future arrangements, etc.) Some informants use their mobile phone as a diary and write down their arrangements in the calendar function of the mobile phone;
- especially if one parent is behind schedule (e.g., due to overtime at work or because of traffic congestion), the parents communicate intensively by phone, mobile phone, text message or even e-mail to organise the afternoon activities (shopping, collecting the children and preparing dinner);
- keeping each other informed about individual plans and schedules (and any changes made to these);
- children call their parents if they are going to bring a friend home with them (so that the parents know and can prepare dinner for an extra person).

The practice of 'holding things together' involves frequent use of the mobile phone, often as part of what Ling and Yttri call 'micro-coordination' – that is, the use of the mobile phone for 'nuanced instrumental coordination' (Ling and Yttri 2002: 139). Particularly in situations where unexpected events change one's schedule, or if agreements have not been made beforehand – for example, about who is going to do the shopping – the mobile phone is used by parents and children for coordination and recoordination. In this regard, modern ICT (and especially the mobile phone) present two contrasting aspects. On the one hand, these technologies make it possible to reorganise plans within a few minutes. Thus, problems caused by unexpected and sudden events can be solved – or at least reduced – thanks to modern ICT. On the other hand, modern ICT (like other modern technologies) makes a new kind of time planning possible that is 'sensitive' to even the smallest unforeseen event. This sensitiveness is due to different time planning strategies such as narrowing the time frame around different activities by squeezing them into a tight schedule, performing more than one activity at the same time (multitasking), and detailed and careful planning.

There is a certain ambiguity in relation to the delimitation of and distinction between different practices – for example, phone calls between parents regarding who is going to prepare dinner and do the shopping. Although such calls can be seen as belonging to the practice of 'preparing dinner' given that daily shopping and preparing dinner are interdependent practices, they can also be regarded as activities related to the practice of 'holding things together' (planning and coordination). The question, therefore, is whether different practices can 'share' the same activity. Or – to put it the other way around – does it make sense to say that the same activity, in some cases, can be interpreted as part of more than one practice? The example above indicates that such ambiguity plays a role in some cases.

Maintaining Social Networks

The discussion of shopping and holding things together clearly shows that the use of modern ICT for mediated communication between family members is closely related to the practical reproduction of the family as a social unit. Other studies and our own interviews show that ICT-mediated communication also plays an increasingly important role in the continuous production and reproduction of close and meaningful relations within the family. While physically separated during most of the daytime, family members establish a feeling of closeness or 'connected presence' through the communicative practice of frequent phone calls and text messages (Licoppe 2004; Christensen 2009). In a similar way, many of our interviewees use modern ICT to maintain non-familial relations and to 'stay in touch' with friends and relatives. Today, the mobile phone in particular is an ingrained element of young people's interaction with their peers (Ling 2004) as they use it to communicate with friends and make appointments (often on a short-term basis). But the internet is also used for this kind of communication, especially instant messaging services like MSN Messenger, internet telephony services like Skype and social networking sites like Facebook. For young people, mediated and non-mediated interactions are intertwined and modern ICT has changed the 'practice' of peer-group interaction.

For adults, e-mail, the phone and mobile phone are frequently used to communicate with friends and relatives whom they do not meet on a regular basis (such as old schoolmates, old friends, distant relatives or children who have left home). Thus, one woman – a fifty-year-old mother – explains how she regularly sends short text messages to her nieces who recently lost their father (the interviewee's brother). She uses these text messages as a way of showing care without being intrusive; they help to maintain regular contact and are intended to show that they can always contact her if needed. This woman feels that phone calls, compared to text messaging, would be much more intrusive, since they might interrupt her nieces in their activities. Another informant – a 41-year-old mother – explains how she regularly sends e-mails to her eldest daughter who now lives far away. The mother writes about the latest news in her life and at home, and she sometimes includes pictures of, for instance, the latest home refurbishments. By sending these e-mails and making regular phone calls, the mother and her daughter reproduce their close bond despite the long distance separating them.

All these examples show the importance of including social interaction in the analysis of social practices. In most cases, the successful performance of a practice depends on the active participation of several persons.

Entertainment

The computer has been used for entertainment for many years, with computer games having gained a strong position as many children and some adults (predominantly men) spend considerable time playing games on the computer or the internet. It makes no sense to talk about 'entertainment' as a single practice. In fact, the word 'entertainment' is often used to bundle up a number of different practices such as playing games, watching television or going to the cinema. One of these entertainment practices, playing games, has obviously a long history and is an ingrained practice of social life. However, new ICTs (especially the computer and the internet) have created new possibilities for the individual to engage in highly complicated games without necessarily playing against significant others. In some computer games, the player participates in an environment with 'virtual' – that is, computer-generated – players. Thus, the computer game has made it possible for individuals to engage in interactive games even without fellow players. And with the integration of computer games into mobile phones it has become possible to play games almost anywhere at any time. Another group of computer games – such as multi-player online role-playing games like World of Warcraft – makes it possible to play in real time with other players via the internet. These fellow players on the internet might be friends and acquaintances as well as 'strangers'.

Another interesting use of ICT for entertainment emerged from our interviews: A fifteen-year-old boy explains how he uses his mobile phone to 'kill time' when he is alone or not together with significant others like friends or family. When waiting for the bus, sitting on the bus or while sitting in his room doing homework, he very often exchanges text messages with his friends. This activity keeps him occupied for many minutes and is – according to him – a superb way of 'killing time'. This example shows the same kind of 'ambiguity' of the activity–practice relation mentioned earlier in relation to 'holding things together': It makes sense to interpret the boy's description of his activity as part of a practice oriented towards 'killing time' in situations where he is alone as well as part of the practice of peer-group interaction. At a more general level, it seems that communication and media technologies (mobile phones, MP3 players and the like) are often used by adolescents to create an ambience of ever changing stimuli which they carry with them nearly everywhere. In many situations, a number of technologies interact and develop a 'backcloth' for other activities such as doing homework. This is most obvious in children's rooms at home where a number of technologies such as television sets, radio/CD-players, mobile phones, computers and the internet often run at the same time, creating multiple layers of changing stimuli and involving passive as well as active communication and entertainment. This can be seen as a way of dispelling boredom and 'killing time'.

More lengthy discussion is needed to decide whether or not it makes sense to use the concept of practices to understand and analyse the use of ICT for 'killing time' and creating ambience. There are obvious similarities between playing a game on the mobile phone at the bus station to while away the time and surrounding oneself with multiple layers of changing stimuli at home to make it less boring to do home-work. However, is it meaningful to talk about a 'killing-time practice' involving different ICT technologies, or is it just the idea of 'killing time' through the use of ICT that has become integrated in different integrative practices such as 'doing homework'?

Personal Documentation

For many years it has been a common practice to store information or artefacts that remind one of persons, places, events or situations in one's life. A prominent example of this practice is the family photo album. Other examples would be keeping old letters, writing a diary, or making one's own videos. Modern ICTs enable new ways of storing personal communication. For instance, one informant – the above-mentioned fifty-year-old mother – writes down all the text messages she receives from her children. She finds it amusing to retrieve old messages and conversations that remind her about specific situations in the past. These messages act like small 'tags' related to particular events, situations and persons in the past. Sometimes they not only serve as reminders of the past but are reactivated and recirculated in the communication between the mother and her children. One example concerns a story about a lost drill: Several months before the interview, one of the adult daughters had lost and retrieved a drill she had borrowed from her mother. At the time of the interview, the mother asked her daughter to return the drill, but – once again – the daughter could not find it. To remind her daughter that this was the second time she had lost the machine, her mother sent her old text messages about the first time. Thus, the old messages became part of a new correspondence between mother and daughter – a communication with a clear undertone of teasing on the mother's part.

In relation to personal documentation, e-mail is particularly interesting as this form of communication is automatically stored on the user's personal computer. But other ICTs also enhance and renew the practice of personal documentation. For instance, digital cameras and mobile phones with cameras have changed the practice of photography. One result is an explosion in the number of pictures taken (Shove et al. 2007: 69–92). Furthermore, the pictures' digital format makes it easy to circulate them among relatives and friends and even on websites on the internet. One of our interviewees – a 51-year-old woman – tells that when she and her husband have guests for dinner on their boat she often takes pictures with her digital camera of the party or the surroundings (for instance, a beautiful sunset). She explains that the pictures 'capture' the 'atmosphere' of the situation. Afterwards, she uploads the pictures on her web-based photo album and invites the friends from the dinner party to look at them. This example illustrates how the integrative practice of photography is changed through the integration of a new set of technologies (the digital camera, computer and internet).

Concluding Remarks

We have explored the potential benefits of applying practice theory to the study of the construction of a new normality in everyday life – particularly in relation to the daily inclusion of ICT – and to highlight some of the problems involved in the practical application of practice theory. The first guiding question has been whether it is possible to obtain a deeper understanding of the construction of a new normality by studying social practices rather than by considering the diffusion of ICT as the result of changing consumption drivers. Like Shove and her collaborators (Shove and Pantzar 2005; Shove et al. 2007), we suggest that a practice theory approach adds more detail and subtlety to the analysis, and that the approach provides a better basis for assessing long-term perspectives related to changing consumption patterns. Obviously, there is a large overlap between the two approaches: general consumption dynamics emanating from individual motivations and the conditions of everyday life – such as the search for individual independence, the interest in time management, and the need for real-time coordination – reappear in relation to different practices, so in this sense it is just a different way of saying the same thing. However, the focus on specific practices highlights in more detail the dynamic coevolution between technological, social and discursive changes, and a broader range of dynamics are brought into the picture. For instance, in the case of shopping we saw how changing gender relations within the family seem to interact with enhanced possibilities of communicating at any time and any place that modern ICT brings about. This more detailed insight can be helpful when the construction of a new normality is considered as it becomes easier to assess whether new consumer acquisitions are a matter of fashion or whether they point towards more durable changes in everyday life. Our findings echo the findings of Shove and associates (Shove and Pantzar 2005; Shove et al. 2007), who broaden the understanding of consumption dynamics through their studies of other fields such as digital photography, Nordic walking, floorball, do-it-yourself activities and kitchen renewal.

The second question we raised is whether the practices of everyday life become more materialised as a result of the increased use of ICTs. This question cannot be answered at a general level since different practices change in different ways; so we need to go into more detail with the changing 'materiality' of each relevant practice. In one of the practices where new ICT products play a decisive role for the performance of the practice – adolescents' intensive use of ICT for peer-group communication and social interaction – we can safely say that the practice appropriates more material resources than before, but in other cases it is less clear cut. It is particularly difficult to take long-term impacts into account, which would be relevant in such cases as changing shopping patterns where goods are bought on the internet and delivered to the home. However, an important observation can be made at the general level: The use of ICT has become integrated into so many practices in everyday life that ICT is developing into a fundamental part of the infrastructure of modern family life. Removing ICT would not only cause annoyance and inconvenience to most people but would almost literally 'undermine' their 'way of living'. In this regard, modern ICT has within a few decades attained a position in the material structures of everyday life comparable to that of the car.

Thirdly, it has been the intention of the chapter to contribute to the development of the practice theory approach by exploring some of the issues arising when practice theory is applied in empirical studies. Our preliminary analyses of practices involving the use of ICTs have revealed some issues that need more elaboration:

1) We have stressed the need to emphasise social interaction (e.g., peer-group interaction of adolescents) in empirical studies of practices. The theoretical focus on individuals as 'carriers' of practices – as emphasised by Reckwitz (2002) – may divert attention from the interplay that is involved in most practices, and it may be important to highlight this interplay in order to understand the process of change. Our approach thus makes the importance of social interaction more visible than it is in the account of Shove and Pantzar (2005).

2) Like Warde (2005) we identify some difficulties in applying the philosophical accounts of practice theory in empirical analyses. For instance, it can be difficult to delimit a particular practice from other practices and to decide at which level a practice should be defined. Some activities can be part of different practices at the same time, and many objects are parts of more than one practice. Of course, the delimitation of practices must be related to the ana-

lytic purpose of a study, but this guideline may be insufficient for a precise delimitation.

3) Some of the practices described raise the question of whether it is relevant to talk about a practice (as distinct from other practices) or to construe what people do in specific situations as related to an overall idea. Particularly in the case of 'holding things together', it is not sufficiently clarified in this chapter to what degree it is meaningful to define this as a practice *per se* (comprised of different activities), or whether it is more relevant to understand 'holding things together' as an abstract (cultural) concept that people use to interpret a diversity of activities and actions related to different practices.

4) Furthermore, it can be difficult to distinguish between the practice *per se* and its context: What should be included in the definition of the practice? Again, the analytic purpose of the study is decisive for delimitation, but there is still a need for a more sophisticated conceptualisation of how practices are embedded in – and interact with – the context of social and economic institutions, technological infrastructures and discourses. A related point is made by Randles and Warde when they argue that practices 'do not float free of technological, institutional and infrastructural contexts', and that political intervention in the formation of practices – for instance, motivated by environmental concerns – has to address these contexts (Randles and Warde 2006: 229).

Perhaps the most obvious and strongest argument for applying a practice theory approach in studies of consumption and everyday life is that consumption is 'derived' from practices. As Warde (2005) argues, people do not usually think of themselves as consuming but as being engaged in different activities; consumption then follows as an integral part of these activities. In this way, practice theory broadens the analytic scope and makes empirical analyses sensitive to the heterogeneous complex of interacting components that constitute the dynamics of everyday practices.

Notes

1. The discussion of 'materialisation' is particularly relevant from an environmental perspective: does the integration of ICTs in everyday life imply that different practices become 'materialised' to an increasing extent, and does this integration in many different practices contribute on the whole to new environmentally demanding standards for the normal way of life? In other

publications we have focused more on the environmental implications of ICT (Christensen et al. 2007; Røpke, Christensen and Jensen 2010).
2. Consumption dynamics related to the emergence of mobile phones are explored in Røpke (2003).
3. Using a term from technology studies, such practices could be called generic practices.
4. See: Hand, Shove and Southerton (2005), Pantzar and Shove (2005), Shove and Pantzar (2005), Hand and Shove (2007), Shove et al. (2007) and Shove and Pantzar (2007).

References

Bonke, J. 2002. *Tid og Velfærd*. Copenhagen: Socialforskningsinstituttet.
Christensen, T.H. 2008. 'Informations- og Kommunikationsteknologi i Familiens Hverdag [Information and Communication Technology in Family Life]', PhD. thesis, Department of Management Engineering. Kgs. Lyngby: Technical University of Denmark.
——— 2009. '"Connected Presence" in Distributed Family Life', *New Media and Society* 11(3): 433–51.
Christensen, T.H., M. Godskesen, K. Gram-Hanssen, M. Quitzau and I. Røpke. 2007. 'Greening the Danes? Experience with Consumption and Environment Policies', *Journal of Consumer Policy* 30: 91–116.
Frissen, V.A.J. 2000. 'ICTs in the Rush Hour of Life', *Information Society* 16: 65–75.
Hand, M. and E. Shove. 2007. 'Condensing Practices: Ways of Living with a Freezer', *Journal of Consumer Culture* 7: 79–104.
Hand, M., E. Shove and D. Southerton. 2005. 'Explaining Showering: A Discussion of the Material, Conventional, and Temporal Dimensions of Practice', *Sociological Research Online* 10. http://www.socresonline.org.uk/10/2/hand.html.
Jørgensen, P.S. 1999. 'Familieliv – i Børnefamilien', in L. Dencik and P.S. Jørgensen (eds), *Børn og Familie i det Postmoderne Samfund*. Copenhagen: Reitzels Forlag, pp.108–31.
Licoppe, C. 2004. '"Connected" Presence: The Emergence of a New Repertoire for Managing Social Relationships in a Changing Communication Technoscape', *Environment and Planning D: Society and Space* 22: 135–56.
Ling, R. 2004. *The Mobile Connection: The Cell Phone's Impact on Society*. San Francisco, CA: Elsevier.
Ling, R. and B. Yttri. 2002. 'Hyper-coordination via Mobile Phones in Norway', in J.E. Katz and M. Aakhus (eds), *Perpetual Contact: Mobile Communication, Private Talk, Public Performance*. Cambridge: Cambridge University Press, pp.139–69.
Pantzar, M. and E. Shove (eds). 2005. *Manufacturing Leisure: Innovations in Happiness, Well-being and Fun*. Helsinki: National Consumer Research Centre.

Randles, S. and A. Warde. 2006. 'Consumption: The View from Theories of Practice', in K. Green and S. Randles (eds), *Industrial Ecology and Spaces of Innovation*. Cheltenham: Edward Elgar, pp.220–37.

Reckwitz, A. 2002. 'Toward a Theory of Social Practices: A Development in Culturalist Theorising', *European Journal of Social Theory* 5: 243–63.

Røpke, I. 1999. 'The Dynamics of Willingness to Consume', *Ecological Economics* 28: 399–420.

——— 2001. 'New Technology in Everyday Life: Social Processes and Environmental Impact', *Ecological Economics* 38: 403–22.

——— 2003. 'Consumption Dynamics and Technological Change – Exemplified by the Mobile Phone and Related Technologies', *Ecological Economics* 45: 171–88.

Røpke, I., T.H. Christensen and J.O. Jensen. 2010. 'Information and Communication Technologies – A New Round of Household Electrification', *Energy Policy* 38: 1764–73.

Schatzki, T. 1996. *Social Practices: A Wittgensteinian Approach to Human Activity and the Social*. Cambridge: Cambridge University Press.

Shove, E. 2003. *Comfort, Cleanliness and Convenience: The Social Organisation of Normality*. Oxford: Berg.

Shove, E. and M. Pantzar. 2005. 'Consumers, Producers and Practices: Understanding the Invention and Reinvention of Nordic Walking', *Journal of Consumer Culture* 5: 43–64.

——— 2007. 'Recruitment and Reproduction: The Careers and Carriers of Digital Photography and Floorball', *Journal of Human Affairs* 17: 154–67.

Shove, E., M. Watson, M. Hand and J. Ingram. 2007. *The Design of Everyday Life*. Oxford: Berg.

Southerton, D. 2003. '"Squeezing Time": Allocating Practices, Coordinating Networks and Scheduling Society', *Time and Society* 12: 5–25.

Warde, A. 2005. 'Consumption and Theories of Practice', *Journal of Consumer Culture* 5: 131–53.

PART IV

New Media Production Practices

CHAPTER 12

Playful Practices: Theorising 'New Media' Cultural Production

Elisenda Ardèvol, Antoni Roig,
Gemma San Cornelio, Ruth Pagès
and Pau Alsina

The aim of this chapter is to contribute to the current debate on media practices specifically focusing on changes regarding the spheres of production and consumption in the context of new media. We will draw on Schatzki's theory of practice in order to approach cultural production as a 'field of embodied, materially interwoven practices centrally organized around shared practical understandings' (Schatzki 2001: 3). In particular, we will argue that Schatzki's notion of practice – as a set of actions that entails ways of doing and saying – allows one to ask questions relating to what people do with media for which current theories of audiences and reception do not provide satisfactory answers. This general framework, together with other related theoretical approaches – such as the perspective on consumption practices proposed by Alan Warde (2005) and the definition of media practices proposed by Nick Couldry (this volume) – offer an insight into the playful practices associated with digital technologies and the engagement of users in a great array of new media practices characterised by appropriation, production and sharing.

Our chapter is based on three different case studies of self-produced videos and depicts not only different media practices but also different motivations and relationships between the spheres of production and consumption. The first case is *The French Democracy*, a well-known example of 'machinima', the name given to (usually) short animated film clips produced through the manipulation of 3D video game engines, altering original elements such as backgrounds, characters and so on. *The French Democracy* depicts the transformative potential of these kinds of practices regarding their political implications. The second case is that of *Bus Uncle*. Originating as a simple mobile-phone-camera recording of an argument on a Hong Kong bus, it became a popular hit through remixing and editing by YouTube users in 2006.[1] The success of the *Bus Uncle* video reveals some interesting synergies between an emerging social network site and the traditional mass media. Finally, the *Acrobats* case is centred on a much less successful (and much more common) example of appropriation practices related to self-produced videos and their dissemination through YouTube. *Acrobats* is part of a set of videos made by a group of friends for fun. This self-produced performance is not only conceived for a 'YouTube audience', but also uses the possibilities of the site to extend the playful experience of the performers.

These three cases are all examples of what is currently known as 'user generated content', specifically audiovisual self-production, that is easily available on the internet. But what is more interesting here is that these products reflect different ways of challenging 'production' and 'consumption' practices from creative and production processes to audience conception. Digital technologies allow people to engage in new and simple ways of producing their own content, as well as appropriating mass-media cultural products in creative ways. This 'new media' environment demands a redefinition of media consumption practices in order for us to consider not only how corporate products are received but also how diverse, complex and playful self-productions are circulating and being consumed.

Media Practices and Cultural Production

People's media consumption has to be understood in the context of everyday life, embedded in practices of sociality, identity construction and popular cultural performances that take place mostly during leisure time. In this context, Nick Couldry's approach to media as practice is particularly relevant in order to understand how people live in a media-saturated world. Couldry (this volume) proposes understanding media practices as an open set of practices relating to or being oriented toward media, and decentring media research from the study of text or its production structures. Decentring the text makes it possible to analyse people's media activity in its own terms. However, Couldry does not seem to take into account in his approach that what people are actually doing with media also includes media production – that is, actively contributing to the everyday (new) media landscape. In other words, those who are media-saturating everyday life are not only 'others'. People are playfully engaging in media production practices in different ways and with different motivations, including political activism, fun, fame, creating social bonds or even the pleasure of playing with the media system itself.

In this sense, Mark Hobart's argument that practice is not supplementary to notions such as system, structure, order or individuals but replaces them (see Hobart this volume) is highly challenging: first, because it considers any productive practice undertaken by any kind of agent – be it an individual, a corporation or an institution – as equally relevant for study; and secondly, because it understands media production and media consumption from the perspective of social organised practices. In Hobart's words, 'there is no sharp dichotomy between the practices of producers, audiences and commentators, of the knowers and of those who are subjects of knowledge'; going somewhat further, he proposes that we 'question totalizing accounts of, say, culture … structure or ideology, and human subjects, in favour of analysing the practices through which these are constituted and antagonisms articulated'.[2] Thus, in order to understand new media practices we have to pay attention to people's experiences and examine the whole process of media production and consumption as well as how this process is articulated with cultural production and the media system.

One of Hobart's particular interests lies in the articulation between mass media as institutional practices of production and media-related practices, such as practices of reception. In his own words, the notion of media-related practices also includes 'women cooking meals so the family can view favourite programmes, family decisions on capital investment on radio, television or computers, preferences in dress or other consumer items shown in advertising or programmes. It also allows for a consideration of absences: the refusal to read a particular newspaper, to watch soccer or whatever' (this volume: 63). However, this conception maintains a complementary relationship between institutional media practices and media-related practices; between producers and audiences.

As Elizabeth Bird (this volume) points out, one of the main problems of studying media in relation to cultural production has been that audience research has too easily based itself on the concept of 'audience response' to specific media. In a previous work she also argues that 'we cannot really isolate the role of media in culture, because the media are firmly anchored into the web of culture, although articulated by individuals in different ways' (Bird 2003: 3). Consequently she proposes a study of practice focusing on moments of articulation between individuals and 'the media'. This approach allows for the study of how media outlets are embedded in everyday communicative and cultural practices, looking at local, grounded activities; these activities thus cease to be necessarily regarded merely as 'audience practices' but as an interplay between media models and people's cultural performances.

Bird proposes a shift from 'media-related practices' to 'mediated practices'. That would mean understanding mediated practices as everyday practices (including ritual practices such as weddings) that are somehow 'mediatised' – that is, influenced by a media gaze or a text in the sense that they emulate media scripts or media genres. Bird's definition of mediated practices also includes people's performances that are transformed or encapsulated as a 'media event' via diffusion on the internet, including through sites like YouTube. Although she recognises people's productive practices, these productions are in some way considered an imitative practice without any kind of transformative appropriation of media conventions. What is not fully explored in this approach to audience practices is the reverse case; for example, when the media industries or professionals copy the popular aesthetics of home video in film-making – well-known examples include *The Blair Witch Project* (1999), *Cloverfield* (2008) and *Paranormal Activity* (2009) – or in advertising – as we will later see in *Bus Uncle*. The point here is that media produced by ordinary people must be considered a constitutive part of media practices that are rooted in creative production processes from the very beginning, not as secondary practices (or mediated practices in the sense given by Bird) but as primary sources. This way, media practices – as we propose understanding them – encompass all the practices around media, including media production and reception by individuals, governments, global corporations and other social agents.

This being said, we see Bird's critique of the notion of 'audience' in studies of cultural practices related to media production and sharing as being critically important to any understanding of 'new media' ecology from a perspective of practices.

Recently, several authors have explored the relationship between audiences and cultural production (Harries 2002; Marshall 2002, 2004; Jenkins 2004). Although they define this relationship in different terms, they agree on the fact that one of the most important transformations aided by digital technologies involves the blurring process between the spheres of production and consumption, giving birth to a productive audience and a certain 'democratisation' of media that would define the 'new media' scenario as opposed, or at least different, to the 'mass-media' model. For example, Dan Harries defines 'viewsing' as: 'the experiencing of media in a manner that effectively integrates the activities of both viewing and using ... "Viewers" are the new "connected consumers" who find entertainment pleasure in the multitasking activities being promoted through their computer and television screens' (Harries 2002: 17). Although this term can be useful to explain emerging forms of media consumption, it still makes direct reference to a traditionally defined concept of reception.

P.D. Marshall suggests that 'reception, of whatever media form, is a kind of work, a kind of cultural production' (Marshall 2004: 8). Paraphrasing him, new media implies a changed spectrum of what defines production and consumption because these cultural forms have expanded the capacity for the viewer/user to produce, appropriating and making cultural forms their own (ibid.: 8–11). This is what Marshall defines as the 'cultural-production thesis', characterised by a 'writerly' approach to the study of new media that is more focused on engagement in practices of cultural production instead of the traditional 'readerly' approach. Like Harries, Marshall recognises the difficulty of finding a single metaphor or neologism that can describe the qualities of these new subjectivities, as this new terminology is not precise enough to 'identify the spectrum of involvement that is possible with new media. While "browser" may be considered as an adequate term in order to refer to distracted uses of new media, "player" becomes particularly relevant as it acknowledges an intensity of experience related to a deep engagement and a dedicated use of new media' (ibid.: 26–27).

The social context of participation, distribution and exhibition that the internet represents, combined with other digital technologies of information and communication from video games to digital video cameras, including podcasts or mobile phones, has prompted the use in many different circles and with different perspectives of the term 'new media'. The popularisation of the 'new media' tag has led Lievrouw and Livingstone to warn against its use as a 'buzzword, shorthand for a volatile cultural and technology industry that includes multimedia, entertainment and e-commerce' (Lievrouw and Livingstone 2002: 1). Contrary to some academic positions which try to define 'new media' in opposition to 'old media' (Bolter and Grusin 2000; Manovich 2001) as mutually exclusive terms,[3] we stand for a notion of new media as a new 'media landscape' (Appadurai 1998), in which new digital technologies and old broadcasting systems, the emerging cultural forms and the traditional mass media, interact and reshape each other, though not without tensions and contradictions.[4]

In order to comprehend this current media context, Jenkins (2004) proposes understanding it in terms of cultural media convergence characterised by the emergence of a participatory culture. Jenkins moves away from a notion of convergence as just technological change, instead highlighting a tension between two opposed but interrelated trends, the confluence of two cultural production logics from the combination of different technologies: 'convergence is both a top-down corporate-driven process and a bottom-up consumer-driven process ... Consumers are learning how to use these different media technologies to bring the flow of media more fully under their control and to interact with other users. They are fighting for the right to participate more fully in their culture' (ibid.: 37). For Marshall, one of the reactions of cultural industries to this new context is what he labels the 'intertextual matrix': a strategy by which the industry offers intricate cross-media environments, formed by different media forms (cinema, television, DVD, the internet, video games), in order to retain the audience, the viewer or the player within a limited system of entertainment options. In this intertextual matrix, institutionalised 'play' is of key importance (Marshall 2002: 69).

What remains problematic in these controversies are questions of power relations, agency and the role of the media industry in shaping 'media' practices. Obviously, in the current media landscape, the relationship between producers, distributors, regulators and consumers is changing in unexpected ways. Internet distribution and content-sharing practices are dissolving the separation between private and public domains and between amateur productions and professional media products. Nevertheless, for Couldry and Langer (2005), these 'new media practices' do not change the asymmetrical set of power relations between producers (media industry) and audiences, arguing against Abercrombie and Longhurst's concept of 'diffused audience' according to which 'the once clearly demarcated role of "audience" (as receivers of media contents) becomes less obviously distinguished in everyday life from the role of the media industry (as the producer of contents) ... people are simultaneously [media] performers and audience members' (quoted in Couldry and Langer 2005: 193). The emphasis on the blurring distinction between producers and audiences hides the power that media corporations still have to decide and legitimate what constitutes relevant cultural content.

On the contrary, we suggest that in the current scenario of the deep interrelation between different media actors and practices, the alignment between media practices and media institutions must be reconsidered and power relations re-examined. We are becoming part of 'the' media. This redefinition does not suggest the collapse of hegemonic media corporations, not even that media power is to be equally distributed, but that media consumers can also act as media producers in their own right. The key point, thus, is production, so we must take into account that audiences are currently often involved in production processes at different levels, creating semi-professional and amateur works that are displayed and distributed on the same channels as media professionals and via the internet.[5] Audiences are also cultural producers inasmuch as individuals and collectives can participate in shaping media products and can themselves be media producers, especially when uploading and sharing content on the internet. The antagonism between 'the media' and 'the audiences' is also a practice that contributes to articulate power and to legitimate the legitimating practices of 'the media'.

Going beyond Bird and Couldry's arguments, we consider self-produced video and its distribution to be a media practice in its own right; this entails moving beyond the restricted context of media consumption. Understanding that 'consumption is not itself a practice but it is, rather, a "moment" in almost every practice' (Warde 2005: 137–38), our aim is to explore how people's media practices mix with institutionalised media practices and how they contribute to define cultural production. For that purpose, we will examine people's practices of media production from a perspective of 'play'. As we shall argue, playful practices mediated the subject experience of producing and sharing media products. In this respect, although we agree with Couldry about the need to decentre the text in the analysis of media practices, we argue that people's production practices also force a re-evaluation of the role of the text – or media object – bringing it back into the picture. We concur with Elizabeth Bird about the need to combine the rhetorical analysis of the media object with on-the-ground ethnography as methodological tools for a full understanding of people's media practice motivations and engagements. An approach from practice theory allows us to understand 'new media' not merely as a 'new' technology, nor as a new kind of audience, not even as a given 'new' context, but as a set of interconnected media practices – entailing the playful use of digital technologies – that shapes the way we produce and consume cultural products.

Play and New Media Pleasures

As Roger Silverstone pointed out, play must be a tool for the analysis of media experience, thereby vindicating its role as a core activity of daily life: 'There are many ways in which we can see the media as being sites for play, both in their text and in the responses that those texts engender' (Silverstone 1999: 59–60). Taking this proposal a little further, media play can be seen as a practice related not only to reception or to game shows or computer games, but also related to the appropriation of media outlets through playful practices of production. Fan activity can be seen as the paradigmatic example of this kind of appropriative practices. Matt Hills has argued that play is at the core of fan activity, involving, for instance, remixing and remaking favourite commercial products: 'it is important to view fans as players in the sense that they become immersed in non-competitive and affective play and that this playful attitude can explain fans' creative engagement and emotional attachment' (Hills 2002: 112). However, fan activity alone does not explain the array of practices surrounding production and sharing in the new media landscape where the means of media production have become accessible to media consumers, and user-created content changes in the nature of media production. Kücklich and Fellow (2004) turn to video games as an exponent of greater changes not only with regard to how media are produced and consumed but also in the way leisure is organised and in the role of play in our everyday lives.

On the one hand, video games place 'play' at the core of the audiovisual experience and introduce innovative changes in the way audiovisual products are experienced. The voyeuristic pleasure of watching a film or television programme is qualitatively different from the pleasure of immersion that derives from the articulation of the audiovisual experience with the embodiment and the feeling of agency and control.

In video games, our relationship with audiovisual representations has to be understood not just as processes of identification with the characters or as aesthetic pleasure through our exposure to images, but also in terms of action, embodiment and interactivity with images. According to Aarseth (1998: 6), the interaction of the player with the narrative elements of the game mobilises a series of coordinated answers – be they auditory, visual, cognitive or kinetic – that erase the distance between the player and their characterisation, so that we can say that we experience things as if we were jumping, running, flying or shooting while clicking our mouse or pressing the buttons on our console. For Andrew Darley (2000) video games involve kinaesthetic performance, which is the primary source of pleasure that they provide.

On the other hand, Fiske (1989) notes the pleasures that may emanate from the fruitful opposition between freedom and control. Thus, the source of the pleasure of games would lie at the interplay between game rules and the room for manoeuvre they allow players, a pleasure which constitutes the quality of openness, essential to video games and new media alike. For Fiske, play oscillates between freedom and control in a continuum similar to Caillois's (1962) concepts of *paidia* (involving fun, improvisation and fantasy) and *ludus* (involving constraints, arbitrary rules and effort). The pleasure of breaking the rules lies in exposing their arbitrariness, so 'the pleasures of play derive directly from the players' ability to exert control over rules, roles and representations' (Fiske 1989: 236).

Following Newman (2004: 21), we must also take into account the pleasure of the player while exploring the limits of the rules, trying at the same time to learn and overcome them. He points out that this relationship with game programmers through the very act of play can be not only pleasurable but also the main challenge for the player.

The cybernetic dimension of games is of particular importance because it reminds us of the tight structure of games and new media systems. In video games, Manovich suggests that 'the user is asked to follow the mental trajectory of a new media designer' (Manovich 2001: 74). As a matter of fact, an important aspect that video games share with other 'new media' cultural forms is their informational structure, which allows modification and customisation. So, we cannot understand video games exclusively as consumption products since they must also be viewed as a means of production. Furthermore, as an informational product, video games are, at one and the same time, a product, tool and toy. Picking up on Manovich's (ibid.: 258) observations, we cannot, therefore, limit our analysis to video games as finished objects; we have to take into account the software tools, their technical architecture and the parameters that are set by default, as well as the possibilities that they open up for transformation and customisation.

There is no doubt that video games, as a cultural form, are increasingly affecting other media, from television to movies to mobile phones and the internet (Boellstorf 2006: 33). As Mihai Coman (2005: 19) has stated with regard to the mass media, video games are not a simple channel through which cultural symbols circulate; they are part of the very cultural system. Certainly, as we have seen, video games can also be understood in terms of an intersection between leisure culture, computer-mediated interaction, visual culture and information societies (Simon 2006). We can also easily find different ways in which the film industry 'remediates' games, such as digital animation, special visual effects and non-linear narrative structures (Bolter and Grusin 2000: 47–48). But what is more interesting here is that there are more and more new media practices imbued with this playful component, as can be seen in blogging practices, fan fiction creation and social practices involving photography and video-sharing sites, as well as, of course, in game modding practices.[6]

Games and Transformative (New) Media Practices

The idea that games can contain transformative practices was noted some time ago by Avedon and Sutton-Smith (1971) and earlier still by John Huizinga (1949), who gave prime importance to games as creators of culture, albeit separated from daily life. Huizinga spoke of a 'magical circle' in order to explain the creation of a temporary sphere of the game, a space where its rules have validity. As Victor Turner (1986: 25) suggested, games are cultural performances that open a social space of liminality where actors can play with factual and commonsense systems in unexpected ways in the mundane sphere. For Turner, 'playfulness is a volatile, sometimes dangerously explosive essence, which cultural institutions seek to bottle or contain in the vials of games of competition, chance and strength, in modes of simulation such as theatre, and in controlled disorientation' (ibid.: 167–68). In Turner's anthropology of performance, play is 'transcendent' in the sense that players can meta-operate over the game rules and, in doing so, they can overpass the confines of the game and transform it, for instance, into another game.

Such transgressions of the rules of games through transformative playful practices can be interwoven with audiovisual content production and consumption as we shall see in our three case studies.

The French Democracy

An example of the transformative potential of video games is 'machinima' (see above). The term machinima is derived from the conflation of 'machine' (referring to the engine of the video game) and 'cinema' (referring to the game's linear narrative structure). According to Robert Jones (2006), an important instrumental element for the early development of machinima was the capacity of game-session recording; for instance, one of the first known machinima movies was *Quake done Quick*, made to showcase a player's abilities. In this way, a short machinima becomes an audiovisual narrative narrated from the space of the game, representing a convergence of ludic practices and audiovisual narratives (ibid.: 271).

Following Jones, creating computer-generated animation based on the use of game engines and of virtual 3D environments can be considered a transforming practice, as it goes beyond the intended use of the game software and leads to a self-produced an audiovisual experience. Unlike 'playing' within the game system – where, despite the control of characters, the range of options is limited to the rules and narratives pre-established by the game design – the 'transforming' game entails the alteration of the game by players so that they introduce new scenarios, change characters and so on (ibid.: 273).

The French Democracy is a thirteen-minute machinima created by the French designer Alex Chan in November 2005 using a game called The Movies. The clip narrates a version of the facts that led to the riots in the *banlieue* (outskirts) of different French cities that same year. Based on the modification of available scenarios of the game, the narration shows the socio-economic situation of the immigrant population in suburban France and tries to explain how the death of two youngsters, after a round-up by the French police, led to a fierce response in their neighbourhood, this in turn leading to demonstrations and outbursts of violence in different French cities. Its critical political stance rapidly attracted users' attention and this paved the way for coverage in the printed and online press. Different items in the *Washington Post, Business Week* and on MTV described how the intention of the young designer was to offer his own explanation of the facts in opposition to the official version, which he believed was made up by the media. As one blog review indicated, *The French Democracy* is a milestone in the history of machinima. However, as Activision own the rights to the content of *The Movies* – including characters, scenarios and so forth – it can legally intervene at any moment and force the removal of this production from the internet.[7] Here, copyright law raises issues about power relations between the media industry and user appropriation and diffusion.

The practices involved in this case are interesting because the user of the original game is not only a player but also a designer, film creator, film producer and social activist. For Jones (2006: 272) machinima video clips literally represent a transformation of the media product from an interactive game into a film, an audiovisual product to be looked at and shared. Until now, the consumption of cinema or television allowed for a certain playful attitude through the interpretation of the text (see, e.g., Fiske 1987: 224). What we find in video games is a modification of the same consumption product and a new use that can go beyond its original design. The player has the possibility to directly intervene, creating a new product and putting it into circulation, and this is what lets us identify a practice that transforms audiences into producers. These practices are not exclusive to video games: we can find them in other forms of new media practices such as video production and sharing. The remakes and reproductions of video clips that can be found on the internet, based on films, advertisements, television programmes and so on, are good examples. Another question is up to what point these transformative practices can be considered as practices of popular cultural resistance.

Jones (2006: 267–68) suggests that the appropriation of original mainstream products must not always be understood as resistance. Jenkins's (1992) argument, on the contrary, is based on the idea that producers' power is questioned since they lose the control over the means of production and distribution, and – up to a certain point – over the very product which is altered and modified.

In this case, the playful practice of appropriation consists of the creation of not only a 'new' text but also a political statement in response to the hegemony of media discourses, as the machinima creator himself made clear.[8] What it is important to observe is that people's behaviour regarding media is not only that of the audience of media apparatuses, but also potentially to be producers of media content. From this perspective, intended or not, these are practices of cultural production that challenge the industry's rules and control. However, this empowerment is connected to a complex back-and-forth tension between corporate and grassroots interests (Jenkins 2004), as exemplified here by the battle for copyright or by what Maxwell and Miller (2005) define as 'cultural labour'; that is, when an industry takes advantage of consumer empowerment for its own marketing purposes, as we shall see in the next example.

Bus Uncle

In the spring of 2006, a passenger on a Hong Kong bus recorded a simple – and fairly surreal – argument between two other passengers using a mobile-phone video camera. Shortly afterwards the video became one of the most popular viewed items on YouTube and became an authentic phenomenon in Hong Kong: some of the sentences became popular taglines among local teenagers, while a multitude of audiovisual replies were generated and uploaded to the YouTube site. These included reproductions of the original video with new sound, music, subtitles, manipulation of the digital images; in short, a multitude of parodies and recreations. At the time of writing there are still more than 300 entries for *Bus Uncle* on YouTube,[9] some very recent and some very interesting, like a film reproducing the event using Javanese shadow-play puppets (*wayang kulit*), and even an interview with the clip's creator to the delight of fans.

Perhaps unsurprisingly, the traditional media did not stay on the sidelines: coverage of *Bus Uncle* ranged from radio debates and TV news reports reflecting on the phenomenon itself and on the pace of metropolitan life to offers for the innocent protagonists-turned-celebrities to appear on reality TV shows; *Bus Uncle* even ended up being the central axis of the advertising campaign for coverage of the 2006 football World

Cup. This video, one among many other locally well-known cases, high-lights the role of ludic culture through new media, which affects both amateur and professional production.

From both these perspectives – from the standpoint of the users and of the media corporations – we can understand the current cultural production scene as the crossover of two logics that collapse on the internet: the 'transmediatic' and transnational logic of cultural indus-tries with respect to, and mixed with, the transmediatic and transna-tional practices of people. The first of these entails the entrepreneurial concentration and diversification of intertextual products, as well as dif-ferent strategies for incorporating users' production into the corporate universe. The second logic entails the appropriation, modification and reproduction of these products as well as the creation of new media objects by users, who openly distribute them on the internet, thus cre-ating social bonds and sharing networks. In any case, it seems that this 'new' scenario is linked to people's productive capacity and skills. And even if it were easy to overestimate the global engagement of media users in these kinds of practices, it seems clear that there is a growing community of consumers who devote part of their leisure time to appropriating, producing, exchanging and sharing audiovisual prod-ucts with others.

However, what is notable about the example of *Bus Uncle* is that it is an example of a successful self-produced video. As in other cases, its 'fame effect' is produced by 'jumping' from the sphere of the internet to the tra-ditional media. In a way, the media industry appropriates these videos for its own audiences and profit. There are two sides of the celebrity effect regarding self-produced videos: on the one hand, they allow YouTube to legitimise itself among other traditional media, being able to reach a large audience and thus able to produce a 'mass phenomenon'; on the other hand, they allow 'the media' (especially press and television) to construct the new media audience in 'traditional media' terms (for instance, through weekly newspapers' publication of rankings of the 'most viewed' videos on YouTube, as if it were just another TV station).

Acrobats

This reflection on the 'fame effect' leads to a final example of self-pro-duction, *Acrobats* (Spanish original *Saltimbanquis*) which is part of a set of self-produced videos uploaded to YouTube in 2006 and shows a group of friends jumping and doing somersaults on the Madrid under-ground.[10] This low-quality recording, made with a mobile-phone video camera, seems a spontaneous action at first sight.

The clip constitutes a sequence of actions without cuts and with the original sound. It seems that the main interest is to capture the action as it takes place, the pirouettes and movements as they are performed in front of the astonished passengers. The characters in this video interact with the public space and the camera, and both the acrobats and the camera operator appeal to a potential audience by saying: 'If you want to see us in action ... YouTube.com' (*Si nos quieres ver en acción ... YouTube.com*, a rhyming slogan in Spanish). They also reinforce the idea of a performance with utterances such as: 'This is a happening'. The person recording the action appears to be also a member of this group of friends and, in a way, provokes the continuity of the action by often shouting: 'Do it again!' or 'Come on!' This transgressive element is also highlighted by the camera operator, who, when referring to an astounded passenger, whispers to an imagined audience: 'Look at that man's face!'

When interviewed for our research, the creator of the film – an architecture student – explained that the presence of the camera recording was essential to their performance and that, in fact, the camera was 'an additional element of fun'.[11] In spite of the apparent spontaneity of the recording, there is no action without the camera: it is a mediated experience of play, which only makes sense when recorded and later displayed for a YouTube audience. In this case, the playful component is present not only in the very nature of the performance but in the pleasure they expect from uploading their works on the internet. When interviewed, the creator told us that part of their 'game' was to upload the video. Their fake hooliganism was not only rooted in the act of transgressing proper behaviour on the underground but in trying to annoy users that found the video by chance on the internet. In fact, they try to reach as many users as possible using 'wrong' tags such as 'sex' or 'hot' to provoke YouTube's audience with their unexpected and 'unbearable' videos. For them, criticism or negative responses on the video site are considered a success as infuriating viewers is a sort of online game. Even if it is far from a success story, *Acrobats* is actually a very complex performance that involves the audience in completing its narrative circle, expanding the playful experience to the audience's response.

Dispersed and Integrative Media Practices

As we have highlighted, play is embedded in current popular new-media practices, especially those involving video games, audio-visual production and sharing on the internet. Game and play pleasures are present in most of the transformative practices such as modding and machinima, but also in practices of remixing media outlets and self-producing and sharing video clips. Through these productive practices, audiences assume the role of producers, creating their own content and shaping their own imagined audiences. Meanwhile, professional producers are also trying to appropriate this playful aesthetic, as is the case in some advertising campaigns such as that mentioned in the *Bus Uncle* case. This back-and-forth process between popular and corporate media production reshapes the professional and domestic content and formats introducing mutual referential ties of playfulness, increasing the complexity of 'the circuit of culture' (Hall 1997).

As a result, the relationship between play and popular productive media practices is underlined: thus, the traditionally underrated bond between game culture and audiovisual media surfaces in a way which is difficult to ignore or underestimate. In this sense, Schatzki's notion of practices can explain this permeability. Schatzki refers to an organised set of bodily and mental activities that form an inextricable assemblage constituted by the understandings about what has to be done and what has to be said, the rules or instructions that regulate them and the teleoaffective structures that orientate them, among which is an emotional component of satisfaction and desire (Schatzki 1996: 89). For Schatzki, the practices can be of two types – dispersed or integrative – and this distinction may be useful not only to understand the interrelated practices of play and game, but also to explain the integration of play in media practices.

Dispersed practices are practices found across different sectors of social life. They rule action not by specifying what particular actions to perform, but by providing evidence to be taken into account when acting and choosing (ibid.: 91, 96). Some examples of dispersed practices would be explaining, describing, asking, examining, greeting, obeying or supposing. Schatzki insists that speaking about dispersion does not mean isolation: thus, a dispersed practice can help constitute another; for example, asking in relation to replying.

Integrative practices are practices that constitute particular domains of social life ('spaces of practices' in Couldry's terms). Some examples are agricultural, culinary and leisure practices, banking, and legal, religious, educational and academic ones. Schatzki does not regard integrative practices as mere collections of dispersed practices since the latter are often transformed when they come to be part of an integrative practice. Thus, the dispersed practices of asking and replying are clearly transformed when they become part of legal practices, for example. It should also be taken into account that the three elements that organise a practice according to Schatzki – in short: understandings; explicit rules (or procedures); and motivations (emotions, goals, beliefs, moods, engagement) – do not necessarily have to intervene to the same extent when governing certain behaviour in a practice (ibid.: 98–103).

Applying Schatzki's model of practice organisation, it could be said that 'play' is a dispersed practice that could obviously be present in the integrative practices of 'games' but also in many other domains of social life. If play is present in video games, and video games are related to other media practices such as watching films, it is not unthinkable that the play practices present in video games may slide into related practices such as video production. Admittedly, the playful dimension of practices related to the production and consumption of images is not really a novelty. What is really 'new' is the way in which video game practices are contributing to the characterisation of a new set of practices related to digital technologies, from digital cameras to the internet and mobile phones. These playful practices are transforming ordinary practices around media consumption and production.

As we have pointed out before, in order to understand media as a set of practices in this context, an inclusive definition of media practices is necessary. Firstly, media practices have to do with media production, distribution and consumption, whether cultural products are made by companies or individuals, since these products are conceived and exhibited for a wide audience in both cases. Secondly, people are not only consuming media for they also engage with media in very different ways that include producing media content, thus becoming 'producers' and creating their own 'audiences'.

Consuming media products is not an integrative practice by itself but it is just a dispersed practice in a set of practices (doings and sayings) related to media that includes the production and sharing of cultural products. This last statement requires further explanation, as it draws on Alan Warde's account of consumption practices. Warde states that consumption is 'a process whereby agents engage in appropriation and appreciation, whether for utilitarian, expressive or contemplative purposes, of goods, services, performances, information or ambience, whether purchased or not, over which the agent has some degree of discretion' (Warde 2005: 137). Here Warde tries to break the necessary identification between consumption and acquisition, foregrounding 'use', which constitutes an essential part of the set of mental and bodily activities inherent in any practice. For instance, this wider conceptualization of consumption could help to overcome some controversies regarding the study of fandom where consumption (thought in terms of 'demand') is seen as antithetical to fan activity (see Hills 2002;

Sandvoss 2005). The same could be said regarding machinima or self-producing images for YouTube.

Thus, a media practice may be understood as an integrative practice that involves a set of dispersed practices of production, distribution and consumption that together constitute a social domain (cultural performance). This interdependence should be taken into account when redefining the relation between producers and audiences, between video game and films, between play and media practices. As Couldry aptly puts it 'what audiences do ("audiencing") is a distinctive set of practices rather than an artificially chosen "slice" through daily life that cuts across how they actually understand the practices in which they are engaged' (this volume: 41–42). Audience is a subject position regarding media production; it is not an entity. People are cultural agents and media producers in so far as they put into circulation self-produced content and remake cultural industry content in their own way for an extended audience.

Couldry also reminds us, quoting Ann Swidler (2001), that some practices anchor, control or organise others, pointing to a possible hierarchy among practices. Usually the anchoring practices in integrative practices are related to the very constitutive object of their motivations. The dispersed practice of 'reporting' has not a clear object, but in the integrative practice of 'motoring', following Warde's example (Warde 2005: 138), practices around vehicles organise and give meaning to the array of other dispersed and integrative practices that characterise the hot-rod enthusiast, including practices of goods, services, performances and information production and consumption. Thus, in media practices the 'text' or the 'media object' plays a crucial role, because the object is exchanged, shared, produced and consumed; it is the practice around the object that anchors and gives meaning to a great amount of diverse interwoven practices. As Knorr Cetina (2001) has pointed out in her analysis of epistemic practices, the interaction with a complex object (say scientific knowledge, video games, soap operas or films) gives way to a different set of practices that entails a deeply affective engagement between subject and object. In this sense, new media practices are not only transforming the productive and consumption practices that define the political economy of the media system, but are also transforming the pleasure and the meaning of these practices and associated socially significant, bodily and emotionally lived experiences.

Play and cultural performance are crucial for understanding people's engagement with creating and sharing media objects. The study of the media system as a complex social domain has to include people's agency in producing media objects and the ability of these objects to perform social relationships as well as cultural meanings. We must analyse to what extent these new-media playful practices are introducing changes in the circle of cultural production. The key issue in the media practice discussion, as we have suggested, is the interrelation of different media practices as they are embedded in the ordinary life of our technologically mediated societies. As we have tried to demonstrate here, the transformative practices of playing with media are cultural performances that create new opportunities to disrupt the existing power relationship between individuals and media institutions.

Notes

1. YouTube was created in 2005 by Chad Hurley, Steve Chen and Jawed Karim and acquired by Google in October 2006. During its first year, the number of users grew dramatically and it became an absolute phenomenon of video sharing on the internet. At the same time, particular videos that have appeared on YouTube have spread widely on the internet and have become paradigm cases for the ongoing video-sharing explosion.
2. Retrieved 3 June 2010 from: http://www.criticalia.org/Texts/Debate-on-Media-Practices.htm
3. The term 'new media' was used in the 1990s as a shorthand for new cultural forms which depend on digital computers for distribution. This simplistic use of the term was problematised by scholars working in the field of media. Principally, the discussion is centred on the 'newness' of the media, as every media was 'new' at the time it first appeared (Manovich 2001: 21). Authors such as Peter Lunenfeld (1999) and Lev Manovich (2001) agree that defining 'new media' by just relying on its digital nature is too limiting and misleading since everything would be new media in the end, including CD-ROMs and DVD-ROMs, websites, computer games, hypertext and hypermedia applications, digital video, audio files, etc.
4. The idea of 'new media', although problematic, captures both, the development of unique forms of digital media and the reshaping of more established media forms to adopt and adapt to digital technologies and 'new media' formats (Flew 2002: 11).
5. Here it is interesting to consider Faye Ginsburg's anthropological reflections on indigenous cultural creation and digital technologies. She questions the ethnocentrism of how we think about the 'new media', pointing out that some indigenous producers use the new circulatory regimes introduced by digital technologies for linking indigenous communities in their own terms, objecting to stereotypes that suggest traditional communities should not have access to cultural forms associated with modernity, but at the same time taking into account the power relations that decide whose knowledge is valued and resisting the commodification of their knowledge under western systems of intellectual property (Ginsburg 2007: 3–4).

6. Game modding practices consist of the modification and customisation of video games through manipulating their engines and codes (see Sotamaa 2003). Machinima can be considered an atypical yet extremely popular form of game modding (Jones 2006: 264–67).
7. Activision was the company that produced the video game *The Movies* at the time of the furore over *The French Democracy*. In October 2007 the company was taken over by Vivendi.
8. According to MTV online magazine, December 2005, Alex Chan stated that 'many French people still don't know or don't want to really understand what happened in their neighborhood ... That's why I chose this ironic title of "The French Democracy" in order to refer to the fact that the youth prefers to use Molotov cocktails than ballot papers to get heard by the government. In this way in my movie, I try to bring people to think or to understand – not to necessarily forgive – what can push a young person or teenager to act like this'. Retrieved 18 May 2008 from: http://www.mtv.com/news/articles/1517481/20051205/index.jhtml. Other online discussions of this case can be found at the following: http://www.businessweek.com/magazine/content/05_51/b3964049.htm, http://www.usatoday.com/tech/gaming/2005-12-15-french-riots-film_x.htm, http://www.wired.com/science/discoveries/news/2006/01/70058?curre ntPage=all, http://www.washingtonpost.com/wp-dyn/content/article/2005/11/30/ AR2005113002117.html.
9. *Bus Uncle*. Retrieved 29 April 2008 from: http://www.youtube.com/ watch?v=EsYRQkmVifg.
10. *Acrobats*. Retrieved 28 April 2008 from: http://www.youtube.com/ watch?v=mB_3ReQ7h-c.
11. This case was analysed in depth in a study conducted by the authors about video self-production on the internet: see San Cornelio et al. (2007).

References

Aarseth, E. 1998. 'Allegories of Space: The Question of Spatiality in Computer Games'. Working Paper, University of Bergen. Retrieved 1 October 2007 from: http://www.hf.uib.no./hi/espen/papers/space/Default.html.

Appadurai, A. 1998. *Modernity at Large*. Minneapolis: University of Minnesota Press.

Avedon, E.M. and B. Sutton-Smith. 1971. *The Study of Games*. New York: Wiley.

Bird, E.S. 2003. *The Audience in Everyday Life: Living in a Media World*. New York: Routledge.

Boellstorff, T. 2006. 'A Ludicrous Discipline? Ethnography and Game Studies', *Games and Culture* 1(1): 29–35.

Bolter, J.D. and R. Grusin. 2000. *Remediation: Understanding New Media*. Cambridge, MA: MIT Press.

Caillois, R. 1962. *Man, Play and Games*. London: Thames and Hudson.

Coman, M. 2005. 'Media Anthropology: An Overview'. Working Paper, EASA Media Anthropology Network e-Seminar. Retrieved 3 May 2007 from: http://www.media-anthropology.net/workingpapers.htm.

Couldry, N. 2004. 'Theorising media as practice', *Social Semiotics* 14(2): 115–32.

Couldry, N. and A. Langer. 2005. 'Media Consumption and Public Connection: Towards a Typology of the Dispersed Citizen', *Communication Review* 8: 237–57.

Darley, A. 2000. *Visual Digital Culture*. London: Routledge.

Fiske, J. 1987. *Television Culture*. London: Methuen.

——— 1989. *Reading the Popular*. London: Routledge.

Flew, T. 2002. *New Media: An Introduction*. Melbourne: Oxford University Press.

Ginsburg, F. 2007. 'Rethinking the Digital Age'. Working Paper, EASA Media Anthropology Network e-Seminar. Retrieved 22 February 2010 from: http://www.philbu.net/media-anthropology/ginsburg_digital_age.pdf.

Hall, S. 1997. *Representation: Cultural Representations and Signifying Practices*. London: Sage.

Harries, D. 2002. 'Watching the Internet', in D. Harries (ed.), *The Book of New Media*. London: British Film Institute Publishing.

Hills, M. 2002. *Fan Cultures*. London: Routledge.

Huizinga, J. 1949[1938]. *Homo Ludens: A Study of the Play Element in Culture*. London: Routledge and Kegan Paul.

Jenkins, H. 1992. *Textual Poachers: Television Fans and Participatory Culture*. London: Routledge.

——— 2004. 'The Cultural Logic of Media Convergence', *International Journal of Cultural Studies* 7(1): 33–43 .

Jones, R. 2006. 'From Shooting Monsters to Shooting Movies: Machinima and the Transformative Play of Video Game Fan Culture', in K. Hellekson and K. Busse (eds), *Fan Fiction and Fan Communities in the Age of the Internet*. Jefferson, North Carolina: McFarland, pp.261–81.

Knorr Cetina, K. 2001. 'Objectual Practice', in T.R. Schatzki, K. Knorr Cetina and E. Von Savingy (eds), *The Practice Turn in Contemporary Theory*. London: Routledge, pp.175–88.

Kücklich, J. and M.C. Fellow. 2004. 'Play and Playability as Key Concepts in New Media Studies', Working Paper, STeM Centre, Dublin City University. Retrieved 1 October 2007 from: http://www.playability.de/Play.pdf.

Lievrouw, L. and S. Livingstone. 2002. *The Handbook of New Media*. London: Sage.

Lunenfeld, P. 1999. *The Digital Dialectic: New Essays on New Media*. Cambridge, MA: MIT Press.

Manovich, L. 2001. *The Language of New Media*. Cambridge, MA: MIT Press.

Marshall, D.P. 2002. 'The New Intertextual Commodity', in D. Harries (ed.), *The Book of New Media*. London: British Film Institute Publishing.

——— 2004. *New Media Cultures*. London: Arnold.

Maxwell, R. and T. Miller. 2005. 'The cultural labour issue', *Social Semiotics* 15(3): 261–6.

Newman, J. 2004. *Videogames*. New York: Routledge.

San Cornelio, G., A. Roig, E. Ardèvol and R. Pagès 2007. 'Broadcast Yourself! Internet and Playful Media Practices'. Paper to the Transforming Audiences Conference, Westminster University, London, September 2007. Retrieved 1 October 2007 from: http://groups.google.co.uk/group/transforming-audiences.

Sandvoss, C. 2005. *Fans: The Mirror of Consumption*. Oxford: Polity Press.

Schatzki, T. 1996. *Social Practices: A Wittgensteinian Approach to Human Activity and the Social*. Cambridge: Cambridge University Press.

——— 2001. 'Introduction: Practice Theory', in T.R. Schatzki, K. Knorr Cetina and E. Von Savingy (eds), *The Practice Turn in Contemporary Theory*. London: Routledge, pp.1–14.

Silverstone, R. 1999. *Why Study the Media?* London: Sage.

Simon, B. 2006. 'Beyond Cyberspatial Flaneurie: On the Analytic Potential of Living With Digital Games', *Games and Culture* 1(1): 62–7.

Sotamaa, O. 2003. 'New Media? New Theories? New Methods?' Nordic Network of Innovating Media and Communication Research, University of Tampere, Finland. Retrieved 1 October 2007 from: http://old.imv.au.dk/eng/academic/pdf_files/Sotamaa.pdf.

Swidler, A. 2001. 'What Anchors Cultural Practices', in T. Schatzki, K. Knorr Cetina and E. von Savigny (eds), *The Practice Turn in Contemporary Theory*. London: Routledge, pp.74–92.

Turner, V. 1986. *The Anthropology of Experience*. Chicago: University of Illinois Press.

Warde, A. 2005. 'Consumption and Theories of Practice', *Journal of Consumer Culture* 5(2): 131–53.

CHAPTER 13

Theorising the Practices of Free Software: The Movement

Christopher M. Kelty

This chapter is excerpted from a larger study that discusses the five core practices that make up free software (Kelty 2008). By 'practice' I mean something roughly similar to the definitions given by Couldry (this volume) and Swidler (2001), where the question of what free-software hackers and users are actually doing with the tools and infrastructures they use and create is central to the analysis. In the book, I approach the significance of free software as the creation of 'recursive publics' – publics which emerge precisely through the active creation of new technologies, new tools and new means of communication – and not only through discourse. Here, I focus on the term 'practice,' which is meant to carry more weight than the term 'culture' typically does today (and despite the original anthropological power of that concept) as it has travelled into other disciplines and places. However, the practices I describe are part of a system, an evolving, experimental (cultural) system. The description bears similarities to the analytic style of analysis associated with the Weberian ideal type, and more recently with concepts developed by Paul Rabinow (2002, 2008). This chapter describes one of the core practices of free software: the free-software movement itself. Elsewhere I discuss the remaining four practices of sharing source code, conceptualizing openness or open systems, writing copyright (and copyleft) licences, and coordinating collaborations (see Kelty 2008).

I define 'movement' here as the practice, among geeks, of arguing about and discussing the structure and meaning of free software: what it consists of, what it is for, and whether or not it is a movement. Some geeks call free software a movement, and some do not; some talk about the ideology and goals of free software, and some do not; some call it free software while others call it open source. Amid all this argument, however, free-software geeks recognise that they are all doing the same thing: the practice of creating a movement is the practice of talking about the meaning and necessity of the other four practices. It was in 1998/9 that geeks came to recognise that they were all doing the same thing and, almost immediately, to argue about why.[1]

One way to understand the movement is through the story of Netscape and the Mozilla web browser (now known as Firefox) because it is a story full of discussion and argument about the very practices that make up free software: sharing source code, conceiving of openness, writing licences and coordinating collaborations.

Forking Free Software, 1997–2000

Free software 'forked' (a term computer hackers use to designate a new version of software) in 1998 when the term 'open source' suddenly appeared (a term previously used only by the CIA to refer to unclassified sources of intelligence). The two terms resulted in two separate kinds of narratives: the first, regarding free software, stretched back into the 1980s, promoting software freedom and resistance to proprietary software 'hoarding,' as Richard Stallman, head of the Free Software Foundation, refers to it; the second, regarding open source, was associated with the dotcom boom and the evangelism of the libertarian, pro-business hacker Eric Raymond, who focused on the economic value and cost savings that open-source software represented, including the pragmatic (and polymathic) approach that governed the everyday use of free software in some of the largest online start-ups.[2]

A critical point in the emergence of free software occurred in 1998/9: new names, new narratives, but also new wealth and new stakes emerged. 'Open source' was premised on dotcom promises of cost-cutting and 'disintermediation' and various other schemes designed to make money from it.[3] VA Linux, for instance, which sold personal-computer systems pre-installed with open-source operating systems, had the largest single initial public offering (IPO) of the dotcom stock-market bubble, seeing a 700 per cent share-price increase in one day. 'Free software' by contrast fanned kindling flames of worry about intellectual-property expansionism and hitched itself to a nascent legal resistance to the 1998 Digital Millennium Copyright Act and Sonny Bono Copyright Term Extension Act. Prior to 1998, free software referred either to the Free Software Foundation (and the watchful, micro-managing eye of Stallman) or to one of thousands of different commercial, avocational or university research projects, processes, licences and ideologies that had a variety of names: sourceware, freeware, shareware, open software, public domain software, and so on. The term open source, by contrast, sought to encompass them all in one movement.

The event that precipitated this attempted semantic *coup d'état* was the release of the source code for Netscape's Communicator web browser. It is tough to overestimate the importance of Netscape to the fortunes of free software. Netscape is justly famous for its 1995 IPO and its decision to offer its core product, Netscape Navigator, for free (meaning a compiled, binary version could be downloaded and installed 'for zero dollars'). But Netscape is far more famous among geeks for giving away something else in 1998: the source code to Netscape Communicator (née Navigator). Giving away the Communicator source code endeared Netscape to geeks and confused investors; but it was ignored by customers. Netscape is important from a number of perspectives. Businesspeople and investors knew Netscape as the pet project of the successful businessman Jim Clarke, who had founded the specialty computer manufacturer, Silicon Graphics Incorporated (SGI). To computer scientists and engineers, especially in the small university town of Champaign-Urbana, Illinois, Netscape was known as the highest bidder for the World Wide Web team at the National Center for Supercomputing Applications (NCSA) at the University of Illinois. That team – Marc Andreessen, Rob McCool, Eric Bina, Jon Mittelhauser, Aleks Totic and Chris Houck – had created Mosaic, the first and most fondly remembered 'graphical browser' for surfing the World Wide Web. Netscape was thus first known as Mosaic Communications Corporation and switched its name only after legal threats from NCSA and a rival firm, Spyglass. Among geeks, Netscape was known as the home to a number of free-software hackers and advocates, most notably Jamie Zawinski, who had rather flamboyantly broken rank with the Free Software Foundation by forking the GNU EMACS code to create what was first known as Lucid Emacs and later as XEmacs.[4] Zawinski would go on to lead the newly free Netscape browser project, now known as Mozilla.

Meanwhile, most regular computer users remember Netscape both as an emblem of the dotcom boom's venture-fed insanity and as yet another of Microsoft's victims. Although Netscape exploded onto the scene in 1995, offering a feature-rich browser that was an alternative to the bare-bones Mosaic browser, it soon began to lose ground to Microsoft, which relatively quickly adopted the strategy of giving away its browser, Internet Explorer, as if it were part of the Windows operating system; this was a practice that the U.S. Department of Justice eventually found to be in violation of antitrust laws and for which Microsoft was convicted, though never punished.

The nature of Netscape's decision to release the source code can be viewed differently depending on which perspective it is seen from. It could appear to be a business plan modelled on the original success: give away your product and make money in the stock market. It could appear to be a strategic, last-gasp effort to outcompete Microsoft. It could also appear, and did appear to many geeks, as an attempt to regain some of the 'hacker-cred' it once had acquired by poaching the NCSA team, or even to be an attempt to 'do the right thing' by making one of the world's most useful tools into free software. But why would Netscape reach such a conclusion? By what reasoning would such a decision seem to be correct? The reasons for Netscape's decision to 'free the source' recapitulates the five core practices of free software – and provided momentum for the new movement.

Sharing Source Code

Netscape's decision to share its source code only seems surprising in the context of the widespread practice of keeping source code secret. This secrecy was a practice largely followed in order to prevent competitors from copying a program and competing with it, but it is also a means to control the market itself. The World Wide Web that Andreessen's team at NCSA had cut their teeth on was itself designed to be 'platform independent' and accessible by any device on the network. In practice, however, this meant that someone needed to create 'browsers' for each different computer or device. Mosaic was initially created for UNIX, using the Motif library of the X11 Window System – in short, a very specific kind of access. Netscape, by contrast, prided itself on 'porting' (making versions that would work on any operating system or computer) Netscape Navigator to nearly all available computer architectures. Indeed, by 1997, plans were underway to create a version of the browser written in Java – the programming language created by Sun Microsystems to 'write once, run anywhere' – that would be completely platform independent.

However, the Java-based Navigator (called Javagator, of course) created a problem with respect to the practice of keeping source code secret. Whenever a program in Java was run, it created a set of 'bytecodes' that were easy to reverse engineer (or re-construct from the output made up of those bytecodes) because they had to be transmitted from the server to the machine that ran the program and were thus visible to anyone who might know how and where to look. Netscape engineers flirted with the idea of deliberately obfuscating these bytecodes to deter competitors from copying them. How can one compete, the logic goes, if anyone can copy your program and make their own ersatz version?

Zawinski, among others, suggested that this was a bad idea: why not just share the source code and get people to help make it better? As a longtime participant in free software, Zawinski understood the potential benefits of receiving help from a huge pool of potential contributors. He urged his peers at Netscape to see the light. However, although he told them stories and showed them successes, he could never make the case that this was an intelligent business plan, only that it was an efficient software-engineering plan. From the perspective of management and investors, such a move seemed tantamount to simply giving away the intellectual property of the company itself.

Frank Hecker, a sales manager, made the link between the developers and management: 'It was obvious to [developers] why it was important. It wasn't really clear from a senior management level why releasing the source code could be of use because nobody ever made the business case' (Moody 2001: 193). Hecker penned a document called 'Netscape Source Code as Netscape Product' and circulated it to various people, including Andreessen and Netscape CEO Jim Barksdale. As the title suggests, the business case was that the source code could also be a product, and in the context of Netscape, whose business model was 'give it away and make it up on the stock market', such a proposal seemed less insane than it otherwise might have:

> When Netscape first made Navigator available for unrestricted download over the Internet, many saw this as flying in the face of conventional wisdom for the commercial software business, and questioned how we could possibly make money 'giving our software away.' Now of course this strategy is seen in retrospect as a successful innovation that was a key factor in Netscape's rapid growth, and rare is the software company today that does not emulate our strategy in one way or another. Among other things, this provokes the following question: What if we were to repeat this scenario, only this time with source code? (Frank Hecker, quoted in Hamerly, Paquin and Walton 1999: 198)

Under the influence of Hecker, Zawinski and CTO Eric Hahn (who had also written various internal 'heresy documents' suggesting similar approaches), Netscape eventually made the decision to share their source code with the outside world, a decision that resulted in a famous January 1998 press release describing the aims and benefits of doing so. The decision, at that particular point in Netscape's life and in the midst of the dotcom boom, was certainly momentous, but it did not lead either to a financial windfall or to a suddenly superior product.[5]

Conceptualizing Open Systems

Releasing the source code was, in a way, an attempt to regain the trust of the people who had first imagined the World Wide Web (WWW). Tim Berners-Lee, the initial architect of the WWW, was always adamant that the protocol and all its implementations should be freely available (meaning either 'in the public domain' or 'released as free software'). Indeed, Berners-Lee had done just that with his first bare-bones implementations of the WWW, proudly declaring them to be in the public domain.

Over the course of the 1990s, the 'browser wars' caused both Netscape and Microsoft to stray far from this vision: each had implemented its own extensions and 'features' for the browsers and servers, extensions not present in the protocol that Berners-Lee had created or in the subsequent standards created by the World Wide Web Consortium (W3C). Included in the implementations were various kinds of 'evil' that could make browsers fail to work on certain operating systems or with certain kinds of servers. The 'browser wars' repeated an open-systems battle from the 1980s, one in which the attempt to standardise a network operating system (UNIX) was stymied by competition and secrecy, at the same time that consortiums devoted to 'openness' were forming in order to try to prevent the spread of this evil. Despite the fact that both Microsoft and Netscape were members of the W3C, the noncompatibility of their browsers clearly represented the manipulation of the standards process in the name of competitive advantage.

Releasing the source code for Communicator was thus widely seen as perhaps the only way to bypass the poisoned well of competitively tangled, non-standard browser implementations. An open-source browser could be made to comply with the standards – if not by the immediate members involved with its creation, then by creating a 'fork' of the program that was standards compliant – because of the rights of redistribution associated with an open-source licence. Open source would be the solution to an open-systems problem that had never been solved because it had never confronted the issue of intellectual property directly. Free software, by contrast, had a well-developed solution in the GNU General Public License (GPL), also known as copyleft licence (because it is the opposite of a copyright licence), that would allow the software to remain free and revive hope for maintaining open standards.

Writing Licences

Herein lies the rub, however. Netscape was immediately embroiled in controversy among free-software hackers because it chose to write its own bespoke licences for distributing the source code. Rather than rely on one of the existing licences, such as the GNU GPL or the Berkeley Systems Distribution (BSD) or Massachusetts Institute of Technology (MIT) licences, they created their own: the Netscape Public License (NPL) and the Mozilla Public License. The immediate concerns of Netscape had to do with the existing network of contracts and agreements they had with other, third-party developers – both those who had in the past contributed parts of the existing source code that Netscape might not have the rights to redistribute as free software, and those who expected to buy and redistribute a commercial version in the future. Existing free-software licences were either too permissive, giving to third parties rights that Netscape itself might not have; or they were too restrictive, binding Netscape to make source code freely available (the GPL) when it had already signed contracts with buyers of the non-free code.

It was a complex and specific business situation – a network of existing contracts and licensed code – that created the need for Netscape to write its own licence. The NPL thus contained a clause that gave Netscape special permission to relicense any particular contribution to the source code as a proprietary product in order to appease its third-party contracts; this essentially gave Netscape special rights that no other licensee would have. While this did not necessarily undermine free-software licences – and it was certainly Netscape's prerogative – it was contrary to the spirit of free software: it broke the 'recursive public' into two halves. In order to appease free-software geeks, Netscape wrote one licence for existing code (the NPL) and a different licence for new contributions: the Mozilla Public License.

Neither Stallman nor any other free-software hacker was entirely happy with this situation. Stallman pointed out three flaws: 'One flaw sends a bad philosophical message, another puts the free-software community in a weak position, while the third creates a major practical problem within the free-software community. Two of the flaws apply to the Mozilla Public License as well.'[6] He urged people not to use the NPL. Similarly, Bruce Perens suggested, 'Many companies have adopted a variation of the MPL [sic] for their own programs. This is unfortunate, because the NPL was designed for the specific business situation that Netscape was in at the time it was written and is not necessarily appropriate for others to use. It should remain the license of Netscape and Mozilla, and others should use the GPL or the BSD or X licenses' (Perens 1999: 184).

Arguments about the fine details of licences may seem scholastic, but the decision had a huge impact on the structure of the new product. As Steven Weber (2004) has pointed out, the choice of licence tracks the organisation of a product and can determine who and what kinds of contributions can be made to a project. It is not an idle choice; every new licence is scrutinised with the same intensity or denounced with the same urgency.

Coordinating Collaborations

One of the selling points of free software, and especially of its marketing as open source, is that it leverages the work of thousands or hundreds of thousands of volunteer contributors across the internet. Such a claim almost inevitably leads to spurious talk of 'self-organising' systems and emergent properties of distributed collaboration. The Netscape press release promised to 'harness the creative power of thousands of programmers on the Internet by incorporating their best enhancements', and it quoted CEO Jim Barksdale as saying, 'By giving away the source code for future versions, we can ignite the creative energies of the entire Net community and fuel unprecedented levels of innovation in the browser market'.[7] But as anyone who has ever tried to start or run a free-software project knows, it never works out that way.

Software engineering is a notoriously hard problem.[8] The halls of the software industry are lined with the corpses of dead software methodologies. Developing software in the dotcom boom was no different, except that the speed of release cycles and the velocity of funding (the 'burn rate') was faster than ever before. Netscape's in-house development methodologies were designed to meet these pressures, and as many who work in this field will attest, that method is some version of a semi-structured, deadline-driven, caffeine- and smart-drink-fuelled race to 'ship'.[9]

Releasing the Mozilla code, therefore, required a system of coordination that would differ from the normal practice of in-house software development by paid programmers. It needed to incorporate the contributions of outside developers who did not work for Netscape. It also needed to entice other people to contribute, since that was the bargain on which the decision to 'free the source' was based, and allow them to track their contributions so they could verify that their contributions were included or rejected for legitimate reasons. In short, if any magical open-source self-organisation were to take place, it would require a thoroughly transparent, Internet-based coordination system.

At the outset, this meant practical things: obtaining the domain name mozilla.org; and setting up (and in turn releasing the source code for) the version-control system (the free-software standard concurrent versioning system, or cvs), the version-control interface (Bonsai), the 'build system' that managed and displayed the various trees and (broken) branches of a complex software project (Tinderbox), and a bug-reporting system for tracking bugs submitted by users and developers (Bugzilla). It required an organisational system within the Mozilla project, in which paid developers would be assigned to check submissions from inside and outside Netscape, and maintainers or editors would be designated to look at and verify that these contributions should be used.

In the end, the release of the Mozilla source code was both a success and a failure. Its success was long in coming: by 2004, the Firefox web browser, based on Mozilla, had started to creep up the charts of most popular browsers, and it has since become one of the most visible and widely used free-software applications. The failure, however, was more immediate: Mozilla failed to create the massive benefits for Netscape that the 1995 give-away of Netscape Navigator had. Zawinski, in a public letter of resignation in April 1999 (one year after the release), expressed this sense of failure. He attributed Netscape's decline after 1996 to the fact that it had 'stopped innovating' and become too large to be creative, and he described the decision to free the Mozilla source code as a return to this innovation:

> [The announcement] was a beacon of hope to me … [I]t was so crazy, it just might work. I took my cue and ran with it, registering the domain that night, designing the structure of the organization, writing the first version of the web site, and, along with my co-conspirators, explaining to room after room of Netscape employees and managers how free software worked, and what we had to do to make it work.[10]

For Zawinski, the decision was both a chance for Netscape to return to its glory and an opportunity to prove the power of free software:

> I saw it as a chance for the code to actually prosper. By making it not be a Netscape project, but rather, be a public project to which Netscape was merely a contributor, the fact that Netscape was no longer capable of building products wouldn't matter: the outsiders would show Netscape how it's done. By putting control of the web browser into the hands of anyone who cared to step up to the task, we would ensure that those people would keep it going, out of their own self-interest'[11]

But this promise did not come true. Or, at least, it did not come true at the speed that Zawinski and others in the software world were used to. Zawinski offered various reasons: the project was primarily made up of Netscape employees and thus still appeared to be a Netscape thing; it was too large a project for outsiders to dive into and make small changes to; the code was too 'crufty' – that is, too complicated, overwritten and unclean. Perhaps most significantly, though, the source code was not actually working: 'We never distributed the source code to a working web browser, more importantly, to the web browser that people were actually using.'[12]

Netscape failed to entice. As Zawinski put it, 'If someone were running a web browser, then stopped, added a simple new command to the source, recompiled, and had that same web browser plus their addition, they would be motivated to do this again, and possibly to tackle even larger projects'.[13] For Zawinski, the failure to 'ship' a working browser was the biggest failure, and he took pains to suggest that this failure was not an indictment of free software as such:

> Let me assure you that whatever problems the Mozilla project is having are not because open source doesn't work. Open source does work, but it is most definitely not a panacea. If there's a cautionary tale here, it is that you can't take a dying project, sprinkle it with the magic pixie dust of 'open source,' and have everything magically work out. Software is hard. The issues aren't that simple.[14]

Fomenting Movements

The period between 1 April 1998, when the Mozilla source code was first released, and 1 April 1999, when Zawinski announced its failure, could not have been a headier, more exciting time for participants in free software. Netscape's decision to release the source code was a tremendous opportunity for geeks involved in free software. It came in the midst of the rollicking dotcom bubble and also came amidst the widespread adoption of key free-software tools: the Linux operating system for servers, the Apache web server for web pages, the perl and python scripting languages for building quick internet applications, and a number of other lower-level tools like Bind (an implementation of the Domain Name System, or DNS protocol for mapping human readable names to numerical Internet Protocol addresses) or sendmail for e-mail.

Perhaps most important, Netscape's decision came in a period of fevered and intense self-reflection among people who had been involved in free software in some way, stretching back to the mid-1980s. Eric Raymond's article 'The Cathedral and The Bazaar', delivered at the Linux Kongress in 1997 (Raymond 2001) and the O'Reilly Perl Conference the same year, had started a buzz among free-software hackers. The article was cited by Frank Hecker and Eric Hahn at Netscape as one of the sources of their thinking about the decision to free Mozilla; subsequently both the author Eric Raymond and noted free software advocate Bruce Perens were asked to consult with Netscape on free-software strategy. And in April 1997 Tim O'Reilly, a publisher of handbooks on free software, organised a conference called the Freeware Summit.

The summit's very name indicated some of the concern about definition and direction. Stallman, despite his obvious centrality, but also because of it, was not invited to the Freeware Summit, and the Free Software Foundation was not held up as the core philosophical guide of the event. Rather, according to the press release distributed afterwards, 'The meeting's purpose was to facilitate a high-level discussion of the successes and challenges facing the developers. While this type of software has often been called "freeware" or "free software" in the past, the developers agreed that commercial development of the software is part of the picture, and that the terms "open source" or "sourceware" best describe the development method they support'.[15]

It was at this summit that Raymond's suggestion of 'open source' as an alternative name was first publicly debated (see Hamerly, Paquin and Walton 1999).[16] Shortly thereafter, Raymond and Perens created the Open Source Initiative and penned 'The Open Source Definition' (see Perens 1999). All of this self-reflection was intended to capitalise on attention being directed at free software in the wake of Netscape's announcement.

The motivations for these changes came from a variety of sources – ranging from a desire to be included in the dotcom boom to a powerful (ideological) resistance to being ideological. Linus Torvalds loudly proclaimed that the reason for doing free software was because it was 'fun'; others insisted that it made better business sense or that the stability of infrastructures like the internet depended on a robust ability to improve them from any direction. But none of them questioned how free software got done or proposed any changes to how it was being practiced.

Raymond's article 'The Cathedral and the Bazaar' quickly became the most widely told story of how open source works and why it is important; it emphasises the centrality of novel forms of coordination over the role of novel copyright licences or practices of sharing source code. The article reports Raymond's experiments with free software (the bazaar model) and reflects on the difference between it and method-

292 | *Christopher M. Kelty*

ologies adopted by industry (the cathedral model). The paper does not truck with talk of freedom and has no denunciations of software hoarding *à la* Stallman. Significantly, it also has no discussion of licensing issues. Being a hacker, however, Raymond gave his paper a 'revision-history', which proudly displays revision 1.29, 9 February 1998: 'Changed "free software" to "open source"'.[17]

Raymond was determined to reject the philosophy of liberty that Stallman and the Free Software Foundation represented, but not in order to create a political movement of his own. Rather, Raymond (and the others at the Freeware Summit) sought to cash in on the rising tide of the internet economy by turning the creation of free software into something that made more sense to investors, venture capitalists and the stock-buying public. To Raymond, Stallman and the Free Software Foundation represented not freedom or liberty but a kind of dogmatic, impossible communism. As Raymond was a committed libertarian, one might expect his core beliefs in the necessity of strong property rights to conflict with the strange communalism of free software – and, indeed, his rhetoric was focused on pragmatic, business-minded, profit-driven and market-oriented uses of free software. For Raymond, the essentially interesting component of free software was not its enhancement of human liberty, but the innovation in software production that it represented (the 'development model'). It was clear that free software achieved something amazing through a clever inversion of strong property rights, an inversion which could be expected to bring massive revenue in some other form, either through cost-cutting or, Netscape-style, through the stock market.

Raymond wanted the business world and mainstream industry to recognise free software's potential, but he felt that Stallman's rhetoric was getting in the way. In his view, Stallman's insistence on, for example, calling corporate intellectual-property protection of software 'hoarding' did more damage than good in terms of free software's acceptance among businesses. Raymond's article channelled the frustration of an entire generation of free-software hackers who may or may not have shared Stallman's dogmatic philosophical stance, but who nonetheless wanted to participate in the creation of free software.

Raymond's article, the Netscape announcement, and the Freeware Summit all played on a palpable anxiety: that in the midst of the single largest creation of paper wealth in U.S. history, those being enriched through free software and the internet were not those who built free software, who maintained free software, or who understood how it worked. The internet giveaway was a conflict of propriety: hackers and geeks who had created the software that made it work, under the premise of making it free for all, saw that software could generate untold wealth for people who had not built it and, furthermore, who had no intention of keeping it free for all. Underlying the creation of wealth was a commitment to a kind of permanent technical freedom – a moral order – not shared by those who were reaping the most profit. This anxiety regarding the expropriation of work (even if it had been a labour of love) was ramified by Netscape's announcement.

During 1998 and 1999, a buzz built around open source. Little-known companies such as Red Hat, VA Linux, Cygnus, Slackware and SuSe, which had been providing free-software support and services to customers, suddenly entered media and business consciousness. Articles in the mainstream press circulated during the spring and summer of 1998, often attempting to make sense of the name change from free software to open source and whether it meant a corresponding change in any of the concrete practices of creating software. A front-cover article in *Forbes*, which featured photos of Stallman, Larry Wall, Brian Behlendorf and Torvalds was noncommittal, shifting between free software, open source and freeware (McHugh 1998).

In early 1999, O'Reilly Press published *Open Sources: Voices from the Open Source Revolution* (Dibona et al. 1999), a hastily written but widely read book. It included a number of articles – this time including one by Stallman – that cobbled together the first widely available public history of free software, both as practice and technology. Kirk McKusick's article detailed the history of important technologies like the BSD version of UNIX, while an article by Brian Behlendorf (of Apache) detailed the practical challenges of running free-software projects. Raymond provided a history of hackers and a self-aggrandising article about his own importance in creating the movement, while Stallman's contribution told his own version of the rise of free software.

By December 1999, the buzz had reached fever pitch. When VA Linux, a legitimate company which actually made something real – computers with Linux installed on them – went public, it became the single most valuable initial public offering (IPO) of the era. VA Linux took the unconventional step of allowing contributors to the Linux kernel to buy stock before the IPO, thus bringing at least a partial set of these contributors into the mainstream pyramid scheme of the internet dotcom economy. Those who managed to sell their stock ended up benefiting from the boom, whether or not their contributions to free software truly merited it. In a roundabout way, Raymond, O'Reilly, Perens and others behind the name change had achieved recognition for the central role of free software in the success of the internet – and now its true name could be known: open source.

Yet nothing much changed in terms of the way things actually got done. Sharing source code, conceiving openness, writing licences, coordinating projects – all these continued as before with no significant differences between those flashing the heroic mantle of freedom and those donning the pragmatic tunic of methodology. Now, however, stories proliferated: definitions, distinctions, details and detractions filled the ether of the internet, ranging from the philosophical commitments of free software to parables of science as the 'original open-source' software. Free-software proponents refined their message concerning rights, while open-source advocates refined their claims of political agnosticism or non-ideological commitment to 'fun.' All these stories served to create movements, to evangelise, advocate and convert them to the cause. The fact that there are different narratives for identical practices is an advantageous fact: regardless of why people think they are doing what they are doing, they are all nonetheless contributing to the same mysterious thing.

A Movement?

To most onlookers, free software and open source seem to be overwhelmed with frenzied argument; the heated arguments and disputes online and offline, seem to dominate everything. To attend a conference where geeks – especially high-profile geeks like Raymond, Stallman and Torvalds – are present, one might suspect that the very detailed practices of free software are overseen by the brow-beating, histrionic antics of a few charismatic leaders and that ideological commitments result in divergent, incompatible and affect-laden opposition which must of necessity take specific and incompatible forms. Strangely, this is far from the case: all this sound and fury does not much change what people do, even if it is a requirement of apprenticeship. It truly is all over but for the shouting.

According to most of the scholarly literature, the function of a movement is to narrate shared goals and to recruit new members. But is this what happens in free software or open source?[18] To begin with, movement is an awkward word; not all participants would define their participation this way. Richard Stallman suggests that free software is a social movement, while open source is a development methodology. Similarly, some open-source proponents see open source as a pragmatic methodology and free software as a dogmatic philosophy. While there are specific entities like the Free Software Foundation and the Open Source Initiative, they do not represent all those engaged in free software or open source. Free software and open source are neither corporations, organisations nor consortia (for there are no organisations to consort); they are neither national, subnational nor international; they are not 'collectives' because no membership is required or assumed – indeed to hear someone assert 'I belong to free software or open source' would sound absurd to anyone who engages in free software or open source. Neither are they shady bands of hackers, crackers or thieves meeting in the dead of night, which is to say that they are not an 'informal' organisation because there is no formal equivalent to mimic or annul. Nor are they quite a crowd, for a crowd can attract participants who have no idea what the goal of the crowd is; also, crowds are temporary while movements extend over time. It may be that 'movement' is the best term of the lot, but unlike social movements, whose organisation and momentum are fuelled by shared causes or broken by ideological dispute, free software and open source share practices first, and ideologies second. It is this fact that is the strongest confirmation that they are a recursive public, a form of public that is as concerned with the material practical means of becoming public as it is with any given public debate.

The movement, as a practice of argument and discussion, is thus centred around core agreements about the other four kinds of practices. The discussion and argument have a specific function: to tie together divergent practices according to a wide consensus which tries to capture the 'whys' of free software: Why is it different from normal software development? Why is it necessary? Why now? Why do people do it? Why do people use it? Can it be preserved and enhanced? None of these questions address the 'hows' and 'whos': How should source code circulate? How should a licence be written? Who should be in charge? The 'hows' and 'whos' change slowly and experimentally through the careful modulation of the practices, but the 'whys' are turbulent and often distracting. Nonetheless, people engaged in free software – users, developers, supporters and observers – could hardly remain silent on this point, despite the frequent demand to just 'shut up and show me the code'. 'Figuring out' free software also requires a practice of reflecting on what is central to it and what lies outside it.

The movement, as a practice of discussion and argument, is made up of stories. It is a practice of storytelling; of affect- and intellect-laden lore that orients existing participants toward a particular problem, contests other histories, parries attacks from outside, and draws in new recruits.[19] This includes proselytism and evangelism (and the usable pasts of protestant reformations, singularities, rebellion and iconoclasm are often salient here), whether for the reform of intellectual-property law or for the adoption of Linux in the trenches of corporate America. It includes both heartfelt allegiance in the name of social justice as well as political agnosticism stripped of all ideology (Coleman 2004). Every time free software is introduced to someone, discussed in the media, analysed in a scholarly work, or installed in a workplace, a story of either free software or open source is used to explain its purpose, its momentum and its temporality. At the extremes are the prophets and proselytes themselves: Eric Raymond (2001) describes open source as an evolutionarily necessary outcome of the natural tendency of human societies towards economies of abundance, while Richard Stallman describes it as a defence of the fundamental freedoms of creativity and speech, using a variety of philosophical theories of liberty, justice and the defence of freedom (see Williams 2002). Even scholarly analyses must begin with a potted history drawn from the self-narration of geeks who make or advocate free software.[20] Indeed, as a methodological aside, one reason it is so easy to track such stories and narratives is because geeks like to tell and, more importantly, to archive such stories – creating web pages, definitions, encyclopaedia entries, dictionaries and mini-histories, saving every scrap of correspondence, every fight and every resolution related to their activities. This 'archival hubris' yields a very peculiar and specific kind of field site: one in which a kind of 'as-it-happens' ethnographic observation is possible not only through 'being there' in the moment but also by being there in the massive, proliferating archives of moments past. Understanding the movement as a changing entity requires constantly glancing back at its future promises and the conditions of their making.

Stories of the movement are also stories of a recursive public. The fact that movement is not quite the right word is evidence of a kind of grasping, a figuring out of why these practices make sense to all these geeks, in this place and time; it is a practice that is not so different from my own ethnographic engagement with it. Note that both free software and open source tell stories of movement(s): they are not divided by a commercial/non-commercial line, even if they are divided by ill-defined and hazy notions of their ultimate goals. The problem of a recursive public (or, in an alternate language, a recursive market) as a social imaginary of moral and technical order is common to both of them as part of their practices. Thus, stories about 'the movement' are detailed stories about the technical and moral order that geeks inhabit, and they are bound up with the functions and fates of the internet. Often these stories are themselves practices of inclusion and exclusion – for example, 'this licence is not a free-software licence' or 'that software is not an open system' – and sometimes the stories are normative definitions about how free software should look. But they are, always, stories that reveal the shared moral and technical imaginations that make up free software as a recursive public.

Conclusion

Before 1998, there was no movement. There was the Free Software Foundation, with its peculiar goals, and a very wide array of other projects, people, software and ideas. Then, all of a sudden, in the heat of the dotcom boom, free software became a 'movement'. Suddenly, it was a problem, a danger, a job, a calling, a dogma, a solution, a philosophy, a liberation, a methodology, a business plan, a success, and an alternative. Suddenly, it was open source or free software, and it became necessary to choose sides. After 1998, debates about definition exploded; denunciations and manifestos and journalistic hagiography proliferated. Ironically, the creation of two names allowed people to identify one thing, for these two names referred to identical practices, licences, tools and organisations. Free software and open source shared everything 'material' but differed vocally and at great length with respect to ideology. Stallman was denounced as a kook, a communist, a dogmatic idealist holding back the successful adoption of open source by business; Raymond and users of open source were charged with selling out the ideals of freedom and autonomy, with the dilution of the principles and the promise of free software, as well as with being stooges of capitalist domination. Meanwhile, both groups proceeded to create objects – principally software-using tools that they agreed on, concepts of openness that they agreed on, licences that they agreed on, and organisational schemes that they agreed on. Yet never was there fiercer debate about the definition of free software.

On the one hand, the Free Software Foundation privileges the liberty and creativity of individual geeks, geeks engaged in practices of self-fashioning through the creation of software. It gives precedence to the liberal claim that without freedom of expression individuals are robbed of their ability to self-determine. On the other hand, open source privileges organisations and processes; that is, geeks who are engaged in building businesses, non-profit organisations or governmental and public organisations of some form or another. It gives precedence to the pragmatist view that getting things done requires flexible principles and negotiation, and that the public practice of building and running things should be separate from the private practice of ethical and political beliefs. Both narratives give geeks ways of making sense of a practice that they share in almost all of its details; both narratives give geeks a way to understand how free software or open-source software is different from the mainstream, proprietary software development that dominates their horizons. The narratives turn the haphazard participation and sharing that existed before 1998 into meaningful, goal-directed practices in the present, turning a class-in-itself into a class-for-itself, to use a terminology for the most part unwelcome among geeks.

If two radically opposed ideologies can support people engaged in identical practices, then it seems obvious that the real space of politics and contestation is at the level of these practices and their emergence. These practices emerge as a response to a reorientation of power and knowledge, a reorientation somewhat impervious to conventional narratives of freedom and liberty or to pragmatic claims of methodological necessity or market-driven innovation. Were these conventional narratives sufficient, the practices would be merely bureaucratic affairs, rather than the radical transformations they are.

Notes

1. For instance, Richard Stallman writes: 'The free software movement and the open source movement are like two political camps within the free software community. Radical groups in the 1960s developed a reputation for factionalism: organizations split because of disagreements on details of strategy, and then treated each other as enemies. Or at least, such is the image people have of them, whether or not it was true. The relationship between the Free Software movement and the Open Source movement is just the opposite of that picture. We disagree on the basic principles, but agree more or less on the practical recommendations. So we can and do work together on many specific projects. We don't think of the Open Source movement as an enemy. The enemy is proprietary software' ('Why "Free Software" Is Better than "Open Source,"' GNU's Not Unix! Retrieved 9 July 2006 from: http://www.gnu.org/philosophy/free-software-for-freedom. html). By contrast, the Open Source Initiative characterizes the relationship as follows: 'How is "open source" related to "free software"? The Open Source Initiative is a marketing program for free software. It's a pitch for "free software" because it works, not because it's the only right thing to do. We're selling freedom on its merits' (Retrieved 9 July 2006 from: http://www.opensource.org/advocacy/faq.php). There are a large number of definitions of free software: canonical definitions include Richard Stallman's writings on the Free Software Foundation's website, including the 'Free Software Definition' and 'Confusing Words and Phrases that Are Worth Avoiding': http://www.fsf.org.

From the open source side there is the 'Open Source Definition': http://www.opensource.org/licenses/; see also Perens (1999). Unaffiliated definitions can be found at www.freedomdefined.org.

2. Amazon, HotWired, Yahoo! and others all 'promoted' free software by using it to run their shops.
3. Cygnus Solutions, an early free-software company, playfully tagged itself as 'Making Free Software More Affordable'.
4. GNU EMACS was software created by Richard Stallman as part of the GNU (Gnu's Not Unix) Operating System project. See Kelty (2008: 179–209).
5. See Moody (2001: 182–204) for a more detailed version of the story.
6. Richard Stallman "On the Netscape Public License" http://www.gnu.org/philosophy/netscape-npl.html. Retrieved 10 March 2010.
7. Netscape. 1998. 'Netscape Announces Plans to Make Next-generation Communicator Source Code Available Free on the Net'. Press Release, 22 January. Retrieved 25 Sept 2007 from: http://wp.netscape.com/ news-ref/pr/newsrelease558.html.
8. On the history of software development methodologies, see Mahoney (1990, 2005).
9. Especially good descriptions of what this cycle is like can be found in Ullman (1997, 2003).
10. Jamie Zawinski, "resignation and postmortem," 31 March 1999, http://www.jwz.org/gruntle/nomo.html. Retrieved 10 March 2010.
11. Ibid.
12. Ibid.
13. Ibid.
14. Ibid.
15. Free Summit. 1998. 'Open Source Pioneers Meet in Historic Summit'. Press Release, 14 April. Retrieved 10 March 2010 from: http://press.oreilly.com/pub/pr/796.
16. The story is elegantly related in Moody (2001: 182–204). Raymond gives Christine Petersen of the Foresight Institute credit for the term 'open source'.
17. The change-log is only available online at: <http://www.catb.org/~esr/writings/cathedral-bazaar/cathedral-bazaar/.
18. On social movements – the closest analogue, developed long ago – see: Gerlach and Hine (1970) and Freeman and Johnson (1999). However, the free software and open source movements do not have 'causes' of the kind that conventional movements do, other than the perpetuation of free and open source software (see Chan 2004; Coleman 2004). Similarly, there is no single development methodology that would cover only open source. Advocates of open source are all too willing to exclude those individuals or organisations who follow the same 'development methodology' but do not use a free software licence – such as Microsoft's oft-mocked 'shared-source' program. The list of licences approved by both the Free Software Foundation and the Open Source Initiative is substantially the same.

Further, the Debian Free Software Guidelines (DFSG) and the 'Open Source Definition' are almost identical: compare http://www.gnu.org/philosophy/license-list.html with http://www.opensource.org/licenses/.

19. It is, in the terms of actor network theory, a process of 'enrolment' in which participants find ways to rhetorically align – and to disalign – their interests. It does not constitute the substance of their interest, however. See Callon (1986) and Latour (1987).

20. For example, Castells (2001) and Weber (2004) both tell versions of the same story of origins and development.

References

Callon, M. 1986. 'Some Elements of a Sociology of Translation: Domestication of the Scallops and the Fishermen of St Brieuc Bay', in J. Law (ed.), *Power, Action and Belief: A New Sociology of Knowledge*. London: Routledge and Kegan Paul, pp.196–233

Castells, M. 2001. *The Internet Galaxy: Reflections on the Internet, Business and Society*. New York: Oxford University Press.

Chan, A. 2004. 'Coding Free Software, Coding Free States: Free Software Legislation and the Politics of Code in Peru', *Anthropological Quarterly* 77(3): 531–45.

Coleman, E.G. 2004. 'The Political Agnosticism of Free and Open Source Software and the Inadvertent Politics of Contrast', *Anthropological Quarterly* 77(3): 507–19.

Dibona, C. et al. 1999. *Open Sources: Voices from the Open Source Revolution*. Sebastopol, CA: O'Reilly Press.

Freeman, J. and V. Johnson (eds). 1999. *Waves of Protest: Social Movements since the Sixties*. Lanham, MD.: Rowman and Littlefield.

Gerlach, L.P. and V.H. Hine. 1970. *People, Power, Change: Movements of Social Transformation*. Indianapolis: Bobbs-Merrill.

Hamerly, J. and T. Paquin, with S. Walton. 1999. 'Freeing the Source', in Dibona et al. *Open Sources: Voices from the Open Source Revolution*. Sebastopol, CA: O'Reilly Press, pp.197–206.

Kelty, C. 2008. *Two Bits: The Cultural Significance of Free Software*. Durham, NC: Duke University Press.

Latour, B. 1987. *Science in Action: How to Follow Scientists and Engineers through Society*. Cambridge, MA: Harvard University Press.

McHugh, J. 1998. 'For the Love of Hacking', *Forbes*, 10 August, pp.94–100.

Mahoney, M. 1990. 'The Roots of Software Engineering', *CWI Quarterly* 3(4): 325–34.

——— 2005. 'The Histories of Computing(s)', *Interdisciplinary Science Reviews* 30(2): 119–35.

Moody, G. 2001. *Rebel Code: Inside Linux and the Open Source Revolution*. Cambridge, MA: Perseus.

Perens, B. 1999. 'The Open Source Definition', in Dibona et al. *Open Sources: Voices from the Open Source Revolution*. Sebastopol, CA: O'Reilly Press, pp.171–88.

Rabinow, P. 2002. *Anthropos Today: Reflections on Modern Equipment*. Princeton, NJ: Princeton University Press.

——— 2008. *Marking Time: On the Anthropology of the Contemporary*. Princeton, NJ: Princeton University Press.

Raymond, E.S. 2001. *The Cathedral and the Bazaar: Musings on Linux and Open Source by an Accidental Revolutionary*. Sebastopol, CA: O'Reilly Press.

Swidler, A. 2001. 'What Anchors Cultural Practices?' in T. Schatzki, K. Knorr Cetina and E. von Savigny (eds), *The Practice Turn in Contemporary Theory*. London: Routledge, pp. 74–92.

Ullman, E. 1997. *Close to the Machine: Technophilia and Its Discontents*. San Francisco, CA: City Lights.

——— 2003. *The Bug: A Novel*. New York: Nan A. Talese.

Weber, S. 2004. *The Success of Open Source*. Cambridge, MA: Harvard University Press.

Williams, S. 2002. *Free as in Freedom: Richard Stallman's Crusade for Free Software*. Sebastopol, CA: O'Reilly Press.

CHAPTER 14

Cinematography and Camera Crew: Practice, Process and Procedure

Cathy Greenhalgh

The thoughts expressed here derive from my experience as a practitioner, teaching cinematography practice, my own work as a cinematographer and ethnographic work with feature film cinematographers conducted over many years. I have found it necessary to find a way of coming from practice towards useful theory to make sense of my profession and art form. I will argue that empirical work observing and experiencing the precise character and operations of practices brings dimensions to consider which are difficult to theorise. I organise this argument by using two examples of practices in the film industry which are picked up by those working in the field, but are difficult to capture in books, training manuals or theories of action. I conclude that these case studies, showing how media-as-practice operates, may usefully question theoretical definitions of media practice as well as the duality between theory and practice. My position is inspired by de Certeau's ideas about practice and recent studies of collaboration and knowledge at work undertaken in organisation studies (Gherardi 2006) and psychology (John-Steiner 2000). Schatzki suggests that 'the field of practices is the place to investigate such phenomena as agency, knowledge, language, ethics, power and science' (Schatzki 2001: 13–14). I contend that this idea of practice theory derived from sociology and anthropology could be enhanced by attention to the spatiality and temporalities of practice affected by 'distributed collaboration' (John-Steiner 2000: 197), particularly prevalent in media practices. I work in a media faculty in a capital-city-based, practice-oriented university where creative industries are at the core influence of its education strategy. Within the milieu of the university's colleges, practice as research, interdisciplinary collaboration, researching practices, the pedagogy of art and design practice and definitions of practices and their often codified descriptions, are fre-

quently discussed. My observation is that the teaching of theory integrated with practice is deeply embedded at this institution in a manner
qualitatively different to many traditional universities, where theory
more often defines and validates practice.

The ideas discussed in this chapter were consolidated during a pedagogic research project which analysed the interplay between theory
and students' film-making practice. The Centre for Learning in
Practice (CLIPCETL) is a U.K. pedagogic research centre for educa-
tion, teaching and learning based at University of the Arts, London
(UAL). In 2006/7 it provided a research grant to the Film and
Television department to study teaching collaboration in film-practice
education, which focused on students taking the BA in Film and
Television at London College of Communication (part of UAL), who
study within one of seven designated U.K. Skillset Screen Academies.
Important aspects of the research included 'collaborative dynamics'
(John-Steiner 2001: 204), embodied learning, technique, affective skill,
social interaction and language used amongst student crews in TV and
film studios as a specific learning environment. The project tracked
how students accumulate knowledge of practical skills – such as shooting and crewing expertise with camera, lighting and grip equipment
when shooting film and television drama projects – and then how they
both understand and analyse that learning and relate it to theoretical
concepts. Data included HD and DVCam video footage and stills of student workshops and shoots, reflexive critical review writing and interviews. Student notions of professional camera-department behaviour
were compared with descriptions by members of the film industry.
Skillset funded 35mm short-film projects over two summers at Elstree
and Shepperton studios in simulated professional conditions on full
size sound stages (film sets). These allowed staff to observe how students implemented their understanding and practical knowledge at a
professional level.

For the purposes of this chapter I have concentrated on the immediate physical conditions around the camera whilst shooting a film in
order to show how two case study concepts and activities amplify a synthesis of media theory and practice. The case studies prove the complex
interrelationship between actions, decisions, instructions, understandings and the mobility of these in human transactions in media as practice. The camera department on a feature film involves several personnel. The cinematographer designs the cinematography (lighting, camera movement, composition) of the film, working to the vision of the
director. It varies widely how much directors involve themselves in this.
Work involves managing the lighting and electrical crew, grip and crane

(camera movement) crew and the camera crew. The role is also known as director of photography (DoP or DP). On smaller films the DP sometimes operates the camera, but in the United States this is a unionised role and so not possible. On the camera crew are the camera operator who works under the DP, as do the focus puller (also known as 'A camera' or first assistant), the clapperloader (also known as 'B camera' or second assistant)[1] and camera trainee.

Cinematographers' creative and craft knowledge and rhetoric is produced, accumulated and transferred via performance protocols, affective expertise and physical dexterity with technology, maintained within a specific on-set hierarchy. The two practice exemplars used in this chapter amplify the inter-relationship of these aspects. The first case study, visualisation, affects the narrative of the filmmaking sequence of pre-production, production, and post-production and is considerably altered by the impact of digital convergence. The second, 'cheating', is the term used on set to describe the continuous re-positioning of bodies and sets with different lens views to achieve a believable geographic spatial reality for the film. Details of how cheating and visualisation operate will assist in developing a theory of both the transformative and processual aspects of media practice, a tentative definition and short typology of the characteristics of media-as-practice, and points to consider when theorising media practice. These require an understanding of temporal workflow within the spatial (and cultural) strategy of the film set (borrowing from de Certeau 1984). In order to explicate this workflow, some conceptual distinctions are made, which highlight differences practitioners perceive between process, practice and procedure in the making of a media artefact: a fiction feature film.

The cultural specificity of these practices is as observed in the U.K., which is mainly U.S.-influenced. Documentary film-making with real people, as opposed to actors, requires a very different mode of attention in comparison to fiction. However, the pattern of on-set feature film-making practice would seem to be similar from country to country. Thus stories from cinematographers told at the Camerimage International Festival of the Art of Cinematography, held in Lodz, Poland each year, suggest films vary more in terms of budget and local union rules than cultural differences. On blockbuster-sized films there will be finance from several sources and these have diverse cultural and language crews (usually referred to as cross-crews) (Greenhalgh 2007). The amount of technology, the size and scale of sets, and the costume and special or digital effects is entirely dependent on the budget and expertise of personnel. Relaxed or minimal union rules allow for a greater degree of crossover in roles, for example in Hong Kong

(Greenhalgh 2005). The above-the-line, below-the-line system used only in the U.K. and U.S. for budgeting wage-paid personnel dictates crew roles and numbers. Much also depends on the feel of particular locations and climates as well as the tone and period of the script. Different directors have methods which may affect the order of shooting – such as Mike Leigh, who develops characters with actors before filming begins; or John Cassavetes, who improvised scenes during rehearsal. There may be spatio-temporal factors, which I will expand on later, and these could be culturally affected. For example, Hong Kong film crews tend to be more capable than Hollywood crews of working at speed with martial arts performers as they know how to count with the action, understand *chi* energy, and are practised at following varied kinetic movement of performers, according to cinematographer Peter Pau.[2]

Practice and Theory

Are there ways of theorising media and practice which are useful to practitioners, articulating concepts or extrapolating theory from practitioners' use of language, rather than reliance on overarching abstract concepts and paradigms? I seek descriptions and solutions applicable to teaching film-making. Practice thinking and language has always been used by artists, for example, but it is easily taken over by theory as it is specific, often very localised, and has to do with specific craft skills. Theorists sometimes appear to deem practitioners' descriptions as essentialist; or at least this is a common finding at occasional conferences where the two meet. I believe this is because it is hard to analyse films that contain complex action and special effects. Access to film sets is also restricted to outsiders and personnel sign contracts which forbid them from speaking to the press about the production company, script or actors' private lives, especially when plot and location secrecy is required for the latest Bond or Harry Potter film, for example. Film-making practices inevitably become more mysterious and neglected in discussion. Practitioners and theorists, academics and technicians, are also often separated in teaching institutions. Peter Matthews, a critic and film scholar, explains that:

> [Film t]heorists consider practice as naive, unreflective, not sufficiently brought to a level of self-consciousness. Therefore practice is often a target. It is why the auteur theory is sometimes discredited in film studies in favour of intertextual approaches …. In teaching production we consider students as artists who have creative vision. This already sounds naive to theorists, but

... it's the criterion by which consciousness is centred and if we didn't address the student as a declared subject we'd get nowhere ... Practice sets up romantic ideas of the artist. Film-makers' first strategy is creative, not conceptual. The auteur theory is a convenient way to assume, fulfil the artist argument. You complicate things no end if you start splitting everything up into departments and the material nature of real film-making.[3]

Film and media theory offers scant description of fundamental activities in film-making practice, rarely acknowledging the collaborative nature of a crew. Discussion centres on audience reception, media consumption and cultural representation. Form, text and authorship persist in the analysis of films, but few realise or take interest in how the crew affect the product. Sobchack (1992), writing on the phenomenal properties of film, and Branigan (2006) on the camera, projection and perception, miss vital cues which would aid their discussion of somatosensory dimensions of moving-image reception. This philosophical level is of little import to the practitioner. I am interested here not so much in what is received through the camera by the audience, as in the nature of the practice concerning knowledge of the conceptual and physical space between the actors, camera and crew.

Media anthropologists who have conducted practice-based studies have made deeper inroads towards theorising media practices. Powdermaker (1950) misunderstood the producers and writers she studied in Hollywood, paying little attention to how a film is made on set, but her anthropological interest in social interaction within space and place did lead her to construct a particular picture of Los Angeles as a place of false locations and invented personalities. Worth and Adair (1972) studied Navajo cultural attitudes to space and composition when they observed how their informants used cameras. Peterson (2003) discusses approaches to the ethnography of media production. He covers text, authorship or ownership, cultural and social questions, means of production technology and interpretation by agents. Several areas of both anthropology and organisation studies (using ethnographic fieldwork) have now begun to attend to the senses and somatic dimensions of human experience which bodes well for more fully detailed and empirically richer accounts of media practice. Anthropologists such as MacDougall (2006) and Deger (2006) are able to develop a more corporeal, lived account of film-making practice, perhaps because they are also experienced film-makers. In my own work, how film-making practice is learned and how knowledge accrues through collaborative authorship in very particular physical circumstances and sequences is fundamental to understanding it.

Practitioners' Knowledge

Bourdieu (1980) likens practice to playing a game (see Introduction, this volume); practical faith involves having a feel for the game. For example, the belief in cinematographers as exceptional visualisers assumes that a prerequisite would be to have a good eye. It is typical that such an assumption is not questioned because 'the essential part of the modus operandi that defines practical mastery is transmitted through practice, in the practical state, without rising to the level of discourse', (ibid.: 66). Film-making contains much tacit practice which is beyond language and discourse. Much of it is learned by doing, through osmosis and intuition, habit and repetition. Recipes in cooking are theories of practice, but are used differently as the learner develops. They are a 'set of instructions for designing action' (Schön 1983: 147). All 'deliberate behaviour' is determined by 'theories of action', that is 'espoused theories that individuals can state explicitly and theories-in-use which must be inferred from actual behaviour' (ibid.: 147). Training manuals often miss out a full description of a practice, merely describing protocols, rules, procedures. De Certeau warns that machines that can replicate procedures appear to deplete realisation of human competences: 'know-how (savoir-faire) finds itself slowly deprived of what objectively articulated it with respect to a how-to-do (un faire). Know-how is invisible and remains unrecognised' (de Certeau 1984: 69). Explicit knowledge is internalised as tacit at an individual level. Operating within a practice, individuals are affected by interdependent, mobile, dynamic changing processes. As Leadbetter (1999: 28) puts it, 'knowledge cannot be transferred, it can only be enacted, through a process of understanding'.

The social aspect of practice ensures reflexivity and purpose. Practice 'combines repertoire and experimentation using the past to conjecture the present and future … it is the capacity for "thinking on one's feet" that characterises differential levels of skill in practitioners' (Jarzabkowski 2004: 16). Film production is increasingly a 'cognitively distributed' activity in which cognitive phenomena occur across individuals, artefacts, media and representational languages (Hutchins 1995). Although film production is not a fully computerised activity, there are varying digital inputs which affect coordination, so it requires team memory and overlapping knowledge among individual crew members.

Practical knowledge is precariously held by freelancers in the film industry and is passed from project to project, outside organisations. It is discussed in the 'emergent structures' and identity formations of film industry 'communities of practice' (Wenger 1998: 49). Wenger summarises practice as including:

what is said and unsaid; what is represented and what is assumed ... the language, tools, documents, images, symbols, well-defined roles, specified criteria, codified procedures, regulations, and contracts ... explicit for a variety of purposes ... implicit relations, tacit conventions, subtle cues, untold rules of thumb, recognizable intuitions, specific perceptions, well-tuned sensitivities, embodied understandings, underlying assumptions, and shared world views ... Things have to be done, relationships worked out, processes invented, situations interpreted, artefacts produced, conflicts resolved. [It] involves an ... embodied, delicate, active, social, negotiated, complex process of participation. (ibid.: 49)

A practice becomes a practice in the sense of a profession when enough people doing or observing the activity have noticed characteristics in which rehearsal and achievement though repetition and memories of previous solutions are re-enacted in particular situated contexts; that is, it is a genre of activity. Examples of film-making professions which have arisen during the digital age include: digital effects supervisor (the manager of a team compositing and animating computer-generated imagery to be inserted into the main physical cinematography), digital technician (on-set high-definition camera engineer), and colourist (who began as a telecine operator taking film to video but now colour grades, resizes and cleans up the final picture). The whole crew has to understand digital compatibility over the course of a project.

Hobart (this volume) describes practices as contingent because of their situatedness, and difficult to define as historical or cultural forms. They have 'moments of slippage, change, openness ... They exhibit sprawl, mutual contradiction ... unplanned originality, undecidability'. Media practices particularly display these characteristics. The early film critic Ricciotto Canudo (1911, 1923) described cinema as the seventh art, an art which combined all others. With digital convergence and mobile-media platforms we are nearer now than ever before to the combination of multiple mediums he imagined. Media has learned and become interdisciplinary, performative, interactive, transformative and processual. It requires practical expertise (know-how) that is adept at being polymathic, collaborative, distributive, appropriative, mobile, manipulative, communicative. Media practices insert themselves within other practices, entering without permission, incorporating new information, technology and forms at speed. There are numerous ways in which film crews (and film-practice students) now use media technologies such as mobile and computer software which are changing practices on and off the film set.

Practice, Process, Procedure

Practice is most commonly understood to involve repeating or rehearsing something over and over again to improve performance, as in running or dance. Process describes the transformation of the material properties of objects or systems, or events of presence altering representational states, such as are required from an actor. If a practice is a doing/being type of happening, and if a process is a way of happening, procedure would describe its operations. The practice (for the student) is anything that can be done, including anything that cannot be theorised. It is essential to distinguish between practice, process and procedure from the learning point of view. In the instance of teaching vocational film-making practice, and cinematography in particular, the practice is viewed as the bigger picture of what the person/role/profession does. The process is the state of going on. It is often spoken of with a kinetic type of description containing a sense of action, but it can often be mysterious, such as the actor's rehearsal process, the visualisation process, the creative process and so on. The procedure attempts to identify stages which help the practitioner to understand the know-how of the process. Procedure makes tasks and operations which can be specified and repeated in the manner of an instruction manual.

Practitioners/makers/agents are often vague about process but can describe procedures. Processual incorporation of new forms, re-enactment or technology re-informs the apparently habitual practice. Understanding the process may only come through practising, but the procedural operations may be all the beginner is aware of. One may not discover what one is practising until one has the sense of repeating an action procedure. The interrelation of understandings of practice, process and procedure may develop at different speeds according to how a series of practised events occurs. The temporality, spatiality, affective and embodied qualities of each, as experienced, may be spoken of as interchangeable, but the realisation of knowledge and the ability to share and pass on this knowledge are generally delineated by this wide-to-close picture – practice, process, procedure.

An actor's main tools are their body and voice, whereas the camera crew (cinematographer or director of photography, camera operator, focus puller, clapperloader, key/camera grip), all have to deal with machines and technologies in close proximity to actors. As the actress Anna Ziman puts it: 'The [acting] process … It's action knowledge … we need the event to know. Practice is what you do. Process involves time, development, creativity, it's textual and visual, ensemble and improvisation … unfolding … Procedure is the way you order the bits, it's logical'.[4]

A more scientific or engineering-based description relevant to man-ufacturing film technology would suggest a practice should be seen as something that is recorded and criticised, because it is observed as action carried out. It is material or objective in some way. Process then is action, but correct action at a quality level, reliable enough to pass on in general detail. Design is not an accident and ergonomics are crucial in making machines such as cameras. Inventors come up with proto-types but someone has to write instructions (intellectual assets to aid in the use of machinery). Procedure often needs a practical manager who is skilled at writing instructions for others to use. A skilled technician can be taught how to do it but may not fully understand what the impli-cations are. When a machine breaks down you try this and try that, eventually getting it to work, sometimes wondering why. Teaching is between theory and practice. Practice, process, and procedure weave through each other. There are moments when procedures change, mal-function in some way, which leads to questioning the wider definition of a given practice. Small changes in procedure can gradually occur and build up to the extent that the whole practice changes.

An example of this is what used to be known as the 'production path' in the post-production of a film; that is, the procedures by which the film negative went to the laboratory for processing, editing, cutting, grading and reprinting until the final print was ready for distribution. This is so disrupted now by digital capture and storage at different stages that there are now several routes where film or HD digital footage is shot, film transferred to digital format, copied back to film in a digital intermediate (DI) as well as multiple distribution platforms on TV, cinema, mobile phones and the internet, that the general term has become 'digital workflow', or simply 'workflow'. This incorporates the notion of non-linearity or combinations of analogue and digital tech-nology and hints at distributed cognition. Digital work can sometimes be undone in a way that analogue cannot. If a painterly, fluid look is needed on top of an original optically captured image, layers of effects are added, then rendered. If these are not satisfying then each layer can be reversed (a distinct procedure), enabling one to get back to the orig-inal image in a way which could not be achieved with actual paint. HD digital cameras now have menus where colour can be changed on set during shooting. Some (though not all) of these adjustments can be changed in the edit.

Film-set Environment

Practices are generally 'construed as *materially mediated* nexuses of activity' (Schatzki 2001: 11). Practice-based studies such as Silvia Gherardi's of safety practices in building construction emphasise how abstract knowledge and contextually situated knowledge are fused in application to material circumstances (Gherardi 2006). She defines 'situated' as processual, in that a 'connection-in-action texture of practice is producing enacted and embodied practising individuals and material interaction over time in a physical context' (ibid.: xii). Language – conversation about practice at work – is part of becoming a practitioner. She encapsulates this in the term 'knowing in practice' (ibid.: 131).

Knowing in practice on a film set requires an understanding of how to negotiate artificial worlds and working realities, an 'aesthetic understanding' of organisation (Strati 1999); an ability to engage the senses. It means to reflect on action (Schön 1983) whilst incorporating constant change. Appropriating space is a continuous activity for film-makers in the cheating of space, people, props and tools to achieve fictional reality in actual space, within the support systems of the film unit on a location or within the geography of a studio stage set with its outer entrances, corridors, offices and driveways on the studio lot. Film-makers acquire a special kind of appropriative expertise through practice.

The way studios and sets are built (a measured system for production first designed in the 1930s), cameras designed, lighting rigged, and the work of filming carried out, are all organised within very specific limits and organisational structures. Applying de Certeau's (1984: 19) metaphor of space as strategy and time as tactic (ways of operating which constitute an 'art of practice') is one way of thinking through what happens here. De Certeau conducted fieldwork on everyday practices such as walking and cooking. For him, roles, rules and technologies which tend to be organised by the state and society are choreographed in particular geographical/spatial patterns, such as a grid of streets. However, the speed and thoughts of the individual walker cannot be controlled entirely as they operate tactically. This means that timing, individual trajectory and temporal control can allow for some empowerment and therefore ownership. In other words there is an unknown factor in reading human tactics that naturally have energy and impetus to think, invent and move. Borrowing de Certeau's notion of 'embodied spatial practice', Clifford (1997: 185–86) argues that fieldwork was initially conceived 'as about "terrain" and could be legitimated as "ground interpretation"'. He conceptualises the field as 'space practiced by the active occupation of the anthropologist'. This idea of location involves appropriation. Film locations are 'recced' (short for reconnoitred) and visualised before shooting to assess the suitability of the terrain for transformation into the setting for a film. For this purpose then, the film industry and all its regulations and institutions can be seen as a strategy, as is the order of making a film with its designated stages: pre-production, production, post-production. The film set or location (once so defined) is a spatial strategy designed to implement the procedures of making a film. The film unit as a whole, and the crew's hierarchy and roles, are largely strategies with particular designations tied to equipment and their operation.

Observations can be made about class, gender or other social differences and the varied power relationships between departments and employees in terms of knowledge, skills and applications. The way particular problems involved in making a film are resolved and the specific physical dexterity, psychological manoeuvres and affective mood of crew members are tactical; i.e.. they are temporal decisions based on specific events and circumstances.

Understanding timing is crucial, and the relationship of timing to embodied performance is central to distinct skilled practice. Cinematographer Dean Cundey reveals: 'when we get to the set we begin to choreograph … Any single moment requires the cooperation, the input, the collaboration of so many different people, often prepared for months in advance'.[5] The director Marc Evans describes the filming conundrum thus: 'I know of no other activity that is so obviously split between delicate art form and heavy industrial practice. It's expensive magic, fraught with failure … achieved at what seems breakneck speed to the crew [but] mind-numbingly slow to the casual observer' (Evans 1998: 10). Different mood or tone is driven by the design, props, costume, colour and light of the film as well as the action. The camera operator William Hines claims: 'each production and script has a distinctive continuity – a pace, timing and rhythm – of it's own … The script carries a certain sustaining mood and requires appropriate (speed)' (Hines 1997: 118).

Bakhtin sought kinetic descriptions of the self, world, language, actions; to construct ideas about dialogic relations with an ethical imperative. His notion of the chronotope, or time-space frame, in the novel, describes time becoming flesh, space being charged with the presence of movement. The precise moment of activity in a lived experience has an 'emotional-volitional tone' (Bakhtin 1993: 36). The act is conceived as spatio-temporal performance. There is a chronotope associable with practice work on the film set. Digital convergence technology and physical on-set collaboration produces specific performative relationships and positions practice, organisation and creativity throughout film production as a transformative and dynamic, processual, dialogical, cross-cultural and interdisciplinary activity.

Affective and emotional orders are at play in any practice with many overlapping disciplines working together in a distributed manner with varying values, commitments and responses to working methods. John-Steiner reminds us that 'collaboration is complex and charged both cognitively and emotionally' (John-Steiner 2001: 124). The crew must learn affective expertise to deal with strange and changing proximities dealt with daily on the set (see Greenhalgh 2009). It is easy for the crew to see immediately when a person has not been on a film set before as they are unable to nip around sets, over cables, keep away from hot lights and delicate camera equipment, and so forth. They haphazardly get in frame, block the camera and trespass on the actors' performance space. In the United States and Canada, unions now insist or at least advise future film employees to undergo behavioural training, advertised as 'set etiquette' before going on a set.

Compared to theatre and construction, film-crew specialists have to organise quickly, coordinating complex activity, often without having known one another prior to the project. Their work is contingent on networks, interpersonal skills and negotiated identities, as much as technical skills. Key crew members bring recommended crew and kit with them when hired. Beth Bechky's ethnographic study of role structures and enactment in temporary organisations includes work on film sets. She observes that 'nuances are negotiated in situ … On each film set, role expectations are communicated through enthusiastic thanking, polite admonishing, and role oriented joking, which enable crew members to learn and negotiate role structures' (Bechky 2006: 1). Borrowing Goffman's term 'total institution', she describes the film set as a 'temporary total institution', where individuals are cut off from society for a long period of time, leading an enclosed life. There is physical and temporal isolation; the public are barred, streets are closed off, and locations are far away; and there are union rules which determine wrap times, the eleven-day-per-fortnight work pattern and a 'drifting schedule'. Film set work involves immersion: 'intensive and visible short-term interaction with an expectation of repeated interactions in the future … blurred boundaries between work and play … film sets are characterised by an atmosphere of continual communication … walkie talkies, megaphones, mobiles' (ibid.: 4, 6, 8). Therefore, crew members must learn affective expertise and emotional intelligence to continue their careers. This happens largely through the enactment of roles around the immediate vicinity of the camera and actors; 'crew members upset the balance at their own peril' (ibid.: 12).

Visualisation

Visualisation is the general term for the visual concept of a sequence or whole film. This may be broken down into storyboard, shot list, set plans, rehearsal, lighting diagrams, and visual-effects 'pre-viz' (pre-visualisation), carried out by the visual-effects supervisor (digital work). The status of decisions at any stage of film pre-production and production will be affected by the memory, projection and manifestation of these processes in myriad small procedures, embodied or as memorised action, which characterise how any given shot gets made, repeated in takes, and locked off (finished, completed, also known as wrapped), before going on to the next shot. It is difficult to go back and repeat a shot once objects, actors and the set have been moved.

Both visualisation and cheating (blocking) are difficult to convey through teaching. Embedding the knowledge needs bodily learning as much as knowledge of point of view, film grammar, optics and so on. One cannot know the likelihood of being able to transform a visual idea from two dimensions to three dimensions and then back again to two dimensions – from the script and drawings, through computer storyboard, rehearsal blocking diagrams, to actual set with crew and cast, and back to editing cohesion and projection in the cinema to audience – without knowing whether things on set can be cheated into position. Each time one has experienced cheating, one has more information about the complexity of bodies and technology combinations and how much time and how much space and personnel is needed to achieve them. Each time one visualises, energy must be spent on planning ahead for how things will be cheated in any given situation. Other logistics on location must be taken into consideration, such as the heat or cold, weather and natural light, the use of vehicles, and so on.

The development stage of a feature film involves the synopsis of the story, treatment details of the sequences and a full script, which for a one-hundred-minute feature is one-hundred-pages long. So-called 'American scriptwriting' follows a specific layout that can be easily read by agents, producers, directors, potential cast and principal crew. The script lines separate dialogue on the page from action and set and character description. If there is a lot of set building and studio work, the production designer is often hired weeks or months before the cinematographer.

The next stage, pre-production, involves meetings about the script, location searches (known as recceing) with key personnel, casting, building, organising equipment and crew, and so on. Some films, especially where there is a camera operator as well as a cinematographer (as with union regulation in Los Angeles), cover shooting of many angles

316 | *Cathy Greenhalgh*

as the main production method. If the cinematography allows more creativity there may be several stages of visualisation. First, photographs, drawing, paintings and varieties of graphic references accumulate. Then, video footage, polaroids and HD stills of locations and comparison with art-department images. Rigging and lighting diagrams are prepared to align with production-design scale drawings for carpentry and plaster construction, with notes on textures to be applied and possible costume and make-up colouring. Usually a scale model of the set will be built which is accessible to all personnel. Screen tests of actors and possible rehearsal videos are pored over by key personnel.

The first assistant director prepares with their team – producing a shooting script from the cinematographer's and director's conversations. This may be accompanied by a storyboard. Many films do not use storyboards at all, but when special effects and complicated action scenes are involved these are essential for ensuring that eyeline directions are accurate and digital visual-effects work where compositing images later need accuracy. When they are needed, storyboards may be drawn by a separate storyboard artist. Pre-visualisation or 'pre-viz' is being used more and more on productions with a lot of CGI (computer generated imagery) or digital processing. This involves the script being produced as a computer-drawn animated storyboard by animators and visual effects designers. Call sheets for each day detail special needs such as props, stunts, special equipment, locations and general movement orders for the production units.

During production, production design and lighting crews move one set ahead of the principal photography crew on the set or location. There may also be second and third shooting units. The shots are set up, then technical run-throughs with stand-ins are followed by rehearsals, all watched by the director and cinematographer by the camera. A video assist monitor set-up (camera viewfinder view) shows the shot and can be used as a guide by all, particularly the script supervisor (who looks after continuity), the art, costume and make-up department, and the sound crew. Around the camera and on cranes and steadicams there are also small monitors, showing focus and aspect-ratio details and other technical information such as exposure, lens distance and so on. Some action shots are also shot with several cameras at once. Actors, of course, are expected to have emotional fluctuations when trying to keep a performance in shape and bring presence and dynamism at the time of the take. This is why the crew talk to the actors very little and wear dark clothing to lessen the likelihood of them paying attention to what is going on behind the camera.

The amount of cheating of lenses to space and crew and actor bodies, means that most shots will have to be revisualised in situ, and storyboards may have to be abandoned as real practicalities are worked out. Storyboarding provides a two-dimensional way into 3D, but it is quite hard to read storyboards unless 3D devising of shots in real space is understood first. Seasoned film-makers do not need storyboards for general shooting, but students often need the security of a graphic guide.

The script supervisor (formerly known as continuity) uses a script marked-up with shots (T-crossed lines on the page) to make sure all script sections have been covered. They keep the cinematographer and director on track. The camera crew also log all shots on camera cards, mobile phones or computers, and of course each shot is slated (these days with an electronic clapperboard). Each day the film is processed and either goes to print or more often to digital rushes or dailies, viewed around lunchtime the following day. After production the cinematographer's job is over, except for grading. Tone and colour can now be changed by the editor if the production has several CGI shots. This may involve several visual-effects houses, the coordination of greenscreen shooting and special effects, and it can be difficult to control all the elements. If the initial product has been shot on HD rather than film, projection of intermediate stages is even more vital than with film. The most recent development is the Digital Intermediate (DI); that is, CGI and composite images scanned back to film.

The way in which documents and dialogue accrue during the making of a film shows the various forms in which visualisation travels through the different minds of those involved and how embodiment and technology meet at each stage of the production of a film. The cinematographer Anthony Dod Mantle describes the following stages:

> The director gets hold of the script ... develops it, starts creating secret pictures in his mind ... then you get to the actor stage and start linking up with casting ... and the director guides actors gradually into this space ... and wants to create mentally and physically so they feel comfortable ... That's my job, to look in the story and understand what kind of space the actors and the director have conjured up.[6]

The production designer Carmel Collins explains how practice involves communication which must gradually materialise the film and also keep track of resolving stages:

> The script might be a guideline or a bible ... You know words are very slippy. You must have ... a common understanding of what you're aiming for. It's an evolving process ... open to different kinds of interpretation ... like a jamming session, it can build and roll once you have something concrete ... even impinge back on the way the script is going to be developed.[7]

This repetition, even rhetoric, of magical and creative inspiration-type words to try to describe the feeling of breakthrough moments and resolving stages of making is often found in film-makers' accounts, such as those found in trade journals or guild magazines like *American Cinematographer*. I would conjecture that this is because of the apparent enormity of what can be achieved through collaborative team work, which extends personal skills by enabling crew members to partially appropriate each others' knowledge, creating mutual engagement and shared ownership of much larger tasks. In other words the quality of collaborative dynamics of the personnel on the film set are a key to success of the work undertaken there. It is often said that no one knows what makes a good film. Previous attempts and methods can be followed and much money spent, but this is no guarantee of a film's success with an audience. Practitioners' pleasure lies in the complexity of the achievement. It is in the practising that creativity appears to show up, because the cycle of preparation for action, immersion in action, and reflection on action allows group confidence and practical faith in serendipity and problem-solving.

Cheating

The camera crew may operate from 'tripod, dolly, handheld, steadicam, remotely activated head, cable rig, crane, motorcycle, car, skis, train, ship, animal, airborne, bungee, underwater, cave, scaffolding, tree, suspended, with inclement weather … frequently accomplished under hazardous conditions, that is when there is a potential, if not substantial, threat to physical safety.'(Hines 1997: 67). They work around special (physical) effects such as explosives, firearms, man-made rain, wind, dust, with animals and so on. In their practice the crew live by the shot, often shooting scenes totally out of sequence to the script. They must pay attention to the moment of fabrication, not least because of health and safety issues, probable circumstances, as well as the sheer range of technology they use.

Devising and organising shots for a sequence involving actors, props and furniture, and using cameras, grip (moving tracking equipment) and lighting within a film or television set or location, requires a complex understanding of blocking. 'Blocking' or 'staging' is the term generally used in the theatre. Film crews say they choreograph or block the shot. 'Cheating' is the term used ubiquitously for all the minor adjustments needed to fit action to lenses and to arrange performers, props and settings to the lenses' points of view. Cheating originated in the theatre and involved actors turning their bodies towards the audience whilst keeping their heads facing their fellow actors, enabling sight lines to the audience. The term *mettre-en-scène* is to do with arranging action onstage; meanwhile, *mise-en-scène* in narrative cinema is mainly to do with the placement of action and setting within the composition, otherwise known as 'framing', a film theory term rarely used on set. Cinematic staging 'delivers the dramatic field to our attention, sculpting it for informative, expressive ... pictorial effect' (Bordwell 2005: 8). Cheating is an incorporation, a second nature. 'It's all about keeping the audience ... so they don't get lost or confused ... oriented and grounded in the film space of the scene ... making it easier to go with the narrative or emotional flow' (Brown 2002: 16, 17).

Another common film-crew term is 'believability', used in relation to the storyline, continuity, action, setting and lighting. The essentials of teaching 'cheating' are to make it 'believable' in a film's terms through squashing or expanding space, fitting in performances, subtle repositionings, understanding technology and optics. A moving image means understanding the 180-degree rule – whereby placing actors on either side of an imaginary line from the camera ensures that shots and reverse shots will cut together – trajectories of performers' movements, as well as cinema conventions and their cultural roots. Work on set is all about artifice, manipulation, appropriation; controlling temporal and spatial transformation.[8] Since 'there is no ideal camera composition or movement, manipulation is necessary' (Arijon 1976: 13).

Students are introduced to different ways of shooting shots and the use of different lenses to create points of view. They realise that trajectories, space expansion and crushing are different with different lenses, whether wide angle or telephoto, and that actors' eyelines will be altered. A wide-angle lens may be very close to an actor, much closer than in any normal conversation, with extremes of texture in focus (as in rap-music videos); a telephoto lens, meanwhile, feels uncomfortably physically distant from actors whilst giving a zoomed-in, close-up cerebral effect (as in Ken Loach's films).[9] Students can see it, but at first they cannot quite believe it. The quagmire of possibilities and how much there is to learn opens out before them. To learn, they need to experience and understand a number of different roles and positions: that of the actor, the director watching the actor, the camera operator looking down the camera viewfinder at the actor(s), the cinematographer designing the lighting, the production designer seeing how much set is behind the actors, and the sound designer seeing where booms will be in shot.

Cheating is what in pedagogical research has been called a 'threshold concept' (Meyer and Land 2003). Once learnt, one cannot go back;

but if not learned, it is impossible to move much further forward. It is 'transformative, irreversible, integrative (exposes the previously hidden interrelatedness of something). The physical situation seems so unlikely at first, that students find it hard to incorporate … it's potentially 'troublesome knowledge' (Perkins 1999), 'counter-intuitive or incoherent' (Meyer and Land 2003: 4). Learning moves forward within an embodied memory. Procedures encoded outside the body in a machine, however, are potentially reversible as it may be possible to undo things that have been done, as in many digital processing examples.

Camera operating and focus pulling require precision memory and choreography because there may be many takes for actors to get a performance or crew to get a physical camera effect right. Experienced actors understand and read what the camera, lights and sound equipment around them are doing as intuitively as the crew using them. For newcomers and outsiders it can be confusing as simply watching the crew will not tell you what they are doing, what is going on. DVD 'making-of's' may give some idea, but not the sheer proxemic variety and affective dimension that daily on-set cheating provides for cast and crew. It can be emotionally and physically exciting and challenging or tiring. The body can 'learn and re-create position/location and varying degrees of motion between' (Hershey 1996: 114). The actor also gives unconscious as well as planned signals. A camera operator learns to anticipate 'a subtle tensing of the muscles in the face, neck … eyes' (Hines 1997: 89). The disciplinary skills are similar but differently experienced, as the actor will of course appear on screen, whilst the operator responds and guides the viewfinder and is the hidden body behind the camera. This creates a system of non-verbal cues to communicate small changes needed. Hierarchy usually dictates crew try not to speak too much to actors so that director-actor relationships are not disturbed. The actor Jason Flemyng regards the camera crew: 'the inexplicable contortions and cheats the Operator insists on, always accompanied by a cheery don't worry, it looks alright on camera … (can) give rise to … temperamental tutting, sighing and exasperated mutterings' (Flemyng 1994: 12). William Hines, meanwhile, counsels the camera operator to assist actors misunderstanding through cajoling because:

> You've no doubt encountered actors who almost never: Hit their marks, or make a move, cross or gesture in the same way for each take (same place, point in time, velocity or magnitude). (They) cover each other from camera view, throw key light shadows on each other … hide upstage eye from camera, banana into and out of tight group shots, bounce up and down or sway side to side in a tight close-up. (Hines 1997: 177).

The elements of practice described here and above encompass embodied learning as a central part of the camera-crew practitioner's experience. Increasingly this is combined with the distributed cognitive faculties of the wider crewing unit with forms of virtual memory and technical convergence. The complexity of modern filming requires detailed specialist knowledge and affective expertise to cope with a thoroughly interdisciplinary arena of work. In making and using media there are levels or registers of making things present; a non-linear, transformative, processual, back-and-forth flow of time, memory, spontaneous improvisation and (usually) collective or collaborative components of fabrication, dissemination and interactivity.

Conclusion

The implication of cheating and visualisation for a fledgling theorising of media and/as practice is that the link between these virtual and distributed forms and embodied knowledge accrued in situated places and temporal moments underpins how practitioners see practice. Practitioners activate knowing in practice through collaborative dynamics by paying attention to when they are in the practice environment. These concepts help us to understand what goes on in filmmaking between theory and practice. Gherardi argues 'there is a need for a new vocabulary centred on the term "practice" ... An entire family of explanatory concepts such as "tacit knowledge", "shared understanding", "communities of thought", "epistemic objects", "aesthetic understanding", "negotiated order", ... denote the search for embodied and contextually situated instances of discourse and action, of doing and knowing.' (Gherardi 2006: 14). She calls this 'practice-based theorising' (ibid.: 15). Learning and knowing are not separate in everyday practices or in media as practice. They instead take place 'within the flow of experience' (ibid.:14). Further empirical studies are needed to observe this integrated relationship. Theories of practice without some link to observation of actual practices are likely to be too overarching to notice that practice tends to come up from the bottom (from the street so to speak) to assume cultural forms.

Notes

1. These titles are changing due to the different configuration of digital cameras vis-à-vis celluloid-film cameras.
2. Author's interview with Peter Pau; Camerimage Festival, Lodz, Poland; December 2003. Pau worked on the shooting of *Crouching Tiger, Hidden Dragon* (dir. Zhang Yimou, 2000).
3. Author's interview with Peter Matthews; 20 January 2008.
4. Author's interview with Anna Ziman; 3 May 2007.
5. Author's interview with Dean Cundey; Torun, Poland; 1 December 1999. Cundey worked on *Jurassic Park* (dir. Steven Spielberg, 1993).
6. Author's interview with Anthony Dod Mantle; Torun, Poland; 30 November 1999. Dod Mantle worked on *Slumdog Millionaire* (dir. Danny Boyle, 2008).
7. Author's interview with Carmel Collins; 2005.
8. I cannot cover the subject of lighting in this chapter, which is a much larger and complicated issue.
9. See Greenhalgh (2003, 2005) for details on lenses.

References

Arijon, D. 1976. *The Grammar of Film Language.* London and Boston: Focal Press.
Bakhtin, M.M. 1993. *Toward a Philosophy of the Act.* Austin: University of Texas Press.
Bechky, B. 2006. 'Gaffers, Gofers and Grips: Role-Based Coordination in Temporary Organizations', *Organization Science* 17(1): 3–21.
Bordwell, D. 2005. *Figures Traced in Light: On Cinematic Staging.* Berkeley: University of California Press.
Bourdieu, P. 1992/1980. *The Logic of Practice.* Cambridge: Polity Press.
Branigan, E. 2006. *Projecting a Camera: Language-Games in Film Theory.* London: Routledge.
Brown, B. 2002. *Cinematography Theory and Practice: Image Making for Cinematographers, Directors, and Videographers.* USA: Elsevier Science, Focal Press.
Canudo, R. 1993[1911]. 'The Birth of the Sixth Art', in R. Abel (ed.), *French Film Theory and Criticism: A History/Anthology, 1907–1939.* USA: Princeton University Press, pp.58–66.
——— 1993[1923]. 'Reflections on the Seventh Art', in R. Abel (ed.), *French Film Theory and Criticism: A History/Anthology, 1907–1939.* USA: Princeton University Press, pp.291–303.
Clifford, J. 1997. 'Spatial Practices: Fieldwork, Travel and the Disciplining of Anthropology', in A. Gupta and J. Ferguson (eds), *Anthropological Locations – Boundaries and Grounds of a Field Science.* Berkeley, Los Angeles and London: University of California Press, pp.185–222.

De Certeau, M. 1984. *The Practice of Everyday Life.* Berkeley: University of California Press.

Deger, J. 2006. *Shimmering Screens: Making Media in an Aboriginal Community.* Minneapolis: University of Minnesota Press.

Evans, M. 1998. 'What Every Cameraman Should Know!' *ZERB* (UK Guild of Television Cameramen) Spring: 12–14.

Flemyng, J. 1994. 'An Actor's Eye View', *ZERB* Spring: 10–11.

Gherardi, S. 2006. *Organizational Knowledge: The Texture of Workplace Learning.* Oxford: Blackwell.

Greenhalgh, C. 2003. 'Shooting from the Heart: Cinematographers and their Medium', in S. Nykvist et al., *Making Pictures: A Century of European Cinematography.* London: Aurum Press, pp.94–155.

——— 2005. 'How Cinematography Creates Meaning in *Happy Together* (Wong Kar-Wai 1997)', in J. Gibbs and D. Pye (eds), *Style and Meaning: Studies in the Detailed Analysis of Film.* Manchester: Manchester University Press, pp.195–213.

——— 2007. 'Traveling Images, Lives on Location: Cinematographers in the Film Industry', in V. Amit (ed.), *Going First Class? New Approaches to Privileged Travel and Movement.* Oxford: Berghahn, pp.72–86.

——— 2009. 'Emotion Work in Teaching and Learning, Collaboration in Film Practice Education', in N. Austerlitz and A. Shreeve (eds), *Unspoken Interactions: Emotions and Social Interactions in the Context of Art and Design Education.* London: Centre for Learning and Teaching in Art and Design, University of the Arts, London, pp.171–87.

Hershey, F.L. 1996. *Optics and Focus for Camera Assistants: Art, Science and Zen.* USA: Focal Press.

Hines, W.E. 1997. *Operating Cinematography for Film and Video: A Professional and Practical Guide.* Los Angeles, CA: Ed-Venture Films/Books.

Hutchins, E. 1996. *Cognition in the Wild.* Cambridge, MA: MIT Press.

John-Steiner, V. 2000. *Creative Collaboration*, Oxford: Oxford University Press.

Jarzabkowski, P. 2004. 'Strategy as Practice: Recursiveness, Adaptation and Strategic Practices-in-Use', *Organization Studies* 25(4): 529–60.

Leadbetter, C. 1999. *Living on Thin Air – The New Economy.* London: Penguin Books.

MacDougall, D. 2006. *The Corporeal Image: Film, Ethnography, and the Senses.* Princeton, NJ: Princeton University Press.

Meyer, J. and R. Land. 2003. 'Threshold Concepts and Troublesome Knowledge: Linkages to Thinking and Practising within the Disciplines', in C. Rust (ed.), *Improving Student Learning.* Oxford: Centre for Staff and Learning Development.

Perkins, D. 1999. 'The Many Faces of Constructivism', *Educational Leadership* 57(3): 6–11.

Peterson, M.A. 2003. *Anthropology and Mass Communication: Media and Myth in the New Millenium.* Oxford: Berghahn.

Powdermaker, H. 1950. *Hollywood, The Dream Factory: An Anthropologist Looks at the Moviemakers.* New York: Little, Brown.

Schatzki, T.R. 2001. 'Introduction', in T.R. Schatzki, K. Knorr-Cetina and E. von Savigny (eds), *The Practice Turn in Contemporary Theory*. London: Routledge, pp.1–14.

Schön, D.A. 1983. *The Reflective Practitioner: How Professionals Think in Action*. New York: Basic Books.

Sobchack, V. 1992. *The Address of the Eye: A Phenomenology of Film Experience*. Princeton, NJ: Princeton University Press.

Strati, A. 1999. *Organization and Aesthetics*. London: Sage.

Wenger, E. 1998. *Communities of Practice: Learning, Meaning and Identity*. Cambridge: Cambridge University Press.

Worth, S. and J. Adair. 1972. *Through Navajo Eyes*. Albuquerque: University of New Mexico Press.

Notes on Contributors

Pau Alsina (Ph.D.) is Lecturer in the Department of Arts and Humanities, Open University of Catalonia (UOC) and director of Artnodes Review on art, science and technology. He is currently collaborating on a research project on 'Visual Culture and New Media' funded by the Spanish government. His main research interests are new media philosophy, new media art and digital culture, and cultural innovation policies. He has published various articles and book chapters on art and technology, new media, aesthetics and cultural policies and is the author of *Arte, Ciencia y Tecnología* (2007).

Elisenda Ardèvol is Senior Lecturer in Social and Cultural Anthropology, Arts and Humanities Department, Open University of Catalonia (UOC). She also teaches on the interdisciplinary MA and Ph.D. programmes on Information and Knowledge Society, UOC, on the MA in Creative Documentary at the Autonomous University of Barcelona (UAB) and on the MA in Visual Anthropology at the University of Barcelona (UB). She has been a Visiting Scholar at the Center for Visual Anthropology, University of Southern California (USC) and Lecturer in the social anthropology department of USC. Her current research topics include visual and media anthropology, digital ethnography and cyberculture studies. Her publications include the books *Representación y cultura audiovisual en la sociedad contemporánea* (2004) *Antropología de los media* (2005) and *La búsqueda de una mirada* (2006).

S. Elizabeth Bird is Professor in the Department of Anthropology, University of South Florida. She studies the role of the media in everyday life and teaches media studies, visual anthropology and folklore. Her books include *For Enquiring Minds: A Cultural Study of Supermarket Tabloids*

(1992), *Dressing in Feathers: The Construction of the Indian in American Popular Culture* (1996), *The Audience in Everyday Life: Living in a Media World* (2003), which won the International Communication Association's Outstanding Book Award in 2004, and *The Anthropology of News and Journalism: Global Perspectives* (2009). She has published over fifty articles and chapters and is a frequent consultant for various media. Her current research interests include community-based ethnographic projects on media, memory and cultural heritage.

Birgit Bräuchler (Ph.D.) is Assistant Professor (*Wissenschaftliche Mitarbeiterin*) in Social and Cultural Anthropology at the University of Frankfurt. Her main research interests are media and cyberanthropology, conflict and peace studies, and the revival of tradition. She is the author of *Cyberidentities at War* (2005) and editor of *Reconciling Indonesia: Grassroots Agency for Peace* (2009). She has published several articles on the expansion of the Moluccan conflict (Eastern Indonesia) into cyberspace, the globalisation of local conflicts, Islamic radicalism on the internet, online identity politics, and the challenges of the revitalisation of traditions. Currently she is engaged in a research project on *adat* (custom) revivalism and the peace process in Eastern Indonesia.

Nick Couldry is Professor of Media and Communications at Goldsmiths College, University of London, where he is Director of the Centre for the study of Global Media and Democracy. He is the author of several books, including most recently *Listening Beyond the Echoes: Media, Ethics and Agency in an Uncertain World* (2006). He is also the co-editor of *Media Consumption and Public Engagement: Beyond the Presumption of Attention* (2007) and *Media Events in a Global Age* (2009).

Cathy Greenhalgh is Principal Lecturer and Head of Film and Television at the London College of Communication, University of the Arts, London (UAL). She is Course Director of the MA Investigating Film Practice and previously directed the BA in Film and Video for several years. She writes about cinematographers and filmmaking practices, performance and narrative, creative collaboration and practice language, film aesthetics and cinematographic phenomena. She is co-founder of the Film and Phenomena Group, making collaborative film works with scientists. She originally worked as a cinematographer in the British film industry and now shoots and directs films which incorporate choreography, documentary and animation, using a combination of media for film and gallery spaces.

Toke H. Christensen (Ph.D.) is Researcher at the Danish Building Research Institute, Aalborg University, Denmark. His main research interest concerns the interplay between technology, built environment, social change and the environment. He is the co-author of a recent article in the *Journal of Consumer Policy* (2007), and has recently published another in *New Media and Society* (2009).

Jo Helle-Valle is Head of Research at SIFO (National Institute for Consumer Research), Oslo. He holds a Dr. Polit. in social anthropology (1996) based on fieldwork in a local community in the Kalahari and has also conducted fieldwork in Uganda and Ethiopia. For the last seven years he has been working on digital media in Norway. He has published on a wide variety of topics, including recent articles in *Human IT* (2008) and *New Media and Society* (2008).

Mark Hobart is Professor of Critical Media and Cultural Studies at the Centre for Media and Film Studies, School of Oriental and African Studies (SOAS), University of London. Originally trained as an anthropologist, he has conducted over eight years' research in Indonesia. Since 1988 he has worked on the ethnography of media production and reception in Indonesia as part of a broader critique of approaches to Asian media. His publications are wide-ranging, but often address his longstanding interest in philosophical issues in the human sciences. Recently he co-edited a volume entitled *Entertainment Media in Indonesia* (2007) and is the editor of a forthcoming special issue of the *Asian Journal of Social Science* on 'New Approaches to Asian Media and Film'.

Guido Ipsen is currently completing his *Habilitation* in Philosophy at the University of Witten-Herdecke. He is Lecturer in Linguistics at the University of Wuppertal, and in Intercultural Communication at the University Südwestfalen. Until recently, he was Professor of Scientific Communication and Semiotics at the University of Dortmund and Guest Professor in Semiotics at the Finnish Network University for Semiotics from 2003 to 2008. His main fields of research include the semiotics of culture and media, linguistics, communication studies (with a focus on professional communication), and the history of media culture. His publications include *HybridHyperSigns* (2001), numerous articles on mediation, semiotics, and culture, and the forthcoming monographs *Linguistics for Beginners* and *Semiotics of Professional Communication*.

Christopher M. Kelty is an Associate Professor at the University of California, Los Angeles. He has a joint appointment in the Center for

Society and Genetics and in the Department of Information Studies. His research focuses on the cultural significance of information technology, especially with regard to science and engineering. He is the author of *Two Bits: The Cultural Significance of Free Software* (2008), as well as numerous articles on open-source and free software, including its impact on education, nanotechnology and the life sciences, and issues of peer review and the research process in the sciences and in the humanities.

Jens Kjaerulff holds a Ph.D in social anthropology from Aarhus University, Denmark, and is currently Lecturer in Social Anthropology at the University of Manchester (U.K.) He has previously taught anthropology at Simon Fraser University and University of Victoria (British Columbia, Canada). His monograph *Internet and Change* (2009) is based on fieldwork among people working via the internet from their homes in rural Denmark. His approach to information and communication technologies reflects his wider comparative interest in knowledge and situated practice, and in complexity and change.

Ruth Pagès is Researcher at the Internet Interdisciplinary Institute (IN3), Open University of Catalonia (UOC). She is currently working on a Ph.D. on the legitimation processes of Net.art (internet art) in Catalonia. Her research explores, among other things, the contemporary mechanisms of authorisation and the courses of reception, appreciation and legitimation of digital art practices within art institutions, as well as the broader new media context of the culture industries and user-generated content.

Mark A. Peterson is a former Washington, DC, journalist. Educated at UCLA and Brown University, he is currently Associate Professor of Anthropology and International Studies at Miami University. His articles on Middle Eastern, South Asian and U.S. media have appeared in such journals as *Anthropology Today, Anthropological Quarterly, Childhood, Contemporary Islam, Media/Culture, New Reviews in Hypermedia and Multimedia* and *Teaching Anthropology*. He has published chapters in several books, and is the author of *Anthropology and Mass Communication: Media and Myth in the New Millennium* (2003) and the co-author of *International Studies: An Interdisciplinary Approach to Global Issues* (2008).

John Postill is Senior Lecturer in Media at Sheffield Hallam University and a Fellow of the Digital Anthropology Programme, University College London (UCL). He holds a Ph.D. in anthropology from UCL and is the author of *Media and Nation Building* (2006), based on field-work among the Iban of Borneo and of *Localizing the Internet* (in press), a study of internet activism and local politics in a suburb of Kuala Lumpur (Malaysia). He has published in journals such as *Social Anthropology, New Media and Society* and *Time and Society*, and is currently researching social media activism in Barcelona (Spain) and the socio-economic implications of mobile phones in the global South.

Ursula Rao is Senior Lecturer in Sociology and Anthropology at the University of New South Wales, Sydney. Her fields of expertise are media anthropology and the anthropology of religion. She has worked in India for over fifteen years and has written on Hindi- and English-language journalism, Hinduism and ritual theory. Some of her recent publications in English include *News Cultures: Journalistic Practices and the Remaking of Indian Leadership Traditions* (2010) and the co-edited volume *Celebrating Transgression: Method and Politics in the Anthropological Studies of Cultures* (2006).

Antoni Roig is Lecturer at the Department of Information and Communication Science, Open University of Catalonia (UOC), and holds a Ph.D. in Information and Knowledge Society from UOC. He is currently collaborating in a research project on 'Visual Culture and New Media'. His main research interests are collaborative cinema, new media creative practices, cross-media production, participatory culture and open media creation tools. He has published various articles on new media, participatory culture and cinema practices, and has co-edited the anthology *Comunicación audiovisual digital* (2005).

Inge Røpke is Associate Professor in the Department of Management Engineering at the Technical University of Denmark. She was trained as an economist and holds a Ph.D. in social science. She has worked on the history and development of modern ecological economics and on environmental aspects of economic growth, international trade, technological change and consumption. At present her main field of research concerns changes in everyday life, technology and consumption from an environmental perspective. In recent years she has published in the *Journal of Industrial Ecology, International Journal of Innovation and Sustainable Development,* and *Ecological Economics.*

Gemma San Cornelio (Ph.D.) is Lecturer in the Department of Information and Communication Science, Open University of Catalonia (UOC). She is coordinator of the research project on 'Visual

Culture and New Media' and has recently authored a number of articles on digital aesthetics and media culture, some of them focused on the relation between play and new media practices. She has forthcoming articles in two volumes which she also co-edited: *Convergence* and *Art, Space and Technology in the Digital Age.*

Debra Spitulnik is Associate Professor in the Department of Anthropology at Emory University (U.S.A.) Her publications in the areas of media anthropology, sociolinguistics and African linguistics have appeared in numerous journals and edited volumes, including *Journal of Linguistic Anthropology, Annual Review of Anthropology* and *Visual Anthropology Review.* Her current research spans the areas of media theory, media ethnography, discourse circulation, critical epistemology, and the relationship between media and national publics. A book project on young adults' engagements with media and politics in the U.S. is currently underway.

Index

value of analytic closure 114
see also radio listening, analysis of
anchoring practices 42–3, 47, 49–50,
63, 71, 197–98
cultural production, play and 275
media practices 59
Anderson, Benedict 135, 217
anthropology 105, 106, 111
cultural anthropology 115, 118
cultural studies and 119
culture, conception of 225–26, 228
media anthropology 2, 4–6, 40,
106–7, 111, 120, 192–93, 200,
207–8, 307
media audience, approach to 86–7
object construction in 117
post-paradigm anthropology 119–20
radio listening, analysis of 105, 106,
111
cultural studies and 119
object construction in 117
post-paradigm anthropology
119–20
research-problem design in 117
anti-functionalism 43
Applbaum, Kalman 137
appropriation 17, 25, 130, 243
cinematography 313, 319
cultural production, play and 259–60,
262, 266, 269–70, 271, 274
arbitrariness 140, 267
Ardèvol, Elisenda 24–5, 259–77, 325
articulation and agency 63
artistic freedom 155
as-it-happens observation 265, 296
audiences
agency of 21, 87, 99
audience reception 85, 259, 307
audience research 38
cultural production, play and
259–62, 264–65, 269–75
television, practices in Egypt 99–100
see also media audiences
auteur theory 306, 307
authoritative representations 42, 59

backyard wrestling 3, 31, 90
Balinese culture 64
Barksdale, Jim 285, 288

Barth, Fredrik 16, 23, 24, 26, 213–15,
216, 221, 222–7, 228, 229–30
Barthes, Roland 183–4, 222–7
BASE jumping 3, 14–5
BDSM (bondage and discipline,
domination/submission, and
sadomasochism) 14–15, 18
Beeman, William 142
behavioural flux 221, 226
belief, formation of 171
believability in cinematography 319
Benjamin, Walter 35, 181, 182
Berners-Lee, Tim 286
bilateral communication 174
Bird, S. Elizabeth 21, 85–101, 325–6
bodily hexis 19, 206
bodily-mental activities 239–41
bodily-mental routines 236–7, 239, 243
body 44
body language 112
discipline and 8
habitus and 7, 141
individualism and 204
and media, relationship between
14–15
media and 3, 12, 14, 172
mind and 10, 197–200, 237, 240, 247
nexus of engagements with world 7,
9, 12
practice theorists, second
generation and 9
procedures encoded outside,
reversibility of 320
routinisation and 236–7
skilled body 10
voice and 311
see also embodiment
body language 112
Bourdieu, Pierre 2–3, 6, 7, 8, 9, 10, 11,
26, 78, 135, 144, 152
bodily hexis 19, 206
field theory 15–16, 47, 163n4
habitus 7, 8, 14, 50, 118–19, 129,
140–41, 147, 149–50, 163n4, 206
interactionism, aversion to 16
power, tripartite division of 139
practice models of 22, 128, 129,
149–51, 162–3, 191, 196, 235,
238–9, 308

'smart mobs' 19
social action, notion of 225–6
social aspects of teleworking 219–20
social categories and social order 48
social communication 180
social context 23, 69, 142, 148, 199,
    201–2
  internet and 263
social effects of media 35–6
social field 15, 19, 129, 132–3, 139,
    142, 149, 198
social interaction 16, 24, 234, 237–40,
    249, 253, 304, 307
social network maintenance 248–9
social practice
  mass media and 68–9
  relationship of media-oriented
    practices to 42–3
social structures 7, 19–20, 42, 140, 206
social theory
  centered on practice 1
  practice as buzzword in 191
social world, logic of 143–4
sociology of practice 41–3
software production 3, 281–300
space of practices 42
spatio-temporal performance 314, 317,
    319–20
Spitulnik, Debra 21–2, 23, 105–23, 330
St Petersburg Times 99
stability in meaning 180
Stallman, Richard 282, 287, 291, 292,
    293, 294, 296, 297, 298n1
state power, social power and 139
Statesman 131, 138
storyboards in film-making 315, 316,
    317
storytelling, software and practice of
    295–6
structuralism 9, 23, 36, 181, 183–4, 192
structuration theory 9, 16, 45
structure (and structures) 56, 62,
    70n5, 100–101, 118, 128, 148, 149,
    188n18, 192, 195, 196, 261, 288
  abstraction of 193
  and agency, theoretical division
    between 41, 192, 207
  agency and 9, 41, 45, 99, 119, 192,
    207

of audience agency 87, 99
categorical structuration 49–50
cognitive structures 200, 235
constraints of 21
culture as 150
deterministic models of 119
duality of 9
equivalence structures 60
escape from 151
film industry practice, emergent
    structures of 309
free software, structure and
    meaning of 25, 281–2
of games 267
gender structures 245
hierarchical structures 119
holistic notion of 19–20, 21, 26
informational structure 267
institutional structures 37–8
intellectualism and structured
    oppositions 129
linguistic structure 116
material structures 253
meanings, structured fields of 130
  in media-oriented practices 47–8
  of media texts 37
narrative structures 267–8
organisational structure 289, 312,
    314
outcomes, analysis of practice and
    structuring of 162
power structures 65, 88
production structures 36–7, 183–4,
    260–61
reward structures 115
signification, structures of 135, 184
social structures 7, 19–20, 42, 140,
    206
structuration theory 45
structured context and habituated
    dispositions, dialectical
    relationship between 141–2
structures and temporary
    organisation of film sets 314–15
symbolic field of structured
    distinctions 133
symbolic structures 235
systems and 1, 20, 62, 214, 261
teleoaffective structures 236, 240, 273

www.ingramcontent.com/pod-product-compliance
Lightning Source LLC
Chambersburg PA
CBHW072047020426
42334CB00017B/1415